THE NEW MIDDLE AGES

BONNIE WHEELER, *Series Editor*

The New Middle Ages is a series dedicated to transdisciplinary studies of medieval cultures, with particular emphasis on recuperating women's history and on feminist and gender analyses. This peer-reviewed series includes both scholarly monographs and essay collections.

PUBLISHED BY PALGRAVE:

Women in the Medieval Islamic World: Power, Patronage, and Piety
   edited by Gavin R. G. Hambly

The Ethics of Nature in the Middle Ages: On Boccaccio's Poetaphysics
   by Gregory B. Stone

Presence and Presentation: Women in the Chinese Literati Tradition
   by Sherry J. Mou

The Lost Love Letters of Heloise and Abelard: Perceptions of Dialogue in Twelfth-Century France
   by Constant J. Mews

Understanding Scholastic Thought with Foucault
   by Philipp W. Rosemann

For Her Good Estate: The Life of Elizabeth de Burgh
   by Frances A. Underhill

Constructions of Widowhood and Virginity in the Middle Ages
   edited by Cindy L. Carlson and Angela Jane Weisl

Motherhood and Mothering in Anglo-Saxon England
   by Mary Dockray-Miller

Listening to Heloise: The Voice of a Twelfth-Century Woman
   edited by Bonnie Wheeler

The Postcolonial Middle Ages
   edited by Jeffrey Jerome Cohen

Chaucer's Pardoner and Gender Theory: Bodies of Discourse
   by Robert S. Sturges

Crossing the Bridge: Comparative Essays on Medieval European and Heian Japanese Women Writers
   edited by Barbara Stevenson and Cynthia Ho

Engaging Words: The Culture of Reading in the Later Middle Ages
   by Laurel Amtower

Robes and Honor: The Medieval World of Investiture
   edited by Stewart Gordon

Representing Rape in Medieval and Early Modern Literature
   edited by Elizabeth Robertson and Christine M. Rose

Same Sex Love and Desire Among Women in the Middle Ages
   edited by Francesca Canadé Sautman and Pamela Sheingorn

Sight and Embodiment in the Middle Ages: Ocular Desires
   by Suzannah Biernoff

Listen, Daughter: The Speculum Virginum and the Formation of Religious Women in the Middle Ages
   edited by Constant J. Mews

Science, the Singular, and the Question of Theology
   by Richard A. Lee, Jr.

Gender in Debate from the Early Middle Ages to the Renaissance
   edited by Thelma S. Fenster and Clare A. Lees

Malory's Morte Darthur: Remaking
Arthurian Tradition
    by Catherine Batt

The Vernacular Spirit: Essays on Medieval
Religious Literature
    edited by Renate Blumenfeld-Kosinski,
    Duncan Robertson, and Nancy Warren

Popular Piety and Art in the Late Middle Ages:
Image Worship and Idolatry in England
1350–1500
    by Kathleen Kamerick

Absent Narratives, Manuscript Textuality,
and Literary Structure in Late Medieval
England
    by Elizabeth Scala

Creating Community with Food and Drink
in Merovingian Gaul
    by Bonnie Effros

Representations of Early Byzantine Empresses:
Image and Empire
    by Anne McClanan

Encountering Medieval Textiles and Dress:
Objects Texts, Images
    edited by Désirée G. Koslin and
    Janet Snyder

Eleanor of Aquitaine: Lord and Lady
    edited by Bonnie Wheeler and
    John Carmi Parsons

Isabel La Católica, Queen of Castile: Critical
Essays
    edited by David A. Boruchoff

Homoeroticism and Chivalry: Discourses of Male
Same-Sex Desire in the Fourteenth Century
    by Richard Zeikowitz

Portraits of Medieval Women: Family, Marriage,
and Politics in England 1225–1350
    by Linda E. Mitchell

Eloquent Virgins: From Thecla to Joan of Arc
    by Maud Burnett McInerney

The Persistence of Medievalism: Narrative
Adventures in Contemporary Culture
    by Angela Jane Weisl

Capetian Women
    edited by Kathleen Nolan

Joan of Arc and Spirituality
    edited by Ann W. Astell and Bonnie
    Wheeler

The Texture of Society: Medieval Women in
the Southern Low Countries
    edited by Ellen E. Kittell and
    Mary A. Suydam

Charlemagne's Mustache: And Other Cultural
Clusters of a Dark Age
    by Paul Edward Dutton

Troubled Vision: Gender, Sexuality, and Sight
in Medieval Text and Image
    edited by Emma Campbell and
    Robert Mills

Queering Medieval Genres
    by Tison Pugh

Sacred Place in Early Medieval Neoplatonism
    by L. Michael Harrington

The Middle Ages at Work
    edited by Kellie Robertson and
    Michael Uebel

Chaucer's Jobs
    by David R. Carlson

Medievalism and Orientalism: Three Essays on
Literature, Architecture and Cultural Identity
    by John M. Ganim

Queer Love in the Middle Ages
    by Anna Klosowska Roberts

Performing Women in the Middle Ages: Sex,
Gender and the Iberian Lyric
    by Denise K. Filios

PERFORMING WOMEN IN THE MIDDLE AGES: SEX, GENDER, AND THE IBERIAN LYRIC

Denise K. Filios

PERFORMING WOMEN IN THE MIDDLE AGES
© Denise K. Filios, 2005.

All rights reserved. No part of this book may be used or reproduced in any manner whatsoever without written permission except in the case of brief quotations embodied in critical articles or reviews.

First published in 2005 by
PALGRAVE MACMILLAN™
175 Fifth Avenue, New York, N.Y. 10010 and
Houndmills, Basingstoke, Hampshire, England RG21 6XS
Companies and representatives throughout the world.

PALGRAVE MACMILLAN is the global academic imprint of the Palgrave Macmillan division of St. Martin's Press, LLC and of Palgrave Macmillan Ltd. Macmillan® is a registered trademark in the United States, United Kingdom and other countries. Palgrave is a registered trademark in the European Union and other countries.

ISBN 1–4039–6730–X

Library of Congress Cataloging-in-Publication Data

Filios, Denise K.
    Performing women in the middle ages : sex, gender and the Iberian lyric / Denise K. Filios.
        p. cm.—(The New Middle Ages series)
    Includes bibliographical references and index.
    ISBN 1–4039–6730–X
    1. Spanish poetry—To 1500—History and criticism. 2. Portuguese poetry—To 1500—History and criticism. 3. Women in literature. 4. Sex role in literature. 5. Identity (Psychology) in literature. 6. Impersonation. I. Title. II. New Middle Ages (Palgrave Macmillan (Firm)).

PQ6058.F56 2005
861'.04093522—dc22   2004052796

A catalogue record for this book is available from the British Library.

Design by Newgen Imaging Systems (P) Ltd., Chennai, India.

First edition: February 2005

10 9 8 7 6 5 4 3 2 1

Printed in the United States of America.

CONTENTS

ACKNOWLEDGMENTS

In a book about the performative, constructed nature of identity, I'd like to acknowledge those who have helped construct the identity I perform in these pages. My interests in medieval studies, gender, and performance were piqued as an undergraduate at the University of Massachusetts-Amherst where I studied with Elizabeth Petroff, Maria Tymoczko, Robert Creed, and Harlan Sturm, interests that continued to develop at the University of California at Berkeley under the tutelage of Charles B. Faulhaber, Louise O. Vasvári, Carolyn Dinshaw, Joseph J. Duggan, James T. Monroe, Arthur Askins, and John K. Walsh. I benefited greatly from the support and peer feedback I received in dissertation and research writing groups; thanks to Lisa Darien, Afrodesia E. McCannon, Kim Starr-Reid, Elizabeth Wheeler, Francesca Royster, and Lisa Dresner, my fellow students at Berkeley, and to Eileen Willingham and Laura G. Gutiérrez, my dear colleagues at the University of Iowa. I also want to thank César Pérez for carefully reading and helping revise my translations, Maria José Barbosa for helping me obtain permissions from the Biblioteca da Ajuda, Barbara F. Weissberger and Nancy F. Marino for their advice and support, the anonymous readers whose reports were so helpful in preparing the final version of this book, and my most enthusiastic supporter and ever-patient reader, Jonathan Wilcox. Any remaining errors are, of course, my own.

I would like to acknowledge the Mellon Foundation and the Department of Comparative Literature at the University of California at Berkeley as well as the Provost's Office and the College of Liberal Arts and Sciences of the University of Iowa for their financial support during my research and writing of this book. Selections from chapter 2 were previously published as "Female Voices in the *Cantigas de escarnio e de mal dizer*: Index and Commentary" in *Bulletin of Spanish Studies* 81 (2004): 135–55; parts of chapter 3 previously appeared in "Rewriting History in the *Coplas de la panadera*," *Hispanic Review* 71 (2003): 345–63 (reprinted with permission of publishers).

INTRODUCTION

FEMALE VOICES IN THE MEDIEVAL LYRIC

Medieval Iberian lyric is full of uppity women mouthing off. While courtly ladies tend to be silent objects of poets' desire, the voices of degraded female characters—performers, prostitutes, and peasants, working women of low social status who lack honor and respectability—resound in both popular and courtly lyrics. In thirteenth-century Galician-Portuguese *Cantigas d'escarnho e de mal dizer* (satiric-obscene songs), *soldadeiras* (professional female entertainers/prostitutes) talk back to priests, poets, and even King Alfonso X el Sabio (1221–84), challenging their privilege and criticizing their sexual performances. In the fourteenth-century *Libro de buen amor*, aggressive *serranas* (women who herd cattle or sheep in the mountains) threaten, beat, and rape the male protagonist, Juan Ruiz, who seems to like it. In the anonymous fifteenth-century *Coplas de la panadera*, a *panadera* (female bread baker and vendor/prostitute) provides a satiric account of the Battle of Olmedo (1445), showing the aristocracy of Castile and Aragon farting, vomiting, and shitting as they flee the battlefield in terror. Why would elite male poets cite these unruly and vulgar voices, incorporating resistant female characters into their fictive worlds?[1]

I argue that the answer lies in the performativity of medieval lyric. Poets used the lyric to construct and perform certain identities that they assumed in reaction to other characters' performances within both the poetic and metapoetic worlds. Comic-obscene poetry focuses particular attention on the relationship between body and identity. While male speakers may parade the phallus in order to authenticate masculine superiority, verbally and sexually aggressive women frequently complain that men's weak bodies do not back up their words with action.[2] In performance, the songs' fictive bodies are brought to life by singers and musicians whose voices, gestures, and bodies violate normative codes of decorum and respectability. Throughout the Middle Ages, lyric was disseminated orally before a live audience. The complexity of these performances varied greatly, ranging from formal courtly spectacles complete with costumes, masks, choreography, and special effects, to informal popular tunes sung by humble men and women to entertain themselves and others while they worked. Poets performed their own verses in courts, marketplaces, and streets throughout medieval Iberia. Lyric performances tended to be rather simple spectacles; the number of performers varied, from a single *juglar* (minstrel) who sang and perhaps accompanied himself with a percussive or stringed instrument, to a group of performers who sang, played instruments, danced and/or impersonated various characters.[3]

The meanings created in each performance depended upon the individual performers, the songs they sang, the audience, and the performance space and time. Courtly performances of the thirteenth-century Galician-Portuguese *Cantigas d'escarnho* were rather spontaneous events intended to provoke laughter by exposing courtiers' bodies and inappropriate behaviors. For the most part these were jokes among friends, exchanges of ritual insults that allowed court wits to use taboo words and gestures as part of the game while staging their bodies as well as those of the individuals around them, especially those of courtesans.[4] The urban setting of the fourteenth-century *Libro de buen amor* suggests that its comic songs were performed in public spaces, in markets or *plazas*, by professional performers, not by the noble courtiers who enacted the *Cantigas d'escarnho*. A single *juglar* would perform the role of Juan Ruiz, the amorous cleric whose attempts at seduction consistently fail until he leaves the city and finds himself the target of sexual assault in the mountains. Fifteenth-century comic-erotic *cancionero* poetry returns to the court to stage events that occurred elsewhere, in mountains, towns, or battlefields, reenacting courtiers' pastoral adventures and degraded women's speeches within the elite space of the court. Courtly lyric allowed noble poets to stage themselves, to adopt certain identities vis-à-vis others, and even to impersonate other members of the court, all within the play space of the lyric.

While the dominant thrust of comic-obscene and comic-erotic poetry is misogynist, its fictive portraits of degraded female characters challenge normative constructions of identity and put gender and sexual norms into play. Female roles were frequently performed by men, even by noblemen; by assuming the mannerisms and voices of immodest, oversexed women, male performers broke with their normative identities, "slumming" as they mimicked women's vulgar performances. Transgendered performances, like all performances of identity, are conventional, made up of infinitely repeatable stylized behaviors that signify and express certain recognizable identity traits. Male performers who impersonated degraded female characters reenacted stereotypical behaviors; such performances could reinforce negative commonplaces and thereby naturalize and reify these identity constructions. However, the spectacle of elite men acting like degraded women specifically played with the link between certain bodies and certain conventional identities; transgendered performances challenged dominant constructions of identity as fixed and innate, that is, as determined by one's body, gender, rank, occupation, religion, and place of origin. By impersonating degraded female characters, male performers played with identity construction in general; their onstage lyric performances as others implied that their own, offstage identities could also be mere acts. Within the fictive space of the lyric, transgendered performances by men impersonating *soldadeiras, panaderas,* and *serranas* exposed the socially-constructed nature of identity itself.[5]

While quite frequently men impersonated degraded female characters, women performed these roles as well. My title, *Performing Women,* is deliberately ambiguous. I use it to refer to men who impersonated women, adopting stereotypically feminine traits while voicing female parts in lyric spectacles. These parodic performances of femininity emphasized the difference between the individual performing and the identity he adopted for the moment. I also intend it to refer to female performers, both historical and fictive. *Soldadeiras* and *panaderas* are not only fictive roles; historic women exercised these functions in the courts and marketplaces of medieval Iberia.[6] The poetic depictions of these characters can help illuminate real women's performances, which left few traces in the historical record. Historic *soldadeiras* were central to the Galician-Portuguese lyric spectacle. The documentary and visual evidence for *soldadeiras'* performances show that they sang, played percussive instruments, and danced at court alongside *trovadores* (amateur poets and performers) and *jograis* (professional performers and minstrels). Francisco Nodar Manso suggests that the individuals named in particular *Cantigas d'escarnho* participated in their performance, voicing their part and/or miming reactions to the *trovador's* depiction of them. I argue that when an individual *soldadeira* uttered the words put into her mouth by a *trovador,* her performance was double-voiced, enunciating someone else's words as though they were her own, and ironic, as she impersonated herself. I call such self-performance "parodic mimicry" to underline the exaggerated, partial imitation of one's offstage identity in an onstage performance.[7] The dynamics of parodic mimicry permeate *trovador* spectacles, heightening the play between fictive and actual identities. In playing these identities, poets and performers play with the very idea of identity.

In this book, I focus on depictions of female performers in comic-obscene and comic-erotic lyrics composed and performed in the courts and marketplaces of Castile during the medieval and early modern period (roughly between 1250 and 1550). In order to limit the scope of this study,

I focus on three female performers who are associated with particular spaces and social contexts, namely the courtly *soldadeira*, the urban *panadera*, and the rural *serrana*. While the three characters I discuss are socially marginalized, the spaces they inhabit are not necessarily so; the order in which I discuss these characters is not based on chronology but on the distance between the space the character inhabits and centers of power. These characters also differ in their identity as entertainers. The *soldadeira* is a professional performer who depended upon her entertaining skills for her livelihood; other professional entertainers include the *cantadera*, the *danzadera*, and the *juglaresa* (female singer, dancer, minstrel, and courtesan/courtly performer). I consider the *panadera* a semi-professional performer, since she engaged in entertaining performances as part of her profession; she sang, danced, and orated in order to advertise her wares and supplement her income. Other semi-professional female entertainers include the prostitute, the healer, and perhaps the most famous of all medieval Iberian working women, the *alcahueta* (panderer/go-between).[8] The *serrana* is an amateur entertainer who sang, danced, and/or orated within her usual social circles in order to amuse herself and to alleviate the tedium of daily tasks. Focusing on these three characters enables me to discuss how poets used them to construct different social spaces and identities and to engage in various parodic performances in reaction to them.

These three characters also differ in the scope of lyrics in which they appear. The *soldadeira* appears almost exclusively in thirteenth-century Galician-Portuguese *Cantigas d'escarnho*, especially in lyrics authored at the courts of Fernando III and his son Alfonso X; almost all of the lyrics are themselves set and performed at court by named poets. The specificity of time, space, and personal allusions enables me to address the subtleties of individuals impersonating themselves and others before an audience that knows both the established poetic and personal identities of all the individuals named in the songs. By contrast, *panaderas* and *serranas* appear in a broad range of lyrics, both popular and literary, composed throughout the medieval and early modern periods. Critics have studied the *panadera* almost exclusively as a literary or folkloric character and almost never as a performer, despite the importance of verbal artistry in the medieval marketplace. Most literary *panaderas* are unnamed stock characters and so probably are not fictive depictions of historic individuals like the *soldadeira*. *Panaderas* appear in popular lyrics, in the *Libro de buen amor*, in *cancionero* lyrics composed by Antón de Montoro and Sebastián de Horozco, and in the anonymous *Coplas de la panadera*. Each of these texts depict a *panadera* in performance, negotiating the sale of bread and/or of sex, commenting on her experience in the marketplace, or criticizing her social superiors, presenting her as a social actor interacting with her customers. The *serrana*, unlike the *soldadeira* and the *panadera*, is purely a fictive character; although female herders worked and lived in the mountains of Castile, the poetic depiction of a traveler's encounter with a *serrana* has little to do with historic shepherdesses.[9] While *serranas* appear in popular and literary texts throughout the medieval and Golden Age periods, I have chosen to focus on their depiction in Juan Ruiz's *Libro de buen amor* and in fifteenth-century *cancionero* poetry by Íñigo López de Mendoza, known more commonly as the Marqués de Santillana, and by Carvajal. Limiting my study to these three poets enables me to explore how they use the *serrana* to play with their own identities and with the meaning of social spaces, contrasting the wild *sierra* with the civilized space of court or town. Each of these characters enables performers to assume roles that put their offstage identities into play; they allow elite male poets to assume self-deprecating roles that mock their accustomed privilege, while less elite poet-performers use them to locate themselves within a broad and heterogeneous poetic and social landscape.

I begin chapter 1 with an overview of the performance practices associated with various types of poetic spectacles during thirteenth-, fourteenth-, and fifteenth-century Iberia. Very few medieval descriptions of poetic performances survive, and those that do tend to condemn *juglaresque* spectacles; modern scholars must approach the evidence we do have with care. I turn to performance theory, ethnographical studies of female performers in traditional contexts, and discussions of gender and music to enable me to reconstruct medieval performance practices and comment on the significance of women's performances in particular. I am interested in the link between public performance, social status, and respectability. Professional female performers, especially dancers, were considered prostitutes because they accepted money for physical self-display. Their bodies, loaded with symbolic meaning, were constructed as essentially different from other women's bodies, a difference often compounded by the performers' social and/or ethnic difference. While their status as female performers gained them economic independence and access to elite social spaces, they were also viewed as potential sources of pollution, as members of the audience could be tempted to imitate these women's immodest acts. In this chapter I also provide a theory of medieval performance, exploring the complex interactions between performers, audience, place, and time, each of which affect the dynamics of individual performances.

In chapter 2 I examine the character of the *soldadeira* in the *Cantigas d'escarnho e de mal dizer*, focusing on *cantigas* that show *soldadeiras* in performance. I articulate how these fictive performances could have been staged, by whom, and how the audience could have reacted. As I explain in chapter 1, facetious interpretations of equivocal song lyrics formed an essential part of courtly poetic spectacles; the informal and spontaneous nature of these interpretive games caused them to be excluded from the poetic record.[10] I suggest that individual *soldadeiras* ironically performed stereotypical, vulgar identities both within lyric spectacles and offstage in conversational exchanges. These performances of self conflated their offstage and onstage identities, creating anxiety and leading to confusion as to how "authentic" their behaviors were. The *soldadeira's* presence at court created room to play with inappropriate behaviors and identities, if only in the fictive world of the courtly lyric. I also examine how poets play with their own sexual, gender, and class identities by defining themselves in line with, or in opposition to, *soldadeiras*. Poets of such diverse rank as King Alfonso el Sabio and Joan Baveca, a *jogral*, used their fictive portrayals of *soldadeiras* to enable themselves to perform a fictive identity as the first-person poetic narrator. This fictive identity ironically incorporated elements of poets' offstage identities, enabling poet-performers to impersonate themselves as well as the *soldadeiras* they cited in their verse.

In chapter 3 I turn to the *panadera*, a familiar figure of the marketplace, since women dominated the medieval Iberian bread trade. I examine how *panaderas* in popular and elite lyrics perform as marketplace orators, advertising their wares, negotiating sales, and haranguing crowds during popular protests. *Panadera* lyrics play on the erotic connotations of *pan* (both bread and female genitals [and sometimes male]), creating ambiguity as to the object that is being offered for sale. Since bread making is a manual process, requiring lengthy kneading to develop the dough, the fact that *panaderas* were considered prostitutes created anxiety as to whether the bread they produced was polluted. The principal difference between profane, daily bread and the Host lay in the hands that prepared them, belonging to either degraded *panaderas* or women religious. Popular lyrics that present the Virgin as a *panadera* who makes her "bread" available to all Christians play on contradictory bread imagery. *Panaderas'* association with pollution, sex, and popular protests culminates in the anonymous *Coplas de la panadera*. In this poem the unnamed *panadera* turns her billingsgate discourse to social commentary, attacking the rhetorical strategies adopted by the royal Castilian propagandists in their account of the Battle of Olmedo. The *panadera's* alternative account focuses on the weak, grotesque bodies of the noble combatants, restoring the embarrassing details the court's version omits.

In chapter 4, I discuss the *serrana*, the best known of these three characters and the one with the greatest variety of depictions in fourteenth- and fifteenth-century lyric. Unlike the *soldadeira* and the *panadera*, the character of the *serrana* was almost exclusively impersonated by a man; while the *serrana* as a fictive character certainly performs class, sexuality, and gender, the actual performer was a male poet who sang of his erotic adventures to amuse his courtly or urban audience. Poems on *serranas* project the supine female form onto mountainous landscapes, construing voyages through the *sierra* as adventures of sexual exploration and conquest. The motif of woman as mountain has appeared most recently in *Amante menguante*, (*Shrinking Lover*) the silent film segment of Almodóvar's *Hable con ella* (*Talk to Her*), in which a miniature man joyfully explores the gigantic body of his sleeping lover, losing himself in her cavernous vagina.[11] In medieval erotic topographies, the female form is not passive; like the hostile terrain within which she lives, the *serrana* resists the male traveler's attempts to impose his will upon her. The articulation and outcome of the conflict between man and feminized nature varies greatly in poems on *serranas*. I argue that in the *Libro de buen amor* the male protagonist, Juan Ruiz, chooses to "provar la sierra" (950b, try out the mountains) in order to play the victim of sexually aggressive *serranas*. In the Marqués de Santillana's eight *serranillas*, his aristocratic alter ego dominates both the landscape and body of the beautiful *serranas* he meets. Carvajal, the other great fifteenth-century *serranilla* poet and a Castilian residing in the Aragonese court at Naples, uses the *serranilla* to illustrate his tenuous place in the Italian landscape. While his projection of Iberian poetic conventions onto Italian terrains could be read as an imperialistic gesture, the ineptness of his love-struck travelers and the always-dismissive attitude of the women they encounter instead suggest, as does the work of Ruiz, that feminized landscapes resist conquest by elite male culture.

Performance proves to be the key for appreciating the significance of gender and verbal play in comic-obscene and comic-erotic lyrics. Lyrics on *soldadeiras*, *panaderas*, and *serranas* focus attention on the performative nature of identity. These lyric spectacles rupture the normative links between certain bodies and certain identities. In non-play contexts, the notion of identity as fixed and unchangeable supports the hierarchical social structure and the differentiation of individuals based on birth, gender, religion, and occupation. Acknowledging that identity is performative challenges the dominant notion of identity construction and can create anxiety, especially among those who benefit from unequal social structures. Play spaces and time license the expression of taboo words and notions, especially that of the performative nature of identity; for this reason, I argue, jurists and theologians repeatedly condemn performers whose immodest acts violate decorum as well as fixed identity categories.

Despite female performers' prominence in poetic spectacles, to date there has been no book-length study of women and performance in medieval Spain. Recently medievalists have explored courtly performances of identity in England, France, and Spain; most, especially Hispanomedievalists, focus on male performances of identity.[12] Nonetheless, the recent surge of publications on women and medieval music demonstrates the high level of interest in female performers. The women *trouvères* and *trobairitz* of France have received the most attention; in broad studies of medieval female performers throughout Europe, discussion of Iberian entertainers, if present at all, is often limited to Muslim singers and dancers.[13] Judith R. Cohen has recently written on women performers in the three cultures of medieval Spain; David Ashurst and Catherine Léglu also discuss Iberian *soldadeiras*, yet use them to highlight male performers (in the case of Ashurst) or French performance practices (Léglu). In his encyclopedic and still unsurpassed discussion of minstrel traditions in Spain, Ramón Menéndez Pidal acknowledged that female performers existed, yet he downplayed their importance, focusing instead on male poets and performers throughout the medieval period.[14] This book redresses the neglect of female performers in Spain; examining both historical female performers and female characters in lyric spectacles, I can study performances omitted from medieval documents and from modern scholarly work. My approach, which examines the traditional literary concerns of character and genre definitions through the lens of gender and performance theory, helps bridge a gulf already profitably crossed in medieval French and English studies. This study makes both familiar and rarely read poems meaningful to a modern audience by focusing on how the embodied performances of medieval men and women brought lyric texts to life and played with the performative nature of identity. The *soldadeira*, *panadera*, and *serrana* take their place in medieval Spanish studies alongside the *alcahueta* and Trotaconventos, as female performers whose fictive portraits give modern scholars access to underworlds otherwise omitted from the historical and literary record.

CHAPTER 1

PERFORMING WOMEN IN MEDIEVAL IBERIAN
POETIC SPECTACLES: HISTORY AND THEORY

Lyric poetry is text brought to life in the bodies and voices of performers. The embodied nature of musical performances increases the eroticism of medieval poetry, within which images of idealized courtly love as well as explicit sex acts and taboo body parts abound. Performances of secular lyric permeated daily life in medieval Iberia, ranging from highly respectable, elaborately staged courtly spectacles to vulgar dances and gestures illustrating comic-obscene songs. Sex sells, in the Middle Ages as now; lyric performance included suggestive songs used by vendors to advertise their wares and attract customers' attention. The immodesty of some acts caused their performers to be stigmatized as agents of the devil; theologians and jurists claimed that the pleasure their acts produced could lead spectators to imitate them and thereby to sin as well. The ubiquity of lyric performances, their primarily oral nature, and the breadth of lyric genres led to a sketchy and biased treatment of lyric performers in medieval sources. The marginality of professional performers, especially women, exacerbated this partial treatment, making the job of modern scholars who wish to examine their ephemeral performances particularly thorny.[1]

In this study of comic-obscene and comic-erotic poetry, I explore two levels of performance: lyric spectacles and the performativity of the lyric. By "lyric spectacles," I mean oral delivery before a live audience. While this aspect of the medieval lyric is difficult to analyze due to the lack of evidence, nonetheless the concept of lyric spectacles is relatively straightforward. In the first part of this chapter, I examine the evidence we do have, both visual and documentary, and I discuss other scholars' attempts to reconstruct lyric spectacles. Francisco Nodar Manso's quite ambitious and controversial reconstruction of dramatic sequences from the Galician-Portuguese *cancioneiros* deserves particular attention. In the second part of this chapter, I address the other, more complicated level of performance, the performativity of lyric: the way that lyric texts repeatedly attribute certain conventional traits to fictive characters, thereby playing with conventional constructions of social identity. Luigi Allegri denies that *juglares* impersonated fictive characters in their poetic performances, implying that identity was not at stake in lyric spectacles. I appeal to performance theorists such as Judith Butler, Marvin Carlson, and Richard Schechner to explicate how lyric performances put identity into play. Finally, I address the dominant construction of professional female performers in contrast to amateur male performers. Different attitudes toward different types of performers deeply affected the meanings created in performance.[2]

Poetic Spectacles in Medieval Iberia

I have already alluded to some of the unknowns about medieval Iberian performance practices that result from a lack of documentation and the fragmentary nature of the documents, both historical and poetic, that we do have. We must view the written poetic texts that survive as mere traces of performances lifted from their original context and recontextualized in ways that reflect the preferences of the compilers of *cancioneros* and not the full extent of poetic practices in medieval Spain. Most of the texts I discuss are lyric poems found in fourteenth-, fifteenth-, and sixteenth-century anthologies. Galician-Portuguese profane lyric is found in three principal collections, the *Cancioneiro da Ajuda*, copied at the end of the thirteenth- or beginning of the fourteenth century, and the two anthologies compiled in Rome during the early sixteenth century, the *Cancioneiro Portuguez da Vaticana* and the *Cancioneiro da Biblioteca Nacional* (formerly known as the Colocci-Brancuti).[3] Of these, only the *Cancioneiro da Ajuda* could have been compiled by members of the poetic community that produced the three hundred and ten *cantigas* contained in it, and almost all these lyrics are *Cantigas d'amor*, just one of the genres composed and performed by Galician-Portuguese poets. While the *Cancioneiro da Ajuda* is a luxury manuscript with illuminations of lyric spectacles and room for musical notation, it was never finished; if it were complete, our knowledge of thirteenth-century courtly performance practices would be incomparably enriched.

In fifteenth- and sixteenth-century Castile, *cancioneros* became a boom business; sources for anthologists proliferated, ranging from *cancioneros* in friends' possession to *pliegos sueltos* found at many secular scriptoria. *Cancioneros* sometimes include rubrics that comment on the poet's motivation for composing the poem; nonetheless, these rubrics do not fully contextualize the poetry, nor do they indicate how the lyric was performed.[4] Medieval and early modern popular lyrics were haphazardly preserved in a variety of Golden Age texts. Margit Frenk's *Corpus de la antigua lírica popular hispánica* collects the popular lyrics she has identified in a single volume, which is very useful; however, such a collection further decontextualizes these lyrics, which had already been decontextualized by the writers who cited them.[5] In short, written poetic records cannot capture what must have been the full excitement of the lyric spectacle.

Most *cancioneros* omit musical notation and performance directions, so that we do not know the number of voices that sang any given lyric, the performers' gender, their use of gesture and/or dance, and the musical accompaniment, if any. Monodic musical notation is included in most of the manuscripts of the *Cantigas de Santa Maria*, yet little notation survives for secular Galician-Portuguese lyric. Monodic notation for six of Martin Codax's *Cantigas d'amigo* was discovered in 1914 and that for seven of Don Dinis's *Cantigas d'amor* in 1990.[6] There is no extant notation for the *Cantigas d'escarnho*. For fifteenth-century *cancionero* lyric, musical notation is found principally in the *Cancionero musical de la Colombina* (SV1) and the *Cancionero musical de Palacio* (MP4). The polyphonic notation in these *cancioneros* does not unambiguously indicate the gender of the singers, the number of voices that performed, or the instruments that accompanied them. While musical *cancioneros* were probably used as guides for singers and musicians in performance, they were visual aids that supplemented the singers' previous knowledge of the song and the direction they received from the composer and other experienced musicians.[7] Musical *cancioneros*, like all medieval *cancioneros*, preserve in writing the primarily oral genre of the lyric, and much is lost in the translation.

Perhaps the most promising source of information for courtly poetic spectacles is the visual evidence found in illustrations in the manuscripts of Galician-Portuguese lyric, especially in the *Cantigas de Santa Maria* and the *Cancioneiro da Ajuda*. Many of these illustrations show lyric performances that probably reflect actual performance practices. Since I focus on secular lyric, the illustrations in the *Cancioneiro da Ajuda* are of particular interest. Unfortunately, none of the illuminations in this manuscript are finished. While attire, clothing, and instruments are clearly illustrated, the performers' faces, hair, and hands are often faint; facial features are sketched lightly, and none of the figures' mouths are open to sing. In some cases it is difficult to determine the gender of the figures. I follow Carolina Michäelis de Vasconcelos's identifications of these figures, which I find generally reliable.[8]

Of the sixteen illustrations in the *Cancioneiro da Ajuda*, female performers appear in twelve. All but one of the sixteen depict three figures in a triangular arrangement within a stylized room or building that represents the performance space. To the left sits a male figure usually read as a *trovador* or *maestre*. The central figure stands and plays an instrument; in four illustrations, this figure is a woman whose arms are raised and hold castanets. The far right figure tends to be smaller than the other two, suggesting s/he plays a supporting role; in eight illustrations, this figure is female, and holds castanets (in three), plays a tambourine (in three), or stands not holding any instruments (in two). Carolina Michäelis de Vasconcelos and Ramón Menéndez Pidal read the instrumentalists as *jograis* or professional performers. It is noteworthy that none of the figures holds or consults a text, suggesting that the performance is completely oral; they do glance at each other, suggesting nonverbal communication between the performers. I agree with Menéndez Pidal that performers of different ranks collaborated in the *trovador* spectacle and that the *trovador* occupied a position of authority over the other two; I also see him as performing in a manner appropriate to his elevated rank. While the *trovador*'s hand gestures can be read as directions to the other performers, they could also be designed to illustrate the posture of a speaking character. This division of roles and ranks informs my analysis of the dynamics of lyric performances. While these illustrations are specific to thirteenth-century Galician-Portuguese love lyric, I believe the small number of performers and relatively simple presentation style characterized most lyric spectacles throughout the medieval period, in both courtly and public spaces.[9]

In the four *Cancioneiro da Ajuda* illustrations in which the female performer is the central figure, she is visually the most striking of the three figures. Her raised arms call attention to her upper body, especially in the images on f. 16 and f. 59, in which one hand is raised above her head and she is not wearing a cloak. In the illustrations on f. 4 and f. 17, the female performer's hands are not as high and she wears a cloak that covers her lower torso, reducing the element of self-display. The raised arms suggest all four performers are dancing; their posture and gender lead me to read them as *soldadeiras*. In comparison with the female performers, the bodily display of the male figures is much less overt. The musicians hold their instruments in front of their bodies, and the seated *trovadores*' range of movement is limited, although they do make gestures with their hands and feet.

These illustrations show that female performers played central roles in *trovador* spectacles; they also imply some tension as to who was in charge of the spectacle, the seated *trovador* or the standing, active, spectacular *soldadeira*. It is worth noting that in the *Cancioneiro da Ajuda* as in the famous *Códice de los músicos* of the *Cantigas de Santa Maria*, the female performers almost exclusively play percussive instruments. Tamborines, drums, and castanets require almost no training; they also mark the rhythm to which the *jogral* played and the dancers and audience moved, allowing the percussionist to control the song's tempo. Percussive instruments, especially in the hands of dancers and singers, encourage audience participation, in the medieval lyric spectacle as now; dancers move about the performance space and approach the audience, mediating between the scripted performers and the live audience, increasing the spontaneity of the performance, and opening the stage up to audience interaction. As I discuss later in this chapter, the dancer's greater proximity to the audience made her movements yet more suggestive; they could incite codified public expressions of private desires, on the part of the audience as well as the performers. In the case of comic-obscene songs, taboo lyrics would further encourage salacious acts. Audience participation helps break down barriers between performers and audience, encouraging the spectators to imitate the onstage movements and songs, as the theologian Martín Pérez, cited below, so feared. Later in this chapter I explain how performance space, time, and audience could make such onstage behaviors acceptable and even respectable.[10]

Law codes such as the *Siete Partidas*, compiled by Alfonso X, can also help us understand the social significance of lyric performances. I have already mentioned that performers of various ranks collaborated in courtly lyric spectacles; performers' status is also variable, dependent upon the performance space, the audience composition, and their motivation for performing. While most medievalists argue that performing for money incurs dishonor, *Partida* 7.6.4 puts more emphasis on the performance space and audience composition:

> Otrosi [son enfamados] los que son juglares, e los remedadores, e los faze-dores de los çaharrones que publicamente andan por el pueblo: o cantan, o fazen juego por precio, esto es porque se enuilecen ante todos por aquel pre-cio que les dan. Mas los que tañeren estrumentos, o cantassen por fazer solaz assi mesmos: o por fazer plazer a sus amigos: o dar solaz a los Reyes, o alos otros señores, non serian porende enfamados.[11]

> Also [defamed] are those minstrels and actors and masked performers who publicly wander through the town, singing or playing for money. [They are defamed] because they abase themselves before all for the money which they pay them. But those who play instruments or sing to amuse themselves, to entertain their friends, or to give pleasure to kings or other lords, would not therefore be defamed.

Enfamado means "lacking honor and respectability," a status that carried significant legal and social repercussions.[12] While the fact that *juglares* and other entertainers perform for money is mentioned twice, equally important is the public nature of their acts. Also telling is the silence as to whether those who perform for their peers and social superiors receive payment, nor is the performers' rank mentioned. The audience and the performance space matter; the same act performed before different audiences and in different spaces signifies differently. This distinction favors courtly *trovador* spectacles while denigrating public *juglaresque* performances and reserves for the elite the privilege of music and song.

This distinction also means that noblemen could engage in entertaining performances before their fellow courtiers without degrading themselves; the private, exclusive nature of the court protects the good reputations of the courtiers who entertain their peers. While most Hispanomedievalists argue that the upper nobility did not perform the lyrics they composed (or, perhaps more accurately, attributed to them), I believe that in some cases they did. Guillaume IX, duke of Acquitaine, count of Poitiers, and the 'first' troubadour, performed his own comic-obscene verse at court, without losing the respect of his peers.[13] Songs written by such elite poets as Alfonso X and the Marqués de Santillana frequently play with their elevated rank. Alfonso shows his (persona's) lack of influence over an angry *soldadeira* bent on avenging herself on Pero d'Ambroa, as I discuss in chapter 2; the Marqués, on the other hand, depicts his persona as playing a shepherd to seduce a *serrana*, as discussed in chapter 4. I argue these two magnates performed these and similar lyrics within an intimate courtly circle. Doing so enabled them to participate fully in the pleasure of the lyric spectacle, to put aside their customary superiority, and to play at being equal to the other courtiers, enjoying the temporary and fictive equality created by the play space. Such performances increased the bonds of intimacy and trust between magnate and inferior, as the magnate spoofed himself and trusted his 'friends' not to take this play with rank seriously, that is, not to read his onstage act as giving them license to treat him as their equal during non-play times. This is not to deny that often the elite employed others to perform their works in order to preserve decorum and to increase deniability should a certain song not be well received. Performers of inferior rank who performed these pieces would speak with the voice of their superiors and get license to impersonate them, more or less seriously; they would get to play up, mimicking the great, just as, on other occasions, the elite would play down. In the case of Alfonso X, many of 'his' lyrics were penned by others who attributed their work to the king in order to promote their dependent position at court; in performing these works in the name of the king, they would get to ventriloquize (the character of) the king and mimic him, undoubtedly in a flattering, sycophantic way. While I recognize that the aristocracy did not usually perform for their dependents, nonetheless, depending upon the time, space, audience, and text, members of the highest ranks could perform comic songs without putting their respectability in jeopardy.

Ecclesiastic documents that discuss *juglaresque* performances in *plazas*, marketplaces, and taverns condemn these public displays of agile bodies and lascivious songs. Texts like Martín Pérez's fourteenth-century *Libro de las confesiones* repeat moralistic commonplaces of remote origin. While they do not accurately reflect local practices, they do illustrate certain dominant groups' attitudes toward and perceptions of *juglaresque* performances. They also provide useful information about performers and their acts. The following passage from the *Libro de las confesiones* provides a worthwhile description of various 'immoral' performance genres:

> Ay otros juglares que cantan cantares suzios e de caçorrias e otros cantares vanos de amor, que mueven a los omes a luxuria e a pecado quando los oyen. Otros fazen algunas encantaçiones, commo fazen algunos paresçer, con engaño, que mudan algunas cosas en culebras o en ranas o dados o en otras cosas tales que son contra natura e sobre natura, e estas cosas todas fazen ellos engañosamente, escarnesçiendo los ojos de los locos que se pagan de ver vanidades. E algunos destos traen instrumentos para cantar e algunos destos cantan en tavernas e en torpes e deshonestos lugares. Otrosi, son otros omes e mugeres que cantan sin instrumentos, quebrantando sus cuerpos e saltando e tornayrando, endoblando sus cuerpos e torçiendo los ojos e las bocas o faziendo otros malos gestos e villanias de amor torpe e suzio, commo suelen algunos fazer, que semeja que han quebrantados los mienbros e asi los menean commo si los oviesen descoyuntados. Todos estos tales juglares e juglaresas, cantadores e cantaderas que tienen ofiçio del diablo para ençender los omes e mugeres en amor malo, todos son estriones e biven en grand peligro, ca non se pueden salvar, menos que desanparen aquellos ofiçios del todo e vengan a penitençia.[14]

> There are other *juglares* who sing dirty songs and *cazorrías* [rude songs] and other vapid songs of love which move men to lust and sin when they hear them. Others perform enchantments, like deceitfully making it seem that they change objects into snakes, frogs, dice or other things which are against nature and supernatural, and all these things they do with trickery, mocking the eyes of the foolish who enjoy seeing vanities. And some of those carry instruments and sing, and some sing in taverns and in vile and dishonest places. Also there are others, men and women, who sing without instruments, breaking their bodies and leaping and twisting, folding their bodies and distorting their eyes and mouths and making other evil gestures and indecorous acts of foolish and obscene love, as some tend to do, so that it seems that they have broken their limbs and they shake them as if they were dislocated. All such *juglares* and *juglaresas*, *cantadores* and *cantaderas* who do the devil's work to inflame men and women with evil love, all are *histriones* [entertainers] and they live in great peril, since they cannot save themselves unless they completely abandon that work and do penance.

Despite the condemnatory stance, this extensive listing of various performance skills illustrates the range of instrumental, vocal, and physical skills collectively cultivated by professional entertainers. While singing and playing instruments are prominent in the above passage, yet more prominent are physical skills such as slight-of-hand, contortionism, and acrobatics; Pérez also highlights facial gestures "et villanias de amor torpe et suzio," sexually suggestive body movements performed while singing erotic songs. He does not specifically mention female performers until near the end, where he presents them as performing spectacular physical displays. Pérez emphasizes that acrobatic and facial movements distort the body, 'breaking' it and 'dislocating' its joints. Far from reading these performances as demonstrations of artistic and athletic skills, he sees them as unnatural, obscene, and deceitful bodily movements. The physicality of the display may be what makes Pérez specify that women perform these acts. His association of women with bodily display implies both that he sees acrobatics as coded feminine and that the really disturbing aspect of such acts is the gendered nature of such bodily play. He seems to fear that men who perform acrobatics may be engaging in feminine acts and thereby destabilizing their gender identity.[15]

Given the author's identity and the purpose of the text he is producing, a guide for confessors, Pérez's negative attitude toward *juglaresque* performances is hardly surprising. He constructs *juglares* as the opposite of confessors, whose acts and words should correct sinners; in his scenario, the two performers, priestly confessor and immoral *juglar*, battle each other for the souls of their spectators. These two figures come together in that of the *clérigo ajuglarado*, either a cleric who turns *juglar* or a professional entertainer who dresses as a cleric; just such a figure is Juan Ruiz, the Archpriest of Hita and the narrator-protagonist of the *Libro de buen amor*. I discuss Ruiz's encounter with Cruz the *panadera* in chapter 3, and his four *cánticas de serrana* in chapter 4. Ruiz's identity as a cleric increases the irony of his erotic adventures and of his public reenactments of them; both are behaviors unbecoming to a priest. Ruiz would have enacted all the characters, mimicking himself as well as impersonating various female characters. While these roles may be feminine acts, the female characters are phallic and aggressive; the more passive role is assumed by the male narrator-protagonist. Louise O.Vasvári has discussed Ruiz's humiliating performances as acts of ritual femininity vis-à-vis the masculinized characters who defeat him. The spectacle of this *clérigo ajuglarado* performing feminine acts in a public space collapses conventional oppositions of gender and profession, as I discuss in chapter 4.[16]

Medieval law codes and chronicles combined with modern ethnographic studies can help us reconstruct other lyric performance genres mostly omitted from the written record. The *juego de palabras* ('word-play,' a ritual insult exchange) is described in *Partida* 2.9.30 as an entertaining game of wit and discretion played by courtiers; this game contributed to group cohesiveness yet also established a verbal hierarchy among players. As I have argued elsewhere, the *juego de palabras* is closely related to the *Cantigas d'escarnho*, the comic-obscene genre of Galician-Portuguese lyric.[17] Modern studies of ritual insult exchanges can help us appreciate the dialogic quality of *Cantiga d'escarnho* performances. Since this was an elite, homosocial game, it could be parodied by degraded women, as in RL 193, "Estavan oje duas soldadeiras" by Joan Baveca, in which the male narrator repeats an insult exchange among *soldadeiras*.[18] My discussion of this poem in chapter 2 explores the eroticism latent in insult exchanges, an eroticism revealed when naked *soldadeiras* play the game in the bath. We find a similarly parodic use of chivalric *pasos de armas* (a type of tournament) in a *serranilla* by the Marqués de Santillana, when Menga de Mançanares refuses to let a *cavallero* pass through her valley without wrestling. Medieval chronicles describe many chivalric games, all of which were elaborate affairs in which elite men and women performed ritualistic roles and/or enacted allegorical characters. These displays of conspicuous consumption not only demonstrate the increasing theatricalization of court life but also inform much *cancionero* verse, as I explain in chapter 4.[19] Marketplace performance genres included hawking songs and negotiating dialogues, genres that appear in fictive works like the *Libro de buen amor* yet not in documentary evidence. In chapter 3, I draw on modern studies of female vendors in traditional marketplaces to help me reconstruct performances of marketplace songs. Such lyrics play on the nexus of language, gender, desire, and power; generally, they show female vendors getting the better of their elite male customers, as verbal prowess neutralizes masculine privilege and economic power.[20]

In my reconstruction of poetic spectacles, I rely heavily on the monumental work of Ramón Menéndez Pidal, *Poesía juglaresca y juglares*. As he says in his foreword to the revised edition of 1957, his objective was to recuperate lost oral practices and demonstrate the importance of the anonymous *juglar* in preserving and creating poetic traditions; Menéndez Pidal privileges this figure over that of the *trovador* and other named poets whom positivist critics had credited with the wholesale creation of Romance poetry in the eleventh- and twelfth centuries. While he does not explicate the methodology he used to reconstruct *juglaresque* spectacles, it is clear that he drew upon his knowledge of modern *romancero* performances as well as his studies of ancient and medieval performance and a careful reading of the poetic corpus. Menéndez Pidal provides many brief vignettes of poetic spectacles, yet he reconstructs detailed performances only in a few cases, most notably that of the *Libro de buen amor*, which I discuss in chapters 3 and 4. His focus on the unnamed or unknown *juglar* causes him to omit *serranilla* performances by such an elevated figure as the Marqués de Santillana. While Menéndez Pidal acknowledges the importance of female performers, he relegates them to secondary status, and he does not describe their participation in the Galician-Portuguese *trovador* spectacle. For him, a figure such as María Pérez Balteira inspired the men around her to perform satiric song and self-mocking verse; her performance skills, he assumes, were primarily those of a good-time girl:

> Todo cuanto ella hacía caía en gracia y era motivo de chacota; mas de sus habilidades artísticas en el canto o en el baile ninguno dice una palabra, y, sin embargo, esas habilidades eran las que le daban entrada en la corte. ¡Hasta tal punto en las soldaderas podía ser la juglaría cosa insignificante al lado de su vida alegre y licenciosa!

> All that she did was received with good humor and prompted mockery; but no one says one word about her artistic skills in song or dance, and, nonetheless, these skills had gained her entrance to the court. For *soldaderas*, minstrelsy could be an insignificant thing compared with their happy and licentious lives!

This comment replicates misogynist strategies of extrapolating from one example a truism for all *soldadeiras*; moreover, his attitude toward silence in this case contrasts sharply with his recuperation project as expressed in his foreword. Menéndez Pidal feels no need to recover Balteira's historical performance practices obscured by the silences of the poetic record; instead, he assumes that silence equals insignificance, the same attitude for which he criticizes "la crítica positivista" and "individualista."[21] While Menéndez Pidal's work laid the ground for my own, he also left much for me, and others, to do.

After Menéndez Pidal, many eminent Hispanomedievalists have worked on poetic performances.[22] The work of Francisco Nodar Manso stands out for its daring reconstruction of poetic dramas based on Galician-Portuguese *cancioneiros*. Nodar Manso argues that Galician-Portuguese profane lyric included three dramatic genres, plays or skits performed by actor-singers (*arremedillo*, *juego de escarnio*, and *juego de erteiro*, all of which roughly translate to farce or mocking play). None of these dramas survived, Nodar Manso asserts, due to discriminatory scribal practices:

> no han llegado a nosotros la totalidad de las canciones que abarcaban los textos primitivos, debido a los criterios discriminatorios empleados por los amanuenses, que coleccionaron las cantigas por géneros y orden alfabético de

autor. . .y ya que en la Edad Media. . .le [*sic*] redacción del *texto literario* se hacía en folios sueltos, en los que se copiaba por separado el papel de cada actor, tal hábito facilitó la pérdida de muchas obras dramáticas. El hecho de que los escarnios se copiasen, implica que se utilizaban en varias representaciones (italics in original).[23]

the totality of the songs that the primitive texts included have not come down to us, due to the discriminatory criteria employed by the scribes, who collected the *cantigas* divided by genres and alphabetically ordered by author. . .and given that in the Middle Ages. . .the edition of the *literary text* was done on individual sheets on which were copied the separate parts of each actor, such a practice facilitated the loss of many dramatic works. The fact that the satires were copied implies that they were used in multiple performances.

Nodar Manso reconstructs nine poetic dramas from the extant *cantigas*, based upon unity of theme, characters, and genre; seven are comic-satirical texts, two love dramas. Since Nodar Manso's primary thesis is that Galician-Portuguese lyrics are theatrical texts, he focuses on reconstructing dramatic sequences that were repeated on a number of occasions by the same performers who sang lyrics attributed to them in the *cancioneiros*. His reconstructions of dramatic texts are highly speculative, a fact that has led many theater historians to criticize or ignore his work.[24]

From my point of view, the rigid, fixed aspect of the performances that Nodar Manso reconstructs is more problematic than the speculative aspect of his work. I value Nodar Manso's focus on performance practices, and I believe his reconstructions of the visual text of the *cantigas* he discusses are valid. However, his approach to the performance text denies the spontaneous nature of medieval lyric spectacles. Improvisation was the rule in medieval poetic and musical performance; even when reproducing another composer's work, performers would embellish and alter the music and lyrics to suit the immediate performance context. The line between composition and performance was fine; as Susan Boynton says, "Every musical performance was inherently an act of composition or recomposition."[25]

While Nodar Manso recognizes the importance of interaction among performers, he does not acknowledge that dialogic exchanges between performers and members of the audience played a key role in the poetic spectacle. Laura Kendrick's discussion of the game of facetious interpretations associated with Provençal verse applies equally to Galician-Portuguese lyric, especially to the *Cantigas d'escarnho* that revel in equivocation. Kendrick associates these interpretive games with scholastic debates:

Certain troubadours' *vidas* remark their ability at understanding and explaining their own or others' verse. The public explanation of lyrics seems to have been an integral part of the performance context; perhaps, in court as earlier in school, the performance of the verse was the "pretext" for competitive debate displaying and asserting the explicators' intellectual prowess and wit—the more explications the better, as long as each was found to be good.[26]

While these interpretive games were integral to troubadour performances, they were not accorded the same status as poetic compositions and were not preserved.

In my analysis of *Cantigas d'escarnho* on *soldadeiras* in chapter 2, I address not only how individual songs were performed but also the post-performance discussions in which various members of the audience participated; these discussions created additional room for other voices, including those of the *soldadeiras* named in the songs, to be brought into play. In my reconstructions of lyric performances in the following chapters, I address many components of performance, including space, time, and audience, as well as the identities of the performers and how they may have enacted the roles they played. Of course, my reconstructions are completely informed by my reading of these texts and of the identity and power issues they raise; my readings are also speculative, based on my sense of medieval lyric performances. I offer them as possible performance scenarios, not as prescriptions. I address poetic performance because it is key to understanding and appreciating how lyrics play with identity, as I explain below.

Theater historians tend to approach the question of poetic performances with caution. Most deny that poetic spectacles constitute theater or even para-theater. Ángel Gómez Moreno seems to fear that acknowledging the theatricality of medieval lyric will result in a proliferation of medieval performance texts, thereby reducing the significance of generic categories:

Sin embargo, una vez más, se impone recordar que uno de los rasgos definitorios de gran parte de la poesía románica del Medievo es su talante dramático; por ello, las propuestas de nuevas obras tal vez representadas o de rasgos que determinen su "representatividad" pueden incrementarse de modo considerable. ¿Se diseñó alguna de estas poesías con el propósito de llevarla a escena? ¿Alguna fue a parar a las tablas con posterioridad? ¿Hasta qué punto eran teatrales determinadas recitaciones poéticas? Son preguntas a las que difícilmente se puede responder.

Entre ellas, la última resulta en especial sugestiva por cuanto debieron de existir numerosas formas intermedias entre la simple recitación y el más desarrollado de los espectáculos.[27]

Nonetheless, once again, it is necessary to remember that one of the definitive traits of a good part of Romance poetry in the Middle Ages is its dramatic style; therefore, propositions of new works that perhaps were staged or of traits that determine their 'representability' can increase at a considerable rate. Were any of these poems designed with the intention of staging it? Were any staged at a later date? To what point were certain poetic recitations theatrical? These are difficult questions to answer. Among these questions, the last one is especially suggestive, since there should exist many intermediate forms between the simple recitation and the most developed of spectacles.

I agree that Gómez Moreno's questions are difficult, if not impossible, to answer, given the lack of evidence for repeated performances of specific lyric texts; but, I doubt that "la simple recitación [poética]" was ever "simple," that is, non-theatrical in some sense. In singing or reciting verse, performers speak with the voice of another who is the fictive narrator of the lyric; even if the performer is also the poet, even if the song is somewhat autobiographical, in performing his life before an audience, the performer separates himself from the poetic 'I.' Talking about one's experience differs significantly from having the experience; the act of articulating it in language and communicating it to a listener fictionalizes the experience and the characters involved. The first-person narrator is further distinguished from the protagonist by time, place, and knowledge of the outcome of the experience. The fictive aspect of personal narratives is increased when an experience is versified and sung before an audience. A poet-performer's choice to reveal a personal experience constitutes a performance of self designed to present a certain identity composed of past and present elements; the performance is highly context-dependent, presenting an aspect of self for the consumption of a certain audience.

The Performativity of Medieval Lyric

Lyric is performative and as such is deeply invested in the question of identity. Performance acts are, as we know, loaded with cultural significance; by executing certain acts in certain ways, individuals express and construct their social identity. The fact that entertainers who enact fictive identities can adopt these acts to impersonate different identities underlines the performative nature of identity itself. Judith Butler's work on the performative construction of gender can be extended to include all aspects of social identity, especially those directly related to bodily conduct.[28] Medieval Iberian constructions of identity combine elements that are apparently innate and/or not changeable or affected by behavior, such as lineage, rank, age, and biological sex, with highly performative elements, such as speech, dress, bodily habits (especially self-restraint or lack thereof), religious practices, moral conduct, respectability, gender, and so on. Several traits fall between the two poles of essential and performative elements.

Religious identity, while subject to change through conversion, nonetheless is frequently construed as essential, such that converts to Christianity were often depicted as not really Christian.[29] Gender, on the other hand, is performative, as inappropriate behavior is read as transgendered acts; gender flexibility is often depicted as performance against nature. In RL 22, Alfonso X mocks foppishly dressed men as "come mulheres prenhadas" (like pregnant women), construing their choice of dress as effeminate and unnatural. In JP 41 [RL 25], a song I discuss further in chapter 2, Alfonso mocks Domingas Eanes as assuming the armor and behavior of a knight and engaging in eroticized combat with a Muslim warrior.[30] While she 'defeats' her opponent, he leaves her with a 'wound' that will never heal; this wound presents her vagina as unequivocal proof of her femininity and as punishment for her inappropriate sexual conduct. This poetic evidence demonstrates both that medieval poets were aware of the performative construction of gender and that that awareness caused anxiety, at least in some poets. Anxiety charges their play with identity and performance, both in their own performances of lyric poetry and in their poetic texts, where they show other characters, such as *soldadeiras*, performing transgressive, albeit conventional, identities.

I see comic-obscene poetry as an especially performative genre of medieval lyric because it calls particular attention to the relationship between body and identity. By their nature, comic-obscene songs violate normative rules of decorum and appropriate speech practices. Such lyrics use sexual language and imagery to give the singers license to utter otherwise prohibited words and topics. While the language of comic-obscene songs was construed as offensive, the performance of these songs was not necessarily so; appropriate performance space, time, and techniques were key to the successful representation and reception of these songs. I would argue that the artificial, musical nature of these songs contributed to their acceptability and even respectability, in the case of comic-obscene court lyrics. The *Cantigas d'escarnho* were almost compulsory; in order fully to display their skill, *trovadores* had to compose all genres of Galician-Portuguese secular lyric, *Cantigas d'amor, d'amigo*, and *d'escarnho*. Comic-obscene lyrics play with acceptability and taboo, indicating contradictions in the theory and practice of medieval cultures; by incorporating and expressing the taboo, they create a space for the normally excluded and unspoken and/or unspeakable.[31]

First-person lyric poems construct a speaking subject through language and endow that subject with a certain identity by attributing to it characteristics that signify in terms of rank, gender, cultural authority, religious identity, respectability, and so on. This speaking subject in turn comments on, and may engage in dialogue with, other characters to whom are attributed distinctive identities, identities that differ from that of the poetic 'I.' The narrator interpellates these other characters, that is, assigns them an identity and often a name. I adopt the word "interpellation" from Judith Bulter, who demonstrates how interpellation functions to call others into being as objects of language and to endow them with a certain identity.[32] In lyric dialogues, secondary characters become speaking subjects and may attempt to negotiate the identity imposed upon them by the narrator, if the poet grants them the volition to do so. All poetic characters, including the narrator, are fictive constructions; they have no volition except within the fictive context of the poem. The poet ventriloquizes the characters, putting his words into their mouths and making them perform a certain identity. Unlike a vaudevillian ventriloquist, the medieval lyric poet does not directly engage his characters in dialogue; he hides behind them, often using the first-person male narrator as his representative, although that character's words and acts are not simply those of the poet. The gap between poet and persona is further increased in performance.

Lyric dialogues put into play multiple poetic 'I's whose identities shift throughout the song. The identity attributed to the poetic 'I' influences those attributed to other characters, and vice versa. These identities are conventional, that is, they reproduce identity categories that have already been culturally constituted. Lyrics generally cite authentic identity positions that are occupied by historic men and women; since the lyrics I focus on are comic-obscene/erotic, the identities they represent are often vulgar and degraded, highly sexual and carnal. In most of the lyrics I examine, the narrator is male and more-or-less elite; he interpellates a degraded female character whom he defines as inferior to himself. In some cases, as with *panaderas* and *serranas*, the female protagonist in turn interpellates the male narrator-protagonist; these characters attempt to control their creator's poetic alter egos. While the female character as a fictive speaking subject may challenge his power, she is still constituted as secondary to the male narrator. In the course of negotiating relative identities, the two characters may come to resemble each other, collapsing structural differences, including gender, rank, and respectability.

The fact that medieval lyric is a performance genre complicates this identity play. The identity attributed to the poetic 'I' often corresponds to that of the poet and/or performer, while those attributed to other characters within the poem correspond to the identities of other members of society. The body that performs each character matters; if the performer's identity closely resembles that of the character s/he enacts, the fictive identity play may continue into the metapoetic world and create anxiety as to the stability of identity categories in the real world. The performance of lyric by male and female performers may further reify conventional identity constructions; it can also destabilize them. The effect of the identity play depends upon the interplay of text, performers, performance space and time, and the larger power structures that surround the performance.

Poetic spectacles put identity into play at both the fictive and metapoetic levels; these two levels are deeply entwined and mutually influence each other. At the metapoetic level, a performer's choice of text communicates her/his identity, just as the gestures, movements, and expressions s/he uses in her/his performance of the text communicate the identity of the character s/he is impersonating. In performing a text, the performer impersonates a fictive identity whose relationship to her/his offstage identity is always at issue.[33] The extent to which these identities overlap varies greatly; the complexity and number of factors that affect identity overlap makes generalizations both risky and of limited worth. I explore individual, contextualized performances in my separate discussions of the *soldadeira*, *panadera*, and *serrana* in their respective chapters. Here, I limit my comments to situations in which there is a very high correspondence between the fictive identity and that of the performer, such as when a male performer identifies himself as the author of the first-person, male-voiced lyric that he sings. In such a case, the performed identity corresponds closely to the performer's identity, and if it doesn't, the disparity specifically calls attention to the gap between performed identity and offstage identity, making that a focus of the lyric performance. A similar dynamic is at work in *panadera* hawking-songs performed by a *panadera* as part of her bread-selling activities; whether she actually composed the song or not, the similarities between the poetic 'I' and the performer tend to collapse the differences between fictive and actual identities.

In the case of the courtly *soldadeira*, a professional entertainer who voices all the female roles in Galician-Portuguese lyric, identity play is particularly complicated. Historical *soldadeiras* such as Maria Pérez Balteira appear as fictive characters in the *Cantigas d'escarnho*, often enunciating absurd speeches that provoke the laughter of the audience. If, as Francisco Nodar Manso suggests, a *soldadeira* performed herself in a lyric presentation, voicing words put into her mouth by a *trovador*, the correspondence between her offstage identity and the one that she performs would be highly charged and multivalent.[34] Her performance would infuse multiple meanings into the words put into her (character's) mouth by the *trovador* and call attention to the gaps between conventional *soldadeira* identity, her own identity as a *soldadeira*, and the fictive identity that she performs in performing herself. I call such performances 'parodic mimicry,' since they imitate life yet do so only partially. The *soldadeira* mimics herself, exaggerating so as to underline the parodic nature of her performance of self. All lyric performers mimic the characters whose roles they enact, including that of the first-person male narrator; mimicry becomes parodic both when there is a close correspondence between the role played and the performer's offstage identity, and when performers impersonate their diametric opposites, as when an elite man impersonates a degraded female. The parodic nature of transgendered performances is widely recognized; the dynamics of performing *as* oneself are just as parodic, although the irony of such performances may not be obvious to the uninitiated.[35]

Luigi Allegri argues that, unlike modern actors, medieval *juglares* never disappeared behind the characters they performed, an argument with which I agree; I disagree with Allegri's claim that a such performers merely performed as themselves:

> De hecho, en la tratadística cristiana, el juglar casi nunca es condenado porque pretenda ser lo que no es, porque asuma falsamente la personalidad y el comportamiento de alguien distinto de sí mismo. . .sino porque siempre es exactamente *lo que es*, o sea un individuo que asume el papel social y profesional del juglar, es decir, de un profesional de la exhibición de sí mismo. Aquello que está en juego no es, pues, la categoría de la representación sino la del espectáculo: el actor que expone y vende (porque lo hace por dinero) el propio cuerpo, el actor que induce a la risa descompuesta con chirigotas y chanzas, el actor que provoca malos pensamientos con la deshonestidad de las historias que cuenta y con la lascivia del propio comportamiento, el autor (*sic*) que no posee otra habilidad más que la *improductiva agilidad* corpórea, del canto, del baile, de la narración, y que, en consequencia, no tiene ninguna utilidad social, con lo que produce un agujero o buco en la malla de la estructura social que puede ser rellenado con las fuerzas del mal (italics in original).[36]

> In fact, in Christian tracts, the *juglar* almost never is condemned because he pretends to be what he is not, because he falsely assumes the personality and behaviors of someone other than himself. . .but because he always is exactly *what he is*, that is, an individual who assumes the social and professional role of a *juglar*, that is, of a professional in self-exhibition. What is in play is not, then, the category of representation [or performance] but that of spectacle: the actor who displays and sells (because he does it for money) his very body, the actor who induces immodest laughter with joking and funny speech, the actor who provokes evil thoughts with the dishonesty of the stories he tells and with the lasciviousness of his own behavior, the author (*sic*) who does not possess any skill other than the *unproductive corporeal agility*, of song, of dance, of story-telling, and who, therefore, does not have any social use, with which he produces a hole or opening in the social structure which can become filled with the forces of evil.

The second sentence of this citation is an accurate summary of clerical and legal attitudes toward players, as discussed above. Nonetheless, I find

Allegri's reliance on such attitudes to support his argument unconvincing. Medieval theologians are moralists, not performance theorists; they condemn using broad strokes and do not attempt to represent accurately what they condemn. Christian tracts have an interest in reading professional performers' behaviors as expressions of a sinful self; they collapse the gaps between performing as a sinful individual and being sinful oneself in order to demonize and marginalize *juglares*. Confessors in particular must believe that identity is stable and readable from conduct; otherwise, confession as a religious act would lose its viability and become mere performance engaged in before a particular audience. We see exactly this treatment of confession in RL 247 by Joan Vaásquiz, in which a *soldadeira*, Maria Leve, confesses not her sexual sins but her old age. She engages in a certain performance of self before her confessor in order to achieve reconciliation and reintegration with the courtly community, not by atoning for her sins, but through rejuvenation. Her parodic confession perverts the ritual as she tries to use the clergy's semi-magical speech acts to change not her sinful identity but her aged body, as I discuss in chapter 2.

Allegri's reading of *juglar* performances denies the doubleness of performance acts. As Marvin Carlson explains, performance "is the sense of an action carried out *for* someone, an action involved in the peculiar doubling that comes with consciousness and with the elusive 'other' that performance is not but which it constantly struggles in vain to embody" (italics in original). Carlson goes on to explain what this "other" can be:

> Although traditional theatre has regarded this "other" as a character in a dramatic action, embodied (through performance) by an actor, modern performance art has, in general, not been centrally concerned with this dynamic. Its practitioners, almost by definition, do not base their work upon characters previously created by other artists, but upon their own bodies, their own autobiographies, their own specific experiences in a culture or in the world, made performative by their consciousness of them and the process of displaying them for audiences. Since the emphasis is upon the performance, and on how the body or self is articulated through performance, the individual body remains at the center of such presentations. Typical performance art is solo art, and the typical performance artist uses little of the elaborate scenic surroundings of the traditional stage, but at most a few props, a bit of furniture, and whatever costume. . .is most suitable to the performance situation.[37]

The last sentence, while describing late twentieth-century performance art, equally applies to most medieval lyric spectacles. As Carlson argues, in performing themselves, performers create that self as other to the performing self; they mimic themselves, playing with the gap between their onstage acts and their offstage identities. While I would not say that *juglares* always or even primarily perform themselves, there is often a fine line between the *juglar*'s performing body and the fictive character that is being enacted.

Both Carlson and Allegri call attention to the bodily presence of performers, an embodiment that, as Francesc Massip says, caused *juglares* to be perceived as akin to prostitutes: "De fet el joglar, mim o histrió era posat al mateix sac que la prostituta, tots dos motiu de condemna perquè feien del seu cos objecte de mercadeig i exhibició" (In fact the *juglar*, mime, or actor was placed in the same category as the prostitute, both deserving of condemnation because they made their bodies the object of commerce and exhibition). As I said earlier in my discussion of female acrobats, the embodied nature of *juglaresque* performances genders these acts feminine; as Suzanne G. Cusick has argued, the physicality of singing, which she calls "the most fully embodied kind of music-making," leads it to be coded feminine in our culture, carrying "the negative prestige usually borne by the mark of the feminine." The same phenomenon holds true for medieval musical performances, including singing, dancing, and other displays of physical dexterity, which as we have seen were rigorously and repeatedly condemned. As Mary Russo says, these condemnations construct *juglares'* performances as grotesque and "[perpetuate] the blaming, stigmatization, and marginalizing of groups and persons who occupy this self-perpetuating loop."[38]

Female entertainers were seen as prostitutes due to their embodied performances for money in close physical proximity to their audience, making them highly accessible and available to be touched. Dancers in particular were seen as inciting spectators to lust with their immodest physical displays, as in my discussion of how they encourage audience participation in lyric spectacles and in the passage from the *Libro de las confesiones* cited above. Professional female dancers usually performed solo with musical accompaniment, as in the illustrations from the *Cancioneiro da Ajuda*. Solo dancing marked that act as a professional performance, distinguishing it from social dance, which in the Middle Ages was primarily the *carole* or round-dance in which a group of women or a mixed gender group participated, simultaneously singing and dancing. Salome, whose dance earned her the head of John the Baptist, was a figure for lust, seduction, and the dangers of feminine sexuality; the scene of her dance before Herod is found in medieval Church carvings throughout Europe. Professional dancers' bodies are staged as spectacles worth seeing due to their difference from other bodies. The performer's body is distinguished from those of her audience and may become marked as physically different, as a "competent body"; often the physicality of the performance is transferred onto the performer, a transference that deliberately obscures the conscious mental control exerted by the performer. Reception of a performance as a physical act ignores the effects of training, practice, and mental effort that discipline the body, instead reading the performance skill as innate or natural, the product of an essentially different body. If the performer's body is additionally construed as racially different, as was the case of Muslim *juglaresas* in medieval Europe, the performance skill may be read as yet another bodily difference, as a racial characteristic. Such constructions may have led to the medieval equation of female minstrels and racial difference, as currently is the case with the Hula girl.[39]

The extent to which a performer's body is differentiated from those of the spectators also depends on the interchangeability of their roles. In a participatory context in which spectators also perform, as in the case of the *Cantigas d'escarnho*, the mutuality of performance may reduce differences between bodies, especially if those differences are played on in the performance. A good example of this phenomenon is RL 41, in which the poet-performer, Afons'Eanes do Coton, favorably compares himself with Mari'Mateu, a *soldadeira* whose lesbian desires he envies (see chapter 2). In the case of professional performers who are construed as degraded, the risk of stigma may cause elite participants to perform the same skill less competently, to distinguish themselves from the more competent professionals. If a performance skill carries negative prestige, the person who enacts that skill in public may also become stigmatized; similarly, if a performer is construed as degraded, the skill s/he enacts will accrue negative social prestige. *Partida* 7.6.4, cited above, tries to straddle this line, by emphasizing different performance spaces and audiences in order to reserve entertainment for the elite and condemn public entertainers. On the other hand, performance spaces may grant a performer license to violate social norms, during the time of performance as well as offstage, as is the case with comic-obscene courtly lyrics; such a license to transgress can lead to an ambivalent positioning of the performer as both privileged and degraded. In the case of female performers, the essentialist tendency to equate women with the body increases the stigma of public bodily performance.[40]

The economic aspects of performance also enact and confer meaning on social relations. Placing a monetary value on performance is highly problematic, as a material good is exchanged for an immaterial, ephemeral good; yet, economic exchange marks the performance as meaningful *per se*, as an act that has value. The problematic nature of valuing performance leads to rigidly hierarchical rankings of performance acts and of performers themselves. As we have seen, in medieval Iberia professional performers who publicly displayed their bodies and performance skills for money were *enfamados*, while amateur performances were read favorably, as marks of good breeding and taste that facilitated congenial relations among the elite. Hierarchical rankings of performance reflect and confer cultural value, positioning both performers and spectators, whose preferences carry social meaning. Valuing performance includes evaluating individual performances in verbal interactions between spectators and sometimes performers as well, discussions in which spectators display their taste in their criticisms and appreciations, enhancing or diminishing their prestige. As Richard Schechner comments in his discussion of modern theater, the 'deep structures' of performance

> include preparations for performance both by performers (training, workshop, rehearsals, preparations immediately before going on) and spectators (deciding to attend, dressing, going, settling in, waiting) and what happens after a performance. . . .Cooling off includes getting performers and spectators out of, or down from, the performance; putting the performance space and implements to rest; the aftermath includes spreading the news about performances, evaluating them—even writing books about them—and in many ways determining how specific performances feed into ongoing systems of social and aesthetic life.[41]

The aftermath of performance enacts the identity of spectators, who themselves become performers in evaluating performances, as in the dialogic reception context of *Cantigas d'escarnho*, discussed in chapter 2. Performance is a site for the negotiation of mutual identities in the interaction between performance, performer, and audience; the performer's body encodes identity and affects the identity of those around her/him who must position themselves relative to her/him. This identity play is especially charged with gender and sexual significance, due to the social controls exerted on public displays of female bodily competence.[42]

In my discussions of lyric spectacles, I consider the value of performances primarily in social terms, as performers of various ranks accrue positive or negative prestige. For male poet-performers, participation in courtly lyric spectacles is about attaining and/or maintaining a recognized position of superiority within their poetic community; by participation, I mean, both singing in lyric spectacles and evaluating such spectacles in post-performance dialogic exchanges. Social prestige is particularly at issue in RL 233 by Joan Soárez Coelho, as his poetic alter ego uses his explication of Maria do Grave's equivocal name to display both his identity as an intellectual and his sexual prowess, as I discuss in chapter 2. Soárez Coelho, a middle-rank performer, crosses social barriers by performing as though he were more educated and refined than he is; his campy mimicry of his superiors entertains and flatters them, who form his principal audience. Even self-deprecating roles enhance a male performer's prestige, as he displays his verbal, musical, and acting skills, making a name for himself in playing the part of a buffoon. As E. Michael Gerli has shown, Antón de Montoro, a fifteenth-century *converso* poet whose lyric "Señor, non pecho ni medro" (D1793) I discuss in chapter 3, used his indigent, buffoonish persona to ingratiate himself with his aristocratic patrons and clients, positioning himself as their inferior and thereby enhancing their relative prestige.[43]

For professional female performers, enacting a stigmatized role could earn them acceptance in elite circles. *Soldadeiras* who played along with their assigned role of deviant insider could thereby maintain a place at court; this place, however, was insecure, dependent upon the continuing favor of those in power. The *soldadeira* was more vulnerable than the *panadera*, since her only salable qualities were her beauty and ability to amuse; as a commodity, her value was subject to rapid depreciation. In several *Cantigas d'escarnho*, *soldadeiras* defend themselves against those who threaten their value and prestige, most notably in JP 16 [RL 1] by Alfonso X. Since the *panadera* exercised more than one function, her value was more secure, although it was still dependent upon supply and demand and other forces beyond her control. In popular lyrics on *panaderas*, we see that those who sell themselves cheaply quickly become worthless; on the other hand, many use their verbal abilities to enhance their value and that of their bread, as in Sebastián de Horozco's "Dama de gentil aseo." *Serranas* are also of limited worth; while their singing and dancing may attract the attention of admirers, peasant and noble, *serranas* are primarily low-value sexual commodities. While female performers accrue both positive and negative prestige, as lyric characters, they are commodities employed by other performers to serve their own ends.

In this chapter, I have discussed two levels of lyric performance, namely, the poetic spectacle and the performativity of lyric. I have demonstrated the importance of lyric spectacles in the reception of lyric texts and the centrality of female performers in Galician-Portuguese spectacles in particular. Since lyric spectacles impersonate conventional identities, they play with the mechanisms of identity construction. The embodied nature of lyric performance, and especially that of comic-obscene lyrics, calls attention to the links between certain bodies and certain identities. Performances that violate conventional links, as when an elite male mimics a degraded female, call yet more attention to the constructed and performative nature of identity. It matters which body performs a certain fictive character; the performer's identity deeply affects the significance and reception of his/her song. For example, in RL 331 Pero d'Ambroa impersonates Maria Balteira to ridicule the lowly *beesteiros* (bowmen) she defeats and to elevate himself and the court as a whole. By positioning himself alongside Balteira, d'Ambroa identifies with her. The fact that her victory consists in sexually outperforming the *beesteiro* means that d'Ambroa virtually screws him as well. In a solo performance, d'Ambroa would mime her sexual acts, using gestures to emphasize her phallic behavior; this spectacle plays with the gender and social significance of 'feminine' sex acts. If Balteira were on stage miming her actions as narrated by d'Ambroa, her act would include a transgendered sexual performance, increasing the parodic nature of her mimicry. As I said, the identity of the performer who enacts a female character matters; I explore just how it matters below.

CHAPTER 2

SOLDADEIRAS' DEVIANT PERFORMANCES AND POETS' COUNTERPOSES: COURTLY PLAY IN THE CANTIGAS D'ESCARNHO E DE MAL DIZER

Soldadeiras, in their dual role as *juglaresas* and prostitutes, are constantly staged in the *Cantigas d'escarnho e de mal dizer*. Ramón Menéndez Pidal wittily claimed that in their poetic depictions *soldadeiras* "son mencionadas tan sólo como mujeres de vida alegre, sin alusión alguna a sus artes histriónicas, que, por lo visto, eran muy secundarias al lado de las otras artes cortesanas" (they are mentioned only as easy women, without any allusion to their histrionic arts, which, seemingly, were quite secondary to their other courtesan/courtly arts).[1] While *soldadeiras'* poetic depictions may not celebrate their official function as singers and dancers, the same is largely true for *panaderas*, who are never shown preparing bread, and for *serranas*, whose herds are seldom mentioned. *Soldadeiras* perform other acts in the *Cantigas d'escarnho*, most notably sexual ones:

> Marinha, ende folegares
> tenho eu por desaguysado,
> e soon muy maravilhado
> de ti por non rebentares,
> ca che tapo eu [d']aquesta minha
> boca a ta boca, Marinha,
> e d' estes narizes meus
> tapo eu, Marinha, os teus,
> e das mãos as orelhas,
> os olhos das sobrencelhas;
> tapo-t' ao primeyro sono
> da mha pissa o teu cono,
> como me non veja nenguũ,

> e dos colhões o cuū:
> como non rebentas, Marinha? (LP 136.3 [RL 52] by Pero Viviaez)[2]

> Marinha, I think it's wrong that you fornicate; and I'm amazed that you don't
> explode, since I cover your mouth, Marinha, with my mouth; and with this
> nose of mine I cover, Marinha, your own; and with my hands, your ears, your
> eyes with my eyebrows; at the first sleep I cover with my prick your cunt, as
> long as no one is watching me, and with my balls your asshole: why don't
> you explode [i.e., climax], Marinha?

Upon first glance, the fact that Marinha performs in this song is not at all
obvious. The focus of this piece is on the male speaker's sexual performance; first-person verb forms outnumber second-person forms two to
one. Second-person forms do appear in line final position in the first and
fourth verse; these prominent verbs describe the female character's sexual
performance that becomes the pretext for the narrator's poetic performance. He assumes a disapproving stance toward her sexual behavior based
not on moral outrage but on his disappointment that she doesn't
explode/climax. As he attempts to stuff every orifice of her body and experiences an explosive orgasm, Marinha performs passivity; while he marvels
at his phallic potency, she remains unimpressed. The dominant treatment of
masculine sexuality in medieval Iberian popular culture and literature
configures it as aggressive and violent, as ripping holes in the tight
or closed body of the feminine receptor. Marinha's too open body and
passive-receptive performance frustrate the speaker's desire to use her as
proof of his aggressive-phallic sexuality.[3]

  Marinha's performance causes the narrator to question the significance
of their differently gendered bodies. In the third and fourth verses the
speaker declares that her body is marvelous, or perhaps monstrous, because
it does not react as he wishes. His subsequent catalogue of body parts establishes a one-to-one correspondence between his phallic body and her
receptive one: mouth to mouth, nose to nose, hands to ears, eyebrows to
eyes, prick to cunt, balls to anus. These correspondences play on similarities and differences between male and female bodies, similarities that the
speaker downplays by highlighting their differences as he construes his
orifices as protuberances. Notably, the speaker does not include his anus in
this catalogue, probably because in the *Cantigas d'escarnho* men's anuses are
consistently constructed as receptive orifices.[4] These correspondences play
on grammatical gender and gendered body parts: the speaker's feminine
hands cover Marinha's feminine ears; his feminine eyebrows cover her
masculine eyes; his feminine prick covers her masculine cunt, while his
masculine balls cover her masculine asshole. Of these body parts, the last
two correspondences are particularly significant in illustrating the contrast

between grammatical and biological/social gender; in all, the male speaker has more feminine parts than does Marinha, a fact that further undercuts his phallic construction of his body. While his covering of her would seem to demonstrate dominance along conventional gender and power lines and to reinscribe normative differences, his word choice puts these conventions into play.

Despite their bodily differences, the speaker seems to expect that they ought to have the same reaction to sexual intercourse: he explodes/climaxes, why doesn't she? His rather enigmatic comment in v. 11, "ao primeyro sono," suggests that she even falls asleep on him, a response that makes him work yet harder to demonstrate his impressive masculinity, burying his prick deeply into her so that no one can see him.[5] The final verse is the punch-line, as his repetition of *rebentar* recontextualizes it and the entire poem; the audience must reassess both Viviaez's marveling stance toward Marinha (he marvels far more at his own body) and the portrait of their intercourse that he has painted. Marinha's capacious body provokes anxiety on his part as to whether he can measure up; her passive receptivity, a conventional feminine act, becomes aggressive, as her lack of response challenges his manliness, virtually emasculating him.[6]

Marinha, in reaction to his phallic performance, performs passivity; her unresponsiveness is the crux of the joke and alters the conventional power balance, inverting their relative positions such that she comes out on top. Marinha's unresponsiveness suggests that shafting, the traditional metaphor for demonstrating male dominance of a feminized other, does not signify, or rather, that it only signifies if the shafted one feels shame, or rather, performs shame, which is the real victory as far as the shafter is concerned. As David Nirenberg comments, "when a Christian penetrated a Muslim woman/slave, he reiterated those very acts of conquest and degradation that formed much of the basis for Iberian Christian ideas of masculinity and honor." The identity lines are different in this song; yet, I would argue, the fact that there are fewer differences between the two characters increases the tension as to the political and social significance of the act of heterosexual coitus. If, as Viviaez's speaker implies, his aim in having sex with Marinha is to prove his social superiority through a demonstration of aggressive masculinity, then her refusal to perform an appropriately pained or shamed (i.e., feminine) response is hostile. Marinha's receptivity makes her conventionally passive-feminine performance aggressive and phallic.[7]

In performance, the spectacle of a single male actor-singer on stage would further downplay the female character's performance, although after he finished singing, she could have her say. The performer who enacted this song exposed his body to the shocked, bemused, and admiring eyes of his fellow courtiers as he mimed the male character's sexual acts. While the female character does not speak in this song, the direct question in the final verse suggests she was present for the performance and invites a response on her part. A performer representing Marinha (or Marinha mimicking herself) probably answered the speaker's query by performing a traditional hand gesture, placing her thumb at the first joint of her index finger and wagging the tip of her finger, in imitation of shallow penile thrusts, signifying his small size and unimpressive performance.[8] This female response, both conventional and rebellious, simultaneously reinscribes and subverts gender roles in sexual encounters and in verbal exchanges; the audience's laughter would mark their appreciation of the gender play and also their relief that the two performers fulfilled their expectations. If this song were performed by Viviaez and Marinha themselves, the spectacle would be yet more comic, since the bodies onstage would correspond to those described in the song, increasing the titillating effect. Marinha's participation would show her collaborating with Viviaez and, of course, further undercut his ironic phallic boast, to the amusement of the audience.

This song illustrates some of the games of ambiguity, interpretation, and role-playing the presence of *soldadeiras* at court made possible in the *Cantigas d'escarnho*. It also highlights some of the difficulties in commenting on *soldadeiras'* historical performance practices. While from my point of view Marinha's response is inscribed within the text's invocation of conventional gender and sexual conflicts, her voice is not cited, so my reconstruction of her response is conjectural. Even the fact that in this song she is presented as a performer is not obvious, although Viviaez's alter ego is highly aware that Marinha is choosing to perform a dismissive response. *Soldadeiras'* performances in the *Cantigas d'escarnho* are often downplayed as the male narrator takes her past, offstage performance as the pretext for his present, onstage act; while sometimes women played *soldadeiras'* roles, more often male performers impersonated them. Historic *soldadeiras* named in *cantigas* were probably present at the performance and responded to their fictive depiction, challenging the poet-performer's account and continuing the gendered conflict presented in the song, as I argue Marinha did. While *soldadeiras'* performances were constrained by the power structures of the court, they also played the role of a ritually deviant insider, a role that granted them license to transgress against courtly norms. When a male courtier assumed a conventionally disapproving stance in reaction to a *soldadeira's* unruly performance, as does Pero Viviaez, he did so as an act; the ironic self-awareness of performing as that which he was, an elite male entrusted with preserving social order, underlines the constructed and contingent nature of that authoritative role and implies that elite men are dependent upon unruly women to enable them to assume authoritative roles. Calling attention to the mutually interdependent nature of these complementary roles emphasizes their performative nature; while this awareness does not mean that these poet-courtiers would not play these roles in earnest in non-play contexts, at least in the fictive space of the lyric spectacle, they could admit their awareness of the constructed nature of these roles, and mock them.[9]

The *Cantigas d'escarnho* is the satirical genre of Galician-Portuguese lyric poetry, which flourished in Castile, Portugal, and other regions of the Iberian peninsula during the thirteenth- and early fourteenth century. The major centers of lyric production were the courts of Fernando III el Santo (r. 1217–52), Alfonso X el Sabio (r. 1252–84), and Don Dinis, king of Portugal (r. 1279–1325). The language in which these songs were composed is an artificial, literary language that functioned as an insiders' argot, limiting the producers and consumers to a relatively small cultural elite. Galician-Portuguese lyric includes the sacred *Cantigas de Santa Maria*, composed at Alfonso X's court, and the secular or profane genres, principally the *Cantigas d'amor* (male-voiced love songs), the *Cantigas d'amigo* (female-voiced love songs), and the *Cantigas d'escarnho e de mal dizer*, designed to provoke the laughter of the audience. The third genre is particularly worthy of study due to the important data it offers on social practice despite its often being doggerel verse. Unfortunately, few *Cantigas d'escarnho* have been translated to English. The work of Richard Zenith and Frede Jensen has made some of this corpus accessible to English speakers; however, most of the poems I discuss here have not previously appeared in English.[10]

In this chapter, I analyze eleven *Cantigas d'escarnho* that depict *soldadeiras* performing as degraded women. While these depictions invoke misogynistic commonplaces, they do not unequivocally reinforce negative stereotypes. Instead, the focus of most *Cantigas d'escarnho* on *soldadeiras* is the roles they play and those assumed by other characters, especially the narrator-protagonist, in response to them. Since *soldadeiras'* degraded status could threaten the exclusivity of the court, I first discuss the construction of the medieval Iberian court as a performance space, addressing the importance of speech practices and the heterogeneous nature of the courtly community. I then analyze *soldadeiras* as performers and their role in the *trovador* spectacle. In the rest of the chapter, I analyze poetic depictions of *soldadeiras* in performance. Since many *Cantigas d'escarnho* name historic *soldadeiras*, I discuss three *cantigas* that specifically examine the construction of *soldadeiras'* identities by explicating their names, bodies, and sexual behaviors. I then address the motif of the *soldadeira* at war, which represents sexual intercourse as combat; the two songs in this section assume opposing stances toward the sexuality of phallic *soldadeiras*. Finally, I examine five songs that cite *soldadeiras'* voices, incorporating their speech into the male poet-performer's song. In the conclusion, I return to a consideration of

how performance affects the meanings created by these songs and introduces ambiguities that reduce the hostile stance often assumed by poetic
narrators.

Much of the previous work done on *soldadeiras* in the *Cantigas d'escarnho*
reads their poetic depiction as simply misogynistic, not recognizing the
ambiguities introduced by the performative nature of these songs. I believe
that the *trovador* spectacle emphasized the equivocal nature of the *cantigas*,
especially when professional female performers participated in the spectacle, whether onstage or as members of the audience, and commented on
the poet's depiction of them. The presence and participation of *soldadeiras*
in these spectacles altered the dynamics and in many cases reduced the hostility expressed toward degraded women. As I demonstrated in chapter 1,
soldadeiras were central to the *trovador* spectacle; while their ephemeral performances left few traces, these few can help us appreciate their importance
in promoting play with gender, sexuality, and identity in the specialized
performance space of the medieval Castilian court.

The Court as a Performance Space

The court is a distinctive performance site that simultaneously highlights
and obscures performance acts as codified, ritualized behaviors distinct
from normal behavior; in court, performance *is* normal behavior, and vice
versa. The itinerant Castilian court was marked not by its location in certain spaces but by the presence of certain individuals and their manner of
speaking and behaving. All members of court had to perform appropriately
at all times, to maintain the court as a site of privilege and distinction and
to justify their own presence in this site. The definition of *corte* in Alfonso X's
law code, the *Siete partidas*, highlights speech as a characteristic of the court
itself and as an offense that the court must redress:

> Corte, es llamado el lugar, do es el Rey, e sus vasallos, e sus oficiales, con el
> que le han cotidianamente de consejar, e deseruir, e los omes del reyno, que
> se llegan y, o por honrra del, o por alcançar derecho, opor fazerlo o por
> recabdar las otras cosas que han de ver con el. . . .Otrosi es dicho corte,
> segund lenguaje de España, þorque alli es la espada, de la justicia, con que se
> han de cortar todos los malos fechos, tanbien de dicho, como de fecho, assi
> como los tuertos, e las fuerças, e las soberuias, que fazen los omes, e dizen
> porque se muestran por atreuidos, e denodados. E otrosi los escarnios, e los
> engaños, e las palabras, sobejanas, e vanas, que fazen a los omes enuilescer,
> e ser rahezes. E los que desto se guardaron, e vsaron de las palabras buenas, e
> apuestas, llaman los buenos, e enseñados. . . .Onde los que tales fueren, deue
> los el Rey allegar assi, e fazer les mucho bien, e mucha honrra. E a los otros
> arredrar los de la corte, e castigar los de los yerros que fizieren. Por que los

buenos tomen, ende fazaña para vsar del bien, e los malos se castiguen, de non fazer las cosas desaguisadas, e la corte finque quita de todo mal, e abondada, e complida de todo bien. (*Partida* 2.9.27)

Court is the name of the place where the king is, as well as his vassals and the officials who advise and serve him daily and the people of the realm who come there, either to honor him, to demand justice or to comply with justice, or to deal with other things that have to do with the king. . . .Also it is called *corte*, in the language of Spain, because it is there that is found the sword of justice with which are cut all the evil things, both of word and of deed, that men do and say to show themselves daring and brave, as well as the insults, tricks, and proud and empty words that degrade men and make them worthless. And those who avoid these words and use good, appropriate words instead, are called good and intelligent men. . . .Therefore those who are like this, the king should bring to court and do them good and honor them. And the others, he should bar from court and punish the errors they do. By this means, the good will continue to act well and the bad will be corrected and not do inappropriate things, and the court will be cleansed of all evil and abound with all good.

This description of the court as a utopia populated by good and discreet men focuses on courtiers' performances, their speech and their deeds, which either justify their presence or necessitate their removal from court. Their behavior is constantly observed and assessed by fellow courtiers and by the king, who is responsible for screening those he admits and for ejecting those who do not exemplify courtliness. Offensive speech, whether enunciated at court or elsewhere, is criminally liable; in exercising justice the court polices speech, punishing those who utter offensive statements and rewarding those who speak well. The *Segunda partida*, which contains laws defining and regulating the king and his household, includes many items that demonstrate the key role played by speech at court. *Partida* 2.9.29 defines *palacio* as "qualquier lugar do el Rey se ayunta paladinamente, para fablar con los omes" (anyplace where the king gathers to talk with men publicly), making speech the *raison d'être* of the palace. The king's presence is essential and he must speak and act to maintain an appropriate court environment; nonetheless, it is the courtiers whose collective speech patterns constitute the distinctness of the court as a site of appropriate, courtly behavior.[11]

When the *Segunda partida* turns to the issue of courtly pastimes, it describes a word game that imitates offensive speech:

E en el juego [de palabras] deue catar, que aquello que dixiere, que sea apuestamente dicho, e non sobre aquella cosa que fuere en aquel con quien jugaren, mas auiessas dello, como si fuere couarde: dezir le que es esforçado: e al esforçado jugar le de couardia. E esto deue ser dicho de manera, quel con quien jugaren, non se tenga por escarnido, mas quel aya de plazer, e ayan a reyr dello, tan bien el, como los otros, que lo oyeren. E otrosi el que lo dixere, que lo sepa bien dezir en el lugar que conuiene, ca de otra guisa non seria juego. E por esso dize el prouerbio antiguo, que non es juego, donde ome non rie. Ca sin falla el juego con alegria se deue fazer: e non consaña, ni con tristeza. (*Partida* 2.9.30)

In the game of mocking speech, players must be sure that whatever they say is said appropriately and not about any quality that the man they are mocking actually has, but the opposite of it; if he is a coward, call him a brave man, and mock the brave man for cowardice. And this joke must be said in such a way that the butt doesn't feel insulted but is amused by it and laughs at it, as well as all those who hear it. And also the one who makes the joke must know how to say it in an appropriate place, because otherwise it would not be a game. For as the old proverb says, it isn't a game when no one laughs. Without fail, the game should be played with pleasure and not with anger or sorrow.

The *juego de palabras*[12] is a game of ritual insults exchanged by courtiers for entertainment and relaxation. The insults' potentially disruptive language is contained by their absurd content, mocking the targets for behavior they do not perform. The manner of delivery is key, since the performer must provoke general laughter among all present to ensure the congeniality of the joke; the cited proverb emphasizes the importance of laughter as the proof of a successful *juego*. The *juego*'s congeniality stands in stark contrast to the definition of words that result in *deshonra* (i.e., of *escarnio*) in *Partida* 7.9.1: "desonrra. . .es fecha, o dicha a otro a tuerto, o a despreciamiento del" (dishonor. . .is done or said to another in order to insult or demean him). The intent and effect of these two ways of speaking are distinct: in the *Siete partidas*, *escarnio* is speaking badly of someone in order to harm him; the *juego*, on the contrary, is mocking someone in order to amuse him and to engage him in the game. Alfonso's vision of congenial joking among friends is idealistic and probably coercive, forced upon a world highly sensitive to insults, as demonstrated by the work of Marta Madero and the lists of penalties for conventional insults in the *Fueros* and other law codes. *Partida* 2.9.30 articulates principles for congenial mockery so as to license such speech and to forestall suits against court wits.[13]

The sketchy description of the *juego* offered by the law code does not enable us to understand precisely how the game would work, how many people would participate, the particularities of the exchange, or the length of each session. Modern studies of ritual insults in informal performance contexts suggest that the *juego* would occur during idle moments when a relatively small group of insiders engaged each other in the game; one player would issue a formulaic insult to which the target responded with a similar jibe. Members of the audience would evaluate each insult and encourage the two players; they could judge an insult inappropriate because too close to the truth. A target could also respond to a too-true insult with a denial or another true insult, in which case the audience may have intervened to prevent further escalation. Aside from the momentary diversion offered by the *juego*, the game would contribute to group cohesiveness and structure, establishing a hierarchy of verbal ability among the participants.[14]

The *juego de palabras* can help us reconstruct performances of thirteenth-century satiric poetry. Elsewhere I have demonstrated the connection between the *juego de palabras* and the *Cantigas d'escarnho*; both are dialogic games of hierarchies that promote self-conscious adoption and performance of ritual identities in order to enhance personal prestige and to entertain self and others. In both cases identity negotiation and play are the crux of the game; these identities continue to be performed outside of game spaces and are influenced and shaped by the game. Courtly lyric was performed in a dialogic context in which spectators participated in the presentation and evaluation of each performance. As with the *juego*, appropriate audience response would prove the success of a mocking song; we may assume that all the extant *Cantigas d'escarnho* met with approval, since they were considered worthy of preservation in writing. The content of *Cantigas d'escarnho* can be overtly offensive, especially those that target degraded others, such as cowardly *coteifes* (low-status knights or soldiers), *viejas fududancuas* (old women good for fucking in the ass), and other stock character types who were not generally present at court. These *cantigas* would not violate appropriate speech practices because the target was not present and so could not be offended. Other *cantigas* target marginal or occasional members of court, such as *jograis* and *soldadeiras*, addressing them by name and mocking them for stereotypical flaws such as poor singing or playing and inappropriate behaviors, especially sexual conduct. Modern readers cannot simply construe these insults as false or invert them as implied by the definition of the *juego de palabras*; these *cantigas*, nonetheless, are ritual insults framed by appropriate courtly and poetic conventions. Such *Cantigas d'escarnho* function doubly; by mocking marginal members of court, courtly poet-performers include them in the courtly circle, yet simultaneously mark them as different, as less-than-courtly individuals.

The *Cantigas d'escarnho*'s overt vulgarity may seem incongruous in a courtly context. Francisco Nodar Manso argues that both *trovadores* and *juglares* were professional itinerant musicians who performed in noble households as well as in *plazas* and brothels; he construes them all as *cazurros*, low-status marketplace performers whose artistry was denigrated by court poets. Part of the reason Nodar Manso downplays the social distinctions between these performers is their shared use of taboo words, themes, and gestures in performing *Cantigas d'escarnho*. One of the poetic

dramas that he reconstructs, *Joán Fernández*, focuses on the target's homo-
sexuality and enacts anal intercourse on stage; Nodar Manso proposes that
an actor-singer made suggestive motions with a hand-held phallus or that a
male actor mimed anal attacks against other performers. While it is certainly
possible that *trovador* spectacles were performed in *plazas* and brothels, mere
obscenity is not sufficient to ban such performances from court. Charles
Muscatine has compellingly argued that the concept of obscenity is a
courtly creation designed to differentiate courtly conduct from that of non-
courtiers, especially that of the masses. The concept of obscenity is deployed
through the courtly performance of obscene texts as risible examples of vulgar behaviors; Muscatine examines the *fabliaux*, but the *Cantigas d'escarnho*
serve the same function. The performance of obscenities is both deniable
("that's what *they* do") and useful, because poetically they express, heighten,
and resolve the pressures caused by courtiers' conscious suppression of primal, relabeled as vulgar, urges. While not all *Cantigas d'escarnho* are obscene,
poets' censorious tones and focus on deviant behaviors enable them to stage
vulgarity in order to ridicule and reject it, finally re-establishing the exclusivity and refinement of the court.[15]

In thirteenth-century Iberia, court entertainers were generally divided
into four classes. *Trovadores*, usually noblemen who composed poetry as well
as exercising other functions at court, sometimes would perform their own
compositions and sometimes would have another performer, a *jogral* or
segrel, perform their compositions. *Segreis* usually belonged to the lower
nobility, or *escudeiro* rank; a status in-between *trovadores* and *jograis*, they
composed and performed their own verse as well as that of other poets.
Like *jograis*, *segreis* accepted *soldada* (payment) for their performances, yet
they may have performed other functions in addition to entertaining.
Jograis and their female counterparts, *soldadeiras*, were professionals who
sang, danced, or played instruments for a living. While these individuals may
have been of noble birth, their status as professional entertainers degraded
them.[16] The degraded status of female performers may have, ironically,
increased their desirability, since it made them (at least in theory) sexually
accessible to the men around them; not only did men greatly outnumber
women at court, but honorable women were sexually off-limits. The accessibility of female entertainers contributed to their construction as a licensed
sexual play space within the normative confines of court.

Soldadeiras in Performance

While we know little about the specific performance practices associated
with Galician-Portuguese lyric, I assume that *soldadeiras* performed all three
profane genres. As Ana Paula Ferreira says,

Pois que, na sua grande maioria, as cantigas galaico-portuguesas evocam uma temática erótico-amorosa estritamente convencionalizada no que se refere à representação das figuras femininas, faz sentido pensar que o corpo da soldadeira (para lá de quaisquer palavras que poderia ou não entoar) se torna o ponto fucral da *performance*. . .Esse corpo é pago para atuar, para evocar visualmente as imagens femininas das cantigas no contexto do espetáculo cortesão em que são apresentadas, escenificadas.[17]

Given that, in their great majority, the Galician-Portuguese songs evoke a strictly conventionalized erotic-amorous theme with respect to their representation of female figures, it makes sense to think that the body of the *soldadeira* (aside from whatever words that she may or may not intone) becomes the fulcrum of the performance. . .That body is paid to act, to evoke visually the feminine images in the songs in the context of the courtly spectacle in which they are presented, staged.

The *soldadeira's* singing and dancing body enacted stereotypical female identities as depicted in male-authored songs. While these acts may have reinforced dominant conventions, I argue that the performance context puts identity categories into play by emphasizing the gap between the several identities performed by a given *soldadeira* and her personal or authentic identity. The embodied performance of a *soldadeira* who voiced both the innocent desire of the *amiga* as well as the transgressive desires of a *soldadeira* would highlight the play of textual identity, identity in performance, and the identity of the performer herself; the impersonation of various characters by a single performer in a single session would tend to reify identity characteristics (performing *as* a love-struck girl) while destabilizing the *soldadeira's* individual identity. This play would be heightened should a *soldadeira* mimic herself as a character in a satiric song, a performance I call parodic mimicry. The codified gestures she would use in order to signify her 'own' identity as ventriloquized by a *trovador* would underline the ritual nature of the identity she was enacting.[18]

The *soldadeira* is a performer in the most conventional sense of the word, an artist who uses artificial bodily movements and verbal enunciations to achieve an aesthetic end. As I discuss in chapter 1, her onstage performance is subject to social control, and the stigma attached to displays of physical competence for pay, especially to sexualized displays, is easily transferred to her offstage performances, causing her to be construed as a threat to social order. In law codes and other official narratives, *soldadeiras* are portrayed as dangerously attractive individuals whose potentially corrupting influence must be controlled. *Soldadeiras* were desirable dinner companions and conversationalists as well as professional performers; however, their stay at court was limited by law to three days at a time. According to the provincial council of Toledo in 1324, clerics in particular should avoid *soldadeiras*: "ellas, entregadas a coloquios depravados y charla deshonesta, corrompen las buenas costumbres, y, además, hacen espectáculo de sí mismas; por esto mandamos a todos, y en especial a los prelados, amenazándoles con el castigo del cielo, que no permitan entrar en sus casas a tales mujeres, ni les hagan dones" (these women, given to depraved speeches and dishonest talk, corrupt good behavior, and, moreover, make spectacles of themselves; therefore we order all, and especially prelates, to threaten them with the wrath of heaven and not to allow such women to enter their houses nor to give them gifts).[19] Perhaps anxiety about the potentially polluting effects of *soldadeiras'* offstage performances caused their onstage acts to be passed over in silence in the *Cantigas d'escarnho*.

Fear of *soldadeiras'* influence highlights the problem of distinguishing between artificial acts and authentic behaviors. The spectacles *soldadeiras* make of themselves cause anxiety because, without the framing conventions of a formal performance context, their behaviors are not marked as play. Judith Butler addresses this problem in her essay "Performative Acts and Gender Constitution."

> [A]lthough theatrical performances can meet with political censorship and scathing criticism, gender performances in nontheatrical contexts are governed by more clearly punitive and regulatory social conventions. Indeed, the sight of a transvestite onstage can compel pleasure and applause while the sight of the same transvestite on the seat next to us on the bus can compel fear, rage, even violence. The conventions which mediate proximity and identification in these two instances are clearly quite different. . . .In the theatre, one can say, "this is just an act," and de-realize the act, make acting into something quite distinct from what is real. Because of this distinction, one can maintain one's sense of reality in the face of this temporary challenge to our existing ontological assumptions about gender arrangements; the various conventions which announce that "this is only a play" allow strict lines to be drawn between the performance and life. On the street or in the bus, the act becomes dangerous, if it does, precisely because there are no theatrical conventions to delimit the purely imaginary character of the act, indeed, on the street or in the bus, there is no presumption that the act is distinct from a reality; the disquieting effect of the act is that there are no conventions that facilitate making this separation.

On the bus, or, in a courtly context, across the dinner table, unconventional performances threaten the illusion that identity categories, including gender, are natural and fixed, such that a spectator may need to distance him- or herself from the challenging performance, render it art, and frame it with conventions, to make it safe.[20]

I suggest that the stereotypical portrayals of *soldadeiras* in the *Cantigas d'escarnho* is just such a distancing and framing gesture. The closeness and accessibility of the *soldadeira* and the ambiguous division between her performance acts and her usual behaviors make such poetic representations socially as well as artistically useful, creating a more comfortable distance that the poet and audience can use to counteract *soldadeiras'* disquieting performances. Poetic play with nonnormative sexualities, especially those of *soldadeiras*, shows the usefulness of this distancing technique, to frame unconventionality and enable it to be staged at court, in an appropriate space for sexualized play. Attributing a ritually degraded identity to *sol-dadeiras* and to other not-quite-courtly individuals at court facilitates this process, as poets can name these individuals, single them out for more-or-less congenial scorn, employ taboo language as part of the mechanism of the joke, and mark the targets as members of the court who are different from most courtiers. The target shows her/his appreciation of the joke with laughter, playing along in order to reaffirm her/his place at court; s/he could respond with her/his own jab at the poet-performer, a ritual insult that would enable the target to assume the role of joker, further the dia-logic nature of the joke-exchange, and express any hostility s/he may feel in a socially acceptable way. Playing along with the role of deviant court insider, a *soldadeira* could conform to her assigned role and also play with it ironically; by performing an acceptable response to a *Cantiga d'escarnho*, she would simultaneously reaffirm her courtliness and her role as a ritually deviant member of the court.

Soldadeiras are especially productive characters for identity play because of their stereotypical portrayal as unruly women driven by deviant desires to violate behavioral norms, especially gender norms. In publicizing *soldadeiras'* deviance, poets can themselves adopt various poses that enable them to play with their identity, pointing to the gap between their perfor-mance with respect to the *soldadeira* and their accustomed courtly behav-ior outside of the play space of the *Cantigas d'escarnho*. The *Cantigas*, like the *juego de palabras*, provide a release valve for the tensions accumulated by the reiterated, obsessively self-conscious performances of courtliness necessary to maintain one's place at court.[21] While the court collectively must adhere to the illusion that reiterated performances constitute a true identity, in play that illusion is ruptured, openly mocked by comic performances that parody the structures that govern non-play time. *Soldadeiras* as poetic char-acters promote stances that ironically replicate normative structures of authority and power and allow poet-performers to stage their own deviant performances.[22]

Poets' identities are also at play in the *Cantigas d'escarnho*. The poses they adopt with respect to transgressive *soldadeiras* reflect their ambivalent iden-tification with and/or rejection of them, as poet-performers present an identity parallel to or diametrically opposed to that of the *soldadeira* and play with their own, already-established identity as well. Performance practices increase the distinctions between poet, poetic 'I,' and performer. The fact that we have few anonymous *cantigas* underlines the significance attached to the poet's identity; however, as I mentioned above, Galician-Portuguese lyrics were often performed by another, socially inferior performer, male or female, who sang the poet's composition. The split between poet and performer divides the poetic 'I' into several voices. Performers themselves employed personas distinct from their offstage identities. We have traces of these personas in the names of various *jograis*, such as Cítola, Alegre, and Joan Baveca, whose name I discuss below in relation to the foolish identity he creates in his *cantigas*; Balteira may be Maria Pérez's stage name, as Graciosa was the chosen moniker of another court dancer.[23] The performance practices associated with the *Cantigas d'escarnho* are less well documented, so we do not know whether substitutes performed them in the name of the poets; the description of the *juego de palabras* leads me to believe that the *Cantigas d'escarnho* were performed by their composers and that the performance conventions were themselves sufficient to establish distinctions between play and non-play times, spaces, ways of speaking, and identities. In the case of Alfonso X, we can detect ironic references to his identity as king in his satiric pieces on *soldadeiras*, especially in JP 16 [RL 1], in which he presents himself as censoring an angry *soldadeira* and then finding himself the target of her wrath. As I discussed in chapter 1, Provençal magnates such as Guillaume IX performed their own lyrics, and the *juego de palabras* creates a recreational space for all courtiers to indulge in otherwise unacceptable speech and acts.[24] In my discussion of individual songs I explore the distinctions between poet, lyric 'I,' and performer; I also discuss the poetic personas that poets develop in order to examine some of the complexities of the identity play that, I argue, lies at the heart of the *Cantigas d'escarnho*.

Interpreting *Soldadeiras'* Equivocal Bodies and Acts

As Jorge A. Osório has demonstrated, interpellation or identifying targets by name is a key characteristic that differentiates the *Cantigas d'escarnho* from other genres of Galician-Portuguese lyric, and he argues that such aggressive language does violence to the addressee.[25] The poetic evidence suggests that calling a woman *soldadeira* did indeed injure her. The word *soldadeira* appears in only four *Cantigas d'escarnho*, JP 30 and RL 193, 213, and 321. JP 30 [RL 14] by Alfonso el Sabio is quite well known: "Fui eu poer a mão noutro di- / -a a ũ a soldadeira no conon" (I went to put my hand on a *soldadeira*'s cunt the other day); the taboo word *conon* underlines the speaker's negative attitude toward the *soldadeira*-prostitute. RL 193 by Joan

Baveca, "Estavan oje duas soldadeiras / dizendo ben, a gran pressa, de si" (Today two *soldadeiras* were praising themselves with great sincerity), features two anonymous *soldadeiras* who exchange insults while bathing each other; the male narrator-voyeur watches their performance and cites it in his account. In both poems, the unnamed *soldadeiras'* speech is cited at length; I discuss these poems below in the section on ventriloquizing *soldadeiras*. In RL 213 by Joan Garcia de Guilhade, the male narrator iron-ically instructs Dona Ourana in the art of *foder* (fucking), calling her both a *soldadeira* and a *puta fududancua* (vv. 11, 21; whore good for fucking in the ass); Dona Ourana, although addressed in the second person, does not speak in this song. RL 321 by Pedr'Amigo de Sevilha plays on the name of Maria Pérez Balteira: "Per Ordónhez, torp'e desembrado / vej'eu un ome que ven da fronteira / e pregunta por Maria Balteira" (vv. 1–3; Per'Ordonhez, fool-ish and immodest, I see a man who's come from the front lines asking about Maria Balteira). Balteira rhymes with *soldadeira*, and Amigo replaces her name with that word in the second stanza. Amigo constructs an erotic tri-angle between the narrator, Per'Ordonhez, and Balteira, who is silenced and excluded from the relationship between men.[26] These four *cantigas* show that unnamed *soldadeiras* were granted a generous license to speak; their use of language parodied speech practices associated with dominant groups, as I discuss below. On the other hand, RL 213 and 321 show that, when women were interpellated as *soldadeiras*, that label was invoked specifically to ridicule and silence the women so labeled, at least within the fictive context of the song.

Not all *Cantigas d'escarnho* that name women silence them. The act of interpellation singles out the target, separating her/him from the courtly community, and focuses attention on her/his distinctiveness, usually in an insulting way. Several *cantigas* on *soldadeiras* focus narrowly on the signifi-cance of their names. Names function to distinguish or to identify individ-uals; however, the relationship between a given name and an individual's identity is often unclear, especially when the name itself is equivocal. In the *Cantigas d'escarnho*, poets frequently attempt to resolve the ambiguity of *soldadeiras'* names by explicating them as signifying with respect to their bodies and behaviors. The identities developed in these songs are fictive and exaggerated, playing on some of the *soldadeira's* distinctive traits. Poet-performers' ironic explications do not resolve ambiguities but increase them. This theme enables a poet to assign individual *soldadeiras* an identity that supports his own parodic performance of identity.

In this section, I discuss three *cantigas* that play on the significance of *soldadeiras'* names. Two songs, RL 233 and LP 125.21 [RL 384], focus closely on the meaning of the equivocal name; the third, RL 41, implicitly plays off the *soldadeira's* mixed-gendered name, Mari'Mateu, which could be translated Mary Matthew. Many of the songs that explicate *soldadeiras* do not cite the female character's voice, suggesting that it is much easier to assign meaning to a silent signifier, as in RL 233 by Joan Soárez Coelho:

> Maria do Grave, grav' é de saber
> por que vos chaman Maria do Grave,
> cá vós non sodes grave de foder,
> e pero sodes de foder mui grave;
> e quer', en gran conhocença, dizer:
> sen leterad' ou trovador seer,
> non pod' omen departir este ≪grave≫.
>
> Mais eu sei ben trobar e ben leer
> e quer' assi departir este ≪grave≫:
> vós non sodes grav' en pedir aver,
> por vosso con', e vós sodes grave,
> a quen vos fode muito, de foder;
> e por aquesto se dev' entender
> por que vos chaman Maria do Grave.
>
> E pois vos assi departi este ≪grave≫,
> tenho-m' end' ora por mais trobador;
> e ben vos juro, par Nostro Senhor,
> que nunca eu achei [molher] tan grave
> com' é Maria—e já o provei —
> do Grave; nunca pois molher achei
> que a mi fosse de foder tan grave.[27]

Maria do Grave, it's difficult (*grave*) to understand why they call you Maria do Grave, since you're not difficult (*grave*) to fuck, although you are very costly (*grave*) to fuck [i.e., he who fucks you must face grave consequences]; and I want, in my great wisdom, to say: unless he's learned or a poet, no man can explicate this *grave*.

But I know how to compose and read well, so I want to explicate this *grave*: you aren't slow (*grave*) to ask money for your cunt, and you are *grave* to fuck, for those who fuck you a lot; this is how one should interpret the fact that they call you Maria do Grave.

And now that I've explicated this *grave*, I consider myself a great poet; and I swear to you, by our Lord, that I have never found a woman so *grave* as Maria—as I've now proven—do Grave; I never found a woman who was so *grave* for me to fuck.

Not only does Soárez Coelho interpellate Maria do Grave, he repeats her name four times in three stanzas; the word *grave*, the equivocal part of her name, he repeats thirteen times, nine times in line final position (three times in each stanza). He also repeats the taboo word *foder* five times, each time as part of his explication of Grave's name, and *cono* once, as a synonym for *foder*. This repetitiveness is heightened by the nearly verbatim repetition of "cá vós non sodes grave de foder, / e pero sodes de foder mui grave" in each stanza. This constant repetition concretizes the equivalence of Maria do Grave and *foder/cono*. The rhyme scheme merits particular attention: in the first two stanzas, the scheme is identical, ABABAAB, while in the third, the scheme changes to BCCBDDB. The change in scheme corresponds to other shifts. Most significantly, the referent for *vos* changes from Grave, who in the first two stanzas is addressed directly in the second-person singular, to the audience, while Grave is treated in the third-person singular; in addition, there are more first-person forms in this stanza than in any other. This prominent use of first-person forms and the shift in his treatment of Grave forces her into the background, as she is separated from the audience and distanced from the moment of performance. In retrospect, his earlier uses of *vos* become apostrophic, addressing her as though she were present; the third-person forms in the final stanza suggest she was not present after all.

The speaker's explanation parodies scholastic exercises to justify his claim that he's *letrado* (educated). In explicating *grave* as "costly," "difficult," "slow," "serious" and "grave" (not difficult to get and not slow to demand payment, but costly/heavy to fuck, meaning that he who fucks her must pay a high cost and face the grave consequences; implicitly, she gives him a venereal disease), the speaker underlines the equivocal nature of Grave's name.[28] He repeats his explication once in each stanza, always framing his interpretation with comments that highlight his status as a *trovador* and learned man. Soárez Coelho prominently uses *grave* in a number of *Cantigas d'amor*, including: "As graves coitas, a quen as Deus dar" (LP 79.8/CA 167–168; The grave cares/suffering, which God gives to he who [loves]), which includes the line, "En tan grave dia senhor filhei" (on such a grave day I gave myself to my lady); "Com' og' eu vivo no mundo coitado / nas graves coitas que ei de soffrer" (LP 79.11/CA 170, How I live in a world burdened by cares with the grave cares that I have to suffer); and "En grave dia, senhor, que vus vi" (LP 79.19/CA 158, It was on a grave day, lady, that I first saw you). In his explication of Maria do Grave, Soárez Coelho implicitly refers to his use of these love conventions, parodying them as well as the process of explication itself.[29]

The ostensible point of the speaker's performance is to showcase his ability as a scholar and a poet before the courtly audience. As the song progresses, the real point of his performance becomes clear; he uses the equivocal nature of Grave's name as a pretext to utter taboo words, to showcase his identity as a *trovador*, and to brag about his sexuality. The third stanza is again key to revealing the joke: in the final two verses, he demonstrates the basis for his authoritative pronouncements on Grave, namely, his personal experience of fucking her. Revealing this information at the end makes it the climax of the song, the punch-line of the joke; while the audience probably started laughing in the first stanza and continued throughout, the end, which reveals the joke the poet-performer has played on them, would provoke the most laughter. I say the real joke is on the audience, because in the end they become aware of the coercive nature of the *trovador* spectacle; they were forced to witness the poet-performer's agonistic self-display, which turns out to be sexual, not intellectual, as he had claimed. Whether Grave herself would have been present or not is difficult to tell. Certainly she, like the audience, is coerced by this song, made to participate in this spectacle. If she were present, I expect she would play along with Soárez Coelho's joke, either by commenting on his sexual performance in relationship to his poetic performance to suggest he was the one who was "grave" to fuck.

The coercive role in the *trovador* spectacle that Maria do Grave plays is similarly forced on another *soldadeira*, Maria Negra in LP 125.21 [RL 384] by Pero Garcia Burgalês, as he makes her explicate her own name:[30]

> Maria [N]egra vi eu, en outro dia,
> hir rabialçada per hunha carreyra,
> e preguntey a como hya senlheyra,
> e por aqueste nome que avya,
> e disse-m' ela 'nton: ey nom' assy
> por aqueste sinal con que naci,
> que trago negro come hunha caldeyra.
>
> Dixi lh' eu hu me dela partia:
> esse sinal é suso na moleyra?
> E diss m' ela daquesta maneyra,
> com' eu a vos direy, e foy sa vya:
> este sinal, se Deus mi perdon!
> é negro ben come hun carvon,
> e cabeludo aderredor da caldeira.
>
> A grandes vozes lhi dix' eu, u se hya:
> que vus direy a [D]on [F]ernan de [M]eyra
> desse sinal? ou é de pena veyra
> de como é feyt[o] a [J]ohan d' [A][m]bia?
> Tournou s' ela e dizia m' outra vez:
> dizede lhis ca chus negr' é ca pez,
> e ten sedas de que faran peneyra!
>
> E dixi lh' eu enton: [D]ona [M]aria,
> como vos sodes molher arteyra,
> assy soubestes dizer com' arteyra,

esse sinal que vus non parecia.
E disse m' ela: per este sinal
nom' ey de [N]egr' e muyt' outro mal;
ey per hy pre[ç]o de peydeyra!

I saw Maria Negra the other day going along the road with her tail in the air; and I asked her, since she was alone, about that name that she has, and she said to me: "I've got that name because of a sign that I was born with, black as a cauldron."

I said to her before she left me there: "Is that sign on the top of your head?" And she said to me just as I will say to you, and then went on her way: "This sign, may God forgive me!, is black like coal, and hairy all around the cauldron."

I called to her very loudly, as she was going, "What should I say to Don Fernan de Meira about that sign? whether it's hard to see [?], or what it's like, to Joan d'Ambia?" She turned around and said to me again: "Tell them it's blacker than tar, and it has hairs that act like a sieve!"

And then I said to her: "Lady Maria, since you're a crafty woman, you know well how to talk artfully about that hidden sign of yours." And she said to me: "Because of this sign, I am called Black and worse; because of it, I'm known as a pig [insult of unclear meaning]!"

The male narrator reports on a conversation he initiated with Maria Negra on the interesting topic of the origin of her name. By posing the question, he presents himself as a naive interrogator who looks to Negra as an authority figure; his aggressive interrogation makes her the object of inquiry, even as she is the one who explains the significance of 'Negra.' It is worth commenting on the rhyme scheme of this song as well. Each stanza uses the same scheme, ABBACCB; A (-ía) and B (-eyra) remain the same throughout the song, while C changes in each stanza. The word *soldadeira* does not appear in this song; however, B rhymes with *soldadeira*, and the frequent repetition of that sound at line final position recalls that never-uttered word. Also not uttered are any explicit or taboo words for female body parts; quite the contrary, much of the humor of this song is Negra's refusal to name the body part in question. Given the interest in that which is not said, the omission of *soldadeira* is significant.

The exchange between Negra and the narrator-protagonist focuses on power and verbal relations between the narrator and the *soldadeira* as much as on her identity. While his voice dominates the song and frames her speeches, he does cite her directly, conceding the floor to her; however, as I discuss below, the male performer who voiced the narrator's part probably also voiced Negra's speeches as well, undercutting the dialogic aspect of this song and reminding the audience that the poet is speaking through her. Interestingly, ventriloquized characters seem to have more volition than those who do not speak, since their voices put into question the narrator's version of events. Female citations are "double-voiced," as Doris Earnshaw discusses in her study of female voices in medieval lyric poetry authored by men.[31] While seeming to report Negra's speech, the narrator recontextualizes it, causing her words to carry at least two meanings, the one that she wished to express as well as the narrator's interpretation of her. Negra's use of equivocal language further complicates her speech; she uses circumlocutions whose ambiguity encourages the narrator to continue his line of questioning and his pose of naïveté. The male speaker continues to talk with her because of his appreciation of her verbal artistry, as his final comment shows. The two characters' voices collaborate in developing the explication of Negra's name within a competitive frame. The metaphors Negra uses are conventional images for female genitals, figuring them as black, as a cauldron blackened with soot, as blacker than coal and tar, and surrounded by rough, wiry hairs; the cauldron image is particularly evocative, as she repeats *caldeyra/caldeira*; the shape connotes a gaping hole or mouth that consumes whatever is put into it and also scalding heat and fire. These images construe her genitals as infernal or diabolical, as burnt by frequent intercourse and as all-engulfing and threatening. Her use of these conventions is ironic, as is marked by the modern editors' use of exclamation points in vv. 12, 21, and 28.[32]

This song presents a *soldadeira* self-consciously in performance; her artful rhetoric and her movements form the central theme of the song, as she performs an identity consistent with her profession and name. Negra's performance of identity is even more exaggerated than the usual parodic mimicry; I read it as a pastiche.[33] The narrator's stance suggests that he reads her performance as straight, that is, as sincerely reflecting her self-perception; the fact that he misreads her is underlined by the contrast with her consciously exaggerated performance. Her eyes are overtly directed toward him, his toward her with side winks at the audience, which he assumes is on his side; however, her performance is staged not just for his sake but for that of the court as a whole. Her awareness of being onstage in their fictive dialogue enables her to appropriate his (future courtly) performance to connect with the audience and contest the narrator's use of her words. The fact that the narrator chose to cite Negra's voice gives the audience less-mediated access to her, enabling it to form its own interpretation of her words. Her ironic speech provokes the laughter of the audience; it laughs at the narrator's naïveté as much as at her use of language.

In a performance context, it is possible that Maria Negra herself could have sung her lines, reenacting their past dialogue in the present before an audience; however, the fact that the male narrator says "E diss m' ela daquesta maneyra, / com' eu a vos direy" (vv. 10–11) suggests that a single, male performer voiced the entire song. In performing as Negra, the poet-performer impersonated her, exaggerating some of her distinctive manner-isms, especially her way of speaking. His transgendered impersonation plays on Negra's parodic performance of self, heightening the irony of the spec-tacle. It is also possible that Negra participated by miming her character's responses to the male protagonist's speech. Her performance would chal-lenge his account, mocking his ventriloquism of her character through nonverbal gestures and movements that communicated her worldly wise impressions of the naive narrator directly to the audience. She would then probably tell her own version of their encounter, a story that would further challenge the narrator's account and increase the comic value of the spec-tacle. Whether Maria Negra participated in the performance or not, the audience would be able to choose between several more-or-less ironic positions with respect to both speakers' campy performances.

Maria Negra's explication of her bodily signs underlines the importance of interpretation and of the value systems that inform the act of interpre-tation. Interpreting *soldadeiras'* bodies is a productive theme in the *Cantigas d'escarnho* since it builds on the ambiguity of women's bodies in general and specifically on how they challenge the binary gender system. Marinha's non-exploding body in Pero Viviaez's LP 136.3, cited at the beginning of this chapter, questions whether gendered body parts signify social inequality. While both characters have the same organs above the waist and different ones below, the male speaker constructs his mouth and nose as protuber-ances and hers as orifices, constructions underlined in their different lower organs. Marinha's nonresponsiveness challenges the speaker's construction of himself as a giant penis; her capacious orifices defy his phallic perfor-mance. While LP 136.3 deflates the speaker's boast, it unfortunately does so by invoking negative commonplaces about female sexuality; the speaker complains that Marinha is too receptive due to her excessive sexual activ-ity. This stereotype helps silence the questions the song had raised as to whether certain body parts dictate different social roles.

I read Afons'Eanes do Coton's song on Mari'Mateu as much more provocative in terms of questioning gender binarisms:

> Mari' Mateu, ir-me quer' eu daquen,
> por que non poss' un cono baratar;
> alguen que mi o daria nõno ten,
> e algũ que o ten non mi o quer dar.
> Mari' Mateu, Mari' Mateu,
> tan desejosa ch' és de cono com' eu!

E foi Deus já de conos avondar
aqui outros, que o non an mester,
e ar feze-os muito desejar
a min e ti, pero que ch' és molher.
Mari' Mateu, Mari' Mateu,
tan desejosa ch' és de cono com' eu! (RL 41)[34]

Mari'Mateu, I want to go away from here, because I can't buy any cunt; he who would give to me it doesn't have any, and he who has it won't give it to me. Mari'Mateu, Mari'Mateu, you want cunt as much as I!

God made many others here abound with cunt, and they don't even need it, while He makes both me and you want it, although you're a woman. Mari'Mateu, Mari'Mateu, you want cunt as much as I!

This song comically presents the problem of the scarcity of cunt on the market due to the dominant economy of desire "here," that is, at the court of Alfonso el Sabio. I cite the manuscript readings of *algũ/algun* in v. 4 and translate that word as "he who," in order to underline the speaker's play on the disjunction between gendered bodies and sexuality. While the male speaker's desire is heterosexual, he is the object of homosexual desire and is unable to find anyone who is willing to "bargain cunt" with him. Implicitly he blames his problem on Mari'Mateu; however, the problem as he outlines it is not caused by her but by an uneven distribution of resources. Nor is it a question of natural or unnatural desires; the speaker's and Mari'Mateu's desires are identical, the same object and equally strong, as ordained by God. The speaker's declaration that she is "tan desejosa. . .de cono com'eu!" is equivocal; she may be "desejosa" because she also is unable to "baratar. . .cono," in which case they are equally unsuccessful on the sexual marketplace. The word "outros" in the second stanza suggests exactly that; others have cunt in abundance, which they don't even lack yet he and she lack, and therefore want. Ironically, Mari'Mateu is also one of those who are endowed yet won't give cunt to the speaker, "algũ que o ten [pero que] non mi o quer dar"; v. 1 underlines this fact by indirectly suggesting that she may wish to console him in order to keep him at court. As Josiah Blackmore has pointed out, Mari'Mateu's name is ambiguous, both female and male, and, we can say, plural; she alone is the mixed-gender "outros" of v. 8.[35] Mari'Mateu's performance of desire affects her gender identity, a fact that is underlined in her equivocal name.

Several critics have noted the narrator's tolerant stance toward same-sex desire in this song; more noteworthy from my point of view is the fact that in this song sex is not phallocentric. The phallocentric model, along with violent sexual practices, predominates in the *Cantigas d'escarnho*, even in other songs that treat same-sex desire.[36] In this song, while the erotic relationship is still constructed by polarized binarisms (active/passive, desiring/desired, etc.), the male organ is not the center of sexual activity; the female organ is. This inversion, as it brings in its wake the elimination of masculine privilege, deeply threatens normative gendered power relations. I can imagine a performance context in which the similarities between Mari'Mateu and the male speaker are downplayed, as Mari'Mateu claims that she gets plenty, unlike our cunt-deprived narrator. Nonetheless, his self-mockingly boastful stance focuses attention on his failings while not at all impugning his virility. The ramifications of this seemingly contradictory yet perfectly tenable position cannot be ignored.

Interpreting *soldadeiras* is a productive theme in the *Cantigas d'escarnho* because it enables poets to focus on their own bodies, desires, and identities in comparison with those of deviant women. While oppositional constructions of masculinity and femininity are consistent elements of these interpretations, also consistent are self-mocking stances on the part of the male speakers who perform their own ambiguous identities that turn out to depend upon those of the *soldadeiras*. This identity play is deeply intertwined with play on structures of power and authority. While the narrator assumes an authoritative stance in order to speak, interpellates a woman, and issues pronouncements on the *soldadeira*'s body and behaviors, he also undercuts his authority by ceding the floor to the female character and by parading his own confusion or failures. These textual traces of ambiguous poses support my reconstruction of performances that celebrate tensions between conventional and deviant identities, behaviors, and sexualities. While these performances are not all affirmatively ambiguous, meaning that not all encourage tolerance for disturbing gender performances, they do put universalizing binarisms into play, calling attention to the constructedness of identity.

In the section that follows, I examine the erotic war motif, which figures coitus as a battle in which one or the other participant must be defeated. Earlier I discussed the agonistic nature of phallic sexuality and an effective feminine counterpose in Pero Viviaez's erotic conflict with Marinha. Throughout the *Cantigas d'escarnho* we find many examples of sexual combats, between men and women as well as same-sex encounters. While often these eroticized battles occur between *soldadeiras* and inappropriate sexual partners such as Muslims, *beesteiros* (crossbowmen), and other marginalized men, any sexual contact can be treated agonistically.[37] The *soldadeira* at war motif presents the sex act as agonistic; at stake is dominance of a feminized other. When the *soldadeira* outperforms the male character, many dominant hierarchies are put into play, showing that the performative nature of sexuality and gender threatens order in general.

Soldadeiras at War

Songs that use the erotic combat motif focus on *soldadeiras'* ambiguously gendered performances as warriors, depicting them as appropriating noble, masculine behaviors as part of a feminine act. Almost all these songs are set at the front lines and are occasional pieces, performed before a mixed audience of courtiers and warriors. The *soldadeiras'* presence at the frontier is both normal, as entertainers regularly traveled with the court, and disruptive, threatening the all-male community of warriors. In the two songs I discuss, the *soldadeiras'* erotic combats either parody Reconquest battles or replicate friendly contests of skill. The outcomes of these combats depend upon the gravity of the threat to order presented by the *soldadeira's* behavior and especially on how her behavior signifies for the community of male courtiers who observe and comment on her performance. In neither song does the narrator participate in the events he describes, as he narrates them in the third person; this distance does not, however, mean both narrators assume a hostile stance toward the female character. In the first song I discuss, JP 41 [RL 25], first-person forms appear only in the narrator's commentary on the scene he describes and then only twice, as the verbal object ("pesa-m' ende," "se Deus me valha," vv. 10, 11); in RL 331, the first person appears only once, "quero lhis eu conselhar ũa ren" (v. 3), marking the narrator's authoritative and homosocial stance, as he advises the non-courtly *beesteiros* to beware of Maria Balteira's ruses. While both narrators pose as eyewitnesses, they don't situate themselves on the battlefield, unlike the *panadera* of the *Coplas de la panadera*, which I discuss in chapter 3. The audience also plays the role of witnesses, of both the *soldadeira's* past, fictive performance and the poet-performer's present display; the *soldadeira* becomes a spectacle, presented for their amusement.

JP 41, authored by Alfonso X, plays with an out-of-place *soldadeira* engaging in mock-heroic combat with an African *genete*, a Muslim horseman. While she defeats him, she emerges seriously wounded, punished for sexual misalliance.[38]

> Domingas Eanes ouve sa baralha
> con ũu genet', e foi mal ferida;
> empero foi ela i tan ardida,
> que ouve depois a vencer, sen falha,
> e, de pran, venceu bõo cavaleiro;
> mais empero é-x'el tan braceiro,
> que ouv' end' ela de ficar colpada.
>
> O colbe colheu per ũa malha
> da loriga, que era desvencida;
> e pesa-m'ende, por que essa ida,

de prez que ouve mais, se Deus me valha,
venceu ela; mais o cavaleiro
per sas armas o fez: com' er' arteiro,
ja sempr' end' ela seerá sinalada.

E aquel mouro trouxe, com' arreite,
dous companhões en toda esta guerra;
e de mais á preço que nunca erra
de dar gran colpe con seu tragazeite;
e foi-a achaar con costa juso,
e deu-lhi poren tal co[l]pe de suso,
que ja a chaga nunca vai çarrada.

E dizen meges que ũus an tal preit'e
que atal chaga ja mais nunca serra
se con quanta lãa á en esta terra
a escaentassen, nen cõno azeite:
por que a chaga non vai contra juso,
mais vai en redor, come perafuso,
e poren muit'á que é fistolada.

Domingas Eanes fought with an African horseman and was seriously wounded; but, she was so ardent that she eventually won, without a doubt, and certainly she defeated a good knight; nonetheless, he is strong that she ended up getting hit.

The blow got to her through a weak spot in her coat of mail, which was untied; and it bothers me, because in this attack, since she was braver (may God aid me), she won; but the knight did it with his weapons; he was so sly that forever after she will be scarred.

And that Moor brought with him, like a studly man, two companions to this combat; and he is famous for never missing when giving a great blow with his lance; and he tumbled her on her back and gave her such a blow from above, that the wound will never close.

And the doctors who understand such matters say that such a wound can never heal, not by warming it with all the wool in this land or with oil; the wound doesn't go straight down, but in circles, like a screw, so that it's been seriously infected for a while.

The third stanza ironically narrates the *genete*'s sexual assault, relying on double-entendres rather than taboo words; his "dous companhões" are his testicles, the "tragazeite" the penis with which he tears open Domingas Eanes's unprotected body. She is figured as passive in the third and fourth stanzas, the object of aggression and of the invasive male gaze; her final passivity rectifies her ambiguously active/passive behavior in the first two stanzas. While she "foi. . .ferida" and "[finca] colpada," she also "venceu,"

presumably by using the same strategy that Balteira does in the following
song, namely, by continuing to demand sex after her partner has climaxed.
She is "ardida," an adjective frequently used favorably to describe an attack
in battle; in this context, it shows that her performance is simultaneously
aggressive-phallic and passive–receptive. Her "loriga . . . desvencida" indicates both the incompetent cross-dressing that makes her vulnerable to
wounding and her already open body. Unlike that of the unexploding
Marinha, Eanes's body bears obvious signs of the *genete's* performance. In
the final stanza, a group of doctors stare at her lower body and in a
detached, ironic way describe the pattern of the wound that makes her
injury so serious. While this description is specific, focusing on this particular female body, the conventionality of the sexual position that produced
this wound suggests to me that this description applies to all sexually active
women, especially to *soldadeiras* whose sexuality both threatens and entertains men of all ethnicities. Eanes's final passivity, an object of violent attack,
invasive gazes, and authoritative pronouncements, neutralizes her, making
her repulsive, diseased, and despised.

The humor of this song lies precisely in its brutal elimination of ambiguity with respect to female sexuality.[39] Domingas Eanes becomes a bur-
lesque show, a spectacle of a disorderly woman put in her place through a
masculine conspiracy that enables Spanish Christians to ally with African
Muslims, if only indirectly. Although she adopts an aggressive role, she is
denied a performance space except as a passive bodily spectacle; her active
impersonation of a knight is ridiculed, as is also her passive performance of
femininity. This song allows Eanes no acceptable performances; while this
could be due to her presence in the homosocial space of the Andalusian
front, the following, more affirmative song suggests instead that this hostility is provoked by Eanes's choice of sexual partner. By engaging with the
genete, Eanes collaborates with the enemy, allowing him to shaft Christian
Spain in an erotic–symbolic renactment of the Muslim conquest. The narrator's praise of the *genete's* aggressive sexuality and his joyous, detailed
account of his attack on Eanes more than counters his brief allusions to her
victory. I explore the symbolic and social significance of sexual misalliance
further in my discussion of Maior Garcia in RL 189 below; in the two
songs, the *soldadeiras'* sexuality is both cause and means of their punishment.

Given this song's hostility toward Eanes and her consistent treatment in
the third person, I expect she did not participate in its presentation.
Whether Alfonso X himself performed it is an interesting question;
below I discuss two more *cantigas* he wrote, either of which he could have
performed. If the king were to perform this song, his impersonation of
Eanes's impersonation of a knight would be especially comic and loaded
with identity play; I comment on a similarly parodic impersonation of an

impersonation in my discussion of the Marqués de Santillana's performance of Menga de Mançanares in chapter 4. In this case, the poet-performer's impersonation of the *genete*'s attack would enable him to showcase his sexuality in the guise of the exotic–erotic, hypermasculine Other. While the narrator does not participate in the fictive spectacle he describes, his distance from the event is undercut by his choice to recount it in suggestive, comic language and to impersonate the characters involved. The metaphoric language enables the poet-performer to avoid taboo words, yet he does pun on forbidden words with *companhões* and *cõno*, vv. 16, 24. His narration presents both Eanes and the *genete* as active verbal subjects; but, from v. 14 on, she becomes either a passive subject ("ela seerá sinalada," v. 14) or a verbal object, as male characters take over the role of active verbal subjects. It is possible that other performers, male and female, could have mimed the characters' actions, in which case the narrator could maintain a distant, ironic stance toward the two actors' behaviors. If Domingas Eanes herself participated, her character's already parodic performance would be yet more so; her active collaboration in making a spectacle of herself would help counteract her passive role in the third and fourth stanzas and encourage the audience's laughter, reducing the tension caused by her presence.

RL 331, which recounts Balteira's phallic performance in a shooting contest with a *beesteiro*, is also set at the front lines, yet not in a combat situation, nor does it cross lines of nationality and race. As in the previous song, the narrator recounts the event in the third person; he frames it with an address to the "beesteiros daquesta fronteira" (crossbowmen here on the front lines), yet that address is also in the third person, creating doubt as to whether any *beesteiros* were present for the poetic spectacle. Second-person forms are also absent, meaning that the audience as well as the narrator are distanced from the event. Maria Balteira's fictive performance is the spectacle they all watch; in this song the grotesque spectacle is produced by one of her victims, a young *beesteiro* whom she shafts. Balteira plays a role similar to that of the *genete* in the previous song and functions to reinscribe conventional hierarchies put into question by the present context, a heterogeneous Christian army gathered on the front lines. In this case, superiority of place trumps gender, as a female courtier defeats an ignoble male soldier.

> Os beesteiros daquesta fronteira
> pero que cuidan que tiran mui ben,
> quero lhis eu conselhar ũa ren:
> que non tiren con Maria Balteira,
> ca todos quantos ali tiraran
> todos se dela con mal partiran
> assi é sabedor e [é] arteira.

Tirou ela con ũu beesteiro,
destes del-Rei, que saben ben tirar;
e, primeira vez, polo escaentar,
leixou-se i logo perder un dinheiro
e des i outr'; e, pois esqueentado,
tirou con el, e á del[e] levado
quanto tragia atẽe no bragueiro.

Os beesteiros dos dous carreirões
tiran con ela, e pon-se sinal;
nen os outros, que tiravan mui mal,
acertaron a dous dos pipeões;
e foron tirando, e bevendo do vinho;
o beesteiro, com' era mininho,
non catou quando s' achou nos colhões! (RL 331 by Pero d'Ambroa)

The crossbowmen of this frontier, although they think they shoot [fuck] very well, I want to give them one piece of advice: Don't shoot with Maria Balteira, because all who do end up badly off, she is so smart and wily.

She shot once with a crossbowman, one of the King's crossbowmen, who know how to shoot and, the first time, in order to warm him up, she let herself lose a coin, and then another; and, once warmed up, she shot with him, and took from him all that he had in his pants.

Two ranks of crossbowmen shot with her, and set up a target; none of the others, who were shooting very badly, hit the bull's eye; and they were shooting, and drinking wine; the crossbowman, being young and foolish, before he knew it, he'd been fleeced [or, got it in the balls]!

This song consistently plays on the sexual connotation of *tirar*, to shoot/to fuck, and configures crossbowmen as extraordinarily phallic, playing on the size of their arrow-shafts and the force of their impact. Maria Balteira is more than equal to the challenge; her excessive sexuality enables her to outperform two ranks of bowmen. The one bowman who presents a challenge to her is also almost insatiable, yet finally he too is exhausted and depleted by her demands. This song develops the literal level of the shooting metaphor throughout, although *bragueiro* and *colhões* (testicles or balls) in vv. 14 and 21 highlight the sexual nature of this contest.

On the literal level, this song comments on Balteira's performance in a test of skill, showing that, while in theory the shooting contest merely tries the accuracy of one's aim, in fact this contest is all about strategy. Her triumph has less to do with her skill at shooting and more to do with her skill at role-playing. As the narrator comments, Balteira is *arteira* because she is sharp; she assesses her opponent's approach to the contest and molds her performance to exploit his weakness, that is, his assumption of superiority due to gender and skill imbalances. Her aggressive performance adopts a feminine pose of weak incompetence vis-à-vis the professional tried in combat and on his own turf, encouraging him to fall into the conventionally masculine role of humoring the silly female. Then, once he is drunk, literally with wine and figuratively with confidence and bravado, she outdoes him, humiliating and emasculating him. She shafts him, as the last verse says, and gets away with it because of the structure of the contest itself, in which the fiction of 'may the best man win' is sustained by quantifiable performances, hitting the target. Not only does she shaft her unwary opponent, but he deserves it, since he let his guard down and underestimated her. Unlike Domingas Eanes, Balteira suffers no punishment for engaging in erotic combat, because, as a representative of the court (like the poet-performer himself, singing his song at the front line, on the *beesteiro's* turf), her triumph reinscribes superiority of place and social status even as it inverts gender hierarchies.

In his presentation of this song, the poet adopts a homosocial pose, warning those unfamiliar with Balteira of her ruses and bonding with the *beesteiros* along gender lines against a disruptive female out of place; the thrust of the joke disrupts this bond, revealing his stance to be as false as Balteira's performance of femininity. The poet performs aggressively through Balteira, replicating her triumph, allying himself with her, and demonstrating his own artful manipulations. Balteira's triumphant performance is a ruse, no more authentic than her feminine pose, which is simply another strategy that helps her achieve a certain end. This song plays with these inauthentic performances, ridiculing the *beesteiro* for his desire to believe in the authenticity of a pleasing performance, and indirectly positing that all performances within a competitive context, including that of the poet at this moment, are mere poses adopted momentarily for their usefulness. The narrator's enthusiastic endorsement of Balteira's victory encourages me to think that she was present for the performance of this song and could have participated by miming her own part while a third, male performer enacted that of the *beesteiro*.

These two songs respond in markedly different ways to aggressive performances of female sexuality on a masculine terrain. The difference is tied to the identity of the *soldadeiras'* opponents and the use the poet-performer wishes to make of his story. Domingas Eanes impersonates a knight in combat with a stigmatized other, an African *genete*; she is punished for sexual misalliance and for appropriating a role reserved for noblemen. At the same time, much of the pleasure of this song is the comic, allusive language used to narrate it, the absence of overt obscenities, and the visual spectacle of transgendered performances at both the fictive and metapoetic levels. Balteira's shooting contest plays on differences among allies, insiders versus outsiders. The poet-performer gets to make a joke at the expense of the *beesteiros*, low-rank professional soldiers who neither ride horses nor engage in hand-to-hand combat; knights' contempt for crossbowmen is notorious. Metaphorical language and comic exaggeration enhance the joke. These two songs are particularly dramatizing of performance, which I see as always central; at the front line, female sexual performances are thematized as masculine martial performances. As with the figure of the *serrana*, who may also adopt aggressive, masculine behaviors in her encounters with travelers, a *soldadeira* who performs aggressive sexuality may or may not be punished for doing so; the narrator's attitude depends on the use he makes of her performance.

In the section that follows, I focus on five songs that put words into *soldadeiras'* mouths. It strikes me as highly significant that in only one of the six songs I have discussed so far does a *soldadeira* speak (Maria Negra in LP 125.21 [RL 384]), which suggests that a poet may more easily adopt an ambivalent pose toward an ambiguous female character if he does not try to incorporate her voice into his composition. The agonistics of voicing are inescapable, especially in a mixed performance context in which the *soldadeira* who is named in the composition is also present for the performance. As I show, allowing a female character to speak affects the power balance within a song, often making for more overtly hostile stances toward the female character.

Ventriloquizing *Soldadeiras* in the *Cantigas d'escarnho*

Ventriloquizing *soldadeiras* in the *Cantigas d'escarnho* is an antagonistic practice, as poets put words into their mouths, making their words equivocal or double-voiced. I use the word 'ventriloquize' advisedly, since female characters do not quite function as dummies; while the audience is aware that her words are not her own, the extent to which the poet-narrator acknowledges this fact depends upon the text and performance of each song. As I mentioned above in my discussion of Maria Negra's equivocal speech, poets often endow ventriloquized characters with more volition than silent ones; we could read Domingas Eanes and Maria Balteira as marionettes more easily than most of the *soldadeiras* I discuss in this section. Poets rarely cite *soldadeiras'* speech; the number of female citations in the *Cantigas d'escarnho*, while statistically higher than in fifteenth-century *cancionero* poetry, is still rather low, especially given the existence of an entire genre of female-voiced songs, the *Cantigas d'amigo*, in the Galician-Portuguese corpus. In the *Cantigas d'escarnho*, *soldadeiras* are directly cited in twelve songs (JP 30 [RL 1] and 16 [RL 14], RL 47, 48, 189, 193, 205, 247,

291, 315, 384, and 426) and indirectly cited or paraphrased in another six (RL 49, 146, 190, 317, and 333). Female speech is framed by the poet's voice, which establishes the context for the citation and encourages an ironic interpretation of her speech. Aggression is foregrounded in this recontextualization, as the narrator cites the *soldadeira* to mark his difference from her; his perspective on her speech dominates and undercuts her own understanding of her words. This stance toward female speech is nearly universal in medieval Romance lyrics, as Doris Earnshaw has demonstrated; it is particularly significant when adopted in reaction to the speech of a female performer. Such a stance implies that the performer misjudges the effect of her performance; the male speaker cites her incompetence to demonstrate his artistry. When female performers voice female characters, the power balance is different; whether a mixed-gender performance can unseat the male narrator's dominance depends on the dynamics of the performance itself.[40]

In this section, I discuss five *cantigas* that cite *soldadeiras'* speech, JP 16 and 30 and RL 189, 193, and 247, exploring the meaning(s) their words carry and the poses the narrators adopt in reaction to female speech. Each of the songs I discuss here parodies a particular speech genre, either judicial language, the *juego de palabras*, negotiating dialogues, confession, or prayer. The first three of these speech genres are mostly practiced by men, so the mere fact of putting such speech into a *soldadeira's* mouth is parodic; it also focuses attention on the gendered nature of language, especially when female speakers address male characters who judge and respond to their speech. Confession and prayer are examples of religious language used to express female sexuality. In all five songs, the male narrator uses the female character's past, and usually private, speech in his present performance, publishing and mocking her speech practices. These narrators may adopt self-mocking poses, as do Pero Viviaez, Joan Soárez Coelho, Pero Garcia Burgalês, and Afons'Eanes do Coton in the songs discussed so far. Alfonso X, the author of the first and last songs discussed here, plays with his role as king, while Joan Baveca, who also composed two of these five songs, mocks himself in one of them. In the remaining two songs, the male narrator does not specifically portray himself as he cites a *soldadeira's* negotiating dialogue or confession, adopting the role of eyewitness and distancing himself from the incident he recounts. Perhaps not coincidentally, in these cases, the poet-performer impersonates the female character, an impersonation that sharply contrasts with the narrator's detached, superior stance. Even when the dominant reception of the *soldadeira's* speech is hostile, the mere act of citing her voice introduces ambiguity; the dialogic aspect of these songs gives the audience access to the female character, although filtered through the perspective of the male speaker.

JP 16 [RL 1] by Alfonso el Sabio includes an extended female monologue in which a *soldadeira* parodies judicial language and comments on
how her speech practices affect the treatment she receives at court:[41]

> [. . .]
> por que lhi rogava que perdoasse
> Pero d'Ambroa, que o non matasse,
> nen fosse contra el desmesurada.
> E diss' ela:—Por Deus, non me roguedes,
> ca direi-vos de min o que i entendo:
> se ũa vez assanhar me fazedes,
> saberedes quaes peras eu vendo.
>
> Ca [me] rogades cousa desguisada,
> e non sei eu quen vo-lo outrogasse,
> de perd[o]ar quen no mal deostasse,
> com' el fez a min, estando en sa pousada.
> E, pois vejo que me non conhocedes,
> de mi atanto vos irei dizendo:
> se ũa vez assanhar me fazedes,
> [saberedes quaes peras eu vendo.]
>
> E, se m'eu quisesse seer viltada,
> ben acharia quen xe me viltasse;
> mais, se m'eu taes non escarmertasse,
> cedo meu preito non seeria nada.
> E en sa prol nunca me vós faledes,
> ca, se eu soubesse, morrer' ardendo;
> se ũa vez assanhar me fazedes,
> [saberedes quaes peras eu vendo.]
>
> E por esto é grande a mia nomeada,
> ca non foi tal que, se migo falhasse,
> que en eu mui ben non-[no] castigasse,
> ca sempre fui temuda e dultada.
> E rogo-vos que me non afiquedes
> daquesto, mais ide-m' assi sofrendo;
> se ũa vez assanhar me fazedes,
> [saberedes quaes peras eu vendo.]

[. . .] because I asked her to forgive Pero d'Ambroa, not to kill him, nor be
so angry with him. And she said: "By God, don't ask me that, 'cause I'll tell
you what I think: if once you make me angry, you'll see what sort of pears
I sell [i.e., you'll see what I'm capable of].

"You ask me an inappropriate thing, and I don't know who would grant you
that: to forgive someone who had insulted them so, like he did to me, while
I was at his lodging. And since I can see that you don't know me, I'll go on
telling you: if once you make me angry, [you'll see what sort of pears I sell.]

"And, if I wanted to be dishonored, I could easily find someone to dishonor me; but, if I don't make an example of those who do, soon my case won't be worth anything. And, don't say anything to me in his favor, because, if I knew how to, he'd go down in flames; if once you make me angry, [you'll see what sort of pears I sell.]

"And because of this, my reputation [for vengeance] is great, since there isn't anyone who offended me that I haven't punished very well, so I have always been feared and respected. And I beg you not to insist on this, but to go on letting me be; if once you make me angry, [you'll see what sort of pears I sell.]"

The speech of the female character (who is unknown since the first verse is lost) constitutes almost the entirety of the song, from v. 4 on; what is presented as her authentic speech is recontextualized and cited by Alfonso X for the amusement of his audience, as he has the angry *soldadeira* threaten his poetic alter ego. Her speech parodies a legal defense, citing the form without the content. She declines to state exactly what Pero d'Ambroa did to offend her, yet she insinuates that the insult was of a sexual nature since it occurred at his lodgings. Her testimony is constrained by the risk of increasing the damage to her if she reveals the insult; because she doesn't reveal it, her case against d'Ambroa is flawed. Given the type of insults to *soldadeiras* we see in the *Cantigas d'escarnho*, I discern two possibilities: either he sexually assaulted her or he rejected her advances.[42] A *soldadeira* could not seek legal remedies for either of these offenses. Since prostitutes were *enfamadas*, lacking honor, they could not be dishonored; their nonexistent honor could not be damaged by verbal or physical assault.[43] The repetition of *viltada/viltasse* in vv. 17–18 underlines the issue of honor and her sense of equity; her behavior is not *desmesurada* (unreasonable or excessive) as the narrator says, but fair, as she gives as good as she gets. Barred from seeking a legal remedy, the *soldadeira's* only recourse is personal vengeance; the interference of the male speaker is especially unwelcome, as the order that he defends would deprive her of any means of redress.

In defending her suit against d'Ambroa, the female speaker addresses both the offense itself and the importance of her complaint. She cites herself repeatedly in the refrain, "se ũa vez assanhar me fazedes, / sabredes quaes peras eu vendo," a citation that gains the force of a personal motto, as it both encapsulates the song's theme and justifies her pursuit of vengeance against d'Ambroa. The *soldadeira* declares that she must punish d'Ambroa in order to reinforce her reputation for swift and implacable anger; from her point of view, her reputation protects her, acting as a deterrent to those who otherwise would insult her. In order to defend herself from future insults, she must defy the king's wishes and pursue her vengeance; she even threatens him with the consequences of her wrath. My reading conflates the lyric 'I' with the poet, a conflation that in this case I feel is justified, since it increases the tension between the *soldadeira* and narrator who embodies the very law that disempowers her. Joseph T. Snow suggests that Alfonso's poetic persona in this song is distinct from his identity as king, although his comment that "from time to time. . .the 'king' peeps through" certainly creates space to read the lyric 'I' as Alfonso himself, a possibility I see as highly relevant to this song and to JP 30, which compares a *soldadeira*'s passion to Christ's, discussed below.[44] This *soldadeira* presents herself as highly aware of the hostility that surrounds her and of how her performance affects the treatment she receives. She must perform as a hot-head, in order to protect herself. Her repeated self-citations indicate the gap between her performance of irrational anger and the rationale for her performance.

In the presentation of this song, the female character's speech would evoke laughter due to the male narrator's ironic stance toward the *soldadeira* who would defend her honor and due to her own ironic self-awareness. This song could be performed by a single male actor-singer who mimicked the voice and gestures of the individual *soldadeira* (if named in the lost first verse), specifically parodying her; the signs of textual femininity in the adjectives that modify the female speaker's I (*viltada*, *temuda*, and *dultada*) means that the character's gender is marked both textually and in the performer's transgendered act. Nevertheless, it seems more likely to me that the performance would be dialogic, with the narrator's part voiced by a male performer and that of the *soldadeira* by a female, due to the length of the female speech and its introduction by the phrase "E diss' ela" (v. 5).[45] The line between the female character and the female performer would be fine, whether the individual *soldadeira* were named or not; the specific trait for which she is mocked, anger, is a stereotypical female attribute. In performing this part, a *soldadeira* would engage in parodic mimicry, exaggerating in order to demonstrate the character's self-awareness and to mock the male character, whose fearful reaction to the *soldadeira* would also be exaggerated; such a performance would be met with gales of laughter. Probably the audience would join in singing the refrain, especially by the third stanza, perhaps clued by the *soldadeira*-performer; in such a participatory performance, all would get to threaten the king's persona by echoing the *soldadeira*'s angry motto. The problem presented in this song is serious, as the legal structure permitted and even endorsed assaults on prostitutes in order to punish them for sexual commerce. This song focuses on a legally/logically untenable position actually occupied by flesh-and-blood individuals at court; in order to disperse the tension created by this fact, this song would have to be performed as high camp. Its humor stems at least as much from the king's inability to control the angry *soldadeira* as from her peculiar perspective on her situation at his court.

In RL 193, the only example of two *soldadeiras* in dialogue in the *Cantigas d'escarnho*, Joan Baveca cites them performing a parodic *juego de palabras*:

Estavan oje duas soldadeiras
dizendo ben, a gran pressa, de si;
e viu a ũa delas as olheiras
de sa companheira, e diss' assi:
— Que enrugadas olheiras tẽedes!
E diss' a outra:—Vós com' as veedes
desses ca[belos sobr' essas trincheiras]?

[. . .]
en esse vosso rostro. E des i
diss' el' outra vez:—Já vós dult' avedes;
mais tomad' aquest' espelh' e veeredes
tôdalas vossas sobrancelhas veiras.

E ambas elas eran companheiras,
e diss' a ũa en jogo outrossi:
—Pero nós ambas somos muit' arteiras,
milhor conhosqu' eu vós ca vós [a] min.
E diss' [a] outra:—Vós, que conhocedes
a min tan ben, por que non entendedes
como son covas essas caaveiras?

E, depois, tomaron senhas masseiras
e banharon-se e loavan-s' a si;
e quis Deus que, nas palavras primeiras
que ouveron, que chegass' eu ali;
e diss' a ũa:—Mole ventr' avedes;
e diss' a outr':—E vós mal ascondedes
as tetas, que semelhan cevadeiras.

Today two *soldadeiras* were praising each other, with great sincerity; and one of them looked at the other one's eyes, and said, "What crow's feet you have!" And the other one said, "How can you see them through those bushy eyebrows that fall over those trenches you have for eyes?"

". . .in that face of yours." And then she said again: "You doubt now, but take this mirror and you will see your eyebrows all streaked with white."

And they were both companions, and one spoke thus in jest: "Although we are both very sly, I know you better than you know me." And the other one said: "You, who know me so well, why don't you see how sunken your cheeks are?"

And, then, they each took a kneading-trough [massaged each other] and they bathed and praised each other; and God wished that, in the first words that they spoke, I arrived there; and one said: "What a flabby belly you have"; and the other said, "And how hard it is to cover your tits, which hang down like feed-bags."

The two *soldadeiras* exchange insults while bathing, to the amusement of the voyeuristic narrator. From the *soldadeiras'* point of view, their dialogue is a *juego de palabras*; neither takes these insults personally, and each responds with another conventional insult, implying the other is old and ugly. The comment "ambas somos muit' arteiras" praises their wittiness; this self-praise is followed by another insult, continuing the game. The *soldadeiras* play this game for their mutual amusement and entertainment; their doing so parodies a noble, masculine game which, as *soldadeiras* with easy access to male recreational spaces, they undoubtedly had witnessed on several occasions. The site of their performance is also parodic, at bath, a single-sex place of pleasure, sociability, and erotic activity. While the word *masseiras* (v. 19, kneading-troughs) is used to denote bowls of water, I read this rather unusual word-choice as suggesting that they knead and massage each other as they bathe. Certainly they have removed their clothes by the fourth stanza; the insults in the first three stanzas focus on their heads, while those in the final stanza name the stomach and breasts. The *soldadeiras'* ritual insults are verbal caresses that build up to their actual physical contact by the end of the song. We see a similarly charged insult exchange between a *panadera* and her male customer negotiating the cost of sex in Sebastián de Horozco's "Dama de gentil aseo," discussed in chapter 3.[46]

The narrator reproduces the *soldadeiras'* private performance in a public performance before courtiers who themselves engage in *juegos de palabras*. The pleasure of his voyeurism stems from his violation of social spaces and sexual taboos; he reveals the *soldadeiras'* in-group speech practices as well as their bodies (represented indirectly through his citations of the *soldadeiras'* words). The narrator's ironic stance toward their abusive speech denies the ritual nature of their insults; he mentions one *soldadeira's* glance at her companion's eyes before the start of the insult exchange in order to frame her comment as a personal insult. His use of ũa and *outra* to mark their two voices emphasizes the *soldadeiras'* interchangeability; by framing their insults as personal, he implies that the *soldadeiras* are factually aged and ugly. The narrator construes their performance as illustrating their degraded nature; an audience may notice that their performance also strips the *juego* of its aristocratic pretenses and reveals its underlying homoeroticism. The narrator's hostile stance may well stem from his desire to deny the significance of their play; he focuses on the *soldadeiras'* grotesque bodies in order to distract attention from the possibility that *juegos* between men are similarly erotic.

If we turn our eye on the male narrator, we may notice that Joan Baveca assumes an ironic stance toward his persona's sexuality. *Baveca* is stage name that emphasizes the poet-performer's foolishness; this mask resembles that assumed by Guillaume IX in his comic-obscene "Farai un vers, pos mi somelh" (I shall make a verse, since I am sleeping), in which the narrator poses as a mute uttering nonsense: "Babariol, babariol, / babarian" (vv. 29–30).[47] Guillaume's narrator-protagonist plays mute in order to have sex with two noblewomen; implicitly, in his absence, they would have satisfied their desires on their own, although they prefer heterosexual activity. In the narrator's subsequent presentation of that encounter at court, he mocks his fictive mask of muteness, demonstrating his verbal artistry and exposing the two women, whom he identifies by name. Guillaume's poem is an ironic phallic and poetic boast; his persona claims he fucked them one hundred and eighty-eight times, yet complains that he cannot express the pain he suffered: "e no·us puesc dir lo malaveg, / tan gran m'en pres" (vv. 83–84). This pose mirrors with a difference Baveca's treatment of the *soldadeiras*, as his alter ego does not take advantage of the opportunity to interact with the two naked women. This may be, in part, due to the very different roles the two male narrators play in the encounters. In Guillaume's case, the female characters accost him, and he performs muteness in order to see how they will react. Later, his lyric 'I' must exert himself to remain silent while they test his muteness by raking him with the claws of a red cat. He continues to perform muteness so that he can benefit both sexually and poetically from his encounter with these grotesque (albeit noble) women.

By contrast, Baveca's narrator conceals himself, allowing his disdain for the degraded women to deprive him of sexual pleasure. Admittedly, in revealing his presence, he would run a risk: the surprised *soldadeiras* could react violently like parodic Dianas at bath and try to kill the intrusive Orion-voyeur; or, they could attack him verbally, given *soldadeiras*' reputation for anger.[48] Baveca's persona's timidity may be an indirect acknowledgment of his inferiority at verbal interactions; he maintains silence rather than be defeated by satiric *soldadeiras*. On the other hand, the two *soldadeiras* may have welcomed his presence and used him as a sexual plaything, as did Agnes and Ermessen in Guillaume's lyric. Even if these *soldadeiras* were actually aged and ugly, the one use of grotesque women is sexual, as Guillaume's lyric demonstrates. Instead, Baveca's narrator remains concealed: he is an ironic voyeur who foregoes sexual pleasure in order to establish and maintain his gender and social superiority and to avoid being tested, as was Guillaume, and, unlike Guillaume, failing. Baveca uses the two *soldadeiras*' dialogue to focus attention on their conventional degradation and over-sexed nature; he also uses it to distract attention from his own persona's sexuality and from the erotic potential of similar verbal games between men.

In performance, these other aspects could be brought out. I consider it probable that two female performers voiced the *soldadeiras'* parts and mimed their gestures; since their voices are clearly set off from that of the narrator, it would be easy to cue them in at the appropriate moments. At the end of the song, they could have lamented that the narrator chose to conceal himself and ridiculed him for doing so, calling attention to his body and sexuality as he had already done to theirs. It is also possible that a male performer impersonated the two *soldadeiras*, imitating their speech and vulgar gestures; such a performance would increase the distance between the female characters and the audience and distract attention from the narrator's stake in their performance. In a solo act, the body of the male narrator-protagonist and those of the *soldadeiras* would merge into the one figure of the male performer as he engaged in both self-mimicry and trans-gendered impersonation; while their voices and gestures would be distin-guished, their bodies would not be. The performer's pleasure in acting like degraded women would contrast starkly with the narrator's ironic distance from them.

Joan Baveca continues his practice of ventriloquizing *soldadeiras* in RL 189; this time Maior Garcia is presented negotiating with three customers, a Christian, a Jew, and a Muslim. While negotiating is a common theme in poems on *soldadeiras*, most negotiating songs are monologic, as the *soldadeira* doesn't respond to the male narrator's attempts to lower the price or get her to fulfill her share of the bargain. Surely it is not coincidental that the only *cantiga* in which a *soldadeira* negotiates directly with a client also features sexual misalliance; as both Benjamin Liu and Roy Rosenstein have observed, Garcia's business practices transgress normative boundaries, leading to mixing and ambiguity.[49]

> Un escudeiro vi oj' arrufado
> por tomar penhor a Maior Garcia,
> por dinheiros poucos que lhi devia;
> e diss' ela, poi-lo viu denodado:
> —Senher, vós non mi afrontedes assi,
> e será' gora un judeu aqui,
> con que barat', e dar-vos-ei recado
>
> De vossos dinheiros de mui bon grado;
> e tornad' aqui ao meio dia,
> e entanto verrá da Judaria
> aquel judeu con que ei baratado
> e un mouro, que á' qui de chegar,
> con que ei outrossi de baratar;
> e, en como quer, farei-vos eu pagado.

E o mouro foi log' ali chegado,
e cuidou-s' ela que el pagaria
dívida velha qu' a ela devia;
mais diss' o mouro:—Sol non é pensado
que vós paguedes ren do meu aver,
meos d' eu carta sobre vós fazer,
ca un judeu avedes enganado.

E ela disse:—Fazede vós qual
carta quiserdes sobre min, pois d' al
non poss' aver aquel omen pagado.

E o mouro log' a carta notou
sobr' ela e sobre quanto lh' achou;
e pagou-a e leixou-lh' o tralado.

I saw a squire today all puffed-up and eager to collect a debt from Maior Garcia, for a few coins that she owed him; and she said, when she saw his great boldness: "Sir, don't abuse me so, because soon a Jew will come here, with whom I have business, and then I'll give you a full accounting

of your money, very gladly; so come back at midday, and in the meanwhile that Jew with whom I will bargain will come from the Jewry, and a Moor too, who will come here, with whom I also have business; and then, however you wish, I will satisfy you."

And then the Moor arrived there, and she thought that he would pay her an old debt that he owed her; but, the Moor said, "I wouldn't even consider paying you anything of mine unless I make a letter on you, since you defrauded a Jew."

And she said: "Make whatever letter you wish on me, since otherwise I won't be able to satisfy that man."

So then the Moor wrote a letter upon her about what he found; and he "paid" her [had sex with her] and left her a copy [i.e., pregnant with his baby].

This song uses economic language as a code for sexual intercourse. *Pagar* is consistently equivocal, meaning both to pay and to satisfy, in verbal, monetary, and sexual exchanges; *recado* and *carta* denote sex, and the *tralado* that the Muslim leaves with Garcia is a copy of himself, his baby. Later I shall discuss the contrast between spoken and written language; for the moment I wish to focus on the voices of the various characters. The narrator recounts two conversations between Maior Garcia and her clients, the *escudeiro* who is paraphrased and the Muslim who is cited directly; the Jewish client does not speak at all, and the fact that the Muslim claims that Garcia defrauded him suggests that his voice is not included because anOther can speak for him. Also interesting is the fact that, in these two dialogues, Garcia gets her way with the *escudeiro* but not with the Muslim, perhaps because his voice, directly cited, is the strongest of the clients' voices in this poem. Garcia utters the greatest number of verses, vv. 5–14 and vv. 22–24, a total of thirteen verses, in contrast with the almost four verses enunciated by the Muslim (vv. 18–21) and the eleven spoken by the narrator (vv. 1–4, 15–18, 25–27). The four male characters must collaborate in order to silence Garcia; the narrator emphasizes Garcia's defeat in the final tercet, where he concludes the song by focusing on her impregnation by the Muslim.

Garcia's activities cause mixing, of races, money, language, and spaces. The three men come to her, leaving their usual spaces to enter her house, a fact emphasized by her comment that the Jew would come from the *juderia*. In the *Cantigas d'escarnho*, as in other traditions of scabrous verse, residences of all kinds symbolize female genitalia. Garcia's house, body, business, and speech are open and accessible to all. Baveca's treatment of Garcia reflects anxieties that Christian prostitutes promoted and enabled the mixing of the three cultures of medieval Iberia. As public women, official prostitutes (prostitutes housed in municipal brothels) could not refuse any client; in towns with mixed populations, this requirement clashed with other laws forbidding relations between Muslim or Jewish men and Christian women on penalty of death. Should a prostitute be accused of violating these prohibitions, the question of whether she knew the customer's identity was paramount; questioning would focus on the customer's appearance, since particular clothing and haircuts were mandated for Jews and Muslims (and for prostitutes as well). David Nirenberg says that "the prostitute's role in identification and the recognition of difference suggests her importance as a boundary marker" between Christian, Muslim, and Jewish communities. He further theorizes that prostitutes created a link between all the men who slept with them:

> the overlap between [the prostitute's] role as receptacle of communal Christian male lust, on the one hand, and medieval theories about the physical and spiritual bonds created by intercourse, on the other, transformed the prostitute into a concrete representation of a community of men united to each other by a common sexual bond. In the case of the fourteenth-century Crown [of Aragon], this was a community delimited in terms of religious identity. All Christian males could, in the words of St. Paul, "become one body" with a Christian prostitute, but through her (and this St. Paul did not say) they also become one with each other.[50]

As in the case of the *panadera* discussed in chapter 3, the prostitute functions like the Host. The consumption of her body, constructed as common property and accessible to all Christians, parallels that of the Host as the absolute marker of (masculine) Christian identity. Prohibitions on sex between Christian women and Jewish and Muslim men also draw on the dominant model of agonistic phallic sexuality: through penetration of the Christian woman's body, the man who due to his religious identity should occupy the space of the conquered performs the role of the conqueror, using gendered differential status to negate religious differential status.[51] In RL 189, Garcia does not hide her transgressive business practices, nor does her misalliance deter her customers; in fact, her trade promotes communication and collaboration among Jews, Muslims, and Christians. The gendered construction of bonds between men overrides their religious differences, as all three conspire to put Garcia in her inferior place.

Benjamin Liu focuses on the ambiguous meaning of the baby with three fathers that Garcia will give birth to; I'm more interested in the song's treatment of the *soldadeira*'s verbal performances.[52] Her discourses both satisfy and frustrate her customers, as she flatters, tells stories, and makes promises in her attempts to achieve and maintain a position of dominance over them. She evades the proud *escudeiro*, an incompetent businessman whom she may never intend to pay, as the dialogue with the Muslim implies; her success is fully due to her rhetoric, as she outtalks the *escudeiro* and gives him only vague promises of future payment. The Muslim, by contrast, uses his narrative of her fraudulent dealings with the Jew to demand a written letter from her. This change from oral to written language marks Garcia's loss of control of the situation, leading to her defeat. The fact that the Muslim writes the letter himself could imply that Garcia is illiterate, another significant difference in addition to gender, race, and social status; it could suggest that he writes the note in Arabic, not Romance, another sign of her loss of power. The Muslim's refusal to pay her without a written record forces Garcia to consent; his verbal performances, as voiced by the narrator who ambiguously identifies with the Muslim, neutralize her rhetorical stratagems. She must perform her normative, passive–receptive feminine role, which signifies her emasculation and shafting by monologic masculinity, albeit triple-faced. While I see the song's focus on miscegenation as significant, more than divisions between races I see bonding between diverse men who mutually exploit each other in order to achieve a higher goal, the just defeat of a verbally dominant woman. The humor of this song is also hostile; while the audience would laugh at the puffed-up *escudeiro*, it would relish Garcia's defeat, especially given the evocatively ambiguous wording Baveca uses, conflating economic, sexual, and verbal transactions and punishing her with her own weapons.

This song is especially suited for performance due to the number of characters and their comic treatment. At least two and perhaps up to five actor-singers could have participated in this presentation, and one of these performers was probably a woman. I think it would be necessary to have a female body on stage impersonating Garcia due to the length of her speeches and their lack of textual femininity. A single male performer could impersonate all the male characters; however, given the references to the *judeu* and the *escudeiro* in the third and fourth stanzas, their visual presence within the performance space would enhance the joke as well as emphasize the homosocial bonding around Garcia. The *escudeiro* would be marked by his preening arrogance, as described in the first verse, and his acceptance of Garcia's terms in the second stanza would be mimed. The *mouro's* sexual performance in the final stanza would certainly be mimed, as well as that of Garcia; all the characters, including of course the audience, would watch, and laugh, at the word-play as well as at Garcia's swollen belly. Such a performance would emphasize collaboration, just as at the fictive level Garcia collaborates with the male characters, accepting the Muslim's terms since only in that way could she satisfy the *escudeiro*.

While *soldadeiras* are seldom depicted negotiating with their clients, they utter parodic confessions in four *Cantigas d'escarnho*, RL 146, 190, 247, and 347. This motif plays on the comic possibilities of the repentant prostitute who, as in the next song cited below, may not confess her sinful sexual practices but some other flaw. All the confession poems play on the logical contradictions between a *soldadeira's* sinful nature and her pious practices, perverted or rendered ineffective by her continued exercise of her profession. Confession also foregrounds performance issues, as the *soldadeira* verbally performs an identity before a specific audience in order to achieve transformation through the power of language. This idea is played on most effectively in RL 247, the only confession poem in which the *soldadeira's* voice is directly cited:

> Maria Leve, u se maenfestava,
> direi-vos ora o que confessava:
> —Sõo velh', ai, capelan!
>
> Non sei oj' eu mais pecador burgesa
> de min; mais vede-lo que mi mais pesa:
> Sõo velh', ai, capelan!
>
> Sempr' eu pequei [i], des que fui foduda;
> pero direi-vos per que [son] perduda:
> Sõo velh', ai, capelan! (RL 247 by Joan Vaásquiz)

Maria Leve, when she confessed, I'll tell you what she confessed: "Alas, I'm old, chaplain!

"There's no greater sinner than myself in all this town; but, what causes me most pain, is that alas, I'm old, chaplain!

"I have always sinned, since I was first fucked; but I'll tell you why I'm truly ruined: Alas, I'm old, chaplain!"

As with the previous examples of ventriloquized *soldadeiras*, the narrator presents himself as a reliable witness to Maria Leve's confession, which in all probability would have occurred in church before witnesses, and he relates her confession to his audience of fellow courtiers. His ironic, distant stance mocks the *soldadeira's* conception of sin and of the transformative possibilities of absolution. Leve uses both the active and passive voices in v. 7, suggesting that she is aware that sin consists of acts of the will and that she takes responsibility for her actions; yet she also says that, once her virginity was lost, an event that happened to her without her volition, her future course was determined. Her use of the passive voice echoes the language of penitentials, in which female sexuality is consistently constructed as passive. Her familiarity with confessional language informs Leve's diction, such that she cites the *capelan's* previous speech although he does not speak in this song. His voice is subsumed in hers, as is hers in that of the narrator. While Jorge Osório cites this text as an example of a female character's speech in the *Cantigas d'escarnho*, the narrator's use of the first-person future (*direi*, v. 2) to introduce his citation of her speech suggests to me that a single male performer would have voiced the entire song.[53] The narrator's choice not to cite the *capelan* transforms their dialogue into a female-voiced monologue (impersonated by a male performer), overturning the gender hierarchy that shapes confessional interactions and reducing the confessor to silence.

This song plays on the ability of language to shape reality and confession as a means of transformation. Maria Leve's use of both active and passive voices elides the difference between sinful acts and being a sinner and leads her to confess her identity as a sin. Her confession, however, is not that she is a *soldadeira*; instead, she confesses that she is old, a state that she would want to emend, if possible. In effect, Leve appropriates the language of confession and puts it to her own use. She does seek reconciliation with and reintegration into a certain community that has excluded her, not that of believers but the sexual (and sinful) community of the court. By confessing her age, Maria Leve hopes to be absolved and rejuvenated, transformed by her language and that of the priest who absolves her. Her parodic confession perverts the ritual as she tries to use the clergy's semi-magical speech acts to change not her sinful identity but her aged body. Her declaration that she is the greatest sinner in the town is a bold assertion of self, a boastful stance that shows her aggressive comparison of herself with other women of her condition. While framed as a lament with her interjection of "ai," Maria's confession of age can also be read as a boast; her age has helped make her the great sinner that she is, since "Sempr' eu pequei [i], des que fui foduda." The chaplain witnesses Maria's boast, as does the poet himself and his audience, who would already know about the legendary vice of this poetic character; her confession enables her to perform contrition and self-assertion, an ironic performance made yet more ironic when double-voiced by the poet–performer.[54]

In performance, the high level of textual femininity, especially in the final stanza and in the taboo word *foduda*, would make for a highly comic female impersonation on the part of the male performer. The refrain could have been sung by the entire audience, especially by the third stanza; such a performance would increase the complicity of all present, as they collaborated in voicing the parodic confession of an old *soldadeira*. Maria Leve herself could have been present for the performance and sung the refrain along with the audience; her participation would reduce the distance between herself as interpellated character and the community formed by the audience and performer. She would still be singled out, yet the fictive role created for her in this song would enable her to present a boastful and proud performance of self, and perhaps also to turn attention onto the poet–performer's role in the fictive confession, to counteract his erasure of self from that narration. As with the performance scenarios I have outlined above, her collaboration would be coerced, yet her participation would also mark the fictive nature of her poetic treatment and enhance the joke.

In JP 30 [RL 14], Alfonso el Sabio puts an extended, parodic monologue in a *soldadeira*'s mouth. She prays during the sex act, crying out to Christ and comparing her passion to His:

> Fui eu poer a mão noutro di-
> -a a ũa soldadeira no conon,
> e disse-m'ela:—Tolhede-la, don
> [. . . -i]
> ca non é esta de Nostro Senhor
> paixon, mais é-xe de min, pecador,
> por muito mal que me lh'eu mereci.
>
> U a voz começastes, entendi
> ben que non era de Deus aquel son,
> ca os pontos del no meu coraçon
> se ficaran, de guisa que logu'i
> cuidei morrer, e dix' assi:—Senhor,
> beeito sejas tu, que sofredor
> me fazes deste marteiro par ti!
>
> Quisera-m'eu fogir logo dali,
> e non vos fora mui[to] sen razon,

con medo de morrer e con al non,
mais non pudi—tan gran coita sofri;
e dixe logu' enton:—Deus, meu Senhor,
esta paixon sofro por teu amor,
pola tua, que sofresti por min.

Nunca, dê-lo dia en que naci,
fui tan coitado, se Deus me perdon;
e con pavor, aquesta oraçon
comecei logo e dixe a Deus assi:
—Fel e azedo bevisti, Senhor,
por min, mais muit' est' aquesto peior
que por ti bevo nen que recebi.

E poren, ai, Jesu Cristo, Senhor,
en juizo, quando ante ti for,
nembre-ch'esto que por ti padeci![55]

The other day I went to put my hand on a *soldadeira*'s cunt, and she said to me: "Take it back, sir, [. . .], 'cause this is not the Passion of Our Lord, but mine, a sinner, for the great punishment that I deserve.

"When you started it, I understood well that that sound was not Godly, because its points stuck into my heart, so that I thought I'd die, and I said: 'Lord, may you be blessed, you cause me to suffer this martyrdom for your sake!'

"I wished to flee then, and not without reason, with the fear of death and with nothing else, but I couldn't, I suffered such a great pain; and I said then: 'God, my Lord, I suffer this passion for your love, for your Passion, which you suffered for me.'

"Never, since the day I was born, have I been so afflicted [sexually aroused], if God forgive me; and with fear, I began this prayer, speaking thus to God: 'You drank bile and vinegar, Lord, for me, but this is much worse, what I drink and receive for you.

" 'And so, alas, Jesus Christ, Lord, when I appear before you in judgment, remember this that I suffered for you!' "

As Manuel da Costa Fontes has demonstrated in his carefully contextualized decoding of this song, the *soldadeira* initially resists the speaker's advances, but her refusal is ironic, referring to the inappropriateness of the hour as that of Christ's passion (i.e., 3:00 p.m. on a Friday) and initiating the parodic parallel between her erotic martyrdom and Christ's passion that continues throughout the song.[56] Not only does the *soldadeira* speak from v. 3 on, narrating her experience of intercourse, but she cites her own exclamations at the end of all but the first stanza, crying out to her *Senhor* (a very ambiguous word in this song, authored by the king), punctuating her climaxes with pious ejaculations. The past-tense forms suggests that her speech is a postcoital account of her experience addressed to her partner, perhaps designed to reawaken his desire and to enable her to relive her suffering/ecstasy. This fictive context suggests she enjoys making a spectacle of her orgasms and performing pleasure before another; it further implies that her pleasure during coitus was also an act. The *soldadeira*'s self-citations show that, while these brief prayers may appear to be spontaneous exclamations, in fact they are carefully employed at appropriate moments to increase the authenticity of her performance and to incite the male character's sexual performance. All four exclamations (vv. 12–14, 19–21, 26–28, and 29–31) are equivocal, directed simultaneously to God and her partner, commenting on the role that she plays as the suffering Christ to his cruel God the Father, who continues to torment her until he climaxes. The final tercet indirectly asks her partner to judge her performance, verbal as well as sexual, and reward her accordingly; it reminds us that the *soldadeira* is performing for money, and that all aspects of her speech are designed to satisfy her customer's sense of social, gender, and sexual superiority.

The *soldadeira*'s exclamations of pain and suffering please due to her multivalent language, simultaneously signifying on sacred and profane levels, and due to her configuration of receptive sexuality as pain and humiliation. Louise Vasvári's reading of the Cruz cruzada episode in the *Libro de buen amor*, discussed in chapter 3, addresses the phallic qualities of the cross and the feminine, weak, tortured body of Christ as signs of aggressive phallo-anal sexuality, as Christ is "planked" by the cross.[57] The *soldadeira*'s language replicates the dominant view that phallic sexuality, in order to mark its masculinity, causes pain, and that such pain is pleasurable for women and other effeminate receptors. She configures herself as passive, unable to resist or escape sexual assault and forced to comply with the stronger will of her lord/Lord; her performance of vulnerable femininity complements the male character's performance of violent masculinity. The play on unlicensed sexual behavior on Fridays means that the accessibility of the female speaker's body is at issue; in her discourse, she presents herself as unable to deny access to her body, "Quisera-m'eu fogir logo dali, / . . . / mais non pudi" (vv. 15, 18). The narrator initiates this encounter with a gesture that asserts his right of access, "Fui eu poer a mão noutro di-/ -a a ũa soldadeira no conon" (vv. 1–2) and implicitly questions her right to deny him. The power structures around this encounter seem to deny the *soldadeira* any agency, yet in her speech and especially in her self-citations she asserts herself and her choice to comply; the ironic, Christ-like pose that she adopts is staged, as is her performance of ecstatic sexual suffering. The success of this ploy is demonstrated by the citability of her speech, both in her self-citations and in the entire text, which purports to be an account of a factual encounter between the narrator and this artful *soldadeira*, whose pleasing performance of sexual suffering becomes his indirect phallic boast.

How this song would have been performed is difficult to conjecture. The lack of textual femininity leads me to suspect that the *soldadeira's* part would have been voiced by a female performer; however, it is equally possible, and perhaps more comic, if the multi-orgasmic *soldadeira* were impersonated by a male performer, even by the king himself. The speaker's self-citations at the end of each stanza underline the gaps between the present moment of enunciation and the past usage of those prayers, heightening the awareness of the fictive nature of the *soldadeira's* performance; in performing this song, the levels of fiction were doubled, calling attention to the male poet-performer's choice to cite, impersonate, and stage the *soldadeira's* fictive performance of pleasure. Since this song does not interpellate a *soldadeira*, after its performance, I suspect members of the audience would speculate as to who this unnamed woman was. If any *soldadeiras* were present, as they probably were, one or more could claim to have been the one and use this song as a pretext for their own performance, praising or impugning the narrator's sexual and poetic performances, playing yet further with the fictive nature of all performance.

I selected the previous five songs as examples of how poets ventriloquized *soldadeiras* and other characters whose voices they incorporated into their compositions. JP 16 and 30, both authored by Alfonso X and featuring extensive framed monologues voiced by *soldadeiras*, begin and end this section, because they focus narrowly on *soldadeiras* in performance. In JP 16, an angry *soldadeira* challenges the king (or his poetic alter ego who also represents law and order) and expresses a keen awareness that her performances of anger are her only means of defense in the existing social system; in JP 30, a pious *soldadeira* performs an ironic *imitatio Christi* to praise the narrator's phallic performance. Both speeches are worthy of extensive citation due to the *soldadeiras'* ironic self-awareness and to the stances they enable the narrator(s) to assume, alternatively dismissive and gratified. While the dominant narrative stance toward *soldadeiras'* speech is negative, in JP 30 the *soldadeira's* speech pleases because it supports the narrator's sexual performance and his sense of superiority; her language also disturbs due to her insistence that her passion parallels Christ's, challenging distinctions between the profane and the sacred. Maria Leve's confession in RL 247 parodies religious language, as she attempts to achieve transformation through confession. Both JP 30 and RL 247 imply that *soldadeiras'* essentially sinful natures cause them to misunderstand or incompetently perform acts of piety, performances that amuse their social superiors. We find additional incompetent performances in RL 193 and 189, both of which focus on *soldadeiras*' appropriation of aggressive speech practices typically construed as masculine, the *juego de palabras* and business negotiations. In RL 193, the *soldadeiras*' insult exchange illustrates their unworthiness to participate in witty verbal exchanges with their social superiors, although the narrator's refusal to engage them in dialogue implies that he does not feel confident enough to take on satiric *soldadeiras*. RL 189 shows Maior Garcia to be initially successful with the vain *escudeiro* but ultimately defeated by the Muslim whose written contract silences her and forces her to comply with his will; the Muslim's victory punishes Garcia for her verbal, economic, and sexual practices and enables the three cultures of medieval Castile to ally over the figure of an unruly woman. In sum, *soldadeiras*' speech in the *Cantigas d'escarnho* tends to be met with censorious silencing gestures; JP 30 is an exception, because in that case the *soldadeira*'s speech praises the male speaker's phallic sexuality.

As we have seen, the comic-obscene *Cantigas d'escarnho* interpellate *soldadeiras* and stage their performances at both the fictive and metapoetic levels. Since *soldadeiras* participated in the *trovador* spectacle, we can assume they were present for and participated in the presentations of *cantigas* that named them. Their participation did not necessarily include impersonating themselves; yet, when they did, their parodic mimicry would increase the play between fiction and reality and focus additional attention on the constructed, performative nature of identity. Poet-performers celebrated *soldadeiras* for the opportunities they created for other performances and for performances as others; the liberating possibilities of assuming various, conflicting identities, especially those that play on normative constructions of social status, gender, and sexuality, made them endlessly useful characters for lyric play. The affirmative possibilities of *soldadeiras*' disturbing performances are celebrated in Afons'Eanes do Coton's (alter ego's) rivalry with Mari'Mateu, in Alfonso X's use of an ecstatic *soldadeira* to praise his (narrator's) sexual performance, and in Pero d'Ambroa's comic narrative of Balteira's shooting contest. In these songs, the narrator endorses the *soldadeira*'s behavior, allying himself with her and taking pleasure in her self-display. Many poetic personas assume self-mocking poses in response to female acts, as in Pero Viviaez's playful complaint that Marinha's passive–aggressive response deflates his phallic boast and Joan Soárez Coelho's parodic explication of Maria do Grave's name in relationship to her identity as a prostitute. Other poet-performers' self-mocking poses focus on female speech, as when Pero Garcia Burgalês has Maria Negra describe her genitals with riddling circumlocutions, putting the dirty jokes into her mouth while he poses as a naive interlocutor; Alfonso X makes fun of his (lack of) kingly authority, making himself the target of a *soldadeira*'s angry threats; Joan Baveca recounts two *soldadeiras*' *juego de palabras* while his timid alter ego conceals himself. Even in cases in which the narrator maintains a distant, critical pose, as in Alfonso X's portrayal of Domingas Eanes as a grotesque sexual spectacle, Joan Vaásquiz's citation of Maria Leve's parodic confession, and Joan Baveca's account of Maior Garcia's business practices, the poet-performers' onstage acts, ventriloquizing that which they (claim to) despise and indulging in female impersonations, negate the narrators' distance. By reading *Cantigas d'escarnho* as performance texts, we can better appreciate how the embodied nature of performance focuses attention on all the bodies interpellated by the text and especially those of first-person narrators who try to conceal their stakes in the events they recount.

In the heterogeneous medieval Iberian court, *soldadeiras* played the role of deviant insider, a role that served the ritualistic nature of *Cantiga d'escarnho* performances well. Their construction as oversexed and generally uninhibited women made them diametrically opposed to the ideal courtier who had to maintain constant vigilance over his behavior in order to merit a place at court. The presence of *soldadeiras* created a space within which courtiers could mock the identities they had to play in earnest in daily court life, including that of king. While such mocking play mainly benefited the king and his officials, providing a release valve for the myriad pressures of court life, *soldadeiras* also benefited. By playing their assigned role, individual *soldadeiras* gained access to the court as a male recreational space and left their mark on the Galician-Portuguese lyric. Through parodic mimicry, *soldadeiras* put into play their stereotypical identity, calling attention to its fictive nature; their disturbing, embodied acts, across the dinner table, in the audience, and on stage in the *trovador* spectacle, reified the conventional identity traits of a (generic) *soldadeira* while destabilizing their own identities. All *cantigas* on *soldadeiras* offer opportunities for transgendered performances and for play with identity, by male as well as female performers; they open up the restrictive environment of the court through their use of taboo words and sexually explicit themes. The presence of *soldadeiras* at court, both in the fictive world of the *Cantigas d'escarnho* and in the actual physical space, introduced a degraded element that poets used to open up the restrictions of courtly culture. *Soldadeiras'* presence also enabled them to voice the roles of degraded female characters, to increase the volition poets granted these characters, and to play with their own stigmatized identity, simultaneously affirming and denying that that is what they were.

In chapter 3 I address how the figure of the *panadera*, like that of the *soldadeira*, contributes to the construction of the marketplace as a performance site. Since the market is an open, public space, unlike that of the court, the *panadera's* mere presence does not threaten dominant authorities. Her association with prostitution and her eroticized hawking discourses do imply that she engages in illicit sexual commerce in addition to performing her licit function of selling bread. In many *panadera* lyrics, the object under negotiation is ambiguous; the contradictory connotations of bread in medieval Iberian culture contribute to the construction of the *panadera* as a prostitute and as the Virgin Mary. As a verbal performer accustomed to judging her customers by their speech practices, the *panadera* is a sharp critic who can turn her rhetoric against that of the dominant authorities, including the king himself, as in the *Coplas de la panadera*. Like the *soldadeira*, the *panadera* challenges her social superiors' authority, so much so that she can become a spokesperson for popular discontent; unlike the *soldadeira*, her proper sphere is public, not courtly. As a figure of the marketplace, she can deride the abuses of the powerful without having to admit her complicity in their power; she can also transform the marketplace into a stage for her oratory, wrestling control of it from the authorities she criticizes.

CHAPTER 3

NEGOTIATING WORTH AND SELLING SEX:
PANADERAS AS MARKETPLACE ORATORS

Panaderas make the marketplace their stage in popular and *cancionero* lyrics. Although they appear with less frequency in literary contexts than do the *soldadeira* and the *serrana*, *panaderas* proliferated in medieval Iberian markets, filling the air with their haggling discourses and hawking songs, holding forth to entertain passersby, to attract customers, and to show off their performance skills. Their depictions play on the historical reality of the bread trade as well as *panaderas'* perennial association with prostitution:

> Galán,
> tomá de mi pan.
>
> Tomalde en la mano,
> veréis qué liviano;
> bolvelde el envés
> i veréis qué tal es;
> si no os contentare,
> bolvérmele eis.[1]

> Handsome youth, take my bread.

> Take it in your hand, see how light it is; turn it about and see how it is; if it doesn't please you, return it to me.

This popular lyric is an unframed female monologue enunciated in its totality by a *panadera*. Since *pan* is a double-entendre for genitals, the exact nature of the product on offer is equivocal. Taboo words do not appear in this lyric, nor in most of those I discuss in this chapter; sexual double-entendres proliferate, so I consider these songs comic-erotic. Indirection characterizes *panadera* lyrics as well as poems on *serranas*; these lyrics use coded language in order to conceal their erotic content from the uninitiated and to increase the pleasure of those who do understand the word-play.[2] This *panadera* entices with her verbal and visual self-display; holding up the literal loaf, she encourages the customer to take it in his hand, to examine it visually and manually, to assess its weight, size, and appearance. Praising and displaying the loaf enables her to praise and display her body, such that the distinction between the two commodities, if there is one, is fine. Ambiguity permeates her song, which simultaneously signifies on at least two levels, the literal (selling bread in accordance with medieval Iberian trade regulations) and the figurative-erotic.

On the literal level, the *panadera's* song constructs her interlocutor as a shrewd customer, carefully examining the bread before buying; he must do so to protect himself from fraud, which medieval Spanish law codes depict as rampant. By law, a loaf of bread sold in the marketplace must conform to official standards of weight, size, and purity; if not, the vendor risks financial and shame punishments:

> Otrosi, que las panaderas, que fagan el pan derechamente, por el peso que les dieren los alamines con los fieles; y la que no lo fiziere assi, por la primera vez que pierda todo el pan que tal le fallaren; y por la segunda, que la pongan a la verguença en la picota por todo un dia; y por la tercera que le den cien açotes, y que la echen fuera de la villa.

> Also, *panaderas* must make bread correctly at the weight determined by the *alamines* [officials responsible for verifying weights and measures]; and she who doesn't do so, for the first violation, will lose all the bread she has with her there, and for the second she will be exposed to shame on the pillory for an entire day; and for the third violation, she will be given one hundred strokes of the whip and expelled from the town.

The manual examination shows the lightness (*liviano*) of the loaf, proving that the *panadera* did not mix in extra water or under bake it:

> [Q]ue las panaderas quezan bien el pan, y no le echen demasiada agua, ni le dexen de cozer à fin de que pese mas.

> *Panaderas* must cook the bread well, and not mix in too much water or stop cooking it early so that it weighs more.

Visual examination enables the customer to assess the purity of the flour, looking for signs of cheap and inferior quality grains mixed in with the wheat flour. Also noteworthy is the fact that the cost of the loaf is not mentioned, probably because in this marketplace, as in most, the price of bread was fixed by municipal authorities:

> [Q]ue ninguna panadera no haga precio en el pan el dia del mercado. . .
> hasta que por alcalde e regidores sea hecho el dicho precio so pena de dos
> reales.[3]
>
> No *panadera* shall set a price on bread on market day. . .until a price has
> been set by the mayor and aldermen, under penalty of two *reales*.

In sum, this popular lyric, whose erotic connotations make it seem a literary fabrication, incorporates many historical aspects of medieval Spanish marketplaces. The *panadera* sings the praise of her bread and offers it to passersby; she relies on the quality of her goods, and perhaps on her good reputation based on previous customers' satisfaction, to make the sale.

At the figurative or performative level, the power of this *panadera*'s voice is striking. She uses imperatives to control both the customer's actions and his perception of her bread. She directs his behavior, scripts his actions, and then claims that he is free to buy or not. Her address of him is interpellative, calling him into being and endowing him with a certain subjectivity in relationship to the product she sells.[4] The rhyme pattern in the *estribillo* (refrain) tightly links the interpellated customer and her bread: "Galán, / tomá de mi pan." *Galán* is neutral in terms of social class, yet it constructs him as her lover/customer, playing on her ambiguous identity as a *panadera*. Her call brings her customer into being, giving her great power over him; he does not exist as a *galán* prior to her address to him and he remains dependent upon her for this identity, especially since within this lyric he is not given a voice that could allow him to assert his own agency as a speaking subject. The stanza glosses the *estribillo*, expanding on the *galán*'s actions with the bread: taking it in his hand, weighing it, turning it around, and gazing upon it; finding pleasure in its physicality, in how it feels in his hand. This visual and manual examination makes the bread a separable item capable of producing great pleasure in its consumer. The moment of ingestion is delayed until after the conclusion of this song, increasing yet more the tension of anticipation; if manual and visual consumption is so pleasurable, ingestion will be yet more so. *Liviano*, the only adjective that is used to describe the bread, connotes lightness as in of little importance, inconstant, lascivious, and easy in sexual matters; this adjective applies to the female speaker as much as to her product. These erotic overtones, illustrated by the *panadera*'s suggestive hand and bodily movements, conflate the two consumables. She packages herself as a sexual object, albeit an active one who objectifies herself as much as she does the *galán* whom she interpellates.

The *panadera*'s song is seductive; it reaches out and draws the *galán* into ever closer contact with her, first aural, then visual, and finally physical. The form of the poem as song is significant. According to James Aho, music frequently is constructed as particularly threatening to the social body since ears are always open to the outside world and so are highly vulnerable to invasion, more so than other bodily orifices. The rhythm and rhyme scheme of the *panadera*'s song create a mesmerizing effect that can reduce listeners to passivity; her voice enchants the customer and induces him to obey her commands and hand over his money. The *panadera* doubly constructs the *galán* as an autonomous agent who is free to buy or reject her goods and as a passive (and silent) object of language who follows the script she wrote for him. This lyric constructs the *panadera* as a man-trap, making her responsible for the desires she provokes and putting her in control of the reactions of those who interact with her. Or rather, she attempts to control the *galán*'s actions, an inappropriate assumption of power given her marginal social and moral status. While seeming to offer herself for his consumption, she attempts to consume him by making him as she wants him, a passive agent, one who believes he is free to act yet is subject to the desires she produces in him. This *panadera* embodies marketplace rhetoric, which beautifies and makes desirable the contemptible, causes rational men to lose their judgment, and shapes the encounter in accordance with her desires.[5]

This lyric offers a vignette of a *panadera* in performance. Like most popular lyrics, it invokes a certain social context without detailing it. All the lyrics in Margit Frenk's collection, *Corpus de la antigua lírica popular hispánica (Corpus of the ancient Hispanic popular lyric)*, are examples of entextualization, which Vincent Barletta defines as "the process by which participants make a strip of discourse extractable from its original setting, in effect converting it into a semi-autonomous, transferable 'text.' "[6] This lyric purports to reproduce a performance genre, a hawking song; its metrical unity makes it separable from its dialogic context. The reader/listener must supplement this decontextualized lyric, drawing on his/her experience of markets and food vendors' hawking songs to recontextualize it. The sketchiness of the portrait it paints, combined with its equivocal language and the power of the speaker's voice, enable it to evoke a powerful reaction. The *panadera*'s ambiguous identity ("is she really a prostitute, or merely using sex to sell a banal product?") plays on audience expectations; like the *panadera*'s voice, this lyric teases and titillates. As such, it is a very citable citation, one that was put to many different uses. As Frenk's notes indicate, this lyric and its variants appear in four Golden Age texts and are parodied in an additional four. Two variants alter the *panadera*'s words to make her bread the Host, playing on the sacred and profane extremes of bread symbolism, which I discuss below.[7]

Popular lyrics were put in the mouths of various characters in Golden Age dramas, novels, and poems. These fragmentary songs triggered a wealth of cultural associations, causing the audience to recall their usual meanings and also to recognize the new meanings they carried in their literary context. Since popular lyrics were a shared cultural base, almost anyone could sing this lyric, pretending to be a seductive *panadera* in a riotous marketplace or altering the context so as to infuse the words with new meaning. *Panaderas* are far less individualized than *soldadeiras*; in lyrics, the *panadera* is a speaking voice that expresses a certain economic, gendered, and sexual identity, one with which the performer and audience may identify or not. More than a stock character, the *panadera* is a persona adopted by poet-performers in medieval and Golden Age Spain, and even into the present. As a performance identity, the cultural connotations it puts into play are highly context dependent. This fact makes lyrics on *panaderas* equivocal, yet it is also why this figure is so productive and worthy of study. *Panaderas'* association with the market makes them both represent and critique the various processes that establish worth of all kinds, social, economic, and symbolic. In their hawking songs and negotiating discourses, they inflate the value of their contemptible goods (including themselves); in turn, smart *panaderas* sharply assess others' goods, ignoring flowerly words and focusing on the quality of the product on offer. This dual and somewhat contradictory function highlights *panaderas'* verbal artistry and their shifting, contingent performances as they assert their value systems and their best interests and defend themselves against exploitation by others.

In this chapter, I discuss a range of *panadera* performances in medieval and Golden Age Iberia. Before analyzing additional poems on *panaderas*, I explore the cultural associations that inform these lyrics. I start with the construction of the marketplace as a performance site and the *panadera's* role as vendor and performer within this space. Bread-making was itself a performance, as the *panadera's* touch transformed flour and water into bread; I discuss the cultural uses of bread in medieval Iberia to explore the sacred and profane connotations of *pan* and the Virgin as *panadera*. In the second half of this chapter, I analyze popular and literary depictions of *panaderas*. Popular lyrics tend to equate *panaderas* with their sexual bread that rapidly grows stale; dependent upon others for their identity and worth, popular *panaderas* seldom contest the identity imposed upon them. By contrast, literary *panaderas* tend to be active agents who assess the elite men with whom they interact and consistently find them wanting. Poets as diverse as Juan Ruiz, Antón de Montoro, and Sebastián de Horozco use *panaderas* to enable their narrator-protagonists to play the fool, trod upon by the downtrodden. Finally, I discuss the *Coplas de la panadera*, which depicts the *panadera* as a spokesperson for popular discontent. Her performance challenges King Juan II's authoritative account of the Battle of Olmedo and offers her audience an alternate version that they can use to resist royal propaganda. Lyrics on *panaderas* underline their construction as speaking subjects whose rhetorical skills make them emblemize the slightly dangerous space of the market.

The Marketplace as a Performance Site

The *panadera* symbolizes the marketplace. While the *soldadeira* simultaneously contributes to and threatens the courtliness of the space she inhabits, the *panadera* embodies the heterogeneous quality of the marketplace within which she performs. Unlike the exclusive and restricted court, the market is public and open to all:

> Apartadamente son del comun de cada vna cibdad o villa, las fuentes e las plaças ofazen las ferias e los mercados e los lugares o se ayuntan a concejo e los arenales que son en las riberas de los rios, e los otros exidos e las carreras o corren los cauallos: e los montes e las dehesas, e todos los o otros lugares semejantes destos que son establecidos e otorgados para pro comunal de cada cibdad o villa o castillo o otro lugar. Ca todo ome que fuere y morador puede vsar de todas estas cosas sobredichas e son comunales a todos tanbien a los pobres como a los ricos. (*Partida* 3.28.9)

> The following are common spaces in each city or town: the fountains and plazas where fairs and markets occur, and the places where the council meets, and the sandy areas on the riverbanks, and other highways and roadways where horses run, and mountains and pastures; all these and other similar places which are established and conceded for the common good of each city or town or castle or other place. Every man who is a resident there can use all these abovementioned things and they are common to all, both to the poor and the rich.

Like the court, the market is a performance space defined by the activities that take place within its confines. These activities are primarily verbal, including hawking songs, negotiating dialogues, official proclamations, and popular protests. Mikhail Bakhtin calls the distinctive marketplace discourse "billingsgate" and depicts the market as an all-inclusive performance space in which official culture is parodied and challenged. This portrait ignores the fact that markets were highly regulated spaces patrolled by representatives of regal, seigniorial, and/or municipal authorities; the king's presence often was marked symbolically by a cross adorned with his glove. James Masschaele's portrait of the medieval marketplace as a public site within which power and authority were subject to negotiation is a much more accurate characterization of marketplace performances and language.[8]

Just as the court was defined by the presence of certain individuals engaged in certain behaviors, the market was peopled by those who gathered together to conduct trade within a particular space at a particular time. Medieval markets could convene daily, weekly, or annually; the ephemeral nature of bread meant that *panaderas* primarily worked in daily or permanent markets. Such markets were urban phenomena located in central *plazas* or in open spaces outside of the city walls; vendor stalls could be permanent structures or tents and benches erected only for that day's activities. Marketplaces were organized according to the products sold and their social prestige; this hierarchical organization established distinctly different areas within the market. Food vendors were grouped together, concentrating their products and the odors and waste they generated into a single area; this area was further subdivided into sections for red meat, poultry and eggs, fish, dairy products, vegetables and fruit, cereals and bread. Livestock vendors occupied a particular section, differentiated according to the type of animal sold, herding animals being less costly and prestigious than mules, oxen, and horses; animals contributed their share of waste to the sights and smells of the marketplace. Professional entertainers also frequented the marketplace, often restricted to a performance area where they sang, played instruments, danced, and/or orated; such marketplace performers were generally considered *cazurros*, the most ignoble and degraded of all entertainers, as I mentioned in chapter 2. The marketplace, then, was both a public space accessible to all and an organized area in which commodities are grouped according to hierarchies of value.[9]

Specific laws and expectations governed the marketplace, making it a site for the demonstration of authority. In medieval Castile and Leon, a special police force maintained the *paz del mercado* (marketplace peace), forbidding the baring of weapons, physical attacks, and private arrests within the market. According to Luis García de Valdeavellano, the *paz del mercado* was dependent upon the king's authority exercised locally by his lieutenants, the *señor del zoco*, the *alcalde*, the *almotaçen* (the lord of the market, the mayor, and the official who verified weights and measures), and other market/municipal authorities. The *paz del mercado* extended protection from assault and theft to merchants both within the marketplace and during their travel to and from market. The *paz* made the market a protected space for public encounters, freeing vendors and buyers to focus on the business of trade, that is, on verbal interactions and negotiations. While the *paz del mercado* served vendors' interests, other laws limited the free exercise of trade. Trade regulations dictated legal weights and measures, protected consumers against fraud, prohibited sales outside of the marketplace, and even forced food producers to sell their goods at the local market rather than at a more distant market where they could charge higher prices; of course, commerce was subject to taxation. In most towns, marketplace authorities set official prices, especially for foodstuffs, eliminating negotiated prices; the *almotacén's* duties included inspecting merchandise to ensure quality and compliance with official weights and measures.[10]

Regulations also constructed the marketplace as a site for public speaking, by authorities as well as the masses. Law codes name the market as a site for official proclamations, including announcements of exiles and judicial sentences made *in absentia*, changes in law codes, and political propaganda. Weekly markets often coincided with the convening of judicial courts whose decisions were proclaimed in the marketplace. Issuing such proclamations in the market guaranteed an audience for demonstrations of official power; however, dominant authorities could not control the reception of these proclamations. The main function of speech in the marketplace was to negotiate; by entering into the marketplace, official speech became negotiable by those who were its primary audience. The presence of several voices commenting on the monologic official voice resulted in a dialogic reception situation; I read the *Coplas de la panadera* as a literary representation of the resistant reception of royal propaganda, as I discuss below. Marketplace speech was not free, as baseless slander and insults were prohibited in the market just as in other spaces; within the specially protected and constructed space of the market less direct verbal agonistics, such as haggling rituals and popular protests, replaced overt physical and verbal aggression.[11]

Shame punishments like whipping and exposure on the *picota* (pillory) were administered in the marketplace. As mentioned above, fraudulent vendors could have their goods seized, be exposed on the *picota*, or whipped publicly. Some offenses, such as the seizure of royal lands, merited particularly humiliating punishment: if the guilty individual could not pay the quite severe fine, he would be "desnudado & puesto desnudo en la picota publica mente dende que saliere el sol fasta que se pusiere" (stripped and placed, naked, on the pillory, in public, from sunrise to sunset). Shame punishments singled out deviant individuals for derision; since those so exposed were local residents, reputations were destroyed. As James Masschaele comments in his discussion of public penance rituals in English marketplaces,

> Shame results from the interaction between individual and society; it is predicated on the presence of witnesses who know the individual being shamed and who will continue to know the individual. A shaming ritual done in front of complete strangers might have been a demeaning experience, but the full impact of the stigma depended on the loss of reputation the individual suffered among friends and acquaintances, people who would retain in memory an image of the shameful acts the sinner had performed.

Public shame punishments created a coercive situation for those in the marketplace; they became witnesses to official violence and may well have felt pressured to demonstrate their acquiescence to authorities by ridiculing or abusing the offenders. The pillory immobilizes the offender, making him defenseless and passive; passersby, and especially victims of consumer fraud, could easily avenge themselves with verbal or physical assault, which was often the only redress they were afforded, as any fines were paid to authorities, not to victims. Sentencing to the pillory also indicates the offender's degraded class status, as only in rare cases (such as defrauding the king) were more elevated offenders so punished. In the case of fraudulent *panaderas*, shame punishments could reify the difference between them and their customers, a difference that was not otherwise absolute, since *panaderas* also made purchases within the market and often occupied a social space alongside their humble customers.[12]

History of the Medieval Iberian Bread Trade

Women dominated bread production. Medieval Spanish law codes frequently refer to *panaderas*, as in the examples cited above, and only rarely to *panaderos*. The *panadera* performed an essential role in the maintenance of a community, as most individual homes did not have bread-baking ovens. While residents could bring their home-made dough to the municipal oven where it was baked by the *fornera* for a small fee, strict price controls made bread an inexpensive item, so many townspeople preferred to buy their daily bread. Bread was particularly prominent in medieval diets; Castilian peasants ate about five hundred grams of bread a day, while monks throughout Spain were allocated about one kilogram of bread a day. The demand for bread within any given town was tremendous. While individual *panaderas*' earnings varied, most barely eked out a living; municipal records are full of *panaderas*' complaints against too-low official prices. Whether this control was motivated by the need to balance competing economic and social interests, a general distrust of *panaderas* and other food vendors, or a desire to limit working women's power, it is clear that official restrictions on the bread trade made for constant conflicts between *panaderas* and marketplace authorities as well as negative depictions of *panaderas*, especially in elite texts.[13]

As a logical extension of their profession, *panaderas* played leading roles in popular protests against grain and other food shortages. Bread or hunger riots were frequent during the Middle Ages and particularly in fifteenth-century Castile, which suffered several famines. Women often participated in bread riots. José Andrés-Gallego suggests they did so in their capacity as "las gobernantes del hogar, en último término las que efectúan personal y directamente las transacciones necesarias para el abastecimiento alimentario de cada familia" (governors of the home, essentially those who personally and directly conducted the necessary transactions to supply food for each family), that is, as a reflection of their economic and social responsibilities. Natalie Zemon Davis has argued that in early modern France and England, "women turn up telling off priests and pastors, being central actors in grain and bread riots in town and country, and participating in tax revolts and other urban disturbances," enacting the role of the unruly woman who has license to express the discontent of the powerless. *Panaderas* in bread riots acted out their gender and profession; their oratorical skills, honed in frequent negotiations with customers and officials, helped them manage the mob's anger, directing it toward those responsible (in the *panaderas'* eyes). They had frequent contact with municipal authorities in the normal exercise of their profession, since these same authorities monitored the marketplace and set prices; their familiarity with the authorities gave *panaderas* access to power that their customers may not have had, encouraging alliances between customers and bread vendors and pushing the latter into a leading role as representatives of the whole community. As a public woman whose presence in the marketplace was expected, who had frequent conflicts with market and municipal authorities over price controls, and who was accustomed to playing the role of intermediary between different social groups, the *panadera* became an emblem of popular discontent, as we see in the *Coplas de la panadera*. The above-mentioned shame punishments of fraudulent *panaderas* could be read as an official attempt to divide vendors from their customers, to discourage their collaborating against the authorities.[14]

Stringent controls on the bread trade may have encouraged *panaderas* to engage in illegal sexual commerce as a gesture of resistance and as a shrewd economic calculation. Whether historical *panaderas* actually practiced prostitution or not, the association between *panaderas* and prostitutes is a medieval and early modern commonplace.[15] Marketplace prostitutes tended to be clandestine ones whose official function as entertainers or vendors gave them access to the market; official prostitutes were often banned from marketplaces to avoid the public disturbances persistently associated with prostitution in medieval law codes and to keep prostitutes, who were viewed as ritually unclean, from contact with food and market personnel.[16] Official prostitutes lived in brothels under the supervision and control of an official often designated by the city. These prostitutes were forced to pay for their room, board, and laundry, and the amount they could charge a client was set by law; in addition, they could refuse no customer (provided he was Christian, as mentioned in chapter 2). Prostitution was closely associated with the marketplace and trade in general; brothels often lined the roads to and from commercial centers and ports.[17] Both the marketplace and the brothel served the city's health, the market by bringing foodstuffs into the city, the brothel by purging sexual excesses.

David Nirenberg discusses medieval constructions of the prostitute as a sewer: "For many medieval commentators, the prostitute was the terminus of a complex plumbing system, emptying (male) society of the fetid waters of fornication that always threatened to overwhelm it. Hence the view that the prostitute exercised a *ministerium*, an office 'ordained for the service of the commonality.' "[18] This view constructs the prostitute's body as public space, an idea already implicit in her status as a public or common woman. The public nature of the prostitute allied her closely to the marketplace, despite official attempts to bar her.

Panaderas in Performance

For *panaderas*, the marketplace was the stage upon which they performed publicly, singing, gesturing, and orating. While these performances may have been secondary to their primary profession of baking and selling bread, such was not necessarily the case; in the *Coplas de la panadera* the female narrator, called a *panadera soldadera* (v. 1), is a marketplace orator whose lengthy diatribe meets with public approval and (probably) hard cash. There are other examples of entertainers who exercised more than one profession. The medieval English waferer, like the modern Mexican *panadero* I discuss below, was as much an entertainer as an artisan; the two skills merge in the single figure, whose professional identity emphasizes his bread production more than his entertainment skills.[19] *Panaderas*' verbal performances included street-cries and other advertising songs to hawk her wares as well as bargaining or haggling, individual dialogic interactions with buyers, in which the *panadera* would attempt to effect a successful exchange. As the popular lyric I cite above shows, her advertising performances included rhythmic speech, song, and physical gestures, spectacular behaviors to attract attention and to differentiate herself from other vendors. The existance of fixed prices did not eliminate bargaining: "Al operar con un sistema de equivalencias fijas, resulta que los precios no se discuten. A pesar de ello, hay un cierto tira y afloja, un cierto regateo; ahora bien, éste tiene por materia las medidas, calidad, medios de pago, etc., pero el precio ya no se debate" (Operating within a system of fixed values, prices are not discussed. Nonetheless, there is a certain give and take, a certain bargaining; now the theme of bargaining is measures, quality, method of payment, etc., but the cost is not subject to debate).[20]

Haggling required the *panadera* to respond directly to an individual customer, encouraging his/her interest in her product, gaining trust, and managing the negotiation so as to arrive at an appropriate outcome. The dialogic exchange conferred relative identity positions, that of vendor and of customer, contingent identities that continued to mark the two individuals after the negotiation was completed; haggling also negotiated relative positions of power and social status. The *panadera* would choose to present a certain image of herself, altering it according to her experience and her sense of which mask would best enable her to achieve her goals in the present negotiation. She could perform authority, wisdom, and power, emphasizing her knowledge of bread and of how business is done; alternatively, she could present herself as equal to her customer, sympathize with his/her desires and needs, and try to establish a local community through the economic transaction. Most likely, she used a combination of relative positioning techniques during the course of negotiations. A primary objective of the *panadera*'s performance was to create a trustworthy voice to facilitate the exchange, an objective complicated by her presence in a heterogeneous site of mixture and exchange. We see a literary representation of just such a haggling exchange in Sebastián de Horozco's "Dama de gentil aseo," discussed below. In that case, since the *panadera* is a clandestine prostitute, the language of both speakers is loaded with coded language and ritual insults; the *panadera* uses her abusive and allusive language to ensnare her customer, impugning his masculinity in order to provoke his anger/desire and cause him to consent to an exorbitant price for her favors.[21]

Most of the *panadera* performances depicted in medieval and early modern lyrics take place on the public stage of the market; but, we should not forget that their backstage activity, that of making bread, is also a performance. The bread-making process is alluded to in "Galán, / tomá de mi pan," yet because it occurs in the secluded space of the home and the oven, it is unseen and seldom depicted. The private nature of the bread-making process perhaps is what made authorities so interested in regulating the product. Their visual and manual assessment assumed that the process was detectable in the product, which isn't necessarily so, as modern jokes and medieval tales show. In Alicia María González's study of itinerant *panaderos* in contemporary Mexican and Mexican American culture, she cites a joke that plays on the seen and the unseen:

> Panaderos sometimes incorporate gesture into their speech play, particularly when they discuss the ways in which certain breads were invented. For example, the *bísquete* is a round biscuit with a small protruding button shape on top. The panadero may ask, "*¿Sabes cómo se hacen los bísquetes?*" ("Do you know how biscuits are made?"), and answer by flattening out an imaginary ball of dough with his hands. Then, pressing the dough to his belly he leaves you to imagine the biscuit being molded by his navel. He then asks, with unmistakable doble sentido [double-entendre], "*Adivina cómo se hacen las donas*" ("Guess how doughnuts are made") (italics and translations in parentheses in original).[22]

González had already emphasized how *panaderos* make bread by hand; the shaping process is particularly manual, as they roll dough between their hands to make various shapes. This joke suggests they use other parts of their bodies, especially of their lower bodies, to shape different loaves; it also replicates *machista* images of phallic and aggressive sexuality, penetrating closed (feminine) bodies and leaving them ripped open. There may well be a double-entendre in the name *donas*, women; the grammatical gender of the two loaves in question, *bísquetes* and *donas*, lead one to read them as gendered, the "small protruding button shape" on the former acquiring phallic connotations, the hole in the latter vaginal.[23] This joke plays with the seen and the unseen: the gestures and words force the viewer to imagine how these loaves are made, a process that s/he cannot observe because it happens at night and behind closed doors. Given the stereotypical construction of the oversexed *panadero* as unclean, the joke hints at the pollution that could enter the bread through contact with the *panadero*'s body, especially with his unclean, lower-body parts; in consuming the bread, the customer could become polluted as well.

The possibility that bread bought in the medieval marketplace could be polluted appears in a tale in the *Sendebar*, also known as the *Libro de los engaños de las mugeres* (*Book of the Wiles of Women*). In the fourth tale, narrated by a *privado* (royal counselor), a merchant who is traveling on business orders his servant to buy food; he finds *panes de adárgama* (fine wheat bread) sold by a *moça* (young woman) in the marketplace. The merchant, who is a fastidious eater, is so pleased by this bread that he orders his servant never to buy any other type. One day the *moça* doesn't have that bread to sell and he asks her why. She explains that her father had had festering blisters on his back and the doctor had advised her to mix *adárgama* flour with butter and honey and apply that to his wounds. After each treatment she would make flour with the mixture and sell it in the marketplace. Her father is now cured. The merchant, disgusted by the bread he has eaten, cries out in vain for something to cleanse him of the pollution he has ingested.[24]

While the official moral of this tale is not to take any irrevocable action without careful thought and study, the significance of the tale exceeds this aphorism. The *moça*'s behavior, like that of all women, is wily, making a profit out of her father's disease.[25] The fact that the bread was made with *adárgama*, the finest of wheat flours, underlines the problem of evaluating the bread itself; while according to its ingredients it should be the best of breads, the unseen process of making it and in particular its having come into contact with a diseased, polluted body (not that of the *panadera* but of her father) makes it unclean. The anonymity of the marketplace and the merchant's status as an outsider increase the risk of purchasing tainted foodstuffs; comically, his fastidious taste buds did not detect the disease hidden in the fine bread. While marketplace authorities and trade regulations should protect consumers from fraud, in this case, the fraud would not have been detectable by them, either. This tale is a joke: the merchant deserves what he gets due to his pretensions and peculiarities; it also points out the fact that the process of making bread is unseen, so a customer can never really know if the bread s/he buys is clean or not. The fact that the *panadera* due to her marginality and associations with prostitution already was ritually unclean means that her product may have always been somewhat suspicious. Such pollution contrasts with the special case of the preparation of the Host.

Sacred and Profane Bread

One of the greatest differences between profane bread and that of the sacred Host lies precisely in the hands that produced them. Clerics (male and female) prepared the Host within a sacred space using a particular technique, as established by ecclesiastical and secular authorities:

> Consagrar non deue el clerigo el cuerpo de nuestro señor IESV Christo, quando dixiere la missa, a menos, de auer estas tres cosas pan, e vino, e agua. E este pan, a que llaman Hostia, deue ser fecho de farina de trigo, amasada tan solamente con agua, sin leuadura, e sin otro mezclamiento ninguno: e deue lo fazer el clerigo muy limpiamente. . .E este pan muda se verdaderamente, enel cuerpo de nuestro señor Iesu Christo. (*Partida* 1.4.52)

> The cleric should not consecrate the body of our Lord Jesus Christ, while saying mass, unless he has three things: bread, and wine, and water. And this bread, which is called the Host, should be made with wheat flour mixed only with water, without leavening, and without any other ingredient: and the cleric should make it cleanly. . . . And this bread truly changes into the body of our Lord Jesus Christ.

For preparing bread to be transubstantiated on the alter at mass, the labor was transferred to the realm of those consecrated in chastity whose kitchens and homes were unpolluted by carnal traffic; while *Partida* 1.4.52 uses the masculine singular *clerigo*, the work was often performed by a group of female religious. The wheat dough was baked in irons embossed with religious imagery in ovens not used for leavened bread, so as to avoid contamination. Even before it was consecrated, the Host was different; after consecration it was a holy object. During mass the priest would elevate the consecrated Host before the eyes of the faithful; if the consecrated Host had to be brought to an invalid, it was paraded through the city with an entourage of attendants, and all Christians who observed the procession had to kneel to show respect for the body of Christ. These rituals construct the Host as a taboo object (as I explain below) and as a potent tool for Church and lay authorities.

The Host occupied the highest echelon of the bread hierarchy in the cultural prestige of its ingredients and of its makers and in its mode of consumption. Of the various grains used for bread-making in medieval Spain, wheat was preferred, with rye, barley, and oat respectively less valued for human consumption. Barley bread was principally consumed by peasants and as a penitential rite; barley and oats were used as animal fodder, *cebada* connoting both barley and animal feed. Wheat was further subdivided into classes of various qualities: Berceo speaks of *trigo candeal* (durum wheat) as the best quality, and law codes distinguish between different grades of wheat flour such as *almodón, adárgama*, and *farina seca*.[26] The lowest type of bread, the inverse of the consecrated Host and like it taboo, was sexual *pan*, male or female genitals. I include sexual bread in this hierarchy because it diametrically corresponds to the Host in that both are bread in a figurative sense and because they pertain to radically opposed symbolic domains, idealized Christianity as represented by the Church and the Christian crown, and popular culture incarnate, represented by the grotesque body.

As James Aho has recently demonstrated, both absolutely holy objects and completely unclean ones are taboo in that they are culturally constructed along parallel lines and surrounded by rituals and prohibitions to contain the danger they represent to the societies that venerate and fear them. Building on Mary Douglas's treatment of pollution, Aho argues that both the most exalted and the most despised objects fuse elements usually considered radically distinct, such as life and death, resulting in an object that challenges and confuses dominant systems of social and symbolic order. The human body, and especially its orifices, are the central concern of ordering systems: "Orifices and their products. . .are unclean, and unclean things reside beyond the horizon of normal, everyday expectations. Which is to say, they are extraordinary, paranormal, sacred. . . .[T]he holy embraces the same paradoxical combination of revulsion and fascination, uncleanliness and enchantment." Aho argues that the sacred and the unclean are equivalent in terms of their sociological function, and that the profane, which he defines as "what is of no account, the pointless, what is for man alone, the commonplace," is the opposite of the sacred/unclean. He concludes that the bodily orifice that has received the greatest cultural weight as a simultaneously desirable and horrifying object is the vagina, because it is understood as a hole or nothingness, as the inverse of the penis, and as the origin of both life and death.[27] Aho's theory helps explain medieval Spain's paradoxical treatment of bread, as both the holiest of holy objects and the most polluted/polluting body part.

This paradoxical treatment extends to the construction of the *panadera* as the Virgin Mary and as a prostitute. In his edition of Berceo's *Milagros de Nuestra Señora*, Daniel Devoto cites a few modern popular lyrics that call the Virgin a *panadera:*

> La Virgen es panadera,
> panadera en un portal,
> ella lo amasa y lo cuece;
> ¡quién comiera de su pan!
>
> La Virgen es panadera,
> ¡quién comiera de su pan,
> que está amasado con leche
> de su pecho virginal![28]

The Virgin is a bread-maker, a bread-maker in a stable [reference to the site of Christ's birth], she kneads it/him and she cooks it/him; lucky he who eats her bread!

The Virgin is a bread-maker, lucky he who eats her bread, which is kneaded with the milk of her virginal breast!

These lyrics play on the connotations of *panadera* as prostitute and of Christ as bread in the form of the Host. The shocking juxtaposition of the sacred and the unclean in the first verse of these two lyrics is resolved with the explanation provided in the final three verses. The first lyric also plays on the association of wombs and ovens; the Virgin's womb cooks the sacred bread, which is fetishized as a greatly desirable yet almost unattainable object. The second lyric focuses on the milk of her breast; bread prepared with milk was considered superior to that made with water. This lyric deviates from the correct preparation of the Host; as a popular lyric, its principal interest is the overlaying of connotations, playing with the extremes of bread imagery, not the accurate explanation of doctrine. The inaccessibility of the Virgin's *pan* is telling: its inaccessibility contrasts powerfully with accessibility of the Virgin herself, who champions the greatest sinners, including murders, thieves, and prostitutes.[29] What is inaccessible is the Virgin's body due to her impossible status as a virgin mother; this paradox leads directly to her construction as an ambiguous *panadera.* Mary's paradoxical sexuality fuses opposites, creating a wondrous, extraordinary, sacred (according to Aho) object. Her assumption of all female familial roles raises the specter of incest, a tension that is resolved by her intact virginity which demonstrates that no corporeal sexual contact has violated the necessarily mutually exclusive roles of wife and daughter. The construction of the Virgin is sacred, not unclean, due to her closed, inaccessible, and ever-virginal body; her diametric opposite, or her dark double, is the prostitute, whose body is always already sexual, open, and accessible to all for mere carnal satisfaction.

The profane *panadera* parallels the Virgin in her function as an intermediary between individuals usually separated by social and spatial divides.
The *panadera* linked yet also separated urban consumers and the rural
menial laborers who produced the raw materials she transformed into
bread. This may be another reason the *panadera*'s bread-making activities
were so closely monitored by authorities: she became the central focus in
order to obscure the large number of individuals whose hands played a role
in the production of bread. Her activities were urban, public, close at hand,
and easily monitored, in contrast to those of millers and peasant laborers
who occupied spaces beyond the city walls.[30] Hierarchically, the *panadera*
mediated between upper and lower classes, if not strictly in terms of economic class, at least in terms of social prestige; she herself was lower class,
a marginal figure economically yet central to the task of supplying the city
with basic necessities. As I discuss below, in literary texts *panaderas* are often
portrayed as aggressive middlemen who impose themselves between their
customers and the bread (literal or figurative) they want; in order to obtain
the object of desire, customers must first overcome the obstacle presented
by the *panadera*. *Panaderas* as bread-providers challenged hierarchical divisions
within consumers' bodies. In the process of digestion, the body transforms
clean food into unclean fecal matter; perhaps for this reason, the *panadera*'s
literal bread was identified with her own lower body. The prostitute also
linked individuals usually separated by social and spatial divisions, as in the
example of Maior Garcia in RL 189, whose sexual business brings Christians, Jews, and Moors into her house, that is, her genitals, as discussed in
chapter 2. The Virgin and *panaderas* of all stripes functioned as intermedi-
aries, facilitating virtual contact between different individuals and helping
maintain normative distinctions by interposing their bodies between those
of their clients and suppliers.[31]

Modern riddles play on the dualistic connotations of bread imagery as
the Host and/or human sexual organs:

> Métese duro,
> sácase brando,
> coloradiño
> e pingarexando.[32]
>
> Put it in hard, take it out soft, flushed, and drooping.

This riddle evokes the taboo answer "penis"; the official answer is bread
dipped in wine, as communicants frequently dip the Host rather than
drinking from the chalice. The evocative nature of bread symbolism shows
that it is a site where simplistic dualistic constructions collapse. In popular

culture, bread is *both* the sacred body of Christ *and* the unclean sexual organs of the human body; these organs are both male and female, depending on the speaker's point of view. The vagina can be constructed as an all-consuming mouth, as in the motif of the *vagina dentata*; the penis, then, is the bread consumed by the female organ. Alternatively, conventional sexual position and gender roles construct the woman as passive and penetrated, the man as active and penetrating, and the greater part of pleasure as his, not hers; the female organ, then, is consumed by the man for the satisfaction of his carnal desires.[33] We see this same ambiguity in popular and literary portraits of *panaderas* and their customers. In the rest of this chapter, I discuss these portrayals, focusing on the *panadera* as a performer whose voice, gestures, and actions negotiate value, including their own.

Panaderas in Popular Lyrics: Fresh, Young Bread

At the beginning of this chapter I cite the popular lyric, "Galán, / tomá de mi pan." My reading shows that this lyric constructs the *panadera* as a dangerous and verbally dominant woman who has the power to interpellate and therefore control her male customers. She calls the *galán* into being as a subject of language; although his voice is not cited in the lyric, implicitly he responds verbally or otherwise to her call. This hawking song presents a dangerously powerful and enchanting *panadera*, an image of a sexually confident young woman that resembles many of the female narrators who voice popular lyrics. As I mentioned above, few popular lyrics survive from the Middle Ages, and those that do are preserved in texts written during the late fifteenth- through the seventeenth centuries. These lyrics usually consist of a two- to three-verse *estribillo* (refrain) sometimes accompanied by a stanza or two that glosses the *estribillo*. The content is usually erotic and presents a moment frozen in time, during which the (often female) speaker comments on her emotional state; while she may be melancholic, reflecting on a frustrated love, she may be exultant and boastful. Sexual encounters are often expressed through the coded imagery of blooming flowers, plucked fruit, rough waters, or burning/tanning by the sun, as I discuss below. While many popular lyrics express the sentiment that all are entitled to sexual fulfillment, others portray sexually active women in a negative light, including most of the lyrics on *panaderas*:[34]

> Que yo, mi madre, yo,
> que la flor de la villa m'era yo.
>
> Ývame yo, mi madre,
> a vender pan a la villa,

i todos me dezían:
"¡Qué panadera garrida!"
Garrida m'era yo,
que la flor de la villa m'era yo.

Que yo, mi madre, yo,
que la flor de la villa m'era yo.[35]

I, my mother, I, I was the flower of the village.

I used to go, my mother, to sell bread in the village, and everyone would say to me: "What a good-looking *panadera!*" I was good-looking, I was the flower of the village.

I, my mother, I, I was the flower of the village.

This lyric is an unframed female monologue voiced entirely by a *panadera*. The female speaker presents herself as active, traveling to the village to sell bread she made at home, or, rather, to have sex. In popular lyrics, women who leave the house do so to meet a lover, and the sexual connotations of *pan* reinforce this implication. While she does not cite her own actions or words, she does perform by moving into the public sphere, and she cites the words of the appreciative audience that greeted her. The speaker addresses her song to a female interlocutor, her mother, and narrates how she was addressed in the village. In the *estribillo*, she indirectly cites the *villanos'* (villagers') speech calling her the flower of the village; the fact that the *estribillo* is an indirect citation is indicated by the word *que*. All the verbs she uses are imperfects, indicating past, habitual actions; these time references frame her present comments as reflections upon the past, when she was celebrated as the flower of the village.[36] Her glorious past implicitly contrasts with her bleak present; due to the lack of narrative context, we must infer what her present conditions are. Implicitly, this *panadera* has figuratively been burnt by sex and is no longer desirable, as I explain below. Her mother is now her principal companion and confidante; her silence contrasts with the praise the female speaker received from the *villanos*. The contrasts between past and present, speech and silence, and here and there are suggestive. The speaker grew up in isolation, not aware of her potential to be a *panadera garrida*; traveling to the village, she learned of her sexual value and had repeated erotic encounters with young men; now, she feels worthless and can only regain a sense of value by repeating the voices she used to hear in the past.

The *villanos'* call of recognition endowed the female speaker with an identity that she did not have prior to her trips to the village and no longer has, since they no longer call her a *panadera garrida*. Nothing in the song indicates that she no longer goes to the marketplace to sell bread; the significant change is that the *villanos* no longer address her as they did. As Judith Butler says, "One is, as it were, brought into social location and time through being named. And one is dependent upon another for one's name, for the designation that is supposed to confer singularity." The *villanos'* conferral of an identity upon her gave her a voice and a personal narrative. She is a speaking subject, yet she is not autonomous (no interpellated subject can be autonomous); while she would like to transform her identity once again, she is dependent upon another to confer an identity upon her. Her mother's silence suggests that she is not going to remedy her daughter's problem. The word *panadera* carries negative weight, that is, it is an insult. The speaker clings to this identity as preferable to the silence that now greets her and denies her any identity or social place: "Indeed, one can be interpellated, put in place, given a place, through silence, through not being addressed, and this becomes painfully clear when we find ourselves preferring the occasion of being derogated to the one of not being addressed at all."[37] The female speaker lacks the authority and linguistic power to alter her situation; complaining to her mother, she does not threaten to destabilize the social and gender system that endows her with such fragile and temporary worth, based solely on her ability to satisfy men's carnal desires.

A similar construction of the *panadera* is found in another popular lyric:

> ¡A la gala de la panadera!
> ¡A la gala d'ella
> y del pan que lleva![38]

Hooray for the panadera, hooray for her and for the bread she carries!

This male-voiced celebration of the *panadera* and her bread focuses on the joy she brings others, *gala* meaning pleasure, adornment, or object of beauty; this *panadera*, too, is the flower of the town, surrounded by enthusiastic young men. Both these lyrics construct the *panadera* as an object that creates and satisfies carnal desires, that is mobile and to some extent an outsider, and that is isolated, not a part of the community of men that surrounds and praises her. They also equate the character with her product: her bread, whether sexual or literal, is a perishable, and its consumption is irrevocable; stale bread is contemptible, fresh bread alone has value. The never-ending hunger for the new and the fresh creates a never-ending supply of fresh, young *panaderas*; each is only of value for a short time, before she becomes spoiled goods and worthless in the sexual marketplace:

> ¿Para que quiere el pelo
> la panadera,
> si a la boca del horno
> todo lo quema?

> Eu namoroime de noite
> d'a mais branca panadeira,
> pero co-o fume d'o forno
> foise volvendo morena.

> —Colorada estáis, nuestra ama.
> —Vengo del horno i dióme la llama.[39]

Why does the *panadera* want her hair, if at the mouth of the oven it all burns off?

I fell in love at night with the whitest *panadera*, but with the smoke of the oven gradually she became brown.

"You are all flushed, our maid." "I'm coming from the oven where the flame struck me."

The first two, male-voiced lyrics play on the *panadera*'s association with the oven where she bakes her bread; *forno/horno* is a double-entendre for female genitals and sexual intercourse. The third, dialogic lyric is voiced by an authority figure, probably male, and his servant; the answer she gives is a coded admission of illicit sexual activity. *Panaderas'* beauty, symbolized by hair and white skin, is destroyed by repeated exposure to the heat of the oven, that is, prolonged sexual activity; they become *morenas*, burnt by fire/sex.

Conventionally the *morena* is a degraded object of desire, fit only to satisfy the basest of carnal desires and shunned by more discerning men whose elevated tastes cause them to seek whiter, younger women, that is, virgins.[40] *Morenas* and their lovers defend their beauty, yet in terms that recognize the conventional superiority of fair skin and hair:

> Morenita me llaman, madre,
> desde el día en que nací;
> y [al] galán que me ronda la puerta
> blanca y rubia le parecí.

> Morenica, no desprecies la color,
> que la tuya es la mejor.

They have always called me little dark girl, mother, since the day I was born; but to the young man who hangs around my door I looked white and blonde.

Little dark girl, don't curse your color, because yours is the best.

These examples show that, just like *panaderas, morenas* are dependent upon male admirers to interpellate them and verify their desirability, after which they can praise themselves by citing their interpellators. Brown *panaderas* can also burn others:

> Solivia el pan, panadera,
> solivia el pan, que se quema.[41]

Lift up the bread, *panadera*, lift up the bread, because it's burning.

This male-voiced lyric complains that the strength of the *panadera*'s desire or the excessiveness of her sexual demands exhaust him, whose member is figuratively burnt by the heat of her oven. This image recalls the erotic riddle whose innocent answer is bread dipped in wine, cited above; that postcoital member is *coloradiño*, reddened from sexual activity. *Morenas*, burnt by their sexuality, can themselves burn their partners; their genitals are fiery ovens and/or hungry, tooth-rimmed mouths that consume male members in the guise of bread.

Popular lyrics on *panaderas* construct them according to a simple dualism. They are low-class women who may become fetishized objects of desire for a brief time; once eaten, that is, once they engage in sexual activity, they become valueless (except in a few cases). The other side of the coin is the aggressive, dangerously seductive *panadera* found in the hawking song "Galán, / tomá de mi pan." In that case, the female speaker is at the height of her erotic and verbal power based to a large degree on her desirable body and wares. She is able to interpellate her customer, gaining verbal dominion over him, unlike those *panaderas* who are interpellated by their clients. The power they do have to harm others is bestowed on them by authority figures who construe *panaderas* as threats in order to contain them and discourage others from seeking them out as sexual partners. These lyrics downplay *panaderas*' agency even as they are treated as active performers; while speaking subjects, they do not threaten dominant systems that maintain social order by imposing limits on *panaderas*' profitability as marketplace vendors and as objects of consumption. I would argue that these lyrics were reused in literate contexts specifically because they reinforce the status quo. The uses *panaderas* and their voices are put to reflect the market's function of assigning values that are dependent upon time and place and that are subject to the approval of those in power.

In the following sections I focus on four literary treatments of *panaderas*, Cruz in the *Libro de buen amor*, Antón de Montoro's "Señor, non pecho ni medro" (D1793), Sebastián de Horozco's "Dama de gentil aseo," and the anonymous *Coplas de la panadera* (D1945). To some extent the distinction I make between popular and literary *panaderas* is a false dichotomy. All the medieval and early modern *panaderas* I discuss are found in literary contexts, and the texts in which they appear are deeply influenced by popular culture. Literary *panaderas* are placed within a more complete context, a fact that makes it much easier to discuss their uses and especially their interaction with the poet-narrator and other characters. In addition, the identity and self-representation of the poet affect the interaction between his poetic alter ego and the *panadera*, an aspect largely absent from popular lyrics in which the narrative voices are far less individualized. It is striking that all the literary *panadera* lyrics I discuss feature buffoonish male characters, often that of the poet's alter ego. Both Ruiz and Montoro represent their personas as the ridiculous victims of *panaderas*' negotiating tactics; Horozco's male speaker is not as obviously a poetic self-representation, yet he too plays the fool in his witty, abusive dialogue with a sharp *panadera*. In the *Coplas de la panadera* the *panadera* herself mimics the buffoonish behavior of a series of elite men. I would argue that medieval and early modern poets chose to include *panaderas* in their fictive world to enable themselves to play the fool, just as Galician-Portuguese poets frequently mocked *soldadeiras* in order to adopt self-mocking poses. In contrast to those of popular lyrics, in the following poems, *panaderas* challenge the status quo, especially the pretensions of the male characters with whom they interact. *Panaderas*' identity as speaking subjects whose voices are powerful and resistant yet who occupy a disenfranchised social position make them ideal foils for poets who want to make themselves the butt of their own jokes, trod upon by the downtrodden.

Literary *Panaderas*: Victimizing Men in the Marketplace

Panaderas in the *Libro de buen amor* and *cancionero* lyrics function as resistant performers who actively take control of the roles they play, even if they are minor or peripheral characters in the action. Of the four poems I discuss below, in two the *panaderas* either do not speak or are cited only once, although their characters are the focus of the poem. In the *Libro de buen amor* and "Señor, non pecho ni medro" by Antón de Montoro, *panaderas* function as external stimulants to which the poetic 'I' reacts, defining himself in relation to them; the female role is primarily symbolic, so that their subjectivity is downplayed. In the other two poems, "Dama de gentil aseo" by Sebastián de Horozco and the anonymous *Coplas de la panadera*, the *panaderas*' voices dominate, although an interlocutor, either the poetic 'I' or the anonymous, collective voice of the *panadera*'s audience, initiates the dialogue, framing and responding to her words. These two poems are longer and focus more on the interaction between the *panadera* and her interlocutor, enabling us to develop a deeper appreciation of her rhetorical strategies as she negotiates a deal or narrates her version of the Battle of Olmedo. All four *panaderas* are highly generic. Even in the *Libro de buen amor*, the only poem in which the *panadera* is named, Cruz performs a conventional role as the object of masculine rivalry; the other poems highlight anonymous *panaderas'* functions as food vendors, prostitutes, and leaders of popular protests.

These four literary *panaderas* perform more overtly than those in popular lyrics. They act in their best interests, which may lead them to comply with their interlocutors' desires or to refuse them. A consistent theme in these poems is the power struggle between characters who occupy different social positions. Literary *panaderas* challenge the power and authority of the men with whom they interact; their verbal power forces their interlocutors to come out on the losing side or to alter their rhetorical tactics, adopting the *panadera's* speech practices as a defense mechanism. The poet-narrators who incorporate *panaderas* into their verses present themselves as socially marginal characters who choose to encounter *panaderas* in order to provoke conflicts over social and rhetorical power. These buffoonish poet-narrators seem to enjoy losing; they profit artistically from their defeat, mocking themselves as well as the *panadera* who defeated them. In all four poems, the *panaderas* assess the worth of men and find them wanting. The three poems I discuss in this section feature male narrators who directly interact with the *panadera;* in the *Coplas de la panadera*, the principal speaker is the *panadera* herself. The length and complexity of that poem merit a more extensive examination, so I discuss it in a separate section; I see it as the most complete treatment of the *panadera* as performer, building on both popular and literary traditions.

The *Libro de buen amor's* Cruz is perhaps the best-known *panadera* of medieval Spanish literature; she has received far more critical attention than the other *panaderas* I discuss. I am interested in the mostly overlooked fact that she is an active, resistant performer who wrests control of her role from its author, Juan Ruiz. Ruiz, the *Arcipreste de Hita*, is the narrator-protagonist of the pseudo-autobiographical *Libro de buen amor* (also known as the *Libro del Arcipreste*, 1330/43), a heterogeneous, ambiguous work that has sparked intense critical debate and interest, not least over the meaning of "good love," that of God, or that of a *dueña garrida* (beautiful woman). While the text is mostly written in *cuaderna vía* (four monorhymed lines of fourteen syllables each), the meter used by most learned, didactic works of the *mester de clerecía* (learned and/or religious narratives written or translated into the vernacular), the *cuaderna vía* is interspersed with prose and songs in range of meters. The ever-shifting stance (and identity) of the narrator-protagonist and his constant word-play defy attempts to interpret his book as imparting a consistent, moral message. As with the *Cantigas d'escarnho*, equivocation seems to be the point, as the author parodies a range of high-culture texts while playing the stock comic role of the lascivious priest.[42]

The *Libro's* comic-obscene songs are highly performative. Ramón Menéndez Pidal, John K. Walsh, and Charlotte Stern have discussed the *Libro* as a performance text or as a source book of Goliardic or *juglaresque* skits that were enacted in *plazas* and other public performance spaces in fourteenth-century Castile.[43] Not coincidentally, the Cruz episode occurs in a marketplace. In his attempt to seduce her, Ruiz tries to control the actions of two characters, Ferrán García, whom he employs as a go-between, and Cruz herself, whom he constructs as a passive object of his desire. Ruiz's decision to employ an intermediary at first makes no sense, since Cruz is a public woman, a figure of the marketplace; any one could seek her out under cover of buying her literal bread and conduct a coded negotiation with her, as does Horozco's male speaker in his "Dama de gentil aseo." Ruiz employs a male go-between specifically to create a rival for himself, as Louise O. Vasvári's analysis implies. Ruiz's objective in this, as in many other plots, is to emerge as the butt of the joke, a much more productive comic role than that of the successful rake.

In order to achieve his objective and also depict himself as the victim, Ruiz constructs an elaborate plot, choosing a debased object of desire and a suspect intermediary whose roles he scripts. He assigns himself a backstage role, hiring and training the male lead, García. Ruiz's choices enable him to play the part of a master playwright as well as to remove himself from the encounter between the other two characters. This removal allows him to blame his loss of control on his rebellious characters. Ruiz's script also enables him to inhabit a superior social position above the two degraded characters he attempts to objectify and control in his script. Not surprisingly, his characters rebel, revising the parts he assigns them, inserting their own desires into the plot, and acting accordingly. García's desire for Cruz is mediated, sparked by his awareness of Ruiz's desire; he makes himself a rival for Ruiz, just as Ruiz made García a rival for himself.[44] García does perform his assigned role as Ruiz's agent while offering himself to Cruz and performing a more aggressive masculinity than his employer:

> Prometiól por mi consejo
> trigo que tenía añejo
> e presentól un conejo,
> el traidor falso, marfuz. (119)

At my advice he promised her some year-old wheat that I had, and he presented her a rabbit, the false, sly traitor.

García boasts of his phallic powers, offering Cruz his *conejo* (rabbit/prick) alongside Ruiz's *trigo añejo*, year-old wheat, that is, aged sperm, aged due to

Ruiz's maturity and to his long abstinence. *Prometió* and *presentó* illustrate García's negotiating strategies and play on the seen and the unseen. Verbally he promises Ruiz's wheat, which García does not have at hand, while physically he displays his own body, presenting it to Cruz for her inspection. García's offer translates Ruiz's hypothetical promise into a concrete, immediate, and visual presentation. García, like the shrewd *moça* in *Sendebar* or *Libro de los engaños* discussed above, poaches; he takes advantage of the situation and revises his part, offering Cruz an easy choice: fresh young meat or moldy old wheat.[45]

Both Ruiz and García construct themselves as sexual commodities for Cruz's consumption. Ruiz also treats Cruz as a commodity and depicts García as her consumer: "él comió la vïanda e a mí fazié rumiar" (113d; he ate the meat and made me chew the cud); "él comió el pan más duz" (118d; he ate the sweetest bread). The roles of consumer–consumed are infinitely reversible, especially given the slippery terminology Ruiz uses. García is both a *conejo* and a *conejero* (120d, bunny-eater); Cruz, while equated to her sexual *pan*, is herself a choosy consumer of men. While Cruz performs her assigned role of object of desire, she also resists by asserting her agency, assessing the two offers, and making a decision based upon her value system. She disregards Ruiz's greater social prestige and prefers García's aggressive masculinity. Ruiz makes Cruz the grammatical object of this entire episode, enabling him to downplay her agency and subjecthood while highlighting his own and García's activity; however, Ruiz's rhetorical strategy is undercut by Cruz's active role in choosing and mediating between men. Her choice of García shafts Ruiz, reducing him to feminine passivity and demonstrating the phallic nature of her own sexuality. In the character of Cruz, the sacred and taboo connotations invoked in this episode coalesce, similar to the anonymous *soldadeira* who compares her passion to that of Christ in JP 30 by Alfonso el Sabio, discussed in chapter 2. As Vasvári has shown, in this episode *cruz* signifies the religious symbol and a simple weapon, a shaft or plank, figuratively used to assault Ruiz's anus, to emasculate him, and to demonstrate his ritual feminization relative to his rival.[46] While Ruiz prefers to focus on homosocial rivalry and treats Cruz as a mere instrument, in actuality Cruz is an active player in this erotic triangle. Her behavior reflects her association with the marketplace; she shrewdly assesses both rivals and chooses the better man.

Ruiz doubly stages his drama in the marketplace on both the textual and metatextual level. The marketplace is the site of the encounter between García and Cruz and the space within which Ruiz, as the narrator-protagonist of the *Libro de buen amor*, performs his scurrilous narrative song based on their encounter. Throughout this episode, the only voice we hear is that of Ruiz, the narrator-protagonist, as the voices of García and Cruz are not directly cited. This lack of dialogue suggests that a single performer would have sung and mimed the movements of the various characters. Cruz's exclusion would be nearly complete; however, she would have been present symbolically in the form of the marketplace cross, a prop that would focus attention on the marketplace setting of the episode and underline the play on the various meanings of *cruz*. This play is especially evocative in the concluding *cuaderna vía* stanza:

> Quando la Cruz veía, yo sienpre me omillava,
> santiguávame a ella doquier que la fallava;
> el conpaño de çerca en la Cruz adorava;
> del mal de la cruzada yo non me reguardava. (121)

> Whenever I saw the Cross, I always humbled myself; I crossed myself before her wherever I found her; her close-by companion worshipped on [top of] her; I didn't have to protect myself from the crusaders' disease.

These verses would allow the performer to mime his own and García's movements, using the market cross as a conventional religious symbol, as a sign of secular authority, and as a woman's body. As Vasvári has shown, the word *adorava* connotes cunnilingus, a meaning the performer could illustrate by kissing the cross. The double-entendres that proliferate in this episode would make for a riotous performance that would challenge conventional symbols of authority, secular as well as ecclesiastical. The performance I have outlined downplays the agency of Cruz, but it highlights the use of the marketplace as a space within which to contest power and negotiate value; it would also illustrate how the presence (actual or virtual) of a *panadera* can create opportunities for homosocial rivalry and for comic displays of masculine aggression.[47]

Antón de Montoro (ca. 1404–78; I discuss his biography below) uses *panaderas* to establish or reinforce an unequal relationship with another man, as he calls upon his superior and patron, Gómez de Ávila (or Dávila), the *corregidor de Córdoba* (magistrate of Cordoba). This light, occasional piece purports to be a note written while the speaker takes refuge in a church surrounded by a mob of angry, stone-weilding *panaderas*:

> Señor, non pecho nin medro,
> corred en todas maneras,
> que me tienen en San Pedro
> çercado çient panaderas,
> sus caras color de yedras
> y de otra fea color,
> dellas cargadas de piedras
> diziendo: "paga, traydor."[48] (D1793)

Señor, I neither pay tribute nor prosper [i.e., I neither pay a lord as serfs do, nor receive favors like courtly parasites]; help me by any means, since one hundred *panaderas* have me surrounded in San Pedro, their faces the color of ivy and another ugly color, loaded down with rocks, saying: "Pay up, traitor!"

The *panaderas* attack the speaker to force him to pay them. While they speak only once, in the final verse of the lyric, they do interpellate him, calling him "traydor," assigning him a role that he does play, that of the fool. Their attack on him is a form of negotiation; they use stones as props to lend their verbal aggression greater credibility and to imply that they will kill him if he doesn't make good on his debts. In response, he cowers, performing exaggerated fear. Presumably the speaker, like Maior Garcia in RL 189 discussed in chapter 2, has used his promise to get money out of someone else (the *corregidor* to whom he directs this poetic appeal) as a delaying tactic; unlike the proud *escudeiro* in that poem, the wily *panaderas* have not left him alone but continue to surround the church, keeping him captive until he pays. The attack began in a public space, perhaps even in the marketplace, despite the *paz del mercado*; this song depicts the dangers of daily life in Cordoba, including the eruption of violence in spaces that should be protected by public authorities.

Montoro uses these generic *panaderas* to portray himself as a buffoon. Montoro, like his attackers, is a tradesperson, as shown by his nickname the *ropero de Córdoba* (tailor of Cordoba); he is also a *converso* (Jewish convert to Christianity) who frequently mentions that fact in his poetry, conflating his historical identity with his poetic persona. His *converso* identity increases the significance of his taking refuge in San Pedro, a church founded by Cordoba's Christian conqueror, Fernando III el Santo, the father of Alfonso X; choosing this particular place name serves to underline Cordoba as a site for clashes between Christians, Muslims, and Jews, and underlines Montoro's ambiguous identity in this multiethnic city. In the first verse, the speaker's self-depiction foregrounds what he is not; this construction parallels the *converso* code discussed by Gregory B. Kaplan, who shows that *conversos* in fifteenth-century lyrics were depicted as neither Christians nor Jews. "Señor, non pecho ni medro" also focuses on poverty, another recurrent aspect of Montoro's poetic persona; indigence is, as Francisco Márquez Villanueva has shown, a stereotypical attribute of the court fool, a role that many fifteenth-century *converso* poets play. E. Michael Gerli has demonstrated that at least in this case poverty was a fictive pose, as the historical Montoro was quite wealthy and well connected, albeit stigmatized as a *converso*. Gerli suggests playing this stigmatized role may have improved Montoro's acceptability to the aristocracy. His persona's economic state reflects his position as a *converso* and as a "so-called [*caballero*] *de cuantía*," a wealthy burger not of noble origin, who interacts with the Castilian elite.[49] He uses *panaderas*, marginal figures who mediate between various social groups, to highlight his own in-between status, as he mediates between the *panaderas* and his elevated patron, the *corregidor*. Montoro cowers before the mob and grovels before his patron, begging both for clemency; he depicts himself as caught between the social extremes of the high and low classes, between humble food vendors and the real wielders of power.

I believe Montoro chose *panaderas* for the mob because of their association with popular protests and bread riots. It is not coincidental that Montoro's protector is a *corregidor*, a municipal official who may himself have been the target of angry mobs during famines; Marithelma Costa suggests that Montoro appeals to Ávila in his capacity as protector of the peace. The present conflict is not a hunger riot but an organized demonstration directed against an individual debtor; however, the two forms of violence are not so different, nor are their personnel, the lowest rungs of urban society. In addition to social and economic conflicts, anti-Semitism may be another motivation for the *panaderas'* aggression. As I mentioned above, during the mid- to late fifteenth century there were many protests due to food shortages, debased coinage, and tax increases; Angus MacKay has shown that riots frequently turned on Jews and *conversos*, who stereotypically worked as tax farmers collecting *pecho* (tribute peasants paid their lord). In 1473 *conversos* were massacred in Cordoba, Montoro, and other cities throughout Southern Castile; this pogrom coincided with severe grain shortages and astronomically high prices. Antón de Montoro identified with the victims of this violence and may have himself been at risk of death; he composed poems on the anti-*converso* riots in Cordoba and Carmona, and he probably left Cordoba after the 1473 uprisings when *conversos* were expelled from the city.[50] This *copla*, while comic due to the mock-heroic description of the *panaderas*, also reflects the precarious position of Montoro and other *conversos* during the late fifteenth century. *Panaderas* in general represent popular opinion, insurrection, and resistance to exploitation by their social superiors. Montoro uses them to represent the social upheaval and scapegoating tendencies of late medieval Castile; a result of this violence was to increase *conversos'* dependence upon powerful patrons and exacerbate divisions between several disenfranchised groups. By taking refuge in a church and addressing his plea for help to a *corregidor*, Montoro appeals to both ecclesiastical and civil authorities, allying himself with the powerful against the weak. He presents his persona as caught between warring factions, a hapless victim of the social conflicts that surround him.

In a sixteenth-century poetic debate between a *panadera* and her customer by Sebastián de Horozco (ca. 1510–80), we return to the familiar model of the wily *panadera* who uses her verbal skills to manipulate her customer.

While this poem (composed ca. 1550) is not medieval, its treatment of the *panadera* draws on the same traditions that inform the character of Cruz and the popular lyrics discussed above. I find Horozco's "Dama de gentil aseo" particularly interesting because it is an extensive negotiating dialogue that illustrates how a shrewd *panadera*'s strategies enable her to dominate her customer. As in the case of the *soldadeira*, there are few poetic representations that illustrate haggling, despite the prominence of negotiating dialogues in historic *panaderas*' verbal repertoires. This lyric, like RL 189 on Maior Garcia, offers a rare portrait of a business woman in action. This poetic dialogue between two speakers simply marked as "EL" and "ELLA" focuses attention upon the densely gendered and eroticized nature of their exchange. The refrain in particular establishes a diametrically gendered difference by playing on the gap between desiring and having *chipirrichape*, a word that may refer to a type of bread and in this context means female genitals.[51] While the exact wording of the refrain varies, the male speaker always concludes with the phrase, "del chipirrichape / que tenéis" (of the *chipirrichape* that you have), indicating his desire for what she has. The female speaker, in turn, consistently responds, "del chipirrichape / que queréis" (of the *chipirrichape* that you want), underlining his desire for what he lacks and implicitly showing her indifference to his desire and to the outcome of these negotiations. She occupies a position of power, free to accept or refuse the terms he offers, while he, as the desiring subject, must petition her to supplement his lack. Their debate constructs her as a middleman who interposes her troublesome voice between the male character and his object of desire, which is treated by both as a separable item, a little piece of bread whose relationship to her body is not at all clear. While the female speaker does not construct herself as a desiring subject, she is also not a mere object of desire; as a speaking subject, she is more than equal to the male, defeating him in the debate by playing on yet never fully yielding to his desires, not even to his desire that she simply name a price. Her indifference enables her to play a dual role that increases the powerful ambiguity of her rhetorical positions, while he can only express frustration and powerlessness, showing his sense of coming out of these negotiations badly.

This unframed debate poem (*tensón*) begins with the male character accosting the female, addressing her with the elevated courtly language often incongruously employed by the traveler in *serranillas* to flatter the *serrana*; his speech quickly becomes comic when he indirectly asks what she charges for sex:

> Dama de gentil aseo,
> dezidme por vuestra vida

a cómo dais la medida
de aquese vuestro poleo.
Pues que sabés lo deseo
¿no diréis,
a cómo vendeis (sic) [la onça
del chipirrichape
que tenéis?][52]

Lady of noble condition, tell me, on your life, for how much money do you give the measure of that pennyroyal of yours? Since you know of my desire, won't you tell me, for how much do you sell an ounce of the *chipirrichape* that you have?

The male speaker's absurdly polite speech, addressing a prostitute as *dama*, shows his inexperience in negotiating sex, as does his inquiry as to her price; his language marks him as a fool, a role that Horozco frequently adopted for his poetic alter ego.[53] Throughout their dialogue, he refuses to propose a price, a reluctance that implies that he does not know the going price. His pose of ignorance leaves him open to be played upon by the far more experienced vendor. He does employ coded vocabulary to identify the object of his desire, showing his familiarity with erotic euphemisms and perhaps attempting to dissimulate for the sake of passersby and marketplace authorities. *Poleo* is an unusual image for female genitals, yet it plays on the conventional association of beautiful women with flowers; a flowering herb frequently used as an abortifacient, pennyroyal is associated with prostitution and would be widely available in the marketplace due to its other medicinal uses.[54] The male character's stakes in this negotiation are multiple: not only does he want to contract sex while eluding marketplace authorities, but he wants to prove his worldliness, masculinity, and verbal artistry as well. He cannot do so if he allows himself to be victimized by the *panadera*, paying too much for her wares and figuratively getting screwed.

In her reply the female speaker echoes the male's circumlocutions (as well as his meter and rhyme scheme). She emphasizes *chipirrichape*, the only word she repeats twice, both times in line final position.

Es tan sabroso bocado
este mi chipirrichape,
que no ay naide [sic] que se escape
si alguna vez lo ha probado.
Si bien pagáis de contado,
gustaréis
¿a cómo se da la onça
del chipirrichape
que queréis? (vv. 10–18)

It is such a delicious bite, this *chipirrichape* of mine, that there's no one who can escape from it once he's tried it. If you'll pay cash for it, you'll taste it; how much will you give for an ounce of the *chipirrichape* that you want?

Rather than answering his question, she praises her *chipirrichape*, detailing both the gustatory pleasures it provides as well as the powerful desire it instills once tried; this speech is typical of advertising discourses, yet here it has a double edge. Basically, she brags that she's got many satisfied repeat customers and that she does not need his custom, although she'll sell, if he's willing to pay well. A tasty bite, her *chipirrichape* provokes such a great desire that men can never escape it; her "sabroso bocado" is also a *vagina dentata* that consumes men. While packaging her *chipirrichape* as a sexual commodity, the *panadera* suggests that the male speaker is himself a commodity to be consumed by the *chipirrichape* that he wants. As is typical of haggling strategies, her positioning of them both shifts throughout the stanza. She downplays her agency in this exchange by using an impersonal construction, "a cómo se da la onça" (v. 16), enabling her to avoid first-person verbs; in contrast, the three second-person verbs, *pagáis, gustaréis,* and *queréis,* portray him as an active, desiring subject. Her rhetorical ploys leave him in a weak position: not only has she not answered his question, but she has demanded that he tell her what he's willing to pay, a statement that he's not willing to make.[55]

The exchange continues with his reply, in which he addresses her respectfully as *señora*:

> Ponelde nombre, señora,
> sepamos a cómo pasa,
> que la que tal pan amasa
> de todo es mereçedora.
> Dezídmelo, ya, traidora,
> si queréis,
> ¿A cómo vendéis la onça
> del chipirrichape
> que tenéis? (vv. 19–27)

Name your price, lady, let's know exactly what's going on, since a girl who kneads such a dough is worth everything. Tell me, now, treacherous lady, if you will, for how much do you sell an ounce of the *chipirrichape* that you have?

He continues to ask her to name her price rather than offer one himself, although he ironically declares that he's willing to pay whatever price she sets. His continued use of courtly rhetoric shows his attempt to regain footing based on his superior social standing. He flatters her ironically by praising her bread, although this praise also identifies her as a *panadera* and puts her in a subordinate place with respect to him.[56] The imperatives in this stanza are more direct and much less couched in gentle persuasion than in his first speech, as he tries to use his verbal and social power to force her to name a price. In the fifth verse, *traidora* functions as an insult to mark his increasing impatience with her rhetorical strategies; yet, it also maintains the courtly register, casting her as a *belle dame sans merci* whose reserve is an essential part of the game of love. His gently abusive speech is comic, as incongruous as his use of flowery euphemisms in the first stanza; while he apparently hopes that his combined strategy of flattery and imperatives will persuade her to answer his question directly, his language sets him up for failure.

The *panadera* does reply directly, although she still refuses to name a price. Instead she employs imperatives, for the first time in this exchange, ordering him to reconsider his approach, and her language becomes openly aggressive and insulting:

No penséis que soy ratera
ni me pago de blanquillas:
¿para qué son palabrillas
y el parlar muy desde afuera?
La mano a la faltriquera
y sabréis
¿a cómo se da la onça
del chipirrichape
que queréis? (vv. 28–36)

Don't think that I'm a pick-pocket, nor do I like small coins: what good are words and beating around the bush? Put your hand in your pocket and you will know, how much will you give for an ounce of the *chipirrichape* that you want?

She acts insulted and expresses impatience with his indirect speech, denigrating his courtly dialogue with the diminutive *palabrillas*. She challenges him to show her his coin, or rather, to put his hand in his pocket to assess how much he can pay her, having warned him not to offer small change (*blanquillas*). *Faltiquera* signifies doubly as pocket and scrotum, which, she implies, are both empty; she impugns his virility and mocks his rhetorical strategies. Her challenge also calls his bluff; she continues to defy his desires while downplaying her agency. Again, aside from the first two verses of this stanza, she avoids first-person verbs while emphasizing his agency with three second-person verbs. Her verbal strategy is productively contradictory; she discounts the value of rhetoric even as she artfully evades his desires, or rather, she complies with his desire that she speak directly, yet her direct speech challenges him to replace his artful speech with hard cash/phallic potency.

In his reply, the last stanza in which he speaks, the male character directly expresses anger and frustration with her verbal strategies and insults; he also adopts her strategies, indirectly acknowledging her superior haggling skills:

> De echar mano y de pitar
> no penséis que yo me espanto,
> mas si vos no dezís quánto
> muy mal podré yo contar.
> Dexá ya de porfiar
> si queréis,
> y dezid a cómo se vende
> del chipirrichape
> que tenéis. (vv. 37–45)

Don't think that I'm afraid to put in my hand or to whistle, but if you don't tell me how much, I won't be able to count. Cut out the arguing, if you will, and tell me how much that *chipirrichape* that you have goes for.

In response to her suggestion that he put his hand in his pocket, he uses the same negative imperative construction that she used in the previous stanza (i.e., "no penséis"). I read the first verses as saying that if he does put his hand in his pocket, it will be to masturbate, not to pay her, *pitar* in this context meaning 'to blow his phallic whistle'; his language replicates her *faltriquera* double-entendre, letting her know that he got her message. His frustration with these interminable negotiations is marked by the absence of courtly forms and his adoption of her verbal practices. His use of the impersonal construction "se vende" echoes the *panadera*'s repeated use of the impersonal in the same line position in her speeches and significantly alters the refrain from his two previous speeches, omitting the word *onça*. By adopting the female character's speech patterns, he radically changes his negotiation strategy; he now speaks directly, performs anger and impatience, and indicates his willingness to walk away from the negotiations if she doesn't start complying with his demand that she name a price. He also, paradoxically, acknowledges the effectiveness of her strategies; in order to succeed in this verbal exchange, he must speak as she does. He abandons his courtly pretenses and speaks crudely, presenting a very different identity than he had initially put forward for himself: a masculinity based upon brute force, not on social superiority nor on courtliness.

In the concluding stanza, the *panadera* finally names a price, although she offers several prices that he can choose from.

> Unos da a diez ducados,
> y otros doze, y otros más;
> si vos sois de los honrados

no avés de quedar atrás.
Dende abaxo es por demás,
si queréis,
entrar en la gorrionera
del chipirrichape
que queréis. (vv. 46–54)

Some give ten *ducados*, others twelve, and others more; if you are an honorable man, you don't have to hang back. The lower [bread] costs yet more, if you want to enter in the sparrow's nest of the *chipirrichape* that you want.

She starts with her lowest price and then works up, a strategy that inverts conventional negotiating discourses, in which the vendor establishes the upper limit and the buyer, the lower. This inversion could suggest that the prices she names are not serious offers, and certainly they are excessive. According to María Eugenia Lacarra, in 1535 public prostitutes in Bujía earned no more than twelve *maravedís* an hour, although clandestine prostitutes did earn more; one *ducado* was worth three hundred and seventy-five *maravedís*.[57] Whether she is serious or not, her construction *unos. . .y otros* suggests that those who pay lower amounts are undifferentiated; if the male speaker wants to demonstrate his superiority, he has to pay more. This comment ironically reflects on his changed performance of identity; if he wishes to perform distinction in this exchange, he must do so with his purse, not with words. The poem breaks off here, leaving us hanging as to the resolution of their negotiations. Either the young man performs anger and stomps off, offended by the *panadera's* refusal to take him seriously, a performance that would provoke the laughter of the female speaker and the audience; or, more likely, the two speakers go off together toward her house, where their dialogue continues behind closed doors.

It is interesting to speculate as to whether this poem was performed in a marketplace or other public space. During the sixteenth century, dialogues of this type were composed for private reading and for presentation in public and in noble households. The bawdy character of this dialogue does not make it inappropriate for public performance. Horozco himself describes watching street performances in Toledo during the 1555 celebration of the so-called conversion of England; these performances included comic-obscene skits (*entremeses*) that featured artificial phalluses. The dramatic nature of this exchange, its use of coded language, and the two speakers' apparent awareness of the presence of onlookers and of their being on stage, encourage me to read it as a performance piece intended for public performance, a skit like those Horozco described.[58] This poem lets us listen to a haggling session as though we were ourselves present in the marketplace. The principal interest is the two speakers' negotiating strategies, their shifting positions and verbal parries and thrusts; the object of their negoti-ation, the sex act, recedes behind the act of negotiation itself. Their verbal sparring is a type of foreplay for an agonistic sex act; having stripped the male character of his noble pretensions, the *panadera* will now provide him a space within which he can demonstrate his phallic mastery. By waiting until the sixth stanza to name her price, the *panadera* both increases the male speaker's investment in their verbal exchange and his desire to domi-nate her verbally and sexually. He finally wants to screw her in order to demonstrate to himself his mastery, while we (and she) know that he has not come out of this exchange well. The public context means that the male speaker has an audience, and he's aware of this fact: part of the anger he expresses in his final speech stems from his sense of embarrassment at being out-done by a *panadera*. As with Juan Ruiz and Antón de Mon-toro, the *panadera's* aggressive rhetoric enables Horozco's male speaker to play the fool.

This detailed analysis of the *panadera's* use of abusive language in her negotiations with an interested customer reminds us of Bakhtin's billings-gate, the distinctive marketplace idiom that forces all inhabitants of the market to abandon their pretenses of superiority and use the same abu-sive discourse in order to get what they want. While our male speaker is conscious of his linguistic defeat, his desire is inflamed. Such is the case with Juan Ruiz as well, who (as we see again in his interactions with *serranas* in chapter 4) enjoys being the victim of verbal and physical abuse. Montoro too takes advantage of his victimization to cling to, and under-score the elevated position of, his protector, the *corregidor de Córdoba;* all three male characters profit from their humiliation. The same cannot be said of the abused noblemen in the *Coplas de la panadera.* As the objects of her abusive discourse, they are denied a voice with which they can respond. Most of the targets of her wrath are members of the highest nobility, unlike the male characters in this section. The aristocrats' sense of entitlement requires their unambiguous degradation, as the *panadera* blames them for the political and economic chaos they have caused.

The *Coplas de la panadera*: The Market as Site of Political Commentary

The character of the *panadera* is most fully developed in the anonymous *Coplas de la panadera* (D1945), an extended diatribe on the Battle of Olmedo (1445).[59] This poem represents a *panadera's* marketplace performance, not a hawking song or a haggling dialogue but a satirical song expressing the col-lective discontent of the people of Castile, frustrated with the apparently interminable civil strife centering on the figure of Álvaro de Luna. In her song, the *panadera* performs like a *juglaresa*. She is a soloist who presents her audience with a series of vignettes caricaturing the flower of Castile and Aragon; in each stanza, she focuses on a single figure, a knight or prelate, narrating his words and actions, making him perform as a soloist as well and incorporating his performance into her own. This *panadera* engages in male impersonation, mimicking the words, gestures, and behaviors of elite men. While her performance is campy, she does not imitate in order to flatter, playing up to please her superiors as did the sycophants at the court of Alfonso el Sabio; quite the contrary, she impersonates to ridicule and degrade the nobility. Her imitation is satiric–parodic, such that she does not disappear behind the characters she enacts; like the male poet-performers who imitate *soldadeiras* and *serranas*, she performs as another, using her parodic performance to mark her difference from the identity that she only partially adopts for the moment. The fact that she impersonates her social superiors lends particular significance to her performance. Not only does she show that nobility is a performed identity, but she shows that she can perform nobility better than the knights she imitates; they, on the other hand, demonstrate their ignobility by performing cowardice, incompetence, and incontinence.

The choice of a *panadera* as the narrator of this anonymous poem was not casual. This *panadera* incorporates most of the characteristics I've discussed, including class consciousness, marketplace oratory, shrewd assessment of men, aggressive negotiating strategies, abusive language, and mediating between diverse social groups. She is also a *soldadera*:

> Panadera, soldadera,
> que vendes pan de barato,
> quéntanos de aquel rebato
> que te aconteció en la vera. (vv. 1–4)[60]

> *Panadera, soldadera, you who sell bread in the street, tell us about that attack that happened to you in the plains.*

Soldadera in this context connotes camp-follower, female performer, and prostitute; our *panadera*, like the English waferer discussed above, sells her song, dance, bread, and body to her audience. While she was on the battlefield of Olmedo in her capacity as food-vendor and as prostitute, at this moment she offers her wares to a crowd of her peers; her performance is designed to please the lower social orders, just as (we can imagine) her performance in the camps was tailored to suit those audiences' tastes. As a female entertainer, she has access to a variety of social spaces, a fact that enables her to mediate between the aristocracy and the peasantry.

The product the *panadera* offers to her current audience is her eyewitness account of the knights at battle. Her version imitates the official, propagandistic version produced by the Castilian court, narrated in the first person by the king himself, Juan II, and celebrating Álvaro de Luna as the hero. The official version depicts Luna's performance on and off the battlefield, referring only in passing to other significant players (even the king himself plays a supporting role with respect to Luna); the *panadera*'s version, by contrast, has a much broader and more developed cast of characters, as she depicts more than forty participants. Elsewhere I have argued that the *Coplas de la panadera* is a counternarrative of the Battle of Olmedo that offers a more complete and accurate version of the battle, one that restores the messy details omitted by the Castilian propagandistic version. Here I focus on the *panadera* as a marketplace orator who uses her account of the battle as a commodity. Her version enters into dialogue with the propagandistic account, which was also probably proclaimed in the marketplace; her account reflects the resistant reception of official propaganda and a popular attempt to negotiate the significance of the battle. The *panadera*'s degrading, grotesque, body-focused account of the antiheroic acts of the aristocracy is designed to amuse her audience and provoke their laughter and discourse rather than to silence and astound them, as does the propagandistic version. The fact that her version pleases her audience is marked in the refrain, "Di, panadera," repeated after each stanza. This collective response endorses her account and encourages her to continue; it also incorporates her audience's voice into the anonymous poet's account of the *panadera*'s performance, underlining the multiplicity of voices that collaborate to produce this dialogic account, in contrast to the monologic propagandistic version voiced by Juan II.[61]

The Battle of Olmedo was a climax in the nearly thirty-year rivalry between the Infantes of Aragon and Álvaro de Luna, the favorite of Juan II, king of Castile. Luna's influence over the king created deep divisions among the Castilian nobility; many saw him as threatening their rightful positions and as acting against their interests, while others benefited from his policies. Family in-fighting fed this factional divide, as Juan II's cousins, the Infantes of Aragon, ruled Castile during his minority and saw Luna as an obstacle to their continued power. After several failed attempts to remove Luna from the Castilian court, Juan of Navarre, the older of the two Infantes, sequestered Juan II (his namesake) in 1443. Luna helped Juan escape and the two factions met in battle on May 19, 1445. The Infantes led a coalition of Castilian rebels and Aragonese and Navarrese forces, using the Castilian city of Olmedo as a base. The Castilian loyalists triumphed; the younger Infante, Enrique, was killed, and the elder, Juan, fled. The *panadera*'s account of the battle generally echoes the official version, yet as I mentioned above is more complete; she names participants on both sides of the conflict, whereas the official version names only the principal Castilian rebels and Aragonese leaders and, of the Castilian defenders, mentions only Juan II, his son Enrique (the future Enrique IV of Castile), and Álvaro de Luna. Her satiric vignettes present the magnates as buffoons, performing degrading acts that belie their knightly costumes and props; in her account, the battlefield becomes a world upside-down underlining the social and economic chaos caused by factional strife.[62]

Disorder proliferates throughout the poem, on the level of structure (poetic and social) as well as in the knights' bodies and performances. Structurally, the poem is roughly broken into four parts: the introduction of the *panadera* and her audience, in the first half-stanza, cited above; the prelude to the battle (stanzas 1 to 6), which presents Enrique of Castile being chased from the riverbank near Olmedo, Juan II ordering his troops to battle "con malancolía" (with anger), and the prelates who bless the troops, in a somewhat chronological account of events; the body of the poem (st. 7–45), in which the chronological narration gives way to caricatures of individual combatants on both sides; and the concluding prayer for peace (st. 46). The caricatures are grouped by faction, although allegiances are not indicated within the poem, presumably because the audience already knew them. Stanzas 7–20 focus on Castilian rebels and Aragonese invaders, while 21–37 target Juan II's loyal supporters. Stanzas 38–42 caricature the principal rebels and invaders: the Infantes of Aragon, Juan I of Navarre and his brother Enrique; Diego Gómez de Sandoval, the count of Castro; Fadrique Enríquez, the admiral of Castile; and the brothers Diego and Fernando de Quiñones; Juan of Navarre is targeted again in stanza 45. While stanzas 38–45 primarily mock the leaders of the anti-Luna coalition, stanzas 43 and 44 do not fit this schema; they attack Lope García de Rojas, of the Aragonese side, and Pero Sarmiento, a Castilian who is also mocked in stanza 26. In this back-and-forth structure, the Castilian loyalists are sandwiched between two series of invectives targeting rebels and invaders. The number of participants who change sides during battle further complicates this organization, including Ruy Díaz de Mendoza (st. 10), Pero Sarmiento (st. 26), Juan Ramírez de Guzmán (st. 35, cited below), and Juan de Silva (st. 37). These shifting allegiances reflect the instability of the differences between the two factions. Although the structure of the poem appears to differentiate between factions, the individual representations emphasize similarities, especially in the combatants' cowardice, incompetence, and greed; distinguishing rebel from loyalist and defender from invader becomes nearly impossible, and perhaps irrelevant.[63]

The collapse of meaningful distinctions underlies the poem's famous scatological humor:

> Temblándole la contera
> al repostero mayor,

> del grandíssimo temor
> le recreció cagalera;
> fuyendo en la delantera,
> casi fuera de sentido,
> todo quanto avía comido
> trastornó por la bavera. (44: 393–400)

Shaking in his boots, dead with fright, the *repostero mayor* [Pero Sarmiento] had an attack of the shits; fleeing in the front line [i.e., leading the flight from the battlefield], on the verge of fainting, all that he had eaten came back up through his chin-guard.

This portrait of Sarmiento plays on his identity as the "head pastry chef" (the *repostero mayor*, an elevated household office in the royal court); his association with delicate, refined dishes is mocked as he spews diarrhea and vomit. Both ends of his digestive system run with waste, equating his mouth with his anus; depicting first his lower body and then his upper underlines inversion and confusion. This erasure of bodily hierarchies reflects the confusion of allegiances, lack of leadership, and self-indulgent participation in the factional strife that led to this conflict. As the *panadera's* catalogue continues, it becomes increasingly clear not only that the two sides are equally incompetent, but also that their noble pretensions are easily deflated by the risk of bodily harm. In order to protect their vulnerable bodies, they perform cowardice, not bravery; defecation marks their defections, shitting while they run away. The *panadera* in her performance mimics their fear, implicitly contrasting their flight from the battlefield with her own choice to remain there, watching them. Her presence as an observer plays on the spectacular nature of warfare, designed to enact significant differences and to teach observers (both eye-witnesses and the mass audiences of political propaganda) the correct social organization.

Given the *panadera's* stereotypical carnality and her focus on her targets' bodies, it is ironic that her own body does not appear in the poem. She presents herself as threatened by the violence around her in only one stanza:

> Vi al señor de Jorquera,
> Alonso Pérez Bivero,
> con escribanía y tintero,
> colgada su linjavera,
> y dentro una alcoholera
> con polvos para escrivir:
> quisiera dello reýr,
> si oviera do me acogiera. (23: 204–211)

I saw the lord of Jorquera, Alonso Pérez Vivero, with a portable writing desk and ink well, his quiver hanging loose, and inside a small bottle with writing powder; I'd have laughed at that, if I'd had somewhere to hide.

This stanza illustrates the essential opposition between the *panadera*'s construction of herself and that of her targets. She sees them (*vi*, I saw, is the first word of this stanza), while they don't see her; she incorporates their voices and behaviors into her performance, while they cannot do the same to her. From their point of view, she is invisible; as she acknowledges in stanza 23, her invisibility is performative, as she makes herself invisible so as to be able to watch the risible performances going on around her. This construction plays with the convention of the female witness to male prowess; the woman, in a protected position (in a tower, e.g., like Jimena in the Alcázar of Valencia in the *Cantar de mio Cid*), fearfully looks on masculine heroic behavior, a spectacle intended to reinforce male dominance and female inferiority. In the *Coplas*, the female observer is not in a protected, elevated position; a camp-follower, she is on or near the battle-field and a potential victim of assault.[64] Her profession, class, and gender make her unworthy of attention. Ironically, on the battlefield, her grotesque body (grotesque because feminine, oversexed, and of low social origin) makes her invulnerable; in contrast, the knights' sense of bodily vulnerability makes their bodies grotesque and ridiculous. The knights she watches display a remarkable lack of self-consciousness. As Julio Rodríguez Puérto-las comments, the knights arrive at the field carefully attired as though participating in a mere show of military power.[65] Fear of bodily injury causes them to forget about heroic display and the presence of onlookers, especially of their fellow noblemen as guardians of correct behavior. The battle becomes a spectacle of well-dressed and armed nobles who stage themselves in an attempt to legitimize their hold on political power; comically, they lose control of the spectacle, showcasing grotesque bodies and exposing their inability to rule even themselves.

The *panadera*, by contrast, is highly aware of her vulnerability. As she comments in stanza 23, she suppresses her urge to laugh during the battle since she is surrounded by armed men who could kill her with impunity. Now she is in the marketplace, where the *paz del mercado* prohibits physical violence, private arrests, and the baring of arms; she is no longer at risk, so she freely expresses her contempt. As an unseen witness, she sees and learns the truth that she presents in her public performance, complete with bodily gestures; her perspective is embodied and situated, essentially linked to the character who speaks. I read the poem's fictive frame as replicating the performance and function of carnival song, releasing the *panadera*'s tensions by gleefully mocking her eminent targets. This is, nonetheless, a fiction; this poem is a courtly composition, adopting the perspective of the subaltern in order to depict to the nobility their own degradation. The *panadera*'s practice of citing her targets' speech underlines her narrative control and their loss of power; her speech in turn is cited by the elite male poet who employs her for his own political and artistic ends. Even as a fictional character, the *panadera* expresses a social and gendered perspective on history that counteracts the ordering techniques of the official Castilian account of the battle.

A particularly interesting aspect of the *panadera's* criticism is her use of degraded women as standards of comparison for elite men:

> Viniendo de la frontera
> el mayor comendador,
> desamparó a su señor,
> de quien gran bien rescibiera,
> y como quien desespera
> de toda gran nombradía
> más vergüença no tenía
> que una puta carcabera. (35: 312–19)

The *Comendador mayor* [Juan Ramírez de Guzmán], returning from the front lines, abandoned his lord, from whom he received great good; and like he who despairs of all good renown, he had less shame than a roadside prostitute.

A *puta carcavera* seeks clients among the sewers outside the city walls, a marginal space that links her with excrement; a *comendador mayor* is an elevated rank in a military order, such as the knights of Santiago, a rank second only to that of the *Maestre*. The juxtaposition of such a high-ranked knight with a *puta carcavera* underlines how ignoble Ramírez de Guzmán's behavior was. The presence of degraded women in the camps had already been alluded to in a reference to a *lavandera* who cleans the terrified bishop of Sigüenza's soiled underwear (6: 58); in the same stanza, we hear of a *cobixera* (6: 54, chambermaid) whose attractions outweigh the call to arms. Diego Arias Dávila, the royal treasurer, masquerades as a *partera* (midwife):

> Vi sentado en una estera
> al segundo contador,
> fablando como doctor,
> vestido como partera:
> y si lo que a él paresciera
> se pudiera allí acabar,
> él quisiera más estar
> cien leguas allende vera. (24: 213–20)

I saw the second treasurer [Diego Arias Dávila] seated on a mat, speaking like a doctor, dressed like a midwife; and if he could have done there what seemed best to him, he would have been a hundred leagues from the battlefield.

The contrast between the treasurer's speech and dress goes beyond gender differences to cut across class and education, since a *partera* is a folk practitioner who specializes in childbirth. *Partera* here is a pun, indicating Arias Dávila's desire to flee the battlefield (*partir*, to leave); the *panadera* construes the difference between his elevated words and his fear as cross-dressing. The use of degraded women as standards of comparison is evident in the character of the *panadera* herself; her stance as an authoritative witness plays with her status as a degraded woman who is superior to the men whom she ridicules. In the *Coplas de la panadera*, we hear the voice of a character speaking against those who would ridicule her. In her performance she turns the tables, replying not only to Juan II's propagandistic account but also to dominant negative attitudes toward *panaderas* and other degraded women; she depicts the noble men she impersonates as themselves impersonating *parteras, putas carcaveras,* and *cobijeras.*

In this poem we see a portrait of the *panadera* as a marketplace orator, entertaining the crowds with a comic–satiric account of the Battle of Olmedo. She acts as a mouthpiece for popular discontent and frustration caused by the interminable wars waged among the nobility; in her abusive, degrading caricatures, she puts her billingsgate rhetoric to political use. As the principal speaker in a dialogic poem, her voice represents that of her enthusiastic audience as well; the collective nature of her voice reflects *panaderas'* roles as leaders of popular protests and bread riots. Her account of the battle recreates orally events she claims to have witnessed, enabling her to mediate between her audience and the aristocrats she satirizes; she sells her authoritative discourse, a product she offers to satisfy her listeners' hunger for alternative versions of contemporary history. She even conflates the sacred and the profane in her comic portrait of God the Father in the final stanza of the poem:

> Tú, Señor, que eres minera
> de toda virtud divina,
> saca la tu melezina
> de la tu sancta triaquera;
> porque ya, Señor, siquiera
> aya más paz algún rato,
> ca del dicho desbarato
> a muchos queda dentera. (46: 411–18)

You, Lord, who are the source of all divine power, take your medicine from your holy medicine chest; now, Lord, may there be some peace for a while, since many are still on edge because of this mess.

The *panadera* portrays God as a healer equipped with a holy medicine bag; this image is ironic, especially following her portrait of Arias Dávila as a *partera* in stanza 24. She prays that He heal the collective body wounded by continuous political struggles; this divine cure shall be short-lived, as she comments in the last two verses. Her use of the word *dentera* (an unpleasant sensation felt in one's teeth caused by a bitter taste or a sharp sound; figuratively, on edge) constructs the battle as a bitter pill that leaves everyone with a disagreeable sensation; this sensation will endure, despite the Castilian victory and divine intervention. She depicts God as impotent, unable to impose order on the disordered bodies portrayed throughout the poem. In her ironic appeal to God, the *panadera* speaks for all the people, uttering a collective if hopeless prayer for peace. Not only does she appropriate the people's voice, but she figures herself as a parodic Virgin who has the authority to petition God on others' behalf; appropriately, the God she appeals to, cross-dressed as a healer, appears as ridiculous in His role as she does in hers. The *Coplas* presents the *panadera* as an eloquent spokesperson for popular discontent, as a marketplace orator, and as a figure that mediates between different social groups while collapsing hierarchies of all kinds; she is also, finally, powerless, able to decry but not to affect the abuses of the powerful.

The *Coplas de la panadera* illustrates some key elements of marketplace discourse. As Deborah A. Kapchan says in her discussion of a female vendor in a modern Moroccan traditional market:

> Her oratory is characteristic of the marketplace, a composite of oaths, formulae, axiomatic sayings, and. . .feminine testimony. . . .Despite the quality of monologue in her speech, the social role of the female hawker introduces dialogue and the process of "dialogization". . .into a public space occupied by both men and women—in the marketplace the authority of every voice is put into question by the presence and competition of all others.

While the audience's commentary on the *panadera*'s performance is not cited by the poem's author, this omission does not reduce the dialogic quality of her speech. She enters into dialogue with Juan II's proclamation, which itself enters the marketplace in order to coerce the public into witnessing an official exercise of power. Through parody and citation, the *panadera* persistently consumes the official version, subverting its legitimizing discourse by placing her own authoritative version alongside it and facilitating her audience's negotiation of meaning. They themselves may be resistant consumers of her version: they may reject the testimony of a prostitute and support the king's version; they may read her performance as the highly entertaining ravings of a lunatic; they may suspect that she is merely giving them what she imagines they want in order to profit from their hunger for alternative views. Her performance will give way to others—not coincidentally, the *panadera*-satirist appears in three Catalan satires from the second half of the fifteenth century, uttering similar personal invectives against powerful men.[66] The *panadera* is a consumable as much as the official narration she herself consumes; she, like most of the *panaderas* we have considered, is wily, poaching what she can and turning a profit from her losses, including the prejudicial dominant construction of herself as a literary and popular character.

The figure of the *panadera* brings to the forefront questions of class, gender, value, and rhetoric, as well as performance in a public space. The *panadera* functions ambivalently as a shrewd assessor and evaluator of others' goods, one who cuts through rhetorical embellishments to get at the true worth of their product, and also as a artist who creates worth with her own powerful rhetoric. She is dangerously seductive, accosting and even assaulting clients with her mesmerizing song, enchanting gestures, and desirable body/bread. While in popular lyrics she becomes powerless after a brief flowering of sexuality and freshness, in literate compositions she is far more enduring; as in her most extended and compelling portrait, in the *Coplas de la panadera*, her power stems not from her beautiful body but from her sharp eye and tongue and her love of public performances. Her command of marketplace discourse serves her well, enabling her to move from marketplace to battlefield and back, emerging unscathed from the Battle of Olmedo to herself wreak vengeance on those who consider themselves above popular opinion. The aristocracy's celebrated self-control functions only in the safe arena of the court and utterly fails them in the open field of battle, as revealed in the betwixt and between space of the market. The ambivalent role played by the *panadera* replicates the contradictory construction of bread as both profane and sacred; her billingsgate rhetoric collapses extreme opposites or, as is the case with the *Coplas*, debunks them, showing them to be mere conventions designed to obscure the bodily reality that all humans share. The marketplace is a site for negotiation, of desires, identity, values, and authority. The dialogic quality of marketplace discourse brings many perspectives to bear on official proclamations and other demonstrations of authority; although forced to witness official spectacles, marketplace personnel are able to negotiate the meaning of such displays. The *panadera*, as the presiding figure of the market, emblemizes and enacts this arena of contested misrule.

Like the marketplace, the *sierra* puts elite men to the test; its representative *par excellence*, the *serrana*, brings its hostile terrain to life. Unlike the *panadera* and the *soldadeira*, the *serrana* is a purely fictive construct, as her poetic depiction has little to do with the historic reality of alpine shepherdesses; her fictive quality enhances the performative nature of her character, as male poet-performers impersonate her in *plazas* and courts. Lyrics on *serranas* foreground performance, at the fictive and metafictive levels; as in the *Coplas de la panadera*, the contrast between the fictive performance site and the space within which the lyric is performed focuses attention on the significance of different social spaces and actors. Conventional oppositions of wilderness and civilization, female and male, peasant and elite, are enacted and conflated in the encounter between male traveler and *serrana*. These two characters collaborate in their dialogue as each enacts a role that requires and enables the other to play a complimentary role. These roles often question dominant social norms, as the *serrana* becomes the desiring subject and the male protagonist, the passive object of desire. Poets use the figure of the *serrana* to locate themselves (or rather, their poetic alter egos) in a shifting and multivalent landscape. In depicting and impersonating *serranas*, poet-performers depict and impersonate (versions of) themselves, playing with their usual identities and creating relations with their poetic predecessors, inscribing themselves into Hispanic literary history.

CHAPTER 4

MONSTROSITY IN THE MOUNTAINS, COURTESY AT COURT: CONTESTING SPACE IN POEMS ON *SERRANAS*

Serranas constantly show off in medieval Iberian poetry, singing, dancing, and orating, making themselves objects for the (elite) male gaze. Their entertaining performances are peripheral to their work as herders and agricultural laborers (*pastoras* or *vaqueras*, shepherdesses or cowgirls); as with the *soldadeira*, poems on *serranas* rarely depict their official function. In poetry, *serranas* mostly make spectacles of themselves, as in the following popular lyric:

> ¡Hávalas, hávalas, hala,
> hava la frol y la gala!
> Allá arriba, arriba,
> junto a mi llogare
> viera yo serranas
> cantar y baxlare,
> y entre todas ellas,
> mi linda zagala.
> ¡Hava la frol y la gala![1]

Look at them, look at them, come on!, look at the flower and the beauty! High up there, high up, right by my place, I saw *serranas* singing and dancing, and among them all, my pretty shepherdess. Look at my pride and joy!

The *serranas* in this *villancico* (a song written in the popular style), like all those depicted in medieval lyrics, are amateur performers who sing and dance for their own pleasure. The *estribillo* (refrain) is the song that the narrator heard the *serranas* sing while they danced. In "hava la frol y la gala," *frol* refers to a literal and a metaphorical flower, as in 'the flower of the town' in the *panadera* lyrics discussed in chapter 3. In the *serranas'* song, *frol* expresses the pleasure they derive from dance, the spring flowers, and, by association, their own beautiful bodies; the imperative *hava* directs the gaze of the spectator, as well as their own, toward these objects. While the *estribillo* was originally female-voiced, this *villancico* is a male-voiced monologue; the narrator incorporates the *serranas'* song into his own, appropriating their voices and submerging them in his. When he sings "hava la frol y la gala," he uses their song to single out and praise his *zagala*, the flower of the *sierra*. His response is proprietary; he takes their performance and transforms it into a display designed to inflame his desire.

The speaker is a *serrano* who at the moment of enunciation is not in the *sierra*; his gender and his immediate context distinguish him from the beautiful mountain women about whom he sings. The lyric emphasizes the temporal and geographical distance between the male speaker and the *serranas*; the past tense verbs and the word *allá* underline the contrast between the speaker's present location and that of the *serranas* he watched in the past. The narrator inserts himself into the *serranas'* performance which he then inserts into his own song, foregrounding his experience as spectator over that of the *serranas* as performers. The groupings and voicing reflect this imbalance: a single male voice mimics and comments on the song and dance of a group of women, who are silenced and objectified in his account.

This comic-erotic *villancico* constructs the *serranas'* performance as an emblem of rural life. Like almost all poems on *serranas*, this song contains no taboo words and its eroticism is restrained; the countryside becomes an idyllic space of innocent pleasures and ample leisure time in which to enjoy them. Implicitly, the pleasure-filled countryside contrasts with the industry and cynicism of the town or court. The distance between the speaker's present location and that of his *llogare* suggests that he is out of place, only temporarily in town on business, and that he will return soon to his accustomed place alongside the dancing *serranas*. He recreates the rural scene for his amusement and for that of his audience, who take as much pleasure in his country bumpkin persona as in his portrayal of the *serranas*. The role he assumes in response to the *serranas*, that of an eager lover, is designed to amuse his urban audience; they would perceive his similarities to the *serranas* as he sings their song and takes as his object of desire a woman of his own status. In other words, the fact that he constructs himself as distinct from the objects of his gaze would itself amuse his audience; where he perceives difference, they would see similarity. His song is a parodic *serranilla*; rather than relating an encounter between a noble *cavallero* (knight) and a rustic *serrana*, this *villanico* depicts a *pastor's* desire for a *pastora* (shepherd, shepherdess). This speaker is a traveler, but he travels to town and will return to the countryside, unlike the *cavallero* whose place is at the court where he sings his *serranilla* about his mountain adventures. Nor does it show the *pastor* in interaction with the *zagala*; there is no dialogue between the characters, unlike most *serranillas*. However, like courtly *serranillas*, this *villancico* provides a vignette of *serranas in situ*, in the mountains, performing an appropriately rustic song and dance; they appear as a natural extension of the *sierra*, reinforcing the "woman as nature" topos and illustrating the cultural significance of mountains.[2]

In this *villancico*, the dancing *serranas* are as spectacular as the mountains they inhabit. They display themselves to the narrator, whose presence makes their dance a spectacle, just as mountains become spectacular when gazed upon. Their decorous bodies offer unthreatening pleasure to spectators, both the narrator and his own audience. The male speaker has claimed one of these *serranas* as his sexual property, just as he asserts a territorial claim to his *llogare*, further underlining similarities between *serranas* and *sierras*. While these *serranas* do not defend a pass/their bodies against a male intruder/rapist as in the *Libro de buen amor*, the terrain they inhabit reflects and is reflected in their bodies; both become sexual playgrounds for male travelers, whether noble or *villano* such as our speaker. The coded, suggestive language employed by *serrana* lyrics both points to and conceals the frankly sexual desires of the male narrators. Poetry about *serranas* is always about sex, gender, class and social spheres, and, almost always, violence. Poet-performers project their desires, fears, and frustrations onto the eroticized mountain landscape and onto the *serrana* as well. Narrator-protagonists get to play in the *sierras*, transgressing normative boundaries, geographical, social, and gendered, and indulging in fantasies limited only by poetic conventions. The traveler performs as much as the *serrana* does, and he gets to tell all about it once he returns to court or town, playing a dual role as narrator and protagonist.

Poems about *serranas* tend to foreground the narrator-protagonist's performance and downplay that of the *serrana*, as do many of the *Cantigas d'escarnho* on *soldadeiras* that I discuss in chapter 2. Unlike the *Cantigas d'escarnho*, women probably did not enact the roles of *serranas*, as I explain below, so male performances became the focus at both the fictive and metapoetic level. Nor would any *serrana* be present for the performance of *serrana* lyrics. The female protagonist's absence from the performance space means that the male narrator-protagonist's version of events remained uncontested, despite the dialogic reception context for *cancionero* lyric. Due to her actual absence, the fictive *serrana* was depicted as an active and resistant agent. Within the fictive world, the *serrana*'s performance attracts the narrator's attention and determines the role he assumes in reaction to the one she plays. The *serrana* both fulfills and resists the narrator-protagonist's desires; she acts to define herself and to control the male character's behavior. The *serrana*'s resistant performances make her a complex character, a foil for the narrator-protagonist, and a figure for the *sierra* itself. A *serrana* is ventroliquized by the poet-performer who (probably) also impersonated her; while he gets to indulge in transgendered performances and parodic mimicry, enacting the roles of narrator and *serrana*, she is a mere character, just another act executed by men. The volition she has is fictive, bestowed upon her by the poet; the fact that she is constructed as resistant underlines the narrator-protagonist's desire to surrender control to her and to indulge in otherwise inappropriate behaviors. Whether conquered, conquering, or indifferent, the *serrana*, her behavior, and her treatment signify deeply, expressing poets' attitudes toward land, toward women, and toward the roles they themselves play, both on- and offstage.

Assuming the voice, gestures, and persona of a humble yet strong shepherdess whose self-sufficiency and weapons highlight her phallic qualities enabled male performers to play with gendered behaviors and bodies. *Serranas* frequently embody the best of both genders, beauty and the ability to fight. As a rule, *serranas* are not afraid or intimidated by the men with whom they interact. Their confidence springs not from their class status or gender (unlike that of the elite male traveler), but from their profession and experience fighting savage beasts, especially wolves, to protect their flocks.[3] I would say their confidence arises from their competent bodies, their self-awareness, and their sense of being in the place they belong, in contrast to the out-of-place and often terrified traveler. *Serranas'* physical strength and competent bodies, so different from those of courtly ladies, make them simultaneously masculine and feminine; they have the power to choose how to perform in response to the male interloper, acting according to their own desires and interests. As both La Chata and Gadea say, *serranas* play a game (*juego*, 964d, 979c) with the male character, and a game spirit permeates all poems on *serranas* as well as the performances of such poems. Their play may be rough or gentle, verbal or physical sparring; yet, it is never serious play. They play at trying on various personas, without regard to complying with gender norms, as the characters as well as the performers act like another.

Lyrics on *serranas* stand out for their extensive citations of female speech, as the encounter between *serrana* and traveler develops through dialogue. As in the *Cantigas d'escarnho*, citing female voices is an antagonistic practice; not only does the narrator-protagonist cede the stage to the *serrana*, but he frames her voice with his, making her speech carry at least two meanings. Voicing is particularly important in poems on *serranas* due to the centrality of identity play; the character who speaks first usually interpellates the other, assigning her/him a role that s/he must either accept or attempt to redefine, not always successfully. Vicenta Blay Manzanera has shown that there are rather few examples of female speech in fifteenth- and sixteenth-century *cancionero* poetry. Those female characters who do speak are either queens and princesses (whose voices are cited in ten poems out of the one thousand and eight found in the three *cancioneros* she studies) or peasants, including *serranas* (cited in seven poems), with courtly ladies running a distant third (cited in only three).[4] These numbers underline the uniqueness of the *serranilla* as a genre, due to the importance of the dialogue between the male and female protagonists. The elite male protagonist often respects what the *serrana* says; his obedience parodies that of the subservient courtly lover and is frequently tinged with hostility. In the case of Santillana's "Menga de Mançanares" (V/D3432), the *cavallero* obeys her demand that he fight with her, toppling her on her back to demonstrate his simultaneous subservience and superiority. While the male protagonist respects the *serrana*'s voice, the narrator and the audience generally do not; they laugh at the imperious *serranas* as much as at the traveler who plays along with these verbally unruly women.

In stark contrast with the *Cantigas d'escarnho*, taboo language (by which I mean, disphemisms derived from taboo body parts) rarely if ever appears in poems on *serranas*. Abusive terminology does appear in many *serranillas*, yet these insults are based on social status, not on taboo body parts. Nonetheless, the landscape in which the *serrana* is located resounds with erotic significance. The pass she defends is that between her legs as much as the literal road on which the traveler walks; mounds signify breasts and the forested *mons pubis* or "mound of Venus." Displacing overt erotic language onto the landscape eliminates the need (and the justification) for taboo words, enabling poet-performers to obey courtly codes of linguistic hygiene while expressing sexual themes. Poet-performers exemplify court-liness in their 'clean' language while they indulge in illicit sex acts in the *sierras*, at a great distance from court. Their poetic performances, in which they recreate their mountain adventures in the space of the court, are comic in part due to the contrast between their courtly language and their uncourtly activities, rutting like animals with bestial *serranas* in the countryside. Their accounts are tailored to suit and amuse their present audience; they offer poet-performers the chance for self-display, bragging about their sexual exploits, while conforming to courtly codes.

My comments thus far show that I see little room for female participation in the creation and dissemination of lyrics on *serranas*, raising the question of why I include this figure in my study of performing women. I see the *serrana* as providing an important contrast with the figures of the *soldadeira* and the *panadera* precisely because it is a fictive role ventriloquized and enacted by male poet-performers. The predominate exclusion of real women from performing as *serranas* is as significant as the fact that elite men impersonated *serranas* in the lyric spectacle. The absence of a female body on stage and the exaggerated female impersonation of a male performer underline the fact that both producers and consumers of the *serranilla* insisted on seeing the *serrana* as a fictive character. *Cantigas d'escarnho* on *soldadeiras* and *panadera* lyrics voiced by women play on the fine lines between authentic and performed identity, creating great tension as to the fictive quality of the lyric spectacle; since the *serrana* is purely fictive, this tension is largely absent, or rather, only arises with respect to the first-person narrator-protagonist, whose identity frequently plays on the poet's identity, especially in the case of the Marqués. Part of the pleasure of *serrana* lyrics is the opportunity they give male performers to engage in parodic female impersonation and to recreate a rustic space within the court or town; such performances are about the representation of otherness, not about authentic otherness. The representational quality of *serrana* performances was enhanced by the presence of a single male body enacting multiple roles, none of which were authentic.

I start this chapter by discussing poems on *serranas* in general, examining the significance of place, class, gender, and performance in the genre as a whole. I then turn to an examination of poems on *serranas* in the fourteenth-century *Libro de buen amor* and in the fifteenth-century work of the Marqués de Santillana and of Carvajal, exploring the uses these three poets make of the figure of the *serrana*. While in the second half of this chapter I follow a chronological order and explore how each later poet responds to his antecedents, my intention is not to write a history of the *serranilla*. Rather, my approach is comparative, as I use these three poets to illustrate the similarities and differences in their use of the *serrana*. The figure of the *serrana* is particularly useful to explore the significance of place; the contrasts between the civilized spaces of court and town and the uncivilized space of the *sierra* are enacted in the encounter between the urbane male traveler and the rustic *serrana*. Juan Ruiz, the Marqués de Santillana, and Carvajal all use the *serrana* to situate themselves in a polyvalent landscape; in mapping themselves, they establish relations with others within both their poetic work and the real world.

The Mountain Range as Performance Site

Theorizing the construction of the *sierra* as a performance site in medieval Iberian literature is more complicated than doing so for the court or the market. Mountain performances were mainly productive, agricultural labor performed to sustain life. *Serrano*'s playful performances, such as songs, dances, storytelling, and conversation, were also productive, as they relieved the tedium of repetitive, mindless chores like herding, sowing, and reaping. The elite used the mountains primarily for the hunt, an endeavor both productive and recreational. As many fifteenth-century poetic treatises comment, rulers needed the relaxation afforded by noble entertainments such as the hunt, tournaments, music, and poetry; these entertainments exercised the mind and body and provided opportunities to practice skills necessary for the serious enterprises of war and governing. The hunt constructs the *sierra* as a site for proving oneself and demonstrating one's ability to dominate nature, an attitude frequently made explicit in the *serranilla*, which reads the *serrana* as nature itself. For travelers of all classes, the mountains were not a destination but another landscape through which they had to pass, one that tested their ability to persevere in the face of adversity. While criss-crossed with roads, mountains were frustrating obstacles; they were also famously dangerous, peopled with bandits and unofficial toll collectors, like La Chata and Gadea in the *Libro de buen amor*. In all, medieval discourse constructed mountains as marginal territories, uncivilized and dangerous; while they had their uses, for the most part, *sierras* were regarded with suspicion.[5]

Medieval philosophical and scientific discourses construct mountains as spectacles that resulted from human performance. Mountains are "monstrous" in the sense of showing off or making themselves different from other terrains. Bartholomaeus Glanville's fourteenth-century encyclopedia *De propietatibus rerum*, published in Castilian as *Propiedades de las cosas* (1494), highlight mountains' active spectacularity: "Montaña es vna ynchazon dela tierra leuantada contra el çielo & toca la tierra con la parte ynferior/ & por esta causa son llamadas montañas porque se muestran euidentemente sobre la tierra segund dize ysydoro" (A mountain is a swelling of land raised against heaven. It touches the earth with the lower part, and for this reason they are called mountains, since they obviously show themselves upon the land, as Isidore says). The verbs *toca* and *se muestran* underline mountains' intentionality and subjectivity; the phrase *levantada contra el çielo* implies their sinful nature, challenging the Heavens with their great heights. This implication is further developed in the story of their origin:

> enel comienço la tierra fue redonda & toda llana & ygual sin hauer ny montañas ny valles. ca era redonda como el çielo. E la causa delas montañas & valles fue la comoçion delas aguas que han cauado la tierra en algunos lugares. Enlos lugares firmes & seguros do el agua no pudo obrar ende quedaron las montañas / & donde el agua pudo cauar ende quedaron los valles & por ende pasan agora los rrios & arroyos. . . .Una vez el mar cubrio

toda la tierra & tiro assi lo que era muelle lo qual despues ella allego en vn lugar o en muchos / & despues de secado fueron ende las grandes montañas.

in the beginning the earth was round and completely flat and smooth without mountains or valleys. But it was round like Heaven. And the cause of mountains and valleys was the commotion of the waters that have dug the earth in some places. In the firm and stable places where the water could not erode mountains remained, and where the water could dig there remained valleys, and through them pass now rivers and streams. . . .Once the sea covered the entire Earth and removed that which was soft, which then gathered in one place or in many and after it had dried it formed huge mountains.

Mountains are the visual reminder of Noah's flood, the extinction of nearly all life due to humanity's sinful nature, and an index of the difference between Heaven and Earth; mountains' geological deformity is a product of humanity's moral deformity. Reading mountains as the sign of mankind's propensity to sin leads to a construction of the *sierra* as a sinful place, a space within which the perennial conflict between virtue and sin, culture and nature, and men and women, is reenacted endlessly.[6]

The hardness of mountains, mentioned twice in the above passage, facilitates their use as places to watch and build fortifications:

Las montañas por su altura son abiles para las atalayas que asechan los enemigos / & para mejor guardar la tierra & las gentes. Las montañas por ser mas fuertes & de mas dura materia son muy conuenientes para edificar castillos & torres / & mayormente quando son tan duras que agrand pena las pueden minar & tan altas que hombre no puede façilmente subir.

Due to their height mountains are an apt site for watchtowers from which to ambush enemies and to protect the land and people. Mountains, due to their strength and very hard materials, are very good for building castles and towers, especially when they are so hard that it's too difficult to mine them and so tall that one cannot easily climb them.

Visigothic forces took refuge in the mountains at the north of the peninsula during the Muslim invasions, as the following passage from the *Crónica de Aragón* indicates:"retruxieron se los cristiannos alas mas fuertes y asperas sierras / que podieron fallar: a las montañas delas asturias / dizen muchos. mas a los montes perhineos pienso que mas. por que son los mas altos y mas famosos montes de toda la hespaña" (the Christians withdrew to the strongest and steepest mountain ranges that they could find; to the mountains of Asturias, many say, but I think to the Pyrenees because they are the tallest and most famous mountains of all Spain). This passage shows the natural landscape as patriotic, not to say nationalistic, supporting the rightful inhabitants of the Iberian peninsula as they strove to retain a foothold in

Spain. Mountains acquire cultural and historical significance, helping to create an origin myth for Christian Spain.[7] The use of mountains as look-outs and as frontiers between warring regions appears in Santillana's *serranillas* I/D3429 and II/D3430, as his poetic 'I' plays the part of a Castilian defender against Aragonese aggression. He even makes a joke of the significance of regional identity and sexual activity: "[A]unque vengas d'Aragón, / d'ésta serás castellana" (II/D3430, vv. 16–17; although you may come from Aragon, from now on you'll be Castilian). His joke conflates military and sexual conquest and constructs the *serrana*'s body as a contested landscape, a construction Santillana frequently employs, as I discuss below.

Theorizing mountains as a performance site is complicated further because, in Iberian poetry, the *sierra* is a fictive construct, represented and recreated through words and gesture in courtly and urban performances. *Serranilla* performances are removed from the *sierra* itself; the narrator's account of the *sierra* encounter occurs at a great distance, geographically and ideologically, from real mountains. Even when the verses voiced by *serranas* are popular in origin, these verses are appropriated, framed, and double-voiced in literate compositions dominated by the poetic 'I' who engages in his own performance of self against an alpine backdrop. Courtly lyrics construct the *sierra* as the diametric opposite of the court, as a site of complete freedom of conduct; far removed from the ever-vigilant eyes of fellow courtiers, noblemen can indulge in inappropriate behaviors. The near-total isolation of the mountains is a constant theme in *serranillas*; absolute privacy releases the male narrator from normative constraints, making the *sierra* a place of refuge where he can recover from the social or psychological trauma of, for example, a frustrated love affair. The mountain as a site of retreat and/or madness is a frequent motif in chivalric romances, as in *Amadís de Gaula* and *Don Quixote*. Fifteenth-century court lyric also plays on this motif; Juan de Encina's "Por unos puertos arriba" (D0764) is an extended portrait of a love-sick knight who has taken refuge in the mountains; his "Quien te trajo, caballero" (D3546, D3139) is a dialogic poem voiced by a *caballero* and a *pastor*, both of whom complain of their frustrated love affairs.[8] This motif also appears in *serranillas*; three of Carvajal's narrator-protagonists (in X/D0608, XXII/D0622, and XLVI/D0651) hint at frustrated love affairs.

In Santillana's *serranilla* IV/D3431, "La moçuela de Bores," the narrator-protagonist presents himself as a former lover:

> Cuidé qu'olvidado
> amor me tenía,
> como quien s'avía
> grand tiempo dexado

de tales dolores
que más que la llama
queman, amadores. (vv. 4–10)

I thought that love had forgotten me, like he who had long ago left behind
those sorrows that burn more than flames, lovers.

The speaker's comments suggest that, rather than abandoning the fellow-
ship of lovers due to an unhappy love affair, he may simply be too old to
indulge in a young man's game. In the *sierras*, far from the ridiculing eyes
of fellow court poets, he is once again able to experience the passions of
youth, indulging in a flirtatious dialogue that culminates in a discrete sexual
encounter with a beautiful *vaquera*: "E fueron las flores / de cabe Espinama /
los encubridores" (vv. 43–45; and the flowers near Espinama were our
covers [i.e., we lay together in the flowers on the outskirts of the village]).
The narrator calls his emotions *amores* (v. 3), situating this encounter
within the tradition of courtly love; yet, given the object's degraded social
status, the nobleman can bed her and publicize his conquest without dam-
aging her nonexistent honor. The fact that she is purely a fictive creation
enables him to violate the courtly code of discretion and dissimulation; he
can even play the role of the object of desire and not just that of desiring
subject. Courtiers can find relief from the constant self-awareness that court
life demands and easy access to healthy sex in the pornotopia of the *sierra*,
inhabited by amiable, beautiful, and sexually liberated *serranas*.[9] This, of
course, in an idealized *sierra* full of *loci amoeni*; *sierras* in Castilian lyrics can
be inhospitable, harsh wastelands inhabited by monstrous, violent women
who beat and rape the male traveler. Even abusive *serranas* enable cultured
men to escape their customary roles and performances, letting them
temporarily play the role of victim of sexual violence then reassert their
phallic mastery in satiric verses, as in the *Libro de buen amor*, the *romance* "La
serrana de la Vera" and some fifteenth-century *cancionero* lyrics.[10]

In medieval literature and popular culture, the *sierra*'s hostile climate
contributes to the opposition between civilization and wilderness. As Juan
Ruiz complains, it is always winter in the *sierra*:

Sienpre ha mala manera la sierra e la altura:
si nieva o si yela, nunca da calentura;
bien en çima del puerto, fazía orilla dura,
viento con grand elada, rozío con friura. (1006)

It is always unpleasant in the mountains and the heights: whether it snows or
freezes, it is never warm; there was bad weather at the top of the pass, wind
and snow and very cold dew.

This perpetually hostile climate is treated as intentional, as though the *sierra* had volition and made itself unpleasant. In popular lyrics, the contrast between *sierra* and town is proverbial:

> Quando aquí nieva,
> ¿qué hará en la sierra?
>
> When it snows here, what must it be like in the *sierra*?

This rhetorical question attempts to reinforce the normative contrast between town and wilderness, a difference put in question by the uncharacteristically inclement weather in town. The equivocal question implies both that it is even worse in the mountains and that nothing is as it should be. The contrast between here, a usually hospitable urban space, and there, the cold *sierra*, replicates other proverbial contrasts between people:

> Cuando las aldeanas traen guantes,
> ¡qué harán las señoras grandes!
>
> Si los pastores han amores,
> ¡qué harán los gentileshombres!
>
> ¡Qué harán los que pudieren,
> que los viejos de amores mueren!
>
> Si eres niña y as amor,
> ¡qué harás quando mayor!
>
> When country girls wear gloves, what will the great ladies do!
>
> If shepherds have loves, what will the gentlemen do!
>
> What will the able-bodied do, when old men die of love!
>
> If you are a little girl and you have love, what will you do when you're grown!

These four lyrics focus on the behaviors by those who should not enjoy certain privileges of dress or of erotic desire, and then wonder what those who should enjoy such privileges will do in order to maintain social order. Such depictions construct the *sierra* as an Otherworld, although contiguous with known, civilized territories. The *sierra* is marginal, not because it is always found on the frontier but because it is ideologically peripheral, "the Other pole to a great cultural centre," as Rob Shields says; "as opposed to being merely a topographic margin, the development of cultural marginality occurs only through a complex process of social activity and cultural work." Literary representations of the *sierra* perform an important part of the work of cultural marginalization, contributing to their historical construction as wilderness.[11]

The wildness of mountains makes them terrible and fearful. The wilderness bewilders civilized beings who venture into it, causing them to become confused and lose their way, like the unwary travelers in *serranillas*. The fearful nature of mountains is a frequent motif in popular lyrics:

> Por las sierras de Madrid
> tengo d'ir,
> que mal miedo é de morir.
>
> En el monte la pastora
> me dexó:
> ¡dónde yré sin ella yo!
>
> Paséisme aor'allá, serrana,
> que no muera yo en esta montaña.
> Paséisme aor'allend'el rrío,
> qu'estoy, triste, mal herido.
> Que no muera yo en esta montaña.
>
> Dame acogida en tu hato,
> pastora, que Dios te duela:
> cata que en el monte yela.

I have to go through the *sierras* of Madrid; I'm afraid I'll die.

The shepherdess left me in the mountain; where will I go without her!

Carry me that way, *serrana*, don't let me die in this mountain.
Carry me across the river, because, alas, I'm badly wounded. Don't let me die in this mountain.

Give me refuge in your hut, shepherdess, for God's sake; see how it's freezing in the mountains.

These lyrics are voiced by male travelers who treat the *sierra* as a terrible, life-threatening place, a site of death, abandonment, suffering, danger, and robbery; the aid of a native, a *serrana* or a *pastora*, is essential to survive the journey through the mountains. In "Paséisme aor'allá" an injured knight begs a large, burly *serrana* to carry him out of the mountains, as later in the *Libro de buen amor* the narrator-protagonist is tossed on a *serrana*'s back and carried to her hut; the contrast between civilization and wilderness is represented in the very different bodies of the two protagonists. The traveler's bewilderment is geographical as well as sexual; *morir*, *hato*, and *yela* are double-entendres, *morir* to climax, *hato* female genitals, and *yela*, sexual frustration or frigidity. As Laura R. Bass, Louise O. Vasvári, and other critics have shown, *sierras* are construed as feminine, analogous to a woman lying on her back in the normative position for coitus.[12] Representations of mountains often encode female bodies:

> Montaña hermosa,
> alegre y muy leda,
> la tu arboleda
> cómo es deleytosa.
>
> Serra que tal gado tem
> não na subiráa ninguém.[13]

Beautiful mountain, happy and very content, how pleasant is your grove of trees.
No one will ever climb such a steep *sierra*.

The diction of these lyrics makes it impossible to say whether these mountains are geographical features or women, or rather, parts of a female body. In the first lyric, *alegre* and *leda* describe emotional states, personifying the mountain; *arboleda* refers to hair on a *mons pubis*. The second lyric uses the image of a steep *sierra* to criticize a proud and/or tall woman; her manner and/or her physicality make her undesirable. While these male-voiced lyrics present their speakers in a position of power over passive feminine terrains, many poems on *serranas* present them as aggressive, threatening to engulf the male traveler. For example, in Ruiz's *cánticas de serrana*, his persona is unable to perform to Gadea de Riofrío's satisfaction, overcome by her demands.

The mountainous female body in Pedro Almodóvar's film *Hable con ella* (*Talk to Her*) demonstrates how apparently passive landscapes can become active and menacing in the eyes of the beholder. In the black-and-white silent film sequence, entitled *Amante menguante* (*Shrinking Lover*), the female body serves as a performance space and itself performs, engulfing the miniaturized male body and showing pleasure. In this sequence, Amparo, a scientist, develops a reducing tonic which her plump fiancé, Alfredo, drinks. While the tonic releases their repressed sexuality, it also causes Alfredo to shrink; by the climactic scene, in which Alfredo and a sleeping Amparo are in bed together, he is some five inches in height. Clad in an undershirt and briefs, Alfredo clearly enjoys playing on Amparo's giant body as he crawls up her mountainous breasts and rolls into the valley between them. Then, gazing upon her forested *mons pubis*, he treks down her torso to her lower body. The image in this shot is particularly landscaped, as the miniature male body stands erect on the gigantic female torso and walks down the river-like depression between her ribs; her torso and lower body are included in the frame, so we see her legs, the knees bent upward and separated, forming two ridgelines below her hips. Not only does this image decapitate Amparo, but it foreshadows the conversion of the entire male body into a penis. As in many poems on *serranas*, the male figure is dwarfed by an enormous female body, a fact underlined by the camera's cut to a close-up of the cave-like vagina. The labia are mostly free of hair and form a clear, slit-like opening to the dark vagina that Alfredo proceeds to explore. He starts by inserting one arm, pushing in almost its entire length, as if testing the depth of the dark passage. The camera cuts to the sleeping Amparo's face, and we see her purse her lips with pleasure. This reaction shot equates her upper and lower lips; the images of her teeth (which we notice in each of the three reaction shots in this sequence) imply that her vagina is *dentata*, foreshadowing the inevitable. After withdrawing and examining his arm, Alfredo removes his undershirt and inserts his entire upper body. The camera again cuts to Amparo's face, and we see her part her lips, revealing her teeth. Cutting back to the male figure, we see him remove his briefs and insert his entire, naked body into her vagina; we watch until his feet disappear. The camera cuts back to her face, and we see her, still asleep, cry out and bite her lower lip in orgasm. The male figure never emerges from her body; he remains inside her forever, as the voice of the narrator, Benigno Martín, explains, bringing us out of the silent film/fantasy interlude.[14]

This sequence reflects the powerfully ambivalent emotions a gigantic female body sparks in some men. The erotic landscape is both a playground for innocent bodily pleasure and a menacing site where one can get lost in dark and unfathomable depths. This loss of self is disturbing yet not undesirable; Benigno's narration implies that Alfredo chose to remain forever lost, bewildered by his own sexuality (as is Benigno himself). This giant woman is highly desirable in the eyes of her lover who chooses to annihilate himself in eternal sexual union with her; at first hesitant, he decides to plunge into a female form that, although passive, engulfs him. By contrast, poems on *serranas* do not allow the narrator-protagonist the pleasure of eternal loss of self in a sexual underground; the first-person, past-tense narration does not permit the loss of voice inherent in the loss of self. While the narrative voice may break off mid-narration, frequently just before the sex act, at the moment of enunciation the narrator is back at court or town, having left behind the mountains within which he was free temporarily to lose himself in sexual self-indulgence. His narration expresses his ambivalent feelings about his past experience; while celebrating sexual freedom he has already abandoned it and returned to the normative constraints of his courtly/urban identity. Nor does he express a desire to return, although a single poet often composed and performed several *serranillas*, showing his continued fascination with the possibilities of the *sierra*.

The *Serranilla* as a Performance Text

Serranillas are, like all medieval lyric poetry, performance. The poet-performer's narrative highlights the performances of both the male and female protagonists, the images of self that they project to the other, and the verbal strategies they employ, as each attempts to obtain her/his desires. Nicolás Bratosevich has discussed this aspect in his communicative analysis of Santillana's "La moçuela de Bores" (IV/D3431):

> como sucede en toda comunicación, cada locutor maniobra con una *imagen* de sí mismo que ofrece al otro para ser reconocida y aceptada—para que se justifique su mensaje—, y en relación con ella coloca al otro en una imagen o posición determinada con respecto a sí mismo; o con palabras de François Flahault (que traduzco): ≪todo hablar, por importante que sea el valor referencial e informativo, se formula también a partir de un 'quién soy yo para ti, quién eres tú para mí' y es operante en ese campo≫.[15]

> As happens in all communicative acts, each speaker manipulates an *image* of himself which he offers to the other in order to be recognized and accepted—in order to justify his message—and, in relation to this image he places the other in a certain image or position with respect to himself; or, in the words of François Flahault (which I translate): "as important as is the referential and informative value of speech, all language is also formulated from the perspective of 'who am I to you, who are you to me' and operates in that field."

This formulation emphasizes the communicative and interactive aspect of identity formation and performance. It does not resolve the question of self-awareness, the extent to which a speaker is aware of this dynamic and intentionally manipulates it in order to influence the other's perception of him/her. The level of self-awareness demonstrated by *serranas* varies greatly. The dual nature of the narrator-protagonist's role within the text increases the conscientious and ironic aspects of his self-portrait, as does his temporal distance from the past moment of encounter and the present moment of enunciation. As a ventriloquized character, the *serrana*'s volition and self-awareness are limited; her construction as an extension of the natural landscape within which she is found often causes her words and actions to be read as unself-aware, as impulses that reveal her primitive nature rather than as learned responses to a given situation. This perception downplays the intentionality of *serranas*' words and behaviors and denies their subjectivity. On the other hand, in many poems on *serranas*, the poet-performer depicts her as knowingly self-aware and even in control of the male protagonist. The extent to which an individual *serrana* is a self-aware agent depends upon the use being made of her character in that particular song.

Poetic performance practices determine the social function of the character of the *serrana*. The *serrana* is an outsider and a fictive character, absent from the performance of the poem within which she appears. To what extent is the pleasure of the genre dependent upon her physical absence yet virtual presence, represented in the words and gestures of the performer? Would the *serrana*, determinately female albeit frequently performing typically masculine behaviors, be voiced by a woman or not? Given that not all poems that feature *serranas* are *serranillas*, did performance practices differ, and if so, how? While it may be impossible to answer these questions definitively, we certainly can suggest probable performance practices by considering the question of the composition and transmission of these poems. It has been argued that Juan Ruiz did not compose all the *cánticas de serrana* that he includes in the *Libro de buen amor*—the open nature of that particular compendium of diverse poetic materials and Ruiz's commentary on the performers of his compositions (written for *cantaderas, moras, ciegos, cazurros*, etc.) certainly can be adduced to support the possibility that he incorporated and/or revised a previously extant composition.[16] As I discuss in chapter 1, medieval performance practices tended to blur the lines between composition, improvisation, and repetition; re-presentations of the same song would alter the words, music, and other aspects. Subsequent performances of a song did not simply replicate the original performance. The orality of medieval poetry in general, and of the *serranilla* in particular, further blurs the line between composing and repeating a text.

Miguel Ángel Pérez Priego argues that courtly *serranillas* were primarily oral in nature, both in their performance and transmission:

> Las serranillas eran, en efecto, unos poemillas ocasionales y ligeros, que se componían en la corte ante un auditorio cortesano y diverso, y en las que, con cierto aire apicarado y cómplice, se relataban aventuras viajeras—más o menos procaces, más o menos idealizadas—de amoríos serranos. Ese carácter semicolectivo y palaciego es el que explica. . .que existan serranillas compuestas en colaboración. . .o que el poeta particular con alguna frecuencia se dirija expresamente al auditorio. . .familiarizado como estaría éste con aquel género de cantares y con sus claves literarias.[17]

> *Serranillas* were, in effect, light and occasional poems that were composed in court before a courtly and diverse audience, in which travel adventures about love in the mountains—more or less lewd, more or less idealized—were recounted with a picaresque and complicit air. That semi-collective and courtly character is what explains. . .the existence of *serranillas* composed in collaboration. . .or why the particular poet [Santillana] with some frequency addresses himself expressly to his audience. . .as it would be familiar with that genre of songs and its literary codes.

This scenario is highly evocative, encompassing composition, performance, and context; while Pérez Priego may mean to capture with this description only fifteenth-century courtly *serranillas*, the similarities between this scenario and the composition and performance practices of the thirteenth-century *Cantigas d'escarnho* suggest that this description may well apply to medieval poetic practices in general, at least for comic-erotic and comic-obscene songs. The occasional, oral nature that Pérez Priego emphasizes in the above quotation hints at oral composition or improvisation; the resultant text would enter the oral culture of the court associated with the improviser, which explains *cancioneros'* attribution of poems to particular individuals.

While Miguel Ángel Pérez Priego's phrase "se componían" is somewhat ambiguous as to whether *serranillas* were improvised, Rafael Lapesa suggests that collaborative composition of *serranillas* "era un ejercicio cortesano de improvisación: la iniciaba un poeta con el estribillo y primera estrofa, fijando el metro y la combinación de rimas a que habían de ajustarse los continua-dores, cada uno con una copla" (was a courtly exercise of improvisation: one poet began it with the refrain and first stanza, fixing the meter and the rhyme scheme that had to be adopted by those who continued it, each with a stanza). His further comment, "pero de ordinario la serranilla era obra de un solo autor y servía para sazonar, de regreso en la corte, el relato de un viaje" (but ordinarily a single author composed a *serranilla*, which served to spice up his account of a trip upon his return to court), firmly situates the *serranilla* performance within an oral, dialogic context, although without clarifying to what extent the single-author *serranilla* was spontaneously improvised or composed in advance. Jeanne Battesti's syntactic analysis of thirty-five *serranillas* underlines the genre's formulaic character. Focusing exclusively on the encounter portion of the narrative (usually the *estribillo* and first stanza), Battesti enumerates the striking similarities in word-choice and syntactic structure, especially the almost compulsory "vi una serrana," a formula found, with variants, in thirty-three of the thirty-five poems she studies.[18] This evidence is certainly consistent with oral composition. Vari-ants in *serranilla* formulas can be explained as expressions of individual poets' style, as playing on audience expectations, and as reflecting the specific char-acter of the immediate performance and compositional context, that is, the interaction between performer and audience.

Serranilla compositional and performance practices demonstrate com-plicity among courtly poets and their audience, as the genre created and reinforced bonds between the members of a poetic community. Nicolás Bratosevich provides a nice definition of complicity in his discussion of the interrelations between the performance context and the fictive situation in the Marqués de Santillana's "Moçuela de Bores" (IV/D3431, discussed below). All of Santillana's *serranillas* are located in mountain sites that have some relationship with the Marqués's life; placing fictive encounters in sites that signify in reality creates a concrete link between the poetic and real worlds, such that the fictive encounter carries real significance. The audience's recognition of this dynamic causes them to read the fictive encounter as "una ficción que juega a ser real, anecdótico-biográfica, aunque autor y auditores sepan que no lo es. . .lo cual es parte del pacto entre ambos interlocutores de realidad; lo llamaremos *complicidad*, y él contribuye a conferirle al texto la plenitud de su (doble) sentido" (a fiction that plays at being real, anecdotal-biographical, although the author and audience know that is it not. . .which is part of the pact between both interlocutors in reality; we will call it *complicity*, and it helps to confer on the text the fullness of its [double] meaning) (emphasis in original). *Serranillas* represent for the amusement of a courtly audience an imaginary encounter between a fictive knight and peasant woman set in a particular mountain locale; the performance recreates that distant locale within the confines of the court. The interplay between realism and fantasy depends on the audience willfully suspending disbelief, which they do, in part due to their interest in distinguishing between the court and the not-court, and in part due to their desire to play along with the joke, to enjoy the resolution which is comic only if one accepts the rules of the *serranilla* game. Jeanne Battesti's analysis emphasizes the prominence of the poetic 'I' and his very close relationship with the audience, which is distanced from the *serrana*:

> Este "*yo*" del poeta crea en cierta medida una distancia entre él y la serrana, y al mismo tiempo una como complicidad por parte del lector y oyente. Este se encuentra, si [*sic*] puede decir, del lado del poeta; el mundo del "yo" asimila al del "tú" (el lector) para rechazar en un universo más lejano a "*ella*," la tercera persona, o sea la serrana. Por otra parte este "*yo*" presenta al poeta como el auténtico heroe de la aventura.[19] (emphasis in original)

> This "I" of the poet creates to some degree a distance between himself and the *serrana* and at the same time a type of complicity on the part of the reader and listener, who finds himself, so to say, at the side of the poet; the world of the "I" assimilates that of the "you" (the reader) in order to reject to a more distant universe "she," the third person, that is, the *serrana*. In addition, this "*I*" presents the poet as the authentic hero of the adventure.

In their mind's eye, the poet/performer and his audience gaze upon the *serrana*, who is physically absent and distanced in time and place from the *serranilla* performance; she is excluded from the performance of the poem that depends upon her for its very existence. This dynamic of virtual presence–actual absence, in addition to the probable improvisational character of the *serranilla*, suggests that a single male poet–performer enacted the role of the poetic 'I' and impersonated the *serrana*.

If a given *serranilla* entered the elite oral tradition, it would subsequently be performed by various individuals, male or female, perhaps even in alternating parts in the case of dialogic *serranillas*. How elaborate these subsequent performances would be is an interesting question. Josep Lluís Sirera's discussion of the theatricality of some *cancionero* dialogues sets out criteria that any one poem should have in order to be considered potentially theatrical: dialogue between two or more characters (one of whom can also function as the narrator); stage directions or other secondary text, such as a narrative frame and/or descriptions of movements, gestures, or speaking techniques to express emotions; setting in a particular time (in the past) and in a certain location. He particularly focuses on dialogic exchanges between characters, arguing that poems in which the characters do not simply exchange complete stanzas are more theatrical, as the dialogic interchange is privileged over poetic form.[20] According to these criteria, the *serranilla* as a genre is highly theatrical. Not only are most *serranillas* situated in particular places and times, but at their center lies the dialogue between *serrana* and male traveler, who performs a dual function as participant and narrator; the narrative section usually focuses on the actions of the two characters. The extent to which each individual *serranilla* can be considered theatrical varies greatly; I would argue that the expectations inherent to the genre included a high degree of theatricality. Part of the performers' pleasure lay in the mimicry of degraded others who were excluded from the group that produced and consumed the *serranilla*; the parodic force of performing as a *serrana* was increased if the performer's gender and rank differed from those of the character he mimicked, although female performers, professional or amateur, could also enjoy mimicking *serranas*, thereby staging their difference from them.[21]

Unlike the figures of the *soldadeira* and the *panadera*, who are fictive characters and also historical individuals who performed in the courts and marketplaces of medieval Castile, the *serrana* is a completely fictive character, a collective fantasy of poet–performers and their audiences. Acting like a *serrana* enacted a stereotypical identity category that was a completely fictive construct; her absence from the performance space enabled all those present, the actor–singer as well as his audience, to define themselves in opposition to her. For this reason, I expect the poems I discuss in the following sections were enacted by a single male actor–singer. Such a performance did not lack irony; just as the narrator distinguishes himself from his past self, that is, the male protagonist, so did the actor–singer mark his difference from the narrator, employing exaggerated and stylized behaviors to perform that character. Poems on *serranas* are comic, and all their characters are objects of ridicule, not just the *serrana*; sometimes the audience laughed along with the *serrana* who verbally and physically abused the male protagonist. There is a self-abasing, slapstick quality to the narrator-protagonist's decision to engage with a peasant woman and then to tell others about his experiences. While not all narrator-protagonists played the role of a fool as did Juan Ruiz, they all did aim to provoke laughter in their audience. The audience may even have laughed at itself, if it fell into a trap laid by the poet-performer, as in the case of Carvajal's "Passando por la Toscana" (XLV/D0650), in which the female protagonist turns out to be a figment of the narrator-protagonist's imagination. In the remaining part of this chapter, I analyze performance and role-playing in various poems on *serranas* by the three best-known authors of this genre, Juan Ruiz, the Marqués de Santillana, and Carvajal. These poets used the figure of the *serrana* to establish themselves in poetic and geographic landscapes, yet their narrator-protagonists assume several roles, as do the *serranas* they encounter. While each poet reacts to his antecedents, their response is not simplistic. *Serranas'* performances enabled these three poet-performers to assume various identities, playing with gender, power, social class, and the significance of different social spaces.

The *Cánticas de Serrana* in the *Libro de buen amor*: The Buffoon visits the Sierra

In the development of the *serranilla*, the four *cánticas de serrana* in the *Libro de buen amor* loom large, both because they are the earliest known examples of this theme written in Castilian and because of their decisive influence on later poets. As E. Michael Gerli has noted, the *Libro de buen amor* is a "key subtext of early fifteenth-century Castilian poetic discourse," a statement that holds true for the later fifteenth century.[22] I address Juan Ruiz's influence on Santillana and Carvajal later; in this section, I focus on Ruiz's interest in role-playing, on how both the male and female protagonists assume and act out certain roles in his four *cánticas de serrana*. It is very easy to focus on the narrator-protagonist's performances and ignore those of the *serranas*, although the *serranas'* performances of aggression and monstrosity make possible the narrator-protagonist's performances of submission and passivity. He gets to perform as a weak, impotent fool, and also have sex, because they are monstrous. In turn, the *serranas* get to perform monstrosity because of the narrator-protagonist's presence, enabling them to make demands and abuse him as part of the game.

The narrator depicts the *serranas* as monsters, subhuman in their bestiality and stupidity, superhuman in their size and strength. Monstrosity is in the eye of the beholder; the narrator-protagonist sees the *serranas* as monstrous, while from their point of view, he's the monster, a foreign intruder whose intentions are unknown and therefore suspicious. Notably, the *serranas* are acculturated; to paraphrase v. 967g, they follow "el uso de la sierra" (the *sierra*'s customs), a complex of cultural systems that the narrator-protagonist doesn't know or understand. His lack of understanding causes him to depict their behavior as irrational and incomprehensible, at least in the first encounter, with La Chata. In the second encounter, Gadea violates the rules of the game, causing the narrator-protagonist to rebel. By the third encounter, with Menga Lloriente, the protagonist has developed enough of an understanding of the rules of engagement in the mountains that he is able to trick her. He attempts to do the same with Alda, yet she, who has invested much more of her resources in the traveler, doesn't let him get away with it. The *serranas*' behavior is ritualistic, as James F. Burke, L. Jenaro MacLennan, and Louise O. Vasvári have pointed out. The *serranas* act in accordance with the cult of St. Águeda or Agatha, on whose feast day, February 5, women attack men:

> las mujeres acometen a los transeúntes, pegándoles si se resisten al baile. . .; se hacen cuestaciones: maltratan al dador pinchándole si la donación no satisface; le suben a hombros y le pasean, si les agrada. . .las mozas. . .molestan a los forasteros también con golpes y pellizcos, obsequiándolos después con bailes.

> Women attack passers-by, beating them if they refuse to dance. . .they collect money for charities: they abuse the donors, sticking them with needles if their contribution isn't enough; they lift men to their shoulders and walk with them, if they want to. . .young women. . .bother outsiders too with blows and pinches, then favor them with dances.

According to the ritual, men must play along, suffer the abuse with patience, and obey the women's demands. In this case, the male protagonist either doesn't understand the ritual and so cannot perform his assigned role, or he refuses to do so. The *serranas* force the narrator-protagonist to play out his assigned role through abusive language and acts; while their abuse may be ritual, it hurts, and the protagonist responds appropriately.[23]

That the narrator-protagonist assumes various identities in this sequence is a critical commonplace; the fact that the *serranas* interpellate him, assigning him an identity in accordance with the game, has received less attention. Marina Scordilis Brownlee acknowledges that the female characters label the narrator-protagonist:

> In *serrana* episode I the male figure who is confronted by "La Chata" is identified as an *escudero* (961b): "Alahé' diz' 'escudero. . . .'" In II he is an

anonymous *hombre* (identified as "sandío" in v. 991i, and as "roín, gaho, envernizo" in v. 992c) whom Gadea de Riofrío meets. Of the four, this second episode is the only one in which the traveller is not identified by his vocation—nonetheless, he is not identified as *arcipreste*, either. In III the masculine protagonist with whom Menga Llorente engages in conversation is a *pastor* (994a): "Pregontóme muchas cosas, cuidóse que era pastor." Since she believes him to be a *pastor*, he takes on the identity of one. . . .Finally, in IV he is an *hidalgo* (1031b): " 'Fidalgo', diz'. . . ." No explanation is given for these changes.[24]

Brownlee does not further develop the implications of the fact that the *serranas* confer these identities upon the narrator-protagonist. Aside from demonstrating the *serranas'* control of these interactions—and even Menga is in control of the negotiating dialogue, if not of the narrator-protagonist's subsequent behavior—their interpellation of him underlines yet further the ritualistic or game quality of their behavior, that is, of the performative nature of it. They behave as they do in order to comply with a certain set of rules; these rules explain the presence of the male traveler in a way that makes him comprehensible to the *serranas*. In order to get what he wants from them, the narrator-protagonist must play by their rules, an aspect of the game that he resents yet must accept.

The narrator-protagonist takes advantage of the dual nature of the roles he plays within the lyric to split his self into different characters, that of the identity-shifting protagonist who plays with the *serranas* and that of the narrator who comments on both characters' performances. The narration is biased, explaining and justifying the protagonist's behavior to his urban audience and downplaying the *serranas'* self-awareness. The protagonist performs fear and submission to La Chata, Gadea, and Alda while the narrator refuses to play such a role, voicing his scorn of the dominant women. These three *serranas* succeed in their performance of aggression and power, intimidating the protagonist to such an extent that he does not attack them physically. La Chata's ironic interpellation of the protagonist as *escudero* (squire) underlines his decision not to attack her. In their interaction, she instructs him in the rules of the game they are playing. First she informs him of her role, then when he doesn't respond as he should, she spells out to him his role:

> ≪A la he≫, diz, ≪escudero,
> aquí estaré yo queda
> fasta que algo me prometas;
> por mucho que te arremetas,
> non pasarás la vereda. ≫ (961c–g)

"By my fay," she said; "Squire, I'll stand right here until you promise me something; no matter how much you charge, you won't get through this path."

When he refuses to promise her something (and she demands mere verbal compliance, since in the end he doesn't give her material goods), she beats him, demonstrating her refusal to let him pass without playing/paying: "Págam', si non verás juego" (964d, Pay me, or else you'll see how I play).[25] The protagonist in response tries a different strategy, flattery and a request to "estar al fuego" (964g, be near her fire); this request, like his first statement that he was heading to "Sotosalvos" (960b), is a code for sex, one less veiled to modern eyes. La Chata's response encourages him in this new strategy, letting him know he's performing better, yet she still insists, "prometme algo, / e tenerte he por fidalgo" (965ef, promise me something and I'll consider you a gentleman). This second interpellation is also ironic, implying that, if he plays along with her she'll treat him as a nobleman, an identity that she is well aware is only temporarily assigned as part of the game. In both the *cuaderna vía* narration and the lyric account of this encounter, the protagonist's promise to her is indirectly cited, as though to underline his mere compliance with the form of the game, since of course he doesn't have items to give her with him. She, happy that he is finally playing along, takes him to her cabin, feeds him, and beds him. They both get what they want, as the narrator ironically comments: "Creet que fiz buen barato" (971g; believe me, I got a good deal). As with the abusive dialogue in Sebastián de Horozco's "Dama de gentil aseo" discussed in chapter 3, this game is a prelude to the sex act, as is the erotic food they consume. La Chata is fully aware this is a game and she demands that the protagonist play along in order to license their intercourse.[26]

A similar game sequence underlies all four encounters; what changes is the narrator-protagonist's attitude toward the subservient role he must play. His encounter with Gadea de Riofrío goes less well for both players. The protagonist attempts to assert dominance by interpellating her as a "serrana fallaguera" (975c, affectionate mountain-girl) in the *cuaderna vía* account and as a "cuerpo tan guisado" (988f, quite shapely body) in the lyric version, and by requesting sex. In response, she insults him, calling him "sandío" (976a, crazy) and "radío" (988i; astray), and strikes him for his impudence. When he complains at this abusive treatment, she responds, "non te ensañes del juego" (979c, don't let this game make you angry), meaning that her abuse is just part of the game and that she'll feed him and sleep with him if he's a good sport. Their interaction is mainly a negotiation over how the game is played. When she wants to bed him immediately, he protests, commenting, "si ante non comiese, non podría bien luchar" (982c, if I don't eat first, I won't be able to fight [i.e., perform sexually] well), arguing that, in the game sequence, eating comes before intercourse. Similarly, her demand that they have sex twice is excessive, a violation of the rules, as he protests:

> Rogóme que fincase con ella esa tarde,
> ca mala es de amatar el estopa de que arde;
> díxele yo: ≪Estó de priessa, ¡sí Dios de mal me guarde!≫
> Assañóse contra mí, resçelé e fui covarde (984).

She begged me to stay with her all afternoon, because it's hard to smother tinder that's on fire; I said to her, "I'm in a rush, may God protect me from evil!" She got mad at me, I felt suspicious and became afraid.

He resists and then, in response to her anger, performs fear and submission; as Louise Vasvári has shown, the "dos senderos" (985a, two paths) she then shows him are her two sexual orifices, "anbos son bien usados e anbos son camineros" (985b, both are well used and both well trod), meaning that she insisted he perform again. "Andit lo más que pud aína los oteros" (985c, I went as fast as I could over the heights); he exerted himself to comply with her demands.[27]

The encounter with Menga differs significantly from the other three in that the protagonist most fully plays the role assigned to him, that of a *pastor*; yet, he also refuses to play the game to the end, abruptly breaking off the encounter just before they get to the turning point, the moment she brings him to her cabin. The narrator expresses great satisfaction in this encounter, as the protagonist verbally dominates Menga, interpellating her as "hermana" (997g, sister), an identity she accepts and reinforces by calling him "pariente" (999a, cousin), although she questions "si [sabe] de sierra algo" (999b, if he knows anything of the *sierra*), showing her awareness that he's no shepherd. She plays along with him, accepting his performance as a *serrano* and complying with him by listing the gifts she demands for her hand/body (if, as Juan Cano Ballesta argues, by *casarse* she means, to have sex). Then the protagonist refuses to go any further, abruptly withdrawing from the conversation. The narrator's satisfaction with this encounter is parodic; he boasts of his success in not having sex with Menga, just as in RL 193 Joan Baveca refuses to let himself be tested by the two *soldadeiras* whose bath he watches, as discussed in chapter 2. If the protagonist had complete confidence in himself, he wouldn't "[fabla] en engaño" (1003g, speak deceitfully) as he does; his withdrawal is an act of cowardice, a fact the narrator tries to hide by insulting Menga as "lerda" (993c, stupid). Laura R. Bass's phallic reading of the name 'Menga' in Santillana's *serranilla* V/D3432 is relevant here; the *serrana*'s name connotes aggressive, dominant sexuality, suggesting that the traveler evades her out of fear.[28] If this is the *engaño* of which the protagonist boasts, then the irony is obvious: his is an anti-phallic boast, since he brags of his success in not sleeping with her. The narrator's self-congratulatory attitude may be as ironic as the anger he expresses in the *cuaderna vía* portion of the fourth encounter.

In the lyric portion of the final encounter, the protagonist once again tries to trick the *serrana* by interpellating her and entering into an extended negotiation. This time he asks for *posada* (1026e, lodging), promising to pay with *dineros* (1028d, money) instead of sex. Agreeing to his terms, Alda brings him to her cabin and feeds him; pleased with his performance, she calls him *fidalgo* (1031b), flattering him and offering him her bed, in compliance with the game, if he gives her gifts. He plays along, encouraging her to list her demands, which she does. At that moment, he tries to withdraw as he had done with Menga; but, the game has gone too far. He is in her cabin, he has eaten her food and engaged her in an extended negotiation; she will not allow him to abandon the game at this point. The narrator marks his anger at her move with the insult *heda* (1040a, ugly), the first insult in the lyric. She proceeds to lecture him on how the game is played, marking her dominance and refusing to be paid only with words; while she says *dineros* (1042c), she means sex, and, as his audience is aware, the protagonist's purse is empty (as mentioned earlier in st. 973). The narrator's account breaks off with Alda's lecture, because the end is predictable. The narrator gets his revenge beforehand, by portraying her as the most monstrous of the four *serranas*, in the *cuaderna vía* introduction. While his performance of anger is understandable, the audience is aware that the protagonist got into this situation on his own; he accosted her and refused to leave as she told him (1025). He pushed because he wanted to improve on his supposed success with Menga; he wanted to play more of the game and enjoy controlling their interaction for a longer time. By doing so he, like Gadea, demands too much, forcing Alda to resist the role he assigned her, that of the fool.

In all these encounters, it is the narrator who plays the fool, recounting tales of his humiliation in order to amuse his urban audience. The protagonist's experience in the *sierra* closely resembles that of the Archpriest in the Cruz episode discussed in chapter 3. In his recreation of these experiences, the narrator-performer complains of the abuse he receives and verbally abuses the other, absent characters. This performance of anger is part and parcel of his buffoonish identity; his anger amuses as much as his comic-satiric portrait of the *serrana*. My discussion of these four *serrana* episodes assumes a certain performance scenario, in which a single, male actor-singer performs the *cánticas* and uses gestures, movements, perhaps props, and voice modulations to differentiate between the three characters' parts (i.e., between the narrator, the male protagonist, and the female protagonist). It is possible that more performers participated, perhaps miming the two protagonists' actions while a soloist sang, perhaps providing musical accompaniment, perhaps even singing the different characters' lines; however, the format of this piece causes me to doubt that the performance would have been dialogic. The first-person narrative voice interrupts the characters' speeches with some frequency, reducing the likelihood that several actor-singers voiced the different characters' parts.[29] The focus of the lyrics is on role-playing, on how a single character can momentarily assume and act out various identities; this focus would be heightened if one actor-singer performed all three roles. As narrator, the performer would address the audience directly, interacting with and reacting to his public. In the role of the male protagonist, he would directly address the (imaginary) female protagonist and indirectly address the audience; he would perform exaggerated gestures (enacting fear, sexual arousal, pride, irony, etc.) before the *serrana* on the fictive level and before the audience at the metafictive level. His performance of both protagonists would be exaggerated and ironic, emphasizing the comic buffoonery of the male and the rusticity of the female. The *juglar* enacting the role of the identity-shifting narrator-protagonist would assume the guise of an archpriest to represent visually the narrator's 'official' identity and impersonate the behaviors that signify the other identities imposed upon and/or assumed by the protagonist, especially that of emasculated fool. These contradictory identity clues, especially the contrast between dress and gestures, would not only heighten the comedy, they would focus particular attention on the play with gender, bodies, and behaviors. The humiliated male protagonist performs more of a feminine act than do the phallic *serranas* who abuse him.

I expect that, in enacting the *serrana*, the actor-singer would also wink ironically at the audience, expressing the *serrana*'s awareness of the game they were all playing and encouraging the audience to laugh at the male protagonist. I agree with Jeanne Battesti that the *serrana*'s actual absence from the performance of the *cántica* helps support the narrative bias and promotes complicity between the performer and audience against the fictive *serrana*. Nonetheless, in Ruiz's *cánticas*, the *serranas*' patronizing stance toward the narrator-protagonist supports his buffoonish persona; the *serranas* also speak with an eye on the metapoetic audience, as does the male protagonist. Their words and actions are filtered through the narrator-protagonist; the *serranas* do not directly address the audience, unlike the narrator, nor were they able to respond to their fictive portrayal, unlike the *soldadeiras* discussed in chapter 2. In order to enhance the comic possibilities of the encounter and especially to encourage laughter at the foolish narrator-protagonist, the *serrana*-character must have established complicity with the audience. Clueing the audience into the ritualistic nature of her behavior was one way to do so; another was to mime violent attacks on the male protagonist, encouraging the audience to laugh at him. In these *cánticas*, the urban audience laughed at the rustic, savage *serrana* yet also at the foolish city-dweller who deserves to be punished for transgressing into the *sierras*. The audience's attitude toward all three characters was ambivalent; they laughed at yet also with all three, endorsing the *serranas*' violence as much as the narrator-protagonist's anger.

Performances of these *cánticas* may or may not have been framed with an explanatory narrative. Unlike Ramón Ménendez Pidal, I do not think the *cuaderna vía* portions would have been recited before the *cánticas* were sung. If they were included, I expect they would have been sung; their meter and melody would distinguish them from the *cánticas*.[30] In a live performance, however, the *cuaderna vía* portions would not have been necessary, as the *juglar* either presented the *cánticas* separately or filled in the gaps with a comic narration. I agree with R.B. Tate that the *cánticas* were pre-existent materials (either in whole or in part) that the author incorporated into an extensive and heterogeneous pseudo-autobiography. In order to construct a coherent narrative out of these four *cánticas*, he added the *cuaderna vía* bridges to explain the shift in locale and to create the impression that the narrator-protagonist is consistent with that of the rest of the book. The *cuaderna vía* section is highly literary, as is marked by stanza 996ab: "De quanto que pasó fize un cantar serrano, / éste deyuso escripto, que tienes so la mano" (I wrote a mountain song about what happened; it's written just below, you've got it under your hand). This comment refers to the physical book the reader holds in her or his hand, not to an ephemeral, oral performance. At the end of each of the *cuaderna vía* introductions, a similar reference appears that calls attention either to the book itself or to the witten, visual text on the page (in 958d, 986, 1021d). The fact that in the book these four *cánticas* form a sequence does not necessarily mean they were performed as a sequence. While this sequence could work well as an extended performance text, in practice the singer-actor would alter the text and presentation to suit the immediate context. This does not preclude presenting all four *cánticas* in order; however, such a performance is only one of many ways these *cánticas* could have been presented.

Although in his presentation of the *cánticas* the narrator asserts his verbal dominance of the *serranas*, during the encounter the *serranas* verbally and physically dominate the male protagonist. The narrator-protagonist depicts the *serranas* as interpellating him, assigning him a role that he must enact, and he plays along, making himself a commodity that they consume. The narrator attempts to turn the tables, commodifying the *serranas* and presenting them (and himself as narrator-protagonist) for the consumption of his urban audience/readership. His audience made their own use of his use of the figure of the *serrana*; while Ruiz preferred to enact the role of victim and butt of laughter, his fifteenth-century consumers rewrote his adventures in ways that reflected their sense of place in the political and erotic landscape. Juan Ruiz as an urban *clérigo ajuglarado* (entertainer-cleric, or goliard) plays with the performative nature of identity in order to invert and mock normative hierarchies, of place, of profession, and of gender. The Marqués de Santillana makes a very different use of the *serrana*; he makes them a stage upon which he enacts his privilege and social superiority. The spirit of game and the pleasure of role-playing pervade the Marqués's *serranillas*, as in the *Libro de buen amor*. Santillana's male narrator-protagonist, always a *cavallero*, verbally dominates the *serrana* he interpellates; he even resorts to violence to defend his sense of self and privilege when threatened by Menga de Mançanares. Santillana uses the *serrana* to act out his territorial claims and his class identity; often his poetic persona privileges the performance of gentility over sexual conquest, respecting the *serrana*'s refusal of his attentions. Unlike Ruiz, who depicts his protagonist as the hapless victim of voracious viragos, Santillana emphasizes his protagonist's control of the encounter and his choice to respect the *serrana* or to put her in her place. The Marqués may endow his *serranas* with voices and attitudes that challenge the male protagonist, yet they do not represent a substantive threat to his status or person. They engage with him, playing a role that supports his performance of social, sexual, and geographic superiority.

The *Serranillas* of the Marqués de Santillana: Claiming Contested Landscapes

In the eight *serranillas* composed by Íñigo López de Mendoza, Lord of Hita and Buitrago, first Marqués de Santillana (1398–1458), the location of the encounter between the poetic 'I' and the *serrana* is personally meaningful. A member of one of the most powerful families of Spain and an active player in the Aragonese-Castilian conflicts discussed in chapter 3, Santillana is best known now for his literary works; he was perhaps the most productive, and certainly the most famous, poet of fifteenth-century Castile. Modern readers often find his *serranillas* the most interesting and aesthetically pleasing of his lyric works. He sets these light, occasional pieces in sites marked by a historical conflict over land with familial, political, and/or cultural significance. The correspondence between Santillana's personal history and his use of certain toponyms enable critics to date his *serranillas*. For example, the "Moçuela de Bores" (IV/D3431), located in the valley of Liébana, is usually read as a record of the Marqués's visit during 1434, occasioned by continual conflicts over land between the house of Mendoza and that of Manrique. The question of land symbolism in this poem can be complemented with the reading offered by Nicolás Bratosevich of the roles played by both the male protagonist and *serrana*, roles that serve the interests of the courtly audience who watches, and judges, the present performance of the narrator-protagonist. As Bratosevich suggests, in the fictive world both characters pretend and both are aware that the other is pretending, an awareness that affects their interaction and also the audience's reaction to their dialogue. While the *moçuela* overtly refuses to enact the role of *dama* that the protagonist assigns her, she tacitly does play that role. She is complicit in her conquest, if we read his success with her as analogous to Santillana's success in asserting his power over the landscape.[31]

The encounter between the *moçuela* and the poetic 'I' occurs near La Lama; this word rhymes with *llama, dama, fama, brama*, Frama and Espinama (flame, lady, fame, the lowing of cattle; Frama and Espinama are villages in the Liébana), key words that illustrate the contrast between the court and the country. This contrast, however, is illusory; as Nicolás Bratosevich notes, courtly values completely infuse this poem, such that the country mirrors the court. In this encounter, as in only one other of Santillana's *serranillas* (I/D3429), the narrator and *serrana* negotiate a mutual agreement, consummated in a delicate yet overt image of coitus. The narrator's tale of a sexual adventure in the *sierras*, addressed to a courtly audience of *amadores* and *señores*, construes sex as conquest. Through his depiction of sexual congress with the *moçuela de Bores*, the narrator demonstrates his cultural, political, sexual, and poetic superiority over other men. Within the fiction of the poem his rivals are the two peasant *pastores* who compete for the *vaquera*'s hand; in the social world within which the Marqués disseminates his fiction, his rivals are the Manrique clan and especially Garci González de Orejón, the resident of La Lama who so molested the Marqués.[32] The nonviolent conclusion to the dialogue between *serrana* and protagonist marks the Marqués's assertion of his right of dominion: this land belongs to him, and while he must flatter and cajole in order to get what he wants, he does so without serious resistance. Also noteworthy is the fact that the narrator does not justify his presence in this locale, unlike in other Santillana *serranillas* where the narrator is stationed on the frontier (I/D3429, II/D3430, VI/D3433, VII/D3434), traveling (III/D2427, V/D3432, VIII/D3435), or hunting (X/D1855). In "Moçuela de Bores," the narrator-protagonist does not feel the need to explain his presence; he is present in order to assert his rights of ownership.

Boastful self-assertion is the narrator's principal interest in this poem. As I mentioned above when I cited the first stanza, the narrator is too old to participate in the game of love, but he can still effectively deploy its language and has a thing or two to teach the *amadores* who witness his poetic performance. The narrator's attitude toward the countryside is highly equivocal; although he revels in the opportunity to play the role of a lover once again, he implicitly sneers at the object of his desire and her rustic appearance:

> Mas ví la fermosa
> de buen continente,
> la cara plaziente,
> fresca como rosa,
> de tales colores
> qual nunca vi dama
> nin otra, señores. (vv. 11–17)

> But I saw the beautiful girl, good-tempered, with a pleasing face, fresh like a rose, of such colors as I had never seen in a lady or other woman, gentlemen.

The speaker constructs her as natural with his comment, "fresca como rosa" (v. 14); this image combined with her location in the Liébana further her identification with the countryside. While she is beautiful, his comment on her color is equivocal, implying that she, unlike other women he's seen, is *morena*; her condition as a *serrana* had already made her an unfit object of courtly love.[33] He constructs her as an object of his gaze who only serves to satisfy male desires, and he proceeds to find her desirable; this desire moves him to speak with her:

> Por lo qual: «Señora,»
> le dixe, «en verdad
> la vuestra beldad
> saldrá desd'agora
> dentr'estos alcores,
> pues meresçe fama
> de grandes loores.» (vv. 18–24)

> Because of which: "Lady," I said to her, "truly from this moment your beauty will travel beyond these hills, since it merits fame and great praise."

He accosts her, addressing her courteously as *señora*, and praises her beauty as deserving fame beyond their immediate location. This speech communicates to her her status as an object of the elite male gaze and his power to publicize her beauty, power that should make her welcome his attentions.

Her response is negative although courteous. She calls him *cavallero* and herself *vaquera*, marking the difference in their status and her refusal to play the role of *señora* that he has assigned her:

> Dixo: «Cavallero,
> tiradvos afuera,
> dexad la vaquera

passar all otero;
ca dos labradores
me piden de Frama,
entrambos pastores.≫ (vv. 25–31)

She said: "Knight, step aside; allow the cowgirl to pass to the hillock; because
two laborers from Frama woo me, both of them shepherds."

Her request that he let her pass configures him as an obstacle that blocks
her way; this configuration plays with the tradition of the *serrana salteadora*
that we see in both La Chata and Gadea, who leap out at the male traveler,
and anticipates the parody of this tradition in "Menga de Mançanares."
In this case, it is the *cavallero* who is the aggressor with whose desires the
serrana must contend. She refers to herself in the third person, as a *vaquera*,
in contrast to *cavallero*; identifying her lovers as *labradores* and *pastores* further
underlines her refusal to play the role of a *señora*. Saying that she is desired
by two men lets him know that others outside of La Lama do in fact know
of and admire her, dismissing the fame that he has offered to confer upon
her. This is the only speech she makes in the poem; nor does the narrator
include any description of her actions or gestures, such that the audience
has very little access to her. This lack of detail suggests she is only of interest as an object of desire, not as a character. The narrator cites her refusal,
but later implies that she consented; he treats her as a secondary character
who is worthy of interest only due to her beauty and her location in a certain geographic site.[34]

The speaker, in response to her refusal, continues addressing her as *señora*
and offers to transform himself into a *pastor* if that state is more pleasing to
her. He offers to serve her as though he were a courtly lover, declaring that
he will prefer animal noises to a nightingale's song:

≪Señora, pastor
seré, si queredes:
mandarme podedes
como a servidor;
mayores dulçores
será a mí la brama
que oír ruiseñores.≫ (vv. 32–38)

"Lady, I will be a shepherd if you want; you can command me, like a servant;
the bellowing of bulls will be more pleasant to me than to hear nightingales."

Nicolás Bratosevich suggests that the courtly audience would read the narrator's inversion of normative courtly values as comic and his stance in this
stanza as ironic. I agree, but I read the significance of the narrator's

comment differently. *Brama*, as Miguel Ángel Pérez Priego indicates in his gloss, refers to the bellowing made by bulls, stags, and other animals in heat; nightingales conventionally represent courtly love songs. While the narrator presents himself as listening to these sounds, in fact at the moment he is singing like a nightingale and would prefer to be bellowing like a rutting bull, with the *vaquera* playing the role of *vaca*. The narrator covers his unacceptable desires with psuedo-delicate imagery, in the final stanza:

> Assí concluimos
> el nuestro proçesso,
> sin façer exçesso,
> e nos avenimos.
> E fueron las flores
> de cabe Espinama
> los encubridores. (vv. 39–45)

In brief, we concluded our proceedings and came to an agreement. And the flowers near Espinama covered up for us.

The flowers that function as their "encubridores" equivocally cover their coitus and serve as *encubridores*, *alcahuetes* or go-betweens that facilitate their extramarital relations.[35] Santillana's witty combination of courtly conventions and crude imagery is didactic, teaching *amadores* how to speak to *vaqueras*; it is also a *tour de force*, displaying his poetic and sexual conquests that correspond to his political achievements, defending his domain and position as the Señor de La Liébana.

Nicolás Bratosevich suggests that the narrator and *serrana* read their interaction as a game and that each adopts roles and strategies in accordance with this game. The *moçuela*, aware of the rules of courtly love that prescribe that the lady resist the attempt at seduction, plays hard to get; her negative response is false, a mere move to prolong their dialogue and comply with the demands of the game. The narrator is aware of the *moçuela's* awareness; his false promise to turn *pastor* indicates his awareness that her refusal was false; thus they collaborate in sustaining the fiction that each believes the other is sincere, while both know the other is not. This reading highlights the game aspect of the *serranilla*, which pervades even the characters' attitude toward the fictive encounter. The game aspect underlines Santillana's use of the *serranilla* to displace and fictionalize conflicts between noble factions. Situating his poetic persona's sexual exploits in this territory constructs the body of the *serrana* as land; herself from Bores, located in La Lama, desired in Frama, and deflowered near Espinama, she represents the extent of the Liébana and consents to her possession by Santillana's alter ego. The use of these place names, the significance of which the Marqués's audience would certainly appreciate, justify his aggressive self-display; this poem amounts to a phallic boast, not as overt as those found in the *Cantigas d'escarnho*, but nonetheless a proud demonstration of phallic and poetic mastery.[36]

Santillana's alter ego plays a very different role in another *serranilla* with significant topographic features, "Menga de Mançanares" (V/D3432). In this encounter, both protagonists assume a knightly role, as Menga challenges the *cavallero* to fight. Her pose ironically reflects that assumed by the *cavallero* in the previous poem; not only did the *moçuela de Bores* read him as barring her way, a stance that Menga overtly assumes in this poem, but Menga assumes the knightly role that he rejected in favor of that of *pastor*. Class inversion, Menga's behavior suggests, can work both ways, an attitude that Santillana's poetic persona rejects. While the Marqués limits the *moçuela*'s volition, making her a mostly complacent object of desire, he endows Menga with volition almost equal to that of Ruiz's *serranas*. Ruiz, of course, named one of his *serranas* Menga, admittedly a frequent name for *pastoras* in Castilian poetry; two others, La Chata and Gadea de Riofrío, demand sex using the euphemism *luchar*. These similarities suggest that part of Santillana's agenda in this composition, as perhaps in all of his *serranillas*, is to rewrite Ruiz's *cánticas de serrana*. His revisions are highly significant, especially since in this instance an act akin to rape occurs.[37]

In this poem, the place names resonate with personal significance as well. As José Terrero says, "El valle del Manzanares. . .era un valle de su señorío, un dominio suyo que había permanecido en secuestro varios años, y del que logró verse en posesión en 1442" (the valley of Manzanares. . .was a valley in his domain, a region of his that had remained sequestered for various years, which he succeeded taking possession of in 1442). Terrero suggests this poem was composed to commemorate the favorable resolution of this conflict. Laura Bass argues that this land dispute was resolved earlier: "Upon [his father's] death in 1404, the young Íñigo López de Mendoza was to have inherited the land, but his half-sister and her husband disputed his rights to it in a legal battle that would not be resolved until 1435 when López de Mendoza won possession of the territory." Our poet was granted the title Conde de Manzanares as well as his most famous title, first Marqués de Santillana, in 1445 after the Battle of Olmedo. Miguel Ángel Pérez Priego dates this poem to between 1430 and 1438, Rafael Lapesa to 1423. The Marqués uses this setting to refer to the land dispute as well as to his own identity as the owner of this particular piece of land. The fact that in this dispute he was opposed by a powerful woman is not coincidental; as Bass comments, "it comprises a lyric space in which the poet tropes the battle over the estate as a struggle of gender-power relations."[38] In the poem, Menga asserts her dominance of this valley and of those who attempt to enter it; her stance implies that she and the *cavallero* are social equals, denying the significance of gender and class inequalities.

Before proceeding further in my discussion, I shall cite the entire poem:

> Por todos estos pinares
> nin en val de la Gamella
> non vi serrana más bella
> que Menga de Mançanares.
>
> Desçendiendo 'l yelmo ayuso,
> contra Bóvalo tirando,
> en esse valle de suso
> vi serrana estar cantando;
> saluéla, segund es uso,
> e dixe: ≪Serrana, estando
> oyendo, yo non m'escuso
> de fazer lo que mandares.≫
>
> Respondióme con ufana:
>   ≪Bien vengades, cavallero,
> ¿quién vos trae de mañana
> por este valle señero?
> Ca por toda aquesta llana
> yo non dexo andar vaquero,
> nin pastora nin serrana,
> sinon Pascual de Bustares.
>
> Pero ya, pues la ventura
> por aquí vos ha traído,
> convien'en toda figura,
> sin ningund otro partido,
> que me dedes la çintura
> o entremos a braz partido,
> ca dentro en esta espesura
> vos quiero luchar dos pares.≫
>
> Desque vi que non podía
> partirme d'allí sin daña,
> como aquel que non sabía
> de luchar arte nin maña,
> con muy grand malenconía
> arméle tal guadramaña
> que cayó con su porfía
> çerca d'unos tomellares.

In all these pine groves nor in the valley of Gamella have I seen a more beautiful *serrana* than Menga of Manzanares.

Walking through the wilderness, heading toward Bóvalo, in the lower valley I saw a *serrana* singing. I greeted her, as is customary, and said, "Serrana, listening to you, I can't excuse myself from doing whatever you demand."

She answered me arrogantly:"Welcome, knight; who brings you through this isolated valley so early in the morning? I don't allow anyone to pass through all this plain, not cowboy, shepherdess or *serrana*, except Pascual de Bustares.

But, since luck has brought you this way, by all means it's fit, without any other terms, that you give me a girdle or we wrestle, since in this thicket I want to fight two rounds with you."

When I saw that I couldn't leave there without injury, like he who doesn't know the art or tricks of fighting, with great anger I launched a sneak attack on her so that she fell along with her stubbornness near some thyme plants.

The number of contradictory elements in this *serranilla* makes it highly ironic; nonetheless, the narrator-protagonist clearly asserts his mastery of Menga and the landscape. On one level Menga's challenge doesn't make sense, namely, on the sexual level. The pass she defends is that between her legs as much as the actual valley. Pascual de Bustares, the one she does allow to pass, is her lover; all others she forbids access to the pass and to her body. Then, in the next stanza, she demands sex. I read this apparent contradiction as part of the game in which she tries to engage the *cavallero*; like La Chata and Gadea, Menga de Mançanares tries to establish the rules of engagement and to impose a certain role upon the male protagonist. Her objective is not to avoid sex but to dominate whomever she meets. In response, Santillana's *cavallero* both plays along and resists complying with her desires. He complies with her demand that he fight, but first he pretends to be afraid and unskilled at fighting; the irony of his initial performance as one who didn't know the art or *maña* of fighting is underlined with his sudden, and successful, *guadramaña*. By fighting her as she demands, he fulfills his courtly offer to obey her; he also demonstrates his skill at unarmed fighting and dominates her, wrestling her into sexual submission.[39]

Both protagonists try to claim the same role, that of a *cavallero*, a problem from the male character's point of view. He asserts his identity as a *cavallero* in his speech, dress, and mannerisms; he offers to serve Menga as a courtly lover due to the beauty of her song, a performance he construes as appropriate for a compliant object of the male gaze. To counterbalance and substantiate his identity, he imposes upon her the role of a rustic *dama*, and he interpellates her as a *serrana*. The Marqués has Menga interpret the role of *serrana* resistantly. For her, the *serrana* is not an object of desire but a subject; playing that role enables her to fight with him, acting as the defender of a pass, a role played by *cavalleros* in courtly *pasos de armas*. *Serranas salteadoras* such as La Chata and Gadea also play this role, yet do so in order to assert their independence from town and seigniorial authority structures. Menga does so in order to insert herself into the seigniorial structure and to claim a place within it, not as an inferior to the Conde de Manzanares but on top of him. She calls the male character *cavallero* (v. 14) and doesn't label herself with any particular identity; but, her language suggests that she considers them equals. She challenges him in order to demonstrate her dominance of the valley of Manzanares, dominance that she has repeatedly demonstrated by preventing the passage of *vaqueros, pastoras,* and *serranas.* From his point of view, this information is insulting; she constructs him as equal to the peasants of both genders she has defeated. The almost casual way she phrases her challenge is intentional, a citation of ritual challenges delivered in *pasos de armas.* Menga's language parodies knightly vows of honor and love-service, underlining her appropriation of a masculine and aristocratic role.

Pasos de armas were large-scale courtly entertainments that made a virtue of ostentation and self-display. Amancio Labandeira Fernández explains the *pasos'* rules and the roles assumed by participants:

> En el paso es preciso que haya un mantenedor, quien, situado en un lugar fijo, prohíba el acceso a todos los caballeros que intenten aproximarse al lugar por él defendido. El defensor o mantenedor del paso debe publicar con antelación el reglamiento de la prueba (capítulos), y al ser éste aceptado por los caballeros, se convierten en «aventureros», obligándose en su aventura de conquista a luchar con el mantenedor que les «cierra el paso.»[40]

> In the pass [of arms] there must be a maintainer who, located in a fixed place, prohibits access to all the knights who wish to approach the place he is defending. The defender or maintainer of the pass should publish in advance the rules for the test (chapters), and upon these rules being accepted by the knights, they become "challengers," pledging to fight with the maintainer who "closes the pass" against them, in a trial of conquest.

Ritual combats that brought to life literary motifs, *pasos* were often linked to the game of courtly love, especially in the case of the most famous fifteenth-century example, that of Suero de Quiñones' *Passo honroso* (1434). A *paso* also could serve to display political power; the *Paso de la Fuerte Ventura* (Hard Luck Pass) held in Valladolid in 1428 marked the transition of power from the Infantes de Aragón back to Álvaro de Luna, who had recently returned to Castile after a brief exile. The challenge on that occasion was issued by a *dama* enacting the part of *Ventura* (Chance), who said, "Cavalleros, ¿qué ventura vos traxo a este tan peligroso passo, que se llama de la Fuerte Ventura? Cúnplevos que vos volbades; si non, non podredes pasar syn justa" (Knights, what chance brought you to this very dangerous pass, which is called Hard Luck Pass? It is in your best interest to turn back; if not, you will not be able to pass without jousting). Our poet participated in this *paso* as a judge; he could well have had *Ventura*'s speech in mind when he put similar language into Menga's mouth. In another *paso de armas* held in 1459, the ritual challenge was issued by "ciertos salvajes que no consentían entrar á los caballeros é gentiles hombres que llevasen damas de la rienda, sin que prometiesen de hacer con él [Beltrán de la Cueva, Enrique IV's *privado*] seis carreras, é si no quisiesen justar, que dexasen el guante derecho" (some wild men who wouldn't allow knights and noblemen who lead ladies on horseback to enter the pass, unless they promised to fight six passes with him; if they refused to joust, they had to leave their right glove). The glove served as a token of the knights' humiliation and cowardice, as they admitted defeat rather than trying themselves against the defender of the pass.[41]

Menga parodies this ritualistic language in her challenge, combining the rhetorical question of the first example with the demand for a symbolic garment in the second. Her demand for a *cintura* (belt or girdle) challenges the *cavallero*'s honor and symbolically emasculates him. Menga poses as the *defensora* of this valley, treating the male protagonist as an *aventurero* who has come to prove himself in combat with her. The form of combat is not chivalric, as neither is mounted nor carries spear or sword; Menga's choice of unarmed wrestling marks her as a *salvaje*, like La Chata and Gadea. She performs monstrosity in the contrast between her initial, highly feminized and idealized appearance, idly singing in the green valley, and the aggressive, conventionally masculine pose she assumes in response to the *cavallero*. Her speech is thoroughly informed by courtly culture, yet her identity as a *pastora* has caused the parodic force of her language and behavior to pass mostly unnoticed.[42] Her gender and sexuality infuse erotic connotations into a chivalric formula, making it speak doubly, expressing her desires for sex and for mastery over her partner/opponent.

The *cavallero* responds to Menga's challenge equivocally, first pretending to be incompetent and reluctant, then suddenly attacking; he performs fear in order to gain an advantage over her. Ironically, his strategy parallels that of Maria Balteira in RL 331, discussed in chapter 2. In this case, the male protagonist adopts a weak, inferior pose which he then belies by performing aggressive, violent masculinity. In effect, he mimics Menga, who in the narrator-protagonist's eyes had initially performed femininity and then adopted a masculine pose with her challenge to *luchar*. The narrator presents the male protagonist's performance as defensive, hers as deceptive. He considers her performance unnatural because it violates normative gender and class roles, and he punishes her for transgressing against identity limitations. Santillana's point is, while he has the right to assume different roles in order to surmount obstacles that frustrate his attempts to achieve his desires, Menga, and implicitly all *serranas*, do not have that right. His class and gender shifts reflect his social power; Menga's reflect her desire to obtain power that Santillana refuses to allow her to have. The narrator-protagonist's performance enables him to dominate her, and with her, Manzanares. He asserts not merely his right of access to the valley but also to her body; rape is a weapon in class, gender, and territorial warfare, and he uses it to emasculate and subjugate Menga.

As a revision of Ruiz's *cánticas de serrana*, "Menga de Mançanares" attests to Santillana's appreciation of the social, sexual, and political implications of transgressive gender performances and of erotic topography, two key elements of the *serranilla*. The Marqués endows Menga with volition in order to be able to punish her for her unruly behavior, unlike Ruiz, who grants his *serranas* volition so that they can victimize him. Santillana uses this poem to claim a position of superiority, on top of Menga, of Manzanares, and of Ruiz as well. While the Marqués does allow his poetic persona to play the role of object of desire in I/D3429, "La serrana de Boxmediano," and in IV/D3431, "La moçuela de Bores," he refuses to allow him to be dominated sexually by any *serrana*. Ruiz's alter ego, on the other hand, is repeatedly dominated and subjected to sexual assault. Menga Lloriente is the only *serrana* that he manages to dominate, and that because he plays the role of a *serrano*; she is also the only *serrana* with whom he does not have sex. An irony of Santillana's use of the name Menga for the one *serrana* his persona rapes is the inversion of Ruiz's *cánticas de serrana*. Not only does Santillana's alter ego rape her, but he refuses to negotiate verbally; the *cavallero* is silent in response to Menga's challenge, instead using force to make the argument for him. In his other *serranillas*, Santillana's persona respects the words of the *serrana*, either engaging her in dialogue or desisting after her refusal of him. Ruiz's alter ego never fights back but always tries to talk his way out of trouble, succeeding only with Menga Lloriente. "Menga de Mançanares" illustrates the Marqués's poetic, political, and personal stakes in the *serranilla*: unlike Ruiz's buffoonish and emasculated narrator-protagonist, Santillana stages his superiority over the forces of nature, over land, over peasantry, and over women.

In his portrayal of Menga de Mançanares as a parodic knight, Santillana could be alluding to another literary precedent, the satiric *obra* of Alfonso el Sabio, particularly his portrayal of Dominga Eanes as a Christian warrior taking on a Moorish *genete* in JP 41, discussed in chapter 2. The motif of the *soldadeira* at war occurs with some frequency in Galician-Portuguese satiric lyrics; to my knowledge no one has explored the influence of this motif on the portrayal of *serranas*. Ramón Menéndez Pidal noted the great influence of Galician-Portuguese *pastorelas* on the *serranilla*, especially in the *pastora*'s almost invariable refusal to satisfy the sexual desires of the male traveler; however, his discussion of the *serrana guerrera* draws only on *serranas* (one Galician-Portuguese, the controversial "Serrana de Cintra," sixteenth-century Portuguese lyrics by Gil Vicente, and the Ruiz's four "serranas de Guadarrama") and does not consider more broadly the mock-heroic treatment of women warriors. Menéndez Pidal does consider the Marqués's "Serrana de Boxmediano," "Vaquera de Morana," and "Menga de Mançanares" (I/D3429, II/D3430, V/D3432) to be *serranas guerreras*; he does not consider these *serranas* mock knights, suggesting instead that this character reflected the historical roles played by mountain women. Laura Bass explores the intersection of gender, geography, and class in I/D3429, II/D3430 and V/D3432 and especially male aristocratic domination over feminized landscapes; still, she does not read Menga as adopting knightly behaviors in her challenge to the *cavallero*. Given that "Menga" derives from "Dominga," I am tempted to argue for the direct influence of Alfonso's poem on Santillana's *serranilla*. Unfortunately, the evidence is lacking, especially since a comment in his *Proemio e carta* implies that the Marqués had not read any of Alfonso's *dezires*. Bass suggests that the phallic connotations of "Menga" may have determined Santillana's choice of name; this connotation may inform Alfonso's *Cantigas d'escarnho* as well. Certainly the image of the woman warrior was far from unknown to Santillana, although he portrays them more often as idealized huntresses in the courts of Diana or Venus. Given the *serranilla*'s general tendency to subvert or invert courtly commonplaces, Santillana's portrayal of *serranas guerreras* and especially that of Menga de Mançanares presents the other side of the virgin huntress, an upstart peasant woman who challenges the aristocratic *cavallero*'s proper social, gender, and political superiority.[43]

The *cavallero* can put this degraded and aggressive woman in her place through overt sexual violence, unlike the courtly *damas* to whom he must defer. As Laura Bass says, "Santillana [created] Menga. . .to provide an excuse for challenging more generally the power of women in courtly lyric." Here Bass draws on the work of Kathryn Gravdal, who has shown that in the French *pastourelle* peasant women, unlike aristocratic ladies, are able to talk back to the knight yet pay for their verbal power by suffering rape. I would tie the *cavallero*'s choice to rape Menga to several factors: her speech, her appropriation of the *cavallero*'s role, and her posing as equal, if not superior, to her aristocratic opponent. We should also remember that, in the world of pastoral sex, rape was not merely a demonstration of masculine superiority but a pleasurable sexual experience for the *pastora*: "The pastourelle often shows rape not as a form of violence but as a form of sex, and therefore of female pleasure."[44] Santillana's *cavallero*, in raping Menga, complies with her demands for sex, especially for the type of aggressive phallic sexuality we see in the *Cantigas d'escarnho* and in the *Libro de buen amor*. While Santillana does configure this attack as punishing and castrating Menga, he also constructs it as pleasurable with the image of the crushed thyme bushes. The *serranilla*, as much as Santillana's extended narrative *decires* and witty courtly *coplas*, are aristocratic exercises; they differ from the other genres in that in the *serranilla* he can dispense with the normative restraints of appropriate conduct and vaunt his virility, forcing his audience to play the role of witness to his poetic demonstrations of superiority.

In his performance of this song before an audience of fellow courtiers, the Marqués enacted three roles, those of the narrator, the male protagonist, and Menga. His performance of the two male roles ironically played with the disparities between these fictive characters and Santillana's established identity as an able warrior, courtier, and poet. The irony of the protagonist's pose as an incompetent fighter would provoke laughter; this pose is so clearly feigned that it would create the expectation for him to attack, an expectation he quickly fulfills. The narrator's excuses in the final stanza show his awareness that the protagonist's actions are offensive and transgressive; the narrator dissociates himself from the protagonist's behavior, couching it in so many qualifiers that he is able to deny that his actions define his character (and I deliberately use this string of ambiguous possessive adjectives to underline the blurring of roles in performance). These excuses are ironic: his audience, fellow courtiers whose aristocratic identity was based in part on their ability as warriors and in part on the privileges due to them by birth, laughed at the sexual violence as much as at his depiction of Menga as a would-be *cavallero*. In his impersonation of Menga, the Marqués exaggerated both her femininity and her use of chivalric language; I expect he would proclaim vv. 21–27 like the ritual challenges issued before *pasos de armas*, emphasizing the citational quality of her speech, that is, her citation of chivalric formulas and his citation of her. These several layers of cited speech made his performance both very suggestive and very comic. The protagonist's choice not to reply verbally (a choice the narrator expressed verbally) is the only response that could silence Menga, given her proven ability to twist knights' words, challenging their verbal authority. His attack asserts a different, more concrete basis for his privilege, namely, more successful performance on the field of combat. In impersonating his protagonist's acts, the Marqués acted out his own privilege; and, unlike the very real *soldadeiras* at Alfonso el Sabio's court, the fictive *serrana* he dominated was not present to dispute his claim.

Carvajal's Italian *Serranillas*: Locating the Self in a Foreign Landscape

Carvajal, a fifteenth-century poet at the Neapolitan court of Alfonso V of Aragon, composed the second greatest number of *serranillas* after Santillana, although many do not feature *serranas* but *damas* or *niñas*. Critics disagree as to the number of his *serranillas*, six according to Nicasio Salvador Miguel and Emma Scoles, seven according to Nancy F. Marino.[45] In his poetry, individual portraits of (pseudo) *serranas* play on the significance of landscape, place of origin, performance, and identity; they also employ intertextual references to maintain and create ties with Peninsular poetic practices. The result is a complex elaboration of political, national, class, and gender relations, as well as relations between court and countryside. Carvajal's principal antecedents are Ruiz and Santillana; he incorporates their voices into his own, as well as the voices of the Italian/Iberian *serranas/damas* that appear in his parodic *serranillas*. The history of the *serranilla* in Spanish letters is a more-or-less direct line of imitation and differentiation, part of the competitive poetic practices that, as E. Michael Gerli and Julian Weiss have demonstrated, formed the literary and social basis of *cancionero* poetry.[46] I consider Carvajal's *serranillas* particularly parodic due to their highly ambiguous nature. Ambiguity reigns supreme in the *Libro de buen amor*; Santillana in his *serranillas*, however, tolerates little ambiguity, especially in the area of gender and power relations. In Santillana's work, the male protagonist interpellates the female protagonist in accordance with his needs and desires, using their fictive encounter to demonstrate her place. The audience for this lesson in social structure is not the fictive *serrana* but the court that sees itself reflected positively in the abject mirror of the *serranilla*.

In Carvajal, the focus is not class relations so much as nationality. In his *serranillas*, we see a complex and ambivalent play on nationality, location, gender, and class; as in all *serranillas*, the present locatedness of the male narrator contrasts with his habitual environment, yet whether Carvajal's poetic alter ego belongs any place at all is highly doubtful. By contrast, and in accordance with *serranilla* conventions, the *serrana/dama* seems at home in the landscape, even if the exact site of the encounter is not conventional or not an appropriate place for her. She expresses confidence and self-awareness, in contrast to the narrator's lack of self-confidence, confusion, and anxiety. This results in a particularly authoritative voice on the part of the female speakers. Playing on the didactic aspect of Ruiz's *cánticas*, in which the foolish narrator-protagonist is taught his obligatory role by the dominant *serranas*, Carvajal's female protagonists issue pronouncements on the art of courtly love and direct the male traveler's actions. While these lessons present courtly life as superior to that of the country, they also invert normative social hierarchies, as the rustic *serrana* instructs the naïve courtier. Place, performance, and audience (both that within the fictive world and that situated outside of the fiction) intermingle, raising yet not resolving key issues of difference.

Carvajal's *serranillas* play openly with identity construction and poetic conventions. In XLV/D0650, "Passando por la Toscana," the female protagonist is not a *serrana*, and the playful ambiguity of this lyric contributes to her enigmatic identity. The introductory half-stanza plays on *serranilla* conventions, especially in the phrase "vi dama gentil, galana," a parody of the usual "vi serrana" formula, a similarity underlined with the *-ana* rhyme:

> Passando por la Toscana,
> entre Sena y Florencia,
> vi dama gentil, galana,
> digna de gran reverencia.
>
> Cara tenía de romana,
> tocadura portuguesa,
> el aire de castellana,
> vestida como senesa
> discretamente, non vana;
> yo le fize reverencia
> y ella, con mucha prudencia,
> bien mostró ser cortesana. (vv. 1–12)

Passing through Tuscany, between Siena and Florence, I saw a noble, beautiful lady, worthy of great reverence.

She had the face of a Roman, a Portuguese headdress, the air of a Castilian, dressed like a Sienese, discreetly, not with vanity; I made a reverence to her, and she, with great prudence, well showed that she was courtly.

The location of their encounter in the Tuscan landscape raises the question of national identity, a question played on in the narrator's description of the *dama*. The adjectives focus on characteristics considered typical of certain regions, yet these regions vary from cities (Rome and Siena) to kingdoms (Portugal and Castile), a variation that raises another question, that of the political boundaries that characterize different land masses, Italy and Iberia, both of which happen to be peninsulas divided into various autonomous regions. This list of characteristics suggests that the speaker considers himself an expert in discerning unknown women's place of origin (or, we could say, in *placing* them); yet, with this particular *dama*, he is perplexed by the contradictory traits he sees. This description also plays on Ruiz's first *serrana*, La Chata, whose name is often interpreted as meaning "roma de nariz," snub-nose; she is also called "la chata troya" (972b), *troya* meaning, according to Alberto Blecua, *ruin*, vile, according to Louise Vasvári, prostitute.[47] This very subtle reference may anticipate the surprising name assumed by this *dama*, that of Cassandra, a Trojan woman (*troyana*). Her regional identity traits include physical characteristics (a Roman face), costume (Sienese dress), hairstyle (Portuguese), and bearing (Castilian); while she presumably has no choice as to her face, all these other traits are performative, suggesting that she deliberately assumes an ambiguous identity. The one unambiguous identity that the narrator can ascribe to her is that of courtliness, an identity she performs through her discretion and prudence, that is, in her manner of speech. It is noteworthy that the narrator does not mention which language she speaks, nor does he cite her.

The following stanzas continue to play on the narrator's reading of ambiguous signs, focusing on his ambivalent reactions to her:

> Así entramos por Sena
> fablando de compañía,
> con plazer haviendo pena
> del pesar que me plazía.
> Si se dilatara el día
> o la noche nos tomara,
> tan grand fuego se encendía
> que toda la tierra se quemara.
>
> Vestía de blanco domasquino,
> camurra al tovillo cortada
> encima de un vellud fino
> un luto la falda rastrada
> pomposa e agraciada
> una invención traía
> por letras que no entendía
> de perlas la manga bordada. (vv. 13–29)

In this way we entered Siena chatting companionably, with pleasure feeling pain of the pain that pleased me [i.e., he was falling in love with her]. No matter how long the day lasted or if night overtook us, such a great fire [of desire] was flaming that would burn all the land.

Dressed in white damask, her lambskin coat cut to her ankle, on top of fine fur, her black skirt dragging on the ground, proud and elegant; she had an *invención* in letters that I couldn't understand; her sleeve was embroidered with pearls.[48]

The speaker's contradictory feelings are conventional symptoms of love; he continues to collapse oppositions in his inability to perceive the difference between day and night, due to the fire of his desire. He projects his emotional state onto the landscape and onto the object of his desire. Even her clothing is contradictory, as she wears a rustic *çamarra* and *vellud* on top of elegant garments. Her outerwear could be read as practical traveling clothes, not as a deliberate attempt to obscure her identity; however, her *invención* is a deliberate identity play. *Invenciones* are riddling games in which courtiers wore codified clothing and signs, including text embroidered on their clothes, performing an identity for others to decipher.[49] In this case, the traveler is unable to decipher the *dama's invención*; she is wearing her identity on her sleeve, yet he is unable to read her. By contrast, she seems to read him very well; their amiable conversation shows her to be comfortable and confident, while he is confused and unsure of himself and her. In the final stanza, the narrator asserts that her speech, dress and being show that she is not a shepherdess; yet, he still does not know who she is:

> En su fabla, vestir e ser
> non mostrava ser de mandra;
> queriendo su nombre saber,
> respondióme que Casandra;
> yo, con tal nombre oir,
> muy alegre desperté
> e tan solo me fallé,
> que, por Dios, pensé morir. (vv. 38–45)

In her speech, dress and being she showed that she wasn't a herder; wanting to know her name, she told me that it was Cassandra; upon hearing such a name, I awoke very happy, and found myself so alone that, by God, I felt like dying.

Frustrated by not being able to assign an identity to her, he directly asks her her name; upon hearing it, he awakens from his dream. This resolution plays on the Marqués de Santillana's dream-visions, such as his "Visión," as does the mythological reference to Cassandra. Her name could imply that the traveler's inability to discern her identity and the narrator's inability to cite her result from the original Cassandra's curse of unintelligibility.

This composition is loaded with intertextual references that would challenge Carvajal's audience (as it does us), establish his relationship with Castilian and ancient traditions, and situate him in the Italian landscape. He uses *serranilla* conventions to frame this mysterious, liminal encounter as familiar and even as trite, given the excessive conventionality of the genre. Carvajal's focus on the psuedo-*serrana's* identity is an innovation; rather than questioning her class status as does Santillana (in III/D2427, VIII/D3435, and, ironically, in 11/D3061), Carvajal questions her national origin (as Santillana does in II/D3430). Carvajal plays most directly with the Marqués's "Cantar a sus fijas loando su fermosura" (11/D3061), since in both *serranillas* the narrators explicitly say that the female characters are not shepherdesses: "Dos serranas. . .non vezadas de ganado" (11/D3061, vv. 1, 4 two *serranas*. . .not accustomed to cattle); "non mostrava ser de mandra" (XLV/D0650, v. 37); both give detailed descriptions of the women's adornments.[50] In that lyric the Marqués uses *serranilla* conventions to present a flattering portrait of his two younger daughters, playing with fictive conventions while pointing to the real world. Similarly, in Carvajal's composition, the detailed description of the lady's appearance, clothing, demeanor, and especially her *invención*, would have led his audience to speculate on her identity, presuming she was an actual member of Alfonso V's Neapolitan court. This expectation would be shattered at the end, with the revelation that she was a mythical being and a figment of the protagonist's imagination. By postponing both the name of the lady and the fact that the encounter was a dream until the end, Carvajal maintains the interest of his audience. He also implies that, if mythical women presently walked the earth, they would do so dressed as ladies of Alfonso's court, flattering his patron with hyperbolic praise.[51]

Carvajal's play with *serranilla* conventions extends to his treatment of landscape. In XLV/D0650, the landscape is more urban, as in the course of the poem, the travelers enter Siena (v. 13); theirs is not a rural encounter, strictly speaking, but one on the road between two cities. The temporal setting of this encounter is also in-between, after sunset but before nightfall. This liminal setting raises the question of proper places. Cassandra is Trojan, and her presence in Tuscany can be tied, perhaps, to Aeneas, the Trojan founder of Rome; this may explain her Roman traits. Her hybrid appearance and mannerisms, however, suggest that she is from no one place; she is a product of many places yet belongs nowhere. On the other hand, she, like all *serranas*, seems at home in her surroundings, a natural extension of a landscape that has sustained so many national, regional, and imperial identities. It is the narrator who seems out-of-place, uncomfortable and unable to read adequately the landscape and its residents; his expulsion from the dreamworld in the final stanza underlines his presence in a space that is not his own. All of Carvajal's *serranillas* imply that the narrator-protagonist is out of place. I would argue that Carvajal cultivates this genre in order to comment on the cultural and social significance of place. Conventionally the *serranilla* plays up the contrast between country and court, a contrast Carvajal does play on; but, he primarily uses the *serranilla* to establish his place in the Italian landscape and in Hispanic/Castilian letters.

Not all of Carvajal's *serranillas* are set in Italy. "Saliendo de un olivar," X/D0608 (Leaving an olive grove), is not clearly located, nor does either characters' speech reveal regional traits; similarly, XXII/D0622, "Andando perdido" (While lost), perhaps Carvajal's most-discussed *serranilla*, is generically located in "una montaña desierta, fragosa" (v. 2; a deserted, rocky mountain). In both these poems the *serrana* instructs the male protagonist, in love with another, in the art of courtly love, a lesson that is particularly incongruous in XXII/D0622. XLI/D0650, "¿Dónde sois gentil galana?" (Where are you from, gentle girl?) is vaguely set in Italy, although the site of the encounter is not indicated; the female character speaks a Neapolitan dialect of Italian and identifies herself as *napolitana*. Most of Carvajal's *serranillas* do include Italian place-names: XLV/D0650, "Passando por la Toscana," discussed above; XVIII/D0618, "Entre Sesa e Cintura"; XLVI/D0651, "Veniendo de la Campaña" (Coming from the country) introduced with the rubric, "Acerca de Roma" (Near Rome); and XLIX/D0655, "Partiendo de Roma passando Marino" (Leaving Rome, passing Marino), which, like XXII/D0622, features a grotesque *serrana*. XLIX/D0655 is clearly a parody of Ruiz's portrait of Alda, as is widely recognized.[52] The location itself is parodic, not just in its use of an Italian place, but in the specific site of their encounter, "fuera del monte en una grand plana" (v. 2): outside of the mountains in a great plain, this *serrana* is unambiguously out of place. Of the three *serranillas* set in Italy, only the last features a *serrana*; the other two apply *serranilla* conventions to a lady. Carvajal's use of the *serranilla* is an ambiguous gesture as to the significance of landscape and location; he uses them in order to locate himself in Iberian poetic traditions and to establish his individuality as a Castilian poet in the Aragonese court at Naples.

Robert G. Black has called the Neapolitan taste for things Hispanic "almost chauvinistic," and the question must be raised: is Carvajal's application of Iberian models to an Italian landscape an imperialistic gesture, a reflection of an Aragonese desire to remake Italy in the image of the old country?[53] On one level, the answer surely is yes; however, in these six *serranillas*, the male narrator's sense of entitlement and superiority is either dismissed or challenged by the women he encounters, who seem constantly to order him back to court, where he belongs. In contrast with Santillana's poetic alter ego, Carvajal's persona never beds the female protagonist; his restraint cannot be linked simply to the fact that many of these pseudo-*serranas* are of a higher social status than the male protagonist. In fact, the lower status *serranas* tolerate the outsider's presence far less than do the noble pseudo-*serranas*, who engage him in dialogue and play the role of ladies to compliment his role of courtly lover, as does Cassandra. Shepherdesses overtly reject the traveler's attentions, as in X/D0608:

> Replicó: ≪Id en buen hora,
> non curéis de amar villana;
> pues servís atal señora,
> non troquéis seda por lana;
> nin queráis de mí burlar,
> pues sabéis que só enagenada.≫
> *Vi serrana, que tornar*
> *me fizo de mi jornada.* (vv. 21–28)

She replied: "Now leave, and farewell; don't bother loving a peasant-girl; since you serve such a lady, don't trade silk for wool; and don't try to make a fool of me, since you know that I belong to someone else." *I saw a serrana, who made me turn from my journey.*

This *villana* orders the traveler to return to court and to his lady, instructs him in the art of love, and labels any continued attempt at seduction on his part a *burla* (trick or deceit). The *estribillo* is highly ironic: while the narrator says the *serrana* made him turn from his way, meaning that her beauty distracted him, she also made him return to it with her rejection. A similar dynamic is found in XLVI/D0651, where the *pastora* does not interact directly with the traveler who watches her sing about the joys of her simple life:

≪Entre yo e mi carillo
ganamos buena soldada.
Sonando mi caramillo
bivo yo mucho pagada;
leche, queso e cuajada
jamás non me fallescía.≫
E si bien era villana
fija d'algo parescía.

≪De triunfos e grandes honores
yo non curo en ningund tiempo;
Fortuna nin sus errores
non me davan pensamiento;
de toda pompa mundana
muy poca estima fazía.≫ (vv. 29–42)

"Between my sweetheart and I, we earn a good living. Playing my pan pipes, I live very happily; I will never lack for milk, cheese, and butter." If she was really a peasant, *she seemed a noble woman.*

"I don't ever worry about triumphs and grand honors; Fortune with its changes don't concern me; I hold all worldly pomp in very low esteem."

Not only is she content and worry-free, but she rejects (even before the protagonist can offer) the praises and pleasures of the court. Since she lacks for nothing, he cannot entice her interest; while he admires her and incorporates her song into his, he continues on his way, back to court where he will sing of her contempt for courtliness while exemplifying nobility.[54] As with the previous example, the female speaker seems to know all about court life; while the first construes court ladies as superior to herself, a comment that can be read as a defensive strategy ("non troquéis seda por lana," X/D0608, v. 24), the second focuses on the anxieties of court life in contrast to her worry-free rural life. In both cases, the narrator does not reply to the *serranas*' speeches, implying that their arguments are unanswerable. The poetic persona performed in these *serranillas* is not the supremely self-confident character we see in most of Santillana's *serranillas*; nor is he the fool played by Ruiz. Carvajal, I would argue, uses this genre to inscribe himself in Hispanic poetic traditions, demonstrating both his indebtedness to yet difference from his famous antecedents, not to impose his will on the Italian landscape nor on the courtly *serranas* he depicts.

In the work of these three poets, we see very different uses made of the figures of the *serrana* and of the narrator-protagonist. While both Ruiz and Carvajal play on the narrator-protagonist's precarious position in the landscape, their precariousness is of a very different nature. Ruiz emphasizes the uncivilized nature of the *sierra* and the *serrana*, or rather, their abusive treatment of the urbane traveler; from the *serranas*' point of view they are playing by the rules and it is the out-of-place protagonist who doesn't understand the game. He misinterprets their ritual, personalizes it, and seeks vengeance for the abuse he receives. Nonetheless, he also enjoys the game and wants to play it with various women, enacting different roles and varying his lines to give him a sense of control. The Marqués, on the other hand, assumes and maintains control of the game from the start; he refuses to indulge the upstart Menga, although he does respect the *serranas* who decline his attentions. Carvajal's alter ego plays a more tentative role, in-between those of Ruiz and Santillana. Like Santillana, he exemplifies courtliness, but without the Marqués's confidence and self-assertion; nor is he beaten and raped like Ruiz's narrator-protagonist, although he does play something of a fool, humbled by goddesses on earth and by indifferent peasant women. Each poet uses this genre to carve out for himself a place in poetic and geographic terrains; they also take advantage of the opportunities for role-playing and laughter offered by the genre. The *serranilla's* eroticism enables the poet-performer to parade his sexuality; even Carvajal, whose persona does not sleep with any of the female protagonists, presents an identity as a courtly lover, explaining that he restrains himself out of respect for his *dama* (in X/D0608 and XXII/D0622).

In all cases, the *serrana* embodies the landscape within which she is located; she becomes the stage upon which the narrator-protagonist performs and she herself enacts the landscape, performing aggression, compliance, pride, or courteous resistance, depending upon the time, place, and identity of the traveler she encounters. As poetic characters, *serranas* articulate the shifting significance of geography, sex, and identity; their *sierra* performances, reenacted in the civilized space of court or town by men, promote play with the many elements upon which identity depends. The discursive nature of identity construction, exemplified by the dialogue between the *serrana* and the male traveler, shows that identity is contingent, dependent upon the other with whom one interacts. The dualistic nature of the *serranilla* encounter, that is, the opposition between extremes, including civilization and wilderness, man and woman, noble and peasant, subject and object of desire, belies the complex nature of negotiated identity. The variations in each encounter, which constitute part of the pleasure of the genre, show that identity is constantly being redefined and reasserted through performance in a variety of settings. One male actor-singer playing three different roles in a single song would further illustrate the flexibility of identity. Even if only in play, the *serranilla* focuses attention on the performative construction of identity, on the reciprocal nature of identity construction and performance, and on the pleasure of playing as an other, of enacting femininity and monstrosity, within the play space of town or court.

CONCLUSION

PLAYING WITH IDENTITY IN LYRIC
PERFORMANCES

Lyric spectacles put identity into play. The embodied performances of actor-singers play with fictive and authentic identities; the identities of fictive characters correspond to those of the performers, of members of the audience, and of individuals excluded from the performance space. All performances of self, by elite men and by degraded women, rely on the fact that identity is performative, a fact that so threatened social order that it could be celebrated rather than condemned only in play. The anxieties created by the constructed and performative nature of identity in non-play contexts made it necessary to create a safe, nonserious genre for identity play; the lyric spectacle is just such a genre. The lyric spectacle combined verbal and visual texts, mixing song, dance, gesture, and mime, to produce a unique performance genre. Enacting incongruous identities in a certain space and time and surrounding them with other artificial acts, especially with music, places them in a frame that signals their nonserious nature. This framing enables poets and audience to play with such perceived absolutes as gender and bodies, that is, with apparently nonnegotiable aspects of identity. The lyric abounds with transgendered performances at both the poetic and metapoetic level; female characters enact and parody masculine behaviors and male actor-singers impersonate women who impersonate men. The fact that many different characters can adopt behaviors coded as feminine or masculine underlines the distinction between a behavior and the body that enacts it. The lyric spectacle enabled poet-performers to express taboo, including forbidden words, embarrassing body parts, and, perhaps the greatest taboo of all, the performative nature of identity.

In the preceding three chapters, I have examined the figures of the *soldadeira*, *panadera*, and *serrana*, exploring both how they are depicted as performers and how their characters were performed by men and women.

Each of these characters helps define, and is defined by, the space she occupies. The *soldadeira*, a ritually deviant member of the court, played a central role in the *trovador* spectacle. While her dancing and singing helped construct the court as a site of distinction and taste, the stigma she carried as a professional female performer and prostitute made her presence there a threat to its status as a restricted space inhabited by those who exemplified good behavior and speech. Her sexuality and the vague distinction between her onstage and offstage acts made her disturbing behaviors destabilize normative identity constructions and licensed sexualized play in the court. *Soldadeiras* ironically played with their stereotypical identity through parodic mimicry, simultaneously imitating and criticizing the behaviors that justified their stigmatized status; their parodic self-impersonations encouraged poet-performers to engage in similar self-mocking play. In depicting and impersonating *soldadeiras*, courtly poets, even those of the highest elite, got to engage in female impersonation, crossing lines of gender, rank, and status in play.

The *panadera*, stigmatized due to her association with prostitution and the marketplace, nonetheless wielded power as an experienced public speaker. Her rhetorical skills and identification with the masses led her to challenge municipal authorities, especially during times of social and economic crisis. The marketplace, unlike the court, was public and open to all; conduct within its confines was regulated so as to make the market a safe space within which to conduct exchanges across the barriers of rank, gender, and nationality and/or ethnicity. The *panadera's* mere presence within this heterogeneous space was not threatening; the threat she presented came from her verbal skills, specifically from her power to negotiate, to assess and create value through language, and to assign identities to those she encountered. The multivalent uses and connotations of *pan* in medieval Spain contributed to her construction as a threat to the social body; not pure like the female religious who prepared the Host, the *panadera* symbolized the profane and unclean, as she was equated to her sexual bread. Simultaneously a savvy consumer of men and a sexual commodity, the *panadera* used her rhetoric to embellish her own wares and to devalue those she was offered. Her association with praise and blame poetry, with hawking songs and haggling discourses, made her the ideal satirist to debunk aristocratic pretenses in the *Coplas de la panadera*.

The *sierra*, unlike the court and the marketplace, was constructed as a dangerous place, a wilderness within which civilized men could lose themselves and be preyed upon by monsters. This bewildering space was also lawless, a site of potentially unlimited self-definition and of sexual freedom, far from the confines of court and town. The *sierra* was read as an erotic landscape, contoured as the body of a reclining woman, simultaneously a welcoming sexual playground and an aggressive, engulfing *vagina dentata* that provoked powerfully contradictory reactions in the men who beheld it/her. All these associations were reflected in the purely fictive figure of the *serrana*. Often depicted singing and dancing to amuse herself and others, her body and character presented a challenge to the elite male traveler who wished to prove himself by sexually conquering her. Supremely self-confident due to her strong, competent body, the *serrana*, like the *panadera*, easily deflated noble pretenses by putting the men whom she met to the test, verbally and physically. Although assigned a particular role in accordance with *serranilla* conventions, she resisted this role by asserting her dominance and demanding the traveler play by her rules, as in the *Libro de buen amor*, or by negotiating relative identity positions, as in the work of the Marqués de Santillana. Carvajal in turn played with generic limits, giving various lone women encountered outside of the court the *serranilla* treatment, no matter their rank or status; his work demonstrates the use of this genre to locate poet-performers in a shifting poetic and literal landscape. Courtiers and city-dwellers enlivened their travel narratives with songs of their encounters with isolated and independent *serranas*; within the safe space of the lyric spectacle, poet-performers could flirt with danger by impersonating this transgressive character.

All three female characters I study are depicted as performers who put identity into play; these characters were variously impersonated by men and women whose performance techniques built on the verbal text. Lyric identity play begins at the textual level with word games. Comic-erotic and comic-obscene songs are filled with taboo words and double-entendres. The taboo words found in most comic-obscene songs refer to body parts or bodily acts; this language calls attention to the bodies of the characters and those of the performers who impersonate them. Comic-erotic songs are less direct, using coded language and imagery to express sexual themes. Part of the pleasure of allusive language is the act of decoding it, an act that implicates the audience in the erotic play. Taboo words and double-entendres can trigger a potentially disturbing physical response in the audience, creating shock and embarrassment; music and rhythm provoke additional somatic responses, heightening the bodily awareness of all present, performers as well as audience members. Female performers often mediated between the actor-singers on stage and members of the audience, approaching them and encouraging them to clap or sing along; their movements to incite the audience could quickly become suggestive. The embodied nature of musical performances and the bawdy language of the lyrics I discuss focused particular attention on the interplay of bodies, behaviors, and identities.

Comic-obscene *Cantiga d'escarnho* lyrics reinforce their gender play by playing with grammatical gender, as in Pero Viviaez's list of body parts whose grammatical gender does not correspond to their biological gender. Ties between grammatical gender, biological gender, and sexual preference are fully disrupted in Afons'Eanes do Coton's ambivalent rivalry and identification with Mari'Mateu, whose disturbing sexual and gender identity is inscribed in her double name. The significance of textual femininity, that is, marking the gender of the speaker with feminine adjectives and personal pronouns, was put into question when men enacted female roles and enunciated the speeches of female characters. The heterogeneous or multimedia nature of lyric performances facilitated play with identity construction. These games with language and gender enabled poets to play with various ways of constructing identity, and they allowed performers to enact various personas, putting their offstage identities into play.

Lyric identity play continues through naming. Comic-obscene and comic-erotic songs interpellate characters, naming them, assigning them an identity, and singling them out for attention. In the case of Pero Viviaez's song, he also separates Marinha from the audience of which she was a member and publicizes her private acts. Naming is a powerful speech act, one that imposes an identity, often an insulting one, on the addressee; interpellation demonstrates the linguistic and interactive construction of identity. In a monologic context, such an address is violent and causes injury; a dialogic performance context, however, creates a cycle of address and response. The interpellated subject becomes a speaking subject, and a performing subject, who can respond to and negotiate the identity imposed upon her/him. In courtly lyric performances, the roles of performer, target, and audience shifted, as one lyric performance was followed by another and as the target and audience responded to each performance. In such a context, interpellation was a two-way street: the speaker, by the act of addressing another, singled her/himself out for attention and display, and s/he was dependent upon the audience and the target to play their assigned roles. Others could get into the act by fully collaborating, that is, performing their assigned roles, or by resisting and negotiating their roles. Any response that shifted attention away from the target and focused attention on the speaker reduced the monologic power of the speaker's voice and decreased the violence done to the target. I see this dynamic as central to the dialogic performance and reception context of comic-obscene songs on *soldadeiras*, especially since the courtly audience for thirteenth-century *Cantigas d'escarnho* was not a homogenous group.

In contexts that excluded the target from the performance space, interpellation functioned differently. In the *serranilla*, the traveler and *serrana* negotiate relative identity positions through their dialogue. The dominant player usually forces the other to play a role, as we see Ruiz's personas playing by the rules set by *serranas*, or Santillana's alter ego imposing roles, through flattery or force, on resistant *serranas*. Interpellation is also central to *panadera* lyrics, as the female speaker calls out to potential customers or depicts herself as an interpellated subject. In the *Coplas de la panadera*, the female speaker's naming of the noble participants in the Battle of Olmedo does violence to them; she uses her words as weapons to strip away their aristocratic pretenses and reveal their weak, grotesque bodies. Interpellation is always a power play, but its effects are negotiable; while certainly those so addressed are not autonomous subjects, they do have some maneuvering room within which to resist the roles imposed upon them. One of these techniques is to mimic the imposed identity, acting it out in an exaggerated way, as do many female characters and the women who impersonated them.

Lyric identity play depends upon both word and gesture. The terms I use to describe medieval performance techniques fuse speech and movement to underline the importance of both aspects of the lyric spectacle. These songs were composed to be played in front of a live audience by performers who enacted multiple characters in rapid succession. *Soldadeiras* and other female performers engaged in parodic mimicry, ironically impersonating their imposed, conventional identity as they performed themselves as poetic characters ventriloquized by *trovadores*, playing with the overlaps between their onstage acts and their usual behavior. Male poet-performers similarly played on their authentic identity in their onstage roles as the first-person narrator, ventriloquizing and impersonating their poetic personas. The significance of these performances of self differed radically due to the diametrically opposed constructions of these two performers, the degraded professional female performer/prostitute and the elite, amateur male poet-performer. While performance as oneself is always ironic, as are all staged or artificial performances, I reserve the term 'parodic mimicry' for *soldadeiras* and other stigmatized female performers in order to mark the richness of meanings created by their self-impersonations. When a stigmatized entertainer ironically enacted her stigmatized identity, she both reinforced and challenged conventional identity categories. Her performance underlined the splits and slippages between identities and roles, especially when she impersonated herself (i.e., a poetic character that bore her name) in someone else's composition. For a *soldadeira*, such a performance of self plays on a multiplicity of selves: herself as *soldadeira* (i.e., degraded female performer/prostitute), herself as a certain person, and herself as a stage persona. Particularly important is how her body both determined her identities and was separable from the roles she played on- and offstage. Her *soldadeira* identity was inextricably linked to her particular body, as in the case of

Maria Negra, to the history of her particular body, as in that of Maria Leve, and to her body as female, that is, to how her particular body was generically categorized. Parodic mimicry simultaneously called attention to and blurred the lines between particular and generic identities as well as those between fictive, conventional, and authentic identities. Doing so emphasized both how a *soldadeira*'s identity was externally constructed and imposed upon her and also particular, dependent upon her actually enacting that identity. In lyric play, *soldadeiras* and other stigmatized female performers enacted a part written for them, playing along to please the dominant power structures, and made that part their own, appropriating it in order to engage in a certain performance of self, a self whose relationship to their authentic self (selves) was always elusive.

When elite poet-performers enacted their poetic personas, they also played off their authentic identity; however, the lines between roles demonstrate how their identity as elite men is constructed differently. Their performances simultaneously highlighted and obscured how their bodies determined their privileged status. They displayed their gendered and sexual bodies, staging their masculine privilege, while putting their social privilege into play. The number of phallic boasts in the comic-obscene songs I discuss illustrates the importance of play on the significance of the elite male body. Pero Viviaez plays on his status as a nobleman in his graphic verbal and visual depiction of his phallic body, then deflates his boast by turning attention to Marinha's dismissive response; Alfonso el Sabio does not verbally depict his own sexual body but has a *soldadeira* exaggeratedly praise his agonistic masculinity while he looks on; Afons'Eanes do Coton boasts of his powerful sexual desires while complaining that his masculinity does not grant him access to cunt. All these songs play on the gap between the speaker's gendered and privileged bodies and how these bodies are valued/evaluated by those around them. We see similar play with the value of masculine bodies in comic-erotic songs on *panaderas* and *serranas*; in the later case, male poet-performers both stage and mock their privileged bodies in solo performances, whereas in *panadera* lyrics such as the *Coplas de la panadera* and Sebastián de Horozco's "Dama de gentil aseo," female speakers openly mock the concept that elite male bodies matter. The ways in which different female characters put male bodies into play both inform the relative construction of male and female roles in the comic-obscene and comic-erotic songs I discuss and deeply affect the dynamics of identity play in each song.

Transgendered performances put bodies and gender into play by underlining gaps between the body that acted and the identity being enacted. Such performances often crossed lines of rank and status as well as that of gender, as elite men impersonated degraded women, engaging in camp performances. These impersonations were partial, as the performer did not disappear behind the persona, to mark the incongruity of transgendered acts. Poet-performers alternated between masculine and feminine roles, switching personas and voices in solo acts. Such acts tended to reify conventional identity categories while severing the tie between certain bodies and certain identities, raising the possibility that all performances of identity were mere acts. I do not explore whether female performers enacted male roles in lyric spectacles, in part because such transgendered performances signify differently and in part because I'm far more interested in female characters who appropriate masculine behaviors, engaging in transgendered performances in their performance of self. Their transgendered acts at the fictive level were mostly impersonated by men, as when Alfonso el Sabio impersonated Domingas Eanes's impersonation of a knight in combat with an African *genete* and the Marqués de Santillana impersonated Menga de Mançanares's impersonation of a defender of a pass. In these two cases the narrators adopt hostile poses toward the female characters' transgendered performances and use violent masculine sexuality to impose their inferior feminine passive–receptive role upon them; the poet-performers, however, impersonate the impersonation, engaging in ambiguously gendered acts comparable to those of the female characters. In these two the narrative pose emphasizes the different significance of these transgendered performances, implying that the elite male body has the right to engage in such acts whereas the degraded female body does not; in the case of Pero d'Ambroa's impersonation of Maria Balteira's masculine act, outshooting callow *beesteiros*, d'Ambroa endorses Balteira's transgendered performance, ridiculing instead her victims. These different narrative poses cannot be read as general endorsement or criticism of women's masculine acts; the acts and poses must be situated in the larger power structures that surround these acts and make them signify differently.

My work on lyric identity play builds on previous scholars' work that demonstrates the play with gender construction and performance in the *Cantigas d'escarnho* and in fifteenth-century *cancionero* poetry.[1] This work tends to focus on male poet-performers and/or characters, reading female characters as the objects against which male subjects defined themselves. I read female characters as both objects and subjects of language, an ambiguous status shared by all poetic characters; in performance, fictive characters, fleshed out by the bodies on stage, overtly asserted their subjectivity, within the bounds of previously constituted identity categories. Reading lyric poetry as performance texts designed to be enacted before a live, participatory audience underlines the fragmentary nature of the written text and the contingency of meaning, always dependent upon the immediate context.

In my reconstructions of lyric spectacles, I have suggested ways in which these songs could have been performed. Usually I sketch out the first performance, with the poet enacting the role of the first-person narrator, when appropriate with other actor-singers impersonating other characters named within the text. These reconstructions build on many aspects of performance and suggest possible audience response, recognizing the heterogeneous nature of lyric audiences and the multiple ways in which members of the audience could respond. My readings emphasize the levels of play with identity in lyric performances, as female actor-singers impersonated female characters ventriloquized by male poet-performers in order to amuse a mostly male audience among which would have been female performers with licensed access to male recreational spaces. The larger power structures around such courtly performances was coercive, but did not eliminate room to play with imposed identities; the equivocal, comic language and tone facilitated ironic play with normative identities, on the part of degraded female performers and elite male poet-performers. I insist on recognizing female performers' contribution to the lyric spectacle since their role is so consistently obscured by the written record and by the authoritative stance of narrator-protagonists who present themselves as agents and the female characters as objects.

While scholars have previously studied these three female characters, they have not generally acknowledged these characters are performers or explored the significance of their performances. Most studies of the voices of female characters emphasize that they are ventriloquized by men and overlook how in performance the authority of the poet-performer was challenged.[2] In Alfonso el Sabio's two *Cantigas d'escarnho* that include extensive citations of *soldadeiras'* voices, the female protagonists direct their speech toward the narrator and perform for his benefit, either praising his agonistic sexual performance or deriding his kingly authority; he then cites their performances in his own, filtering their words through his perspective yet ceding the stage to them and allowing them to address a wider audience. If these characters were enacted by female performers, as I believe they were, their self-awareness would be obvious, as they performed ironically with an eye on the male speaker and another on the heterogeneous, appreciative audience. Most *serranilla* performances were male solo acts, but this did not eliminate the audience's ability to see the *serrana*, ventriloquized and impersonated by the poet-performer, as self-aware and engaging in gender and class parody. The Marqués impersonated Menga de Mançanares's impersonation of a knight; by appropriating the role of the defender of a pass, she contests the meaning of her *serrana* identity and refuses to play the part of a complacent object of desire. Even lyrics that do not cite female voices do not necessarily conceal that the female character is performing. Carvajal depicts Cassandra as deliberately performing an enigmatic identity in her dress and in her *invención*. Pero Viviaez complains that Marinha's passive–receptive act is hostile and aggressive since she fails to climax in response to his energetic sexual performance. In the case of this *Cantiga d'escarnho*, the dialogic performance context makes it likely that Marinha was present for Viviaez's song and responded to it by imputing his small size, deflating his phallic boast. These songs have been read in the past as simply misogynistic; in performance, nothing is simple, as the complexities of acting and reception increase textual ambiguities.

Reading lyrics as performance texts counteracts the tendency of written texts to construct the poetic 'I' as a disembodied voice. In performance, the narrator's investment in the episode that he recounts is impossible to ignore. This awareness deeply affects reception and the meanings created in performance. The disdain of Joan Baveca's alter ego for the two *soldadeiras* whose insult exchange he relates becomes comic when we realize the two women are naked and bathing each other; his cowardly persona remains a concealed voyeur rather than risk injury by revealing his presence and perhaps getting to join in their erotic play. Alfonso el Sabio's investment in Domingas Eanes's parodic performance as a knight is underlined when the king impersonates her behaviors as well as those of the African *genete* who 'wounds' her. The fact that the Archpriest prefers losing to a male rival over bedding Cruz is clear when we see him engage in an overly complicated mini-drama and assign himself a backstage role, allowing the other two characters free rein to pursue their own agendas. On the other hand, the Marqués de Santillana's desire to reenact his accustomed superiority and dominion over land and women in the terrain of the *serranilla* led him repeatedly to compose and perform fictive conquests set in factually contested sites. Not only did these men depict their alter egos in relationship with such degraded women, but they also enacted these encounters before an audience of their peers or social superiors, staging themselves as well as their poetic characters and using the ludic nature of lyric spectacles to force others to witness their self-assertive acts.

This study demonstrates the fruitfulness of rereading medieval Iberian literature through the lens of performance. I have chosen to focus on the lyric spectacle, whose performative nature is obvious. My taste for comic-obscene and comic-erotic lyric determined my choice of text, while my interest in gender theory lead me to focus on female performers. This approach would be similarly fruitful for other lyric genres, especially those which foreground gender. Prime candidates for such study are the *Cantigas d'amigo* and *d'amor*, two genres distinguished mostly by the gender of their speaker and that play with conventional constructions of the object and subject of desire. I have, unfortunately, been forced to exclude music from my study; not only do few examples of notation for profane lyric survive, but my focus on text and gesture precluded engagement with music within a reasonable space. The surviving melodies for Martin Codax's *Cantigas d'amigo* and those for Don Dinis's *Cantigas d'amor* could provide the basis for a study of the musical construction of gender; the widespread use of contrafacture in medieval lyric, that is, the practice of setting new words to old melodies, combined with other evidence of gendered discourse, could enable scholars to examine music, meter, and gender in the *Cantigas d'escarnho*, despite the absence of extant notation.[3] In other bodies of work, the approach through music would be yet more fruitful. The late fifteenth-century musical *cancioneros* already contain sufficient evidence in the form of notation and gendered voices, and so are ripe for study from the perspective of gender and performance theory.[4]

Studies of gender and performance would be greatly facilitated by scholarly multimedia editions of *cancionero* poetry. Modern critical editions tend to decontextualize lyric poetry, making it very difficult for readers to access the larger cultural systems that underlay the lyric and to appreciate how these songs were performed. A fully searchable database that includes manuscript images, diplomatic transcriptions, and critical editions as well as modern musical notation and performances of lyrics with extant notation would be a tremendous improvement, especially if users could also browse individual *cancioneros*. Electronic editions that include sound seem primarily marketed as introductory texts, such as the Biblioteca Nacional's *Cantar de mio Cid* and Mount Holyoke College's *Teaching Medieval Lyric with Modern Technology*, which includes twenty-five *Cantigas de Santa Maria* complete with images from the *Códice Rico*, musical notation, transcriptions, and translation into Castilian and English.[5] ADMYTE, an immensely useful, searchable database of medieval Spanish texts, includes browsable diplomatic transcriptions of entire *cancioneros* and in some cases images of the texts, but it does not include sound.[6] I hope that in the future textual critics and musicologists will productively collaborate on multimedia editions of medieval lyric, enabling investigators to articulate more fully the complexity of the lyric spectacle.

Medieval studies in general depend on interdisciplinary approaches bringing together diverse cultural materials to make fragmentary records intelligible. Hispanomedieval studies have benefited lately from feminist, queer, and cultural studies approaches; such work has enabled fruitful discussions of comic-obscene and comic-erotic texts previously excluded from study due to their sexual content and taboo words. Performance theory offers additional tools to aid our exploration of medieval and early modern literature, both written and oral; this approach can help us analyze the situated, contingent nature of the identities constructed in and by literary texts. In this book I have drawn on ethnographic studies of female performers in traditional contexts, on studies of modern performance artists, and on performance theory to fill in the gaps left in the written records. My work shows that medieval poets and performers enjoyed playing with the performative and contingent nature of identity in the lyric. Performance theory allows modern readers to productively engage our own taboo, namely, that we produce our own Middle Ages each time we read, discuss, and write about a medieval text.

NOTES

Introduction

1. On the question of female voices in medieval Iberian poetry, see Vicenta Blay
   Manzanera, "El varón que finge voz de mujer en las composiciones de
   cancionero," *Cultural Contexts/Female Voices*, ed. Louise M. Haywood, Papers
   of the Medieval Hispanic Research Seminar 27 (London: Queen Mary and
   Westfield College, 2000), 9–26, and "El discurso femenino en los cancioneros
   de los siglos XV y XVI," *Actas del XIII Congreso de la Asociación Internacional
   de Hispanistas: Madrid, 6–11 de Julio de 1998*, ed. Florencio Sevilla and Carlos
   Alvar, 4 vols., vol. 1 (Madrid: Castalia, 2000), 48–58, in which she analyzes
   female voices in fifteenth-century *cancionero* lyric. While her work demonstrates
   the relative absence of female voices from late medieval courtly lyric, Blay
   Manzanera also shows that those women who are cited tend to be either
   powerful queens or peasant women, especially *serranas*. In the thirteenth-
   century Galician-Portuguese corpus, an entire genre, the *Cantigas d'amigo*,
   is female-voiced; see Esther Corral, "Feminine Voices in the Galician-
   Portuguese *cantigas de amigo*," trans. Judith R. Cohen with Anne L. Klinck,
   Medieval Woman's Song: Cross-Cultural Approaches, ed. Anne L. Klinck and Ann
   Marie Rasmussen (Philadelphia: University of Pennsylvania Press, 2002),
   82–98. I have shown the importance of female voices in the *Cantigas
   d'escarnho* in "Female Voices in the *Cantigas de escarnio e de mal dizer*: Index
   and Commentary," *Bulletin of Spanish Studies* 81 (2004): 135–55. General
   studies of women's voices in medieval Romance lyric include Doris Earnshaw, *The Female Voice in Medieval Romance Lyric* (New York: Peter Lang, 1988)
   and Pilar Lorenzo Gradín, *La canción de mujer en la lírica medieval* (Santiago de
   Compostela: Universidade de Santiago de Compostela, 1990). Throughout
   this book I use Castilian forms when referring to performers who appear in
   Castilian-language texts: *juglar, trovador*, etc. (professional minstrel, amateur
   poet). I use Galician-Portuguese forms when discussing the characters and
   poet-performers associated with the *Cantigas d'escarnho: soldadeira, jograr/
   jogral* (pl. *jograis*), *segrer/segrel* (a poet-performer who occupied a medial position
   between professional *jograis* and amateur *trovadores*), and *trovador*. I discuss the
   significance of these different ranks in chapters 1 and 2. For the most part,
   I follow Manuel Rodrigues Lapa's choices for the proper names of characters and poets of the *Cantigas d'escarnho*, with the exception of Alfonso X;

cf. Lapa's *indices, Cantigas d'escarnho e de mal dizer dos cancioneiros medievais galego-portugueses*, 4th ed. (Lisbon: João Sá da Costa, 1998; 1st ed., 1965; 2nd rev. ed., 1970), 275–86. I also use Provençal and Occitan terms as appropriate. I generally use *Cantigas d'escarnho* as an abbreviation for *Cantigas d'escarnho e de mal dizer*.

2. By 'comic-obscene lyrics,' I mean songs that contain taboo words and erotic word-play or that depict taboo body parts and/or sexual acts by inference or through the use of coded language. Most of the lyrics I discuss contain taboo words and/or sexual double-entendres; fifteenth-century *serranillas* (lyrics that narrate the encounter between an elite male traveler and a *serrana*) tend not to contain such overt language. I use 'comic-erotic lyrics' to designate songs that use less vulgar language yet nonetheless deal with sex.

3. The best discussion of medieval Iberian poetic spectacles continues to be Ramón Menéndez Pidal, *Poesía juglaresca y juglares. Orígenes de las literaturas románicas*, 9th ed. (Madrid: Espasa Calpe, 1991; 1st ed. 1942). See also John K. Walsh, "The *Libro* de buen amor as a Performance-Text," *La corónica* 8 (1979): 5–6, and his "Performance in the 'Poema de mio Cid,' " *Romance Philology* 44.1 (1990): 1–25; Francisco Nodar Manso, *Teatro menor galaicoportugués (siglo XIII): Reconstrucción textual y Teoría del discurso* (Kassel: Reichenberger, 1990); Miguel Ángel Pérez Priego, ed., *Teatro medieval, volumen 2: Castilla* (Barcelona: Crítica, 1997); and Charlotte Stern, *The Medieval Theater in Castile* (Binghamton, NY: Medieval & Renaissance Texts & Studies, 1996), 145–81.

4. I discuss the *Cantigas d'escarnho* as ritual insult exchanges in "Jokes on *Soldadeiras* in the *Cantigas de Escarnio e de Mal Dizer*," *La corónica* 26.2 (Spring 1998): 29–39.

5. I base this definition of performance on the work of Judith Butler, primarily *Gender Trouble: Feminism and the Subversion of Identity* (New York and London: Routledge, 1990) and *Bodies that Matter: On the Discursive Limits of "Sex"* (New York and London: Routledge, 1993). It is important to emphasize the social ramifications of these characters' transgendered performances, since some critics stridently resist acknowledging the fluidity of gender construction in the Middle Ages. For example, Ulf Malm, *Dolssor Conina: Lust, the Bawdy, and Obscenity in Medieval Occitan and Galician-Portuguese Troubadour Poetry and Latin Secular Love Song*, Historia Litterarum 22 (Uppsala: Uppsala University Library, 2001), concludes his study of the *Cantigas d'escarnho* with the comment, "The man is the one with the penis, the woman the one with the vagina" (285). The essays in *Queer Iberia: Sexualities, Cultures, and Crossings from the Middle Ages to the Renaissance*, ed. Josiah Blackmore and Gregory S. Hutcheson (Durham: Duke University Press, 1999) present a view of medieval sexuality more in line with my own.

6. Studies of historic *soldadeiras* include Menéndez Pidal, *Poesía juglaresca*, 62–65, 228–34, and Ana Paula Ferreira, "A 'Outra Arte' das Soldadeiras," *Luso-Brazilian Review* 30.1 (1993): 155–66. On *panaderas*, see Louise O. Vasvári, "La semiología de la connotación: Lectura polisémica de 'Cruz cruzada panadera,'" *Nueva Revista de Filología Hispánica* 32 (1983): 299–324, and Francisco Márquez Villanueva, "Pan 'pudendum muliebris' y *Los españoles en Flandes*,"

Hispanic Studies in Honor of Joseph H. Silverman, ed. Joseph V. Ricapito (Newark, DE: Juan de la Cuesta, 1988), 247–69.

7. I take the phrase 'parodic mimicry' from my colleague Laura G. Gutiérrez who uses this term to refer to similarly exaggerated performances of stereotypical Mexican and Mexican American identities by modern performance artists; see her article, "Gender Parody, Political Satire, and Postmodern *Rancheras*: Astrid Hadad's *Heavy Nopal*" (unpublished manuscript). My usage is also informed by the work of Elin Diamond, "Mimesis, Mimicry, and the 'True-Real,' " *Modern Drama* 32.1 (March 1989): 58–72, and Homi K. Bhabha, "Of Mimicry and Man: The Ambivalence of Colonial Discourse," in his *The Location of Culture* (London and New York: Routledge, 1994), 85–92. I develop this idea more in chapter 1. Richard Schechner, *Performance Theory*, rev. ed. (New York and London: Routledge, 1988), 50, demonstrates that onstage performances of self always exaggerate certain aspects of one's offstage character; Marvin Carlson, *Performance: A Critical Introduction* (London and New York: Routledge, 1996), 6, discusses the doubleness of performing oneself. Nodar Manso suggests individuals named in comic lyrics either voiced their parts or mimed themselves on stage, *Teatro menor galaicoportugués*, 24, 50–53, 169. Earnshaw, *The Female Voice in Medieval Romance Lyric*, 1–3, 11–15, discusses how women's voices in medieval lyric authored by men are double-voiced. The lyrics I discuss are mostly attributed to men; in the case of anonymous popular lyrics, while female authorship is possible, it is impossible to prove. While professional and amateur female performers certainly composed music and lyrics, few of their works were preserved. On the question of female composition in medieval Europe, see Susan Boynton, "Women's Performance of the Lyric Before 1500," *Medieval Woman's Song: Cross-Cultural Approaches*, 47–65; Matilda Tomaryn Bruckner, "Fictions of the Female Voice: The Women Troubadours," *Speculum* 67 (1992): 865–91; Judith R. Cohen, "*Ca no soe joglaresa*: Women and Music in Medieval Spain's Three Cultures," *Medieval Woman's Song: Cross-Cultural Approaches*, 66–80; Maria V. Coldwell, "Jougleresses and Trobairitz: Secular Musicians in Medieval France," *Women Making Music: The Western Art Tradition, 1150–1950*, ed. Jane Bowers and Judith Tick (Urbana and Chicago: University of Illinois Press, 1986), 39–61; Ria Lemaire, "Explaining Away the Female Subject: The Case of Medieval Lyric," *Poetics Today* 7 (1986): 729–43; and Kimberly Marshall, "Symbols, Performers, and Sponsors: Female Musical Creators in the Late Middle Ages," *Rediscovering the Muses: Women's Musical Traditions*, ed. Marshall (Boston: Northeastern University Press, 1993), 140–68.

8. On the various types of professional female entertainers, see Menéndez Pidal, *Poesía juglaresca*, 61–66. The figure of the *alcahueta* has already been well studied, perhaps most thoroughly by Francisco Márquez Villanueva in his *Orígenes y sociología del tema celestinesco* (Barcelona: Anthropos, 1993); the best recent study of the female healer and *alcahueta* is Jean Dangler's *Mediating Fictions: Literature, Women Healers, and the Go-Between in Medieval and Early Modern Iberia* (Lewisburg, PA: Bucknell University Press, 2001).

9. Critics have occasionally misconstrued the apparent realism of poems on *serranas* as reflecting the historical realities of medieval shepherdesses; see, e.g., José Manuel Nieto Soria, "Aspectos de la vida cotidiana de las pastoras a través de la poesía medieval castellana," *El trabajo de las mujeres en la Edad Media Hispana*, ed. Ángela Muñoz Fernández and Cristina Segura Graíño (Madrid: Asociación Cultural Al-Mudayna, 1988), 303–319.

10. In my discussion of the dialogic performance context of courtly lyric, I draw mainly on Laura Kendrick, *The Game of Love: Troubadour Word Play* (Berkeley: University of California Press, 1988), esp. 62–63.

11. Vasvári, "Peregrinaciones por topografías pornográficas en el *Libro de buen amor*," *Actas del VI Congreso Internacional de la Asociación Hispánica de Literatura Medieval*, ed. José Manuel Lucía Megías (Alcalá: Universidad de Alcalá, 1997), 1563–72; *Hable con ella*, dir. Pedro Almodóvar [El Deseo, 2002], videocassette (Warner Bros. Pictures, 2003).

12. See, e.g., Sarah Kay, *Subjectivity in Troubadour Poetry* (Cambridge: Cambridge University Press, 1990) and Simon Gaunt, *Gender and Genre in Medieval French Literature* (Cambridge: Cambridge University Press, 1995), who explore Provençal troubadours' construction and performance of self and gender; Susan Crane, *The Performance of Self: Ritual, Clothing, and Identity during the Hundred Years War* (Philadelphia: University of Pennsylvania Press, 2002) focuses on courtly performance practices in England. For Hispanomedieval studies of courtly performances by men, see Julian Weiss, "Alvaro de Luna, Juan de Mena and the Power of Courtly Love," *MLN* 106.2 (1991): 241–56; E. Michael Gerli, "Carvajal's *Serranas*: Reading, Glossing, and Rewriting the *Libro de buen amor* in the *Cancionero de Estúñiga*," *Studies on Medieval Spanish Literature in Honor of Charles F. Fraker*, ed. Mercedes Vaquero and Alan Deyermond (Madison: Hispanic Seminary of Medieval Studies, 1995), 159–71; see also the essays in *Poetry at Court in Trastamaran Spain: From the Cancionero de Baena to the Cancionero General*, ed. Gerli and Weiss (Tempe, AZ: Medieval & Renaissance Texts & Studies, 1998).

13. Recent publications on women and medieval music include: *The Voice of the Trobairitz: Perspectives on the Women Troubadours*, ed. William D. Paden (Philadelphia: University of Pennsylvania Press, 1989); Boynton, "Women's Performance of the Lyric Before 1500"; Bruckner, "Fictions of the Female Voice"; Maria V. Coldwell, "Jougleresses and Trobairitz"; and Fredric L. Cheyette and Margaret Switten, "Women in Troubadour Song: Of the Comtessa and the Vilana," *Women & Music* 2 (1998): 26–45. The edited collections *Women in Music: An Anthology of Source Readings from the Middle Ages to the Present*, ed. Carol Neuls-Bates (Boston: Northeastern University Press, 1996), *Women & Music: A History*, ed. Karin Pendle, 2nd ed. (Bloomington and Indianapolis: Indiana University Press, 2001), *Women Making Music: The Western Art Tradition*, and *Medieval Woman's Song: Cross-Cultural Approaches* all discuss women's historical role as patrons, performers, composers, and consumers of music and lyric poetry. Bruce W. Holsinger, *Music, Body, and Desire in Medieval Culture: Hildegard of Bingen to Chaucer* (Stanford: Stanford

University Press, 2001), also studies how medieval sexuality was constructed and performed in music and song.

14. Studies of female performers in the Iberian peninsula include Cohen, "*Ca no soe joglaresa*"; Ferreira, "A 'Outra Arte' das Soldadeiras"; Eukene Lacarra Lanz, "Sobre la sexualidad de las soldadeiras en las cantigas d'escarnho e de maldizer," *Amor, escarnio y linaje en la literatura gallego-portuguesa*, ed. Lacarra Lanz et al. (Bilbao: Universidad del País Vasco, 2002), 75–97; Catherine Léglu, "Did Women Perform Satirical Poetry? Trobairitz and *Soldadeiras* in Medieval Occitan Poetry," *Forum for Modern Language Studies* 37.1 (2001): 15–25; David Ashurst, "Masculine Postures and Poetic Gambits: The Treatment of the *Soldadeira* in the *Cantigas d'escarnho e de mal dizer*," *Bulletin of Hispanic Studies* (Liverpool) 74 (1997): 1–6; and Menéndez Pidal, *Poesía juglaresca*.

Chapter 1   Performing Women in Medieval Iberian Poetic Spectacles: History and Theory

1. Discussions of the oral performance of medieval lyric include Paul Zumthor, *La lettre et la voix: De la "littérature" médiévale* (Paris: Seuil, 1987) and Peter Dronke, *The Medieval Lyric*, 3rd ed. (Woodbridge, UK: D.S. Brewer, 1996). Ian Parker, "The Performance of Troubadour and Trouvère Songs," *Early Music* 5 (1977): 184–207, and Kendrick, *The Game of Love*, discuss Provençal performance practices. Discussions of Iberian poetic performances include Menéndez Pidal, *Poesía juglaresca*; Nodar Manso, *Teatro menor galaicoportugués* and his "El carácter dramático-narrativo del escarnio y maldecir de Alfonso X," *Revista Canadiense de Estudios Hispánicos* 9.3 (1985): 405–444; António José Saraiva, "A poesia dos cancioneiros não é lírica, mas dramática," in his *Poesia e drama: Bernadim Ribeiro. Gil Vicente. Cantigas de Amigo* (Lisbon: Gradiva, 1990), 181–89; and Josep Lluís Sirera, "Diálogos de cancionero y teatralidad," *Historias y ficciones: Coloquio sobre la literatura del siglo XV*, ed. R. Beltrán et al. (Valencia: Universidad de Valencia, 1992), 351–63. Many recent discussions of medieval Castilian theater also address poetic performances, including Ángel Gómez Moreno, *El teatro medieval castellano en su marco románico* (Madrid: Taurus, 1991), Pérez Priego, *Teatro medieval*, and Stern, *The Medieval Theater in Castile*. In order to mark the musical nature of the poetry I discuss, I often use the word 'song' to designate a particular work.

2. References to Nodar Manso, *Teatro menor galaicoportugués*; Allegri, "Aproximación a una definición del actor medieval," *Cultura y representación en la Edad Media*, Actas del II Festival de Teatre i Música Medieval d'Elx, 1992, ed. Evangelina Rodríguez Cuadros (Alicante: Instituto de Cultura "Juan Gil Albert," 1994), 125–36; Butler, *Gender Trouble* and *Bodies that Matter*; Carlson, *Performance*; Schechner, *Performance Theory*.

3. These three *cancioneiros* are all available in modern editions: *Cancioneiro da Ajuda*, ed. Carolina Michäelis de Vasconcelos, 2 vols. (Halle: Max Niemeyer, 1904); *Cancioneiro Portuguêz da Vaticana*, ed. Theófilo Braga (Lisbon: Impresa

Nacional, 1878); and *Cancioneiro da Biblioteca Nacional (antigo Colocci-Brancuti)*, ed. E. Paxeco Machado and J.P. Machado, 8 vols. (Lisbon: Edicio da Revista de Portugal, 1949–64). The two Italian anthologies were probably prepared in the same scriptorium under the supervision of the Italian humanist Angelo Colocci in 1525–26; for a description of these MSS, see the appropriate entries in the *Dicionário da literatura medieval galega e portuguesa* (Lisbon: Caminho, 1993), 119–26. The entire collection of Galician-Portuguese profane lyric has been published in *Lírica profana galego-portuguesa. Corpus completo das cantigas medievais, con estudio biográfico, análise retórica e bibliografía específica*, ed. Fernando Magán Abelleira et al., 2 vols. (Santiago de Compostela: Xunta de Galicia, 1996). The organization and structure of the extant *cancioneiros has* been studied by António Resende de Oliveira, *Depois do espectáculo trovadoresco: A estrutura dos cancioneiros peninsulares e as recolhas dos séculos XIII e XIV* (Lisbon: Colibri, 1994).

4. Vicenç Beltran Pepió, "The Typology and Genesis of the *Cancioneros*: Compiling the Materials," *Poetry at Court in Trastamaran Spain*, 19–46, studies medieval Castilian *cancioneros*; for a complete edition and index of Castilian *cancionero* poetry, see Brian Dutton, *El Cancionero del siglo XV, c. 1360–1520*, 7 vols. (Salamanca: Universidad de Salamanca, 1990–91), which follows on his earlier *Catálogo-Índice de la poesía cancioneril del siglo XV*, 2 vols. (Madison: Hispanic Seminary of Medieval Studies, 1982). Throughout this book I use Dutton's identification system for fifteenth-century *cancioneros* and the poetry contained therein. Most of the *cancionero* poetry I cite comes from single-author editions, including the Marqués de Santillana (Íñigo López de Mendoza), *Poesía lírica*, ed. Miguel Ángel Pérez Priego (Madrid: Cátedra, 1999); Carvajal, *Poesie*, ed. Emma Scoles (Rome: Ateneo, 1967); Sebastián de Horozco, *Cancionero*, ed. Jack Weiner (Bern: Herbert Lang; Frankfurt: Peter Lang, 1975); Antón de Montoro, *Cancionero*, ed. Marcella Ciceri, intro. Julio Rodríguez Puértolas (Salamanca: Universidad de Salamanca, 1990).

5. *Corpus de la antigua lírica popular hispánica (siglos XV a XVII)*, Nueva biblioteca de erudición y crítica 1 (Madrid: Castalia, 1987).

6. The six Martin Codax *cantigas* are found in MS Vindel, MS 979, Pierpont Morgan Library, New York; they are transcribed with modern notation in Manuel Pedro Ferreira, *O Som de Martin Codax: Sobre a dimensão musical da lírica galego-portuguesa (séculos XII–XIV)* (Lisbon: Unisys, 1986). Harvey Leo Sharrer, "Fragmentos de Sete Cantigas d'Amor de D. Dinis, musicadas; uma descoberta," *Literatura medieval*, Actas do IV Congresso da Associação Hispânica de Literatura Medieval, Lisboa, 1–5 Outubro 1991, ed. Aires Augusto Nascimento and Cristina Almeida Ribeiro, 4 vols., vol. 1 (Lisbon: Cosmos, 1993), 13–29, reproduces the manuscript fragments of the seven Don Dinis *cantigas*. The *Cancioneiro da Ajuda* is an unusually elaborate anthology for medieval secular lyrics and did include room for musical notation as well as illustrations of *trovador* spectacles; the manuscript was never completed, so there is no notation and none of the illustrations were finished. I discuss these illustrations as visual evidence for *trovador* spectacles below. The *Cancioneiro da Ajuda* is available in a facsimile edition: *Fragmento do Nobiliario*

do Conde Dom Pedro. Cancioneiro da Ajuda. Edição Fac-similada do códice exis-tente na Biblioteca da Ajuda, ed. Instituto Português do Patrimonio Arquitec-tónico e Arqueológico (Lisbon: Távola Redonda, 1994).

7. See Jineen Elyse Krogstad, "Cancionero Poetry and Its Musical Sources," Diss. University of Illinois at Urbana-Champaign, 1988, 3–6, for a complete (as of 1988) list of manuscript and printed sources of *cancionero* lyrics with musical notation; she includes forty-three items in this list. On the question of the use of musical notation, see Krogstad, "Cancionero Poetry and Its Musical Sources," 77–78, 85–86, and Robert Murrell Stevenson, *Spanish Music in the Age of Columbus* (The Hague: M. Nijhoff, 1960), 303.

8. Michäelis de Vasconcelos, *Cancioneiro da Ajuda*, vol. 2, 162–63; Menéndez Pidal, *Poesía juglaresca*, 63–64, concurs with her reading of the gender and office of the figures. I have consulted the facsimile edition of the *Cancioneiro da Ajuda* and based the following descriptions upon my reading of the illus-trations. I count the folios from the first page that contains verse, omitting the first forty folios, which contain the *Livro de Linhagens do Conde D. Pedro*. For a description of the MS, see M.A. Ramos, "Cancioneiro da Ajuda," *Dicionário da literatura galega e portuguesa*, 115–17. The illustrations are found on f. 4 (seated male, female on foot holding castanets, seated male playing psalter), f. 15 (only two figures, a seated male and a seated male harpist), f. 16 (seated male, female on foot holding castanets, seated male playing psalter), f. 17 (seated male, female on foot holding castanets, seated male playing psalter), f. 18 (seated male, male guitarist on foot, female on foot, perhaps singing and/or dancing), f. 21 (seated male, standing male playing viola with bow, standing female playing a tambourine), f. 29 (seated male, male gui-tarist on foot, female on foot holding castanets), f. 33 (seated male, standing male playing viola with bow, standing female perhaps singing or dancing), f. 37 (seated male, standing male violist, seated male harpist), f. 40v (seated male, standing male guitarist, standing male perhaps singing), f. 47 (seated male, standing male guitarist, seated male harpist), f. 48 (seated male, stand-ing male guitarist, seated female playing tambourine), f. 51v (seated male, standing male guitarist, standing female holding castanets), f. 55v (seated male, standing male guitarist, standing female holding castanets), f. 59 (seated male, standing female holding castanets, seated male psalterist), and f. 60 (seated male, standing male guitarist, standing female playing tambourine).

9. By 'relatively simple presentation style' I mean, few instruments, simple cos-tumes, and performance in a multifunctional space, not in a space reserved for lyric spectacles. Discussions of lyric performances in Spain and France generally conform with my model. Saraiva, who discusses the performative aspect of the Galician-Portuguese *Cantigas d'amigo* (indirectly) posits that a soloist or perhaps two performers sang and gestured in order to illustrate the fictive context and setting of their song ("A poesia dos cancioneiros não é lírica, mas dramática"); Cheyette and Switten, who discuss *trobairitz* per-formances, seem convinced that Provençal lyric was always performed by soloists, male or female ("Women in Troubadour Song," 36, 44); Katharina

Städtler, "The *Sirventes* by Gormonda de Monpeslier," *The Voice of the Trobairitz*, 129–55, suggests that two performers performed a satiric political debate poem (151); Boynton discusses an illustration of the troubadour Gaucelm Faidit and his wife, the *soldadera* Guilelma Monja, in performance together ("Women's Performance of the Lyric Before 1500," 52); Nodar Manso, *Teatro menor galaicoportugués*, alone posits a very different performance format for *Cantigas d'escarnho*.

10. Illustrations from the *Códice de los músicos* are widely reproduced, including on the Internet: see "Las Cantigas de Santa Maria," [no name], http://www.3to4.com/Cantigas/e_index.html (updated February 4, 2004, cited May 10, 2004).

11. All citations of the *Siete partidas* from *Las siete partidas del sabio rey don Alfonso el nono, nueuamente Glosadas por el Licenciado Gregorio Lopez del Consejo Real de Indias de su Magestad*, Salamanca, 1555, Facsimile (Madrid: Boletín Oficial del Estado, 1974); in transcribing this text, I expand abbreviations and omit superscript references to the glosses. All references included in the text. Menéndez Pidal, *Poesía juglaresca*, 46 n. 63, 115–17, and Stern, *The Medieval Theater in Castile*, 80–81, also cite *Partida* 7.6.4. All translations are mine.

12. These repercussions are listed in *Partida* 7.6.7; they include loss of benefices and honors and banishment from royal and seigniorial courts.

13. Martín de Riquer, *Los trovadores: Historia literaria y textos* (Barcelona: Planeta, 1975), vol. 1, 108, presents evidence that Guillaume IX performed his comic and obscene lyrics. In the fifteenth century, aristocrats had yet more license to participate in lyric and other courtly spectacles, as shown by the *Hechos del Condestable don Miguel Lucas de Iranzo*, an official biography of this magnate that describes the almost constant play-acting that he organized and led in his court in Jaen [*Relación de los hechos del Condestable don Miguel Lucas de Iranzo (Crónica del siglo XV)*, ed. Juan de Mata Carriazo, colección de crónicas españolas, 3 (Madrid: Espasa-Calpe, 1940)]. I discuss evidence that the Marqués de Santillana performed his own *serranillas* in chapter 4.

14. Martín Pérez, *Libro de las confesiones: Una radiografía de la sociedad medieval española*, ed., intro., and notes, Antonio García y García, Bernardo Alonso Rodríguez, and Francisco Cantelar Rodríguez (Madrid: Biblioteca de Autores Cristianos, 2002), 445–46. Pérez closely follows other medieval penitentials, such as Thomas of Cobham's *Poenitentiale* (Gómez Moreno, *El teatro medieval castellano*, 36–37, cites passages from both texts; Pérez Priego, *Teatro medieval*, 207–208, also cites Pérez). Pérez's list of *juglaresque* performances is generic and pan-European, not specific to Iberia. For a more extensive overview of *juglaresque* performance practices, see Menéndez Pidal, *Poesía juglaresca*, 86–120, 302–313.

15. See Mary Russo, *The Female Grotesque: Risk, Excess and Modernity* (New York and London: Routledge, 1994), 41–44; her discussion of modern female acrobats, especially of trapeze artists and tight-rope walkers, highlights the ambiguous gender of their gravity-defying performances, virile in their strength yet feminine in their bodily self-display and ability to detach "from the heaviness of the flesh."

16. The opposition between entertainers and ecclesiasts was, Kendrick argues, at the heart of troubadour language and poetic practice (*The Game of Love*, 15–21). Luigi Allegri discusses this opposition in medieval Spain in "El espectáculo en la Edad Media," *Teatro y espectáculo en la Edad Media*, Actas Festival d'Elx 1990, ed. L. Quirante (Alicante: Instituto de Cultura "Juan Gil Albert," 1992), 21–30. Not only were clerics forbidden to perform in public, but entertainers were forbidden to dress as clerics (*Partida* 1.6.35 and 1.6.36). For a discussion of the *clérigo ajuglarado*, see Menéndez Pidal, *Poesía juglaresca*, 57–61 (he discusses Ruiz as a performer, 268–83); see also Stern, *The Medieval Theater in Castile*, 72–80. The question of Juan Ruiz's true identity has provoked much scholarly debate; see Francisco J. Hernández, "The Venerable Juan Ruiz, Archpriest of Hita," *La corónica* 13.1 (Fall 1984): 10–22, and Henry Ansgar Kelly, "Juan Ruiz and Archpriests: Novel Reports," *La corónica* 16. 2 (Spring 1988): 32–54. For her part, Louise Vasvári has suggested that Juan Ruiz was the name of a stock character and that various performers assumed that name when presenting materials associated with that character (personal communication). I agree that the figure of the Archpriest of Hita is a performance persona, not a historic individual. For an analysis of this multiform poetic 'I,' see Alfonso Rey, "Juan Ruiz, Don Melón y el yo poético medieval," *Bulletin of Hispanic Studies* 56 (1979): 103–116. Vasvári explores the levels of semantic play in "La semiología de la connotación."

17. I discuss the *Cantigas d'escarnho* as an exchange of ritual insults in "Jokes on Soldadeiras"; see also Jesús Montoya Martínez, "El carácter lúdico de la literatura medieval. (A propósito del 'jugar de palabra'. Partida Segunda, tít. IX, ley XXIX)," *Homenaje al profesor Antonio Gallego Morell*, ed. C. Argente del Castillo et al. (Granada: Universidad de Granada, 1989), 431–42. Modern studies of ritual insult exchanges, sometimes called Playing the Dozens, include John H. McDowell, "Verbal Dueling," *Handbook of Discourse Analysis, III: Discourse and Dialogue*, ed. Heurs Aven Digle (London: Academic Press, 1985), 203–211, and William Labov, "Rules for Ritual Insults," *Studies in Social Interaction*, ed. David Sudnow (New York: The Free Press, 1972), 120–69.

18. Throughout this book, I use RL to indicate poems cited from M. Rodrigues Lapa's revised edition of the *Cantigas d'escarnho*.

19. See, e.g., the descriptions of courtly spectacles in Gómez Moreno, *El teatro medieval castellano*, 89–97, 144–58; Pérez Priego, *Teatro medieval*, 15–20, 231–246; Stern, *The Medieval Theater in Castile*, 92–108, 176–78, 182–83, 217–18, 259–61; and Francisco Rico, "Unas coplas de Jorge Manrique y las fiestas de Valladolid en 1428," *Anuario de estudios medievales* 2 (1965): 515–24, esp. 515–23. Both Gómez Moreno and Pérez Priego include in their appendices extended excerpts from late medieval chronicles and letters describing courtly spectacles.

20. The studies I rely on are Deborah A. Kapchan, *Gender on the Market: Moroccan Women and the Revoicing of Tradition* (Philadelphia: University of Pennsylvania Press, 1996), and Brigittine M. French, "The Symbolic Capital

of Social Identities: The Genre of Bargaining in an Urban Guatemalan Market," *Journal of Linguistic Anthropology* 10 (2001): 155–89.

21. Citation from *Poesía juglaresca*, 234, 18, 20.

22. One who is particularly significant for me yet whose publications do not reflect the extent of his work on performance is John K. Walsh, with whom I was fortunate to study at the University of California, Berkeley.

23. Citation from Nodar Manso, *Teatro menor galaicoportugués*, 29.

24. Among Nodar Manso's critics is Sirera, "Diálogos de cancionero y teatralidad"; Pérez Priego, *Teatro medieval*, omits Nodar Manso's book from his bibliography. Stern, *The Medieval Theater in Castile*, 157–60, does discuss Nodar Manso's work.

25. Citation from Boynton, "Women's Performance of the Lyric Before 1500," 47.

26. Citation from Kendrick, *The Game of Love*, 62–63. Richard Schechner, *Performance Theory*, xiv, also addresses the importance of post-performance evaluations, as I discuss below. The definition of *escarnio* in the *Arte de Trovar* in the *Cancioneiro da Biblioteca Nacional* underlines the equivocal nature of the *Cantigas d'escarnho*: "Cantigas d escarneo som aquelas que / os trobadores fazen querendo dizer / mal d algue[m] en elas, e dizen lho / [per] palauras cubertas, que aiam dous / entendymentos pera lhe lo non entenderen / . . . ligeyramente; e estas palauras / chaman os clerigos *hequiuocatio*" (15; *trovadores* compose *Cantigas d'escarnho* when they want to insult someone, and they use veiled words that have two meanings, so that they are not easily understood; and clerics call these words *equivocatio*).

27. Citation from Gómez Moreno, *El teatro medieval castellano*, 103.

28. I refer primarily to Butler's work on the performative nature of gender, published in *Gender Trouble* and in *Bodies that Matter*.

29. Joan Fernández, probably a Muslim convert to Christianity, is called "o mouro" (the Moor) and told that a Moor is fucking his wife (i.e., he is cuckolded by his former self), in RL 51, 229, 230, 297, 300, 408, and 409. See Benjamin Liu, "'Affined to love the Moor': Sexual Misalliance and Cultural Mixing in the *Cantigas d'escarnho e de mal dizer*," *Queer Iberia*, 48–72, esp. 61, for a discussion of this character, and Roy Rosenstein, "The Voiced and the Voiceless in the *Cancioneiros*: The Muslim, the Jew, and the Sexual Heretic as *Exclusus Amator*," *La corónica* 26.2 (Spring 1998): 65–75, esp. 68–72, on the treatment of Moors and Jews in the *Cantigas d'escarnho*. See Steven F. Kruger, "Conversion and Medieval Sexual, Religious, and Racial Categories," *Constructing Medieval Sexuality*, ed. Karma Lochrie, Peggy McCracken, and James A. Schultz (Minneapolis: University of Minnesota Press, 1997), 158–79, on the problematics of religious conversion in medieval culture. For the poetic treatment of fifteenth-century *conversos* (Jewish converts to Christianity), see Gregory B. Kaplan, *The Evolution of Converso Literature: The Writings of the Converted Jews of Medieval Spain* (Gainesville, FL: University Press of Florida, 2002).

30. Throughout this book I use JP to refer to Juan Paredes's edition of Alfonso X's profane lyric, *El cancionero profano de Alfonso X el Sabio: Edición crítica, con*

introducción, notas y glosario (Rome: Japadre, 2001). I find his readings more reliable than those of Lapa in his revised edition of the *Cantigas d'escarnho*.

31. Jorge A. Osório, "≪Cantiga de escarnho≫ galego-portuguesa: sociologia ou poética?" *Revista da Faculdade de Letras, Linguas e Literatura* 3 (1986): 153–97, addresses how the use of taboo language enables the expression of the unspeakable. See also Josiah Blackmore, "The Poets of Sodom," *Queer Iberia*, 195–221, who addresses the issue of what constitutes obscenity.

32. Reference to Butler, *Excitable Speech: A Politics of the Performative* (New York and London: Routledge, 1997), 5, 24–28. Osório, "≪Cantiga de escarnho,≫" argues that interpellation is a key characteristic of the *Cantigas d'escarnho* (174–75). I discuss this issue further in chapter 2.

33. While I use the singular form 'identity,' I do so for ease of expression, not to imply that anyone has solely one authentic identity.

34. References to Nodar Manso, *Teatro menor galaicoportugués*, 24, 50–53, 169.

35. I take the phrase "parodic mimicry" from Gutiérrez, "Gender Parody"; see also Diamond, "Mimesis, Mimicry, and the 'True-Real' " and Bhabha, "Of Mimicry and Man," 85–92. Schechner, *Performance Theory*, 50, demonstrates that onstage performances of self always exaggerate certain aspects of one's offstage character.

36. Citation from Allegri, "Aproximación a una definición del actor medieval," 128.

37. Citation from Carlson, *Performance*, 6.

38. Citations from Massip, "L'actor en l'espectacle medieval," *Teatralidad medieval y su supervivencia*, Actas del III Festival d'Elx de Teatre i Música Medieval, ed. César Oliva (Alicante: Instituto de Cultura "Juan Gil Albert," 1998), 27–40, 30; Cusick, "Feminist Theory, Music Theory, and the Mind/Body Problem," *Perspectives of New Music* 32.1 (1994): 8–27, 21, 20; and Russo, *The Female Grotesque*, 22.

39. Jane Desmond, *Staging Tourism: Bodies on Display from Waikiki to Sea World* (Chicago: University of Chicago Press, 1999), examines the racialized construction of the Hula dancer's body; the preferred Hawai'i ethnic look, "hapa haole," is a mix of native and Causian, and slender, a body type rare among Polynesians (23). I take the phrase "competent body" from Kapchan, *Gender on the Market*. Both Coldwell, "Jougleresses and Trobairitz," 44, and J. Michele Edwards, "Women in Music to ca. 1450," *Women & Music: A History*, 26–53, esp. 34, mention literary examples of noble women darkening their skin to pass as minstrels. On dance in the Middle Ages, see Antonio María Mourinho, "A Dança na Antiguidade e na Idade Média," *Revista de dialectología y tradiciones populares* 32 (1976): 373–403, esp. 386–95, and Félix A. Rivas, "El significado de las imágenes de bailarinas en el románico aragonés," *De los símbolos al orden simbólico femenino* (*Siglos IV-XVII*), ed. Ana Isabel Cerrada Jiménez and Josemi Lorenzo Arribas (Madrid: Asociación Cultural Al-Mudayna, 1998), 217–35, esp. 220–23. Rivas denies that all medieval Aragonese images of female dancers represent Salome or condemn dancing.

40. See Kapchan's discussion of *shikhat*, professional dancers, in modern Morocco, *Gender on the Market*, 181–211, and of how amateur dancers

intentionally perform less competently, 199. Cusick, "Feminist Theory, Music Theory," 20, also discusses the dominant negative reception of female performers.

41. Citation from Schechner, *Performance Theory*, xiv.

42. See Kapchan's discussion of performance as a commodity in modern Moroccan marketplaces, *Gender on the Market*, 40. On the controls exerted on public performances, see Pirkko Moisala, "Musical Gender in Performance," *Women & Music* 3 (1999): 1–16, esp. 11–13.

43. Reference to E. Michael Gerli, "Antón de Montoro and the Wages of Eloquence: Poverty, Patronage, and Poetry in 15th-c. Castile," *Romance Philology* 48 (1995): 265–76.

Chapter 2   *Soldadeiras*' Deviant Performances and Poets' Counterposes: Courtly Play in the *Cantigas d'escarnho e de mal dizer*

1. Citation from *Poesía juglaresca*, 62. *Soldadeiras* were professional female court entertainers who danced and sang; generally considered prostitutes, sometimes they are depicted as camp-followers in the *Cantigas d'escarnho*. The word *soldadera/soldadeira* derives from *soldo*, salary or wage, as does also *soldado*, soldier. In his entry for *sueldo* (Galician-Portuguese *soldo*), Joan Corominas shows that *sueldo* is derived from late Latin *solidus*, "a certain gold coin, ducat," and first appeared in the vernacular as *soldo* in 1062–63. *Sueldo* additionally meant "payment for a mercenary soldier"; *soldadero* as "mercenary" appears in Castilian (in Berceo). Corominas links *soldadera* with *soldadero*; however, the only definition he provides is Menéndez Pidal's, *juglaresa* "female minstrel," or *mujer de malas costumbres*, a vicious or immodest woman (Joan Corominas and José A. Pascual, *Diccionario crítico etimológico castellano e hispánico*, 5 vols., vol. 5 [Madrid: Gredos, 1983], 325–26). Liu suggests that the association of *soldadeira* with camp-followers likens their trade to mercenaries ("Affined to love the Moor," 57). For more on the poetic treatment of *soldadeiras*, see Menéndez Pidal, 62–65, 228–34; Lapa, *Lições de literatura portuguesa, Época medieval*, 7th rev. ed. (Coimbra: Coimbra 1970), 184–86; Kenneth R. Scholberg, *Sátira e invectiva en la España medieval*, Biblioteca Románica Hispánica vol. 163 (Madrid: Gredos, 1971), 81–88; Yara Frateschi Vieira, "Retrato medieval de mulher: a bailarina com pés de porco," *Estudos Portugueses e Africanos* 1 (1983): 95–110; Graça Videira Lopes, *A sátira nos cancioneiros medievais galego-portugueses* (Lisbon: Estampa, 1994), 221–29; Esther Corral Díaz, *As mulleres nas cantigas medievais*, Seminario de Estudos Galegos 2 (La Coruña: Castro, 1996), 278–81; Ashurst, "Masculine Postures"; Lacarra Lanz, "Sobre la sexualidad de las soldadeiras"; and Filios, "Jokes on *soldadeiras*" and "Female Voices in the *Cantigas de escarnio*." I use RL to indicate poems in M. Rodrigues Lapa's revised edition of the *Cantigas d'escarnho*, LP for *Lírica profana galego-portuguesa*, JP for Paredes's edition of the *Cancionero profano de Alfonso X el Sabio*, CA for the *Cancioneiro da Ajuda*, CB for the *Cancioneiro da Biblioteca Nacional* and CV for the *Cancioneiro Portuguêz da Vaticana*.

2. I choose to cite the LP version of this song since it is less emended than RL 52; its reading of vv. 9–10 continues the one-to-one correspondence of body parts already established in vv. 6–7. Lapa considers Afons'Eanes do Coton the author of this song, while recognizing that CB attributes it to Pero Veviãez (*Cantigas d'escarnho e de mal dizer*, 51). Coton was undoubtedly associated with Alfonso X's court; Viviaez was probably a Portuguese *trovador* of noble status about whom little is known (see his brief biography in *Lírica profana galego-portuguesa*, 876). While Marinha is not called a *soldadeira* in this poem, the fact that she is portrayed in sexual intercourse with the narrator means that she is being treated as a *soldadeira*, whatever her factual status was (if she were a historic figure, a caveat that holds true for all the characters I discuss in this chapter). See my discussion of the use of the word *soldadeira* in the *Cantigas d'escarnho*, below. In my translation I draw on Richard Zenith's English translation of this song in his *113 Galician-Portuguese Troubadour Poems in Galician-Portuguese and English*, Aspects of Portugal (Manchester: Carcanet, 1995), 25. This song, like almost all the *Cantigas d'escarnho* I cite, is full of word-play and difficult to translate; my translations reflect what I see in these songs, which is one of many possible readings.

3. Reading *rebentar* in this context as a euphemism for orgasm (male or female) seems obvious to me; unfortunately, this word appears only once in the *Cantigas d'escarnho*, in this song. My reading is corroborated by Alan Deyermond's "Sexual Initiation in Woman's Court Lyric," *Courtly Literature: Culture and Context*, Selected papers from the 5th Triennial Congress of the International Courtly Literature Society, Dalften, The Netherlands, August 9–16, 1986, ed. Keith Busby and Eric Kooper (Amsterdam and Philadelphia: John Benjamins, 1990), 126–58, esp. 151–52, in which he reads *crever* (to burst) in "Doulce chose est que mariage," Christine de Pizan's poem on her wedding night, as a veiled reference to female orgasm. Critics who have read this song as a phallic boast include Malm, *Dolssor Conina*, 227, and Ashurst, "Masculine Postures," 3. Xosé Bieito Arias Freixedo, *Antoloxía de poesía obscena dos trobadores galego-portugueses* (Santiago de Compostela: Positivas, 1993), 92–93, argues that this song depicts Marinha as a phallus and that the speaker's covering of her is an attempt to restrict her too-active movement during coitus. Although his reading also comments on the gender and power conflict between the narrator and Marinha, he does not see her as deflating the speaker's boast, as I do.

4. In the *Cantigas d'escarnho*, men's anuses are targets of sexual aggression and sites of gender confusion, as anal rape reveals the target's feminine vulnerability. Blackmore, "The Poets of Sodom," 195–221, and Rosenstein, "The Voiced and the Voiceless," discuss sodomitic assault in the *Cantigas d'escarnho*.

5. V. 13, "como me non veja nenguũ," is difficult to interpret; Lapa reads this line as "como me non vej' a nenguũ," "as I have never seen anyone do" (*Cantigas d'escarnho e de mal dizer*, 51); Zenith renders this line as "no man has my art" (*113 Galician-Portuguese Troubadour Poems*, 25). This verse plays on the seen and the unseen, and in the context of a live performance is highly ironic, as the speaker verbally and visually represents the unseen.

6. Excessive female receptivity is a folkloric commonplace, especially for old women and prostitutes; see Vasvári, " 'Chica cosa es dos nuezes': Lost Sexual Humor in the *Libro del Arcipreste*," *Revista de Estudios Hispánicos* 24.1 (1990): 1–22, esp. 12–14, and Barbara F. Weissberger, "Male Sexual Anxieties in *Carajicomedia*: A Response to Female Sovereignty," *Poetry at Court in Trastamaran Spain*, 221–34, for an overview of this motif in medieval Spanish literature. A similar anxiety is touched on in RL 11, in which Maria Balteira challenges Joan Rodríguiz, implying that he won't be able to measure up to her satisfaction; his subsequent phallic boast silences her. See Vasvári, " 'La madeira certeira. . .a midida d'Espanha' de Alfonso X: un *gap* carvalesco," *Actes del VII Congrés de l'Associació Hispànica de Literatura Medieval*, Castelló de la Plana, 22–26 de septembre de 1997, ed. Santiago Fortuño Llorens and Tomás Martínez Romero, vol. 3 (Castelló de la Plana: Universidad Jaume I, 1999), 459–69, for a reading of this *cantiga*.

7. Citation from David Nirenberg, *Communities of Violence: Persecution of Minorities in the Middle Ages* (Princeton: Princeton University Press, 1996), 141. Vasvári, "Festive Phallic Discourse in the *Libro del Arcipreste*," *La corónica* 22:2 (1994): 89–117, and "The Semiotics of Phallic Aggression and Anal Penetration as Male Agonistic Ritual in the 'Libro de Buen Amor,' " *Queer Iberia*, 130–56, has discussed the use of ritualistic performances of anal rape to signify the dominance of one man over another; she uses the word shafting to identify this phenomenon, and I follow her usage. We see an appropriate feminine response to aggressive male sexuality in RL 14, discussed below.

8. Louise O. Vasvári demonstrated this gesture in her discussion of RL 11 as a phallic boast at the 1997 MLA Convention in Toronto, a talk published as " 'La madeira certeira.' " My discussions of how women, silenced in the poetic text, would speak in a dialogic performance context draw on E. Jane Burns, *Bodytalk: When Women Speak in Old French Literature* (Philadelphia: University of Pennsylvania Press, 1993), esp. 31–70, where she discusses how women speak in old French literature. While Burns considers the female voice to be always hostile and challenging, at least from a masculine point of view, I believe that, in some cases, the female voice would collaborate or support the male speaker, in order to resolve tensions and play along with the joke. See also Kendrick's discussion of the game of interpretation that followed performances of troubadour lyric, *Game of Love*, 16–19.

9. I discuss how naming *soldadeiras* in *Cantigas d'escarnho* simultaneously includes them in the courtly community and excludes them on the basis of difference in "Jokes on *Soldaderas*"; Ashurst, "Masculine Postures," discusses poets' stances toward *soldadeiras* as mere acts.

10. Both Zenith (*113 Galician-Portuguese Troubadour Poems*) and Jensen (*Medieval Galician-Portuguese Poetry: An Anthology* [New York & London: Garland, 1992]) provide good introductions to Galician-Portuguese poetry; Jensen's approach is more scholarly, yet he includes relatively fewer *Cantigas d'escarnho* in his selections. In this paragraph I draw on both Zenith and

Jensen's introductions and on Jensen's entry, "Poetry, Vernacular, Popular, and Learned: Cancioneiros of Portugal" in *Medieval Iberia: An Encyclopedia*, ed. E. Michael Gerli (New York: Routledge, 2003), 665–66. See also Janice Wright, "The Galician-Portuguese *Cancioneiro* Poets: *Cantigas de amor, de amigo, de escarnho e maldizer*," *Castilian Writers, 1200–1300*, ed. Frank A. Domínguez and George D. Greenia, Dictionary of Literary Biography (Detroit: Gale, 2004 [forthcoming]). These works are invaluable resources for English speakers looking for an introduction to medieval Iberian literature and culture.

11. Jesús D. Rodríguez Velasco, *Castigos para celosos, consejos para juglares* (Madrid: Gredos, 1999), also discusses the importance of speaking well as a demonstration of courtliness, 14–20.

12. In the *Partidas*, the specific term applied to this game of joking speech varies; it is initially called the *jugar de palabras* in *Partida* 2.9.29, while in the section I cite, it is simply called the *juego*.

13. See Marta Madero, *Manos violentas, palabras vedadas: La injuria en Castilla y León (siglos XIII–XV)*, Humanidades/Historia 341 (Madrid: Taurus, 1992), and Jerry R. Craddock, "The Legislative Works of Alfonso el Sabio," *Emperor of Culture. Alfonso X the Learned of Castile and His Thirteenth-Century Renaissance*, ed. Robert I. Burns, S.J. (Philadelphia: University of Pennsylvania Press, 1990), 182–97, esp. 186, for discussions of speech practices forbidden by medieval Spanish law codes. See Montoya Martínez, "El carácter lúdico de la literatura medieval," and Filios, "Jokes on *Soldadeiras*" for additional discussions of the *juego de palabras* and the *cantigas d'escarnho*.

14. On ritual insults, see McDowell, "Verbal Dueling," 207; also see Labov, "Rules for Ritual Insults," 239–43, for an extensive discussion of a Dozens session, and Schechner, *Performance Theory*, for a discussion of ritual insults as displaced violence.

15. References to Nodar Manso, *Teatro menor galaicoportugués*, 28, 65, 88, 95–99, 106, 111–12, and to Charles Muscatine, "Courtly Literature and Vulgar Language," *Court and Poet: Selected Proceedings of the Third Congress of the International Courtly Literature Society, Liverpool, 1980*, ed. Glyn S. Burgess et al. (Liverpool: Francis Cairns, 1981), 1–19. On *cazurros*, see Rodríguez Velasco, *Castigos para celosos*, 297, and Menéndez Pidal, *Poesía juglaresca*, 36. Osório, "≪Cantiga de escarnho≫," 176–83, presents a similar analysis of obscene language in the *Cantigas d'escarnho*, arguing that the narrative aspect contributes to the realism of the texts and increases the performer's ability to deny responsibility for the offensive language and/or event. Josiah Blackmore, "Locating the Obscene: Approaching a Poetic Canon," *La corónica* 26.2 (Spring 1998): 9–16, discusses what constitutes obscenity in the *Cantigas d'escarnho*; see also Yara F. Vieira and Brian F. Head, "Obscenidade em Poesia de Língua Portuguesa," *Luso-Brazilian Review* 16.1 (1979): 91–103.

16. See Menéndez Pidal, *Poesía juglaresca*, 33–66, esp. 33–41, 62–65, for a more complete discussion of the ranks of medieval performers. For a reassessment

of the importance and significance of the *segrel*, see António Resende de Oliveira, "Segrel," in *Dicionári da literatura galega e portuguesa*, 609–611. On the question of the noble status of one *soldadeira* in particular, that of Maria Pérez Balteira, see Carlos Alvar, "María Pérez, Balteira," *Archivo de filología aragonesa* 36–37 (1985): 11–40, esp. 11.

17. Citation from Ferreira, "A 'Outra Arte' das Soldadeiras," 158.

18. In the corpus of Galician-Portuguese lyric, feminine identity categories include the *senhor/dama* of the *Cantigas d' amor*, the *amiga* who voices the *Cantigas d'amigo*, and various dishonorable women in the *Cantigas d'escarnho*; see Corral Díaz, *As mulleres nas cantigas medievais*. Schechner, *Performance Theory*, 50, discusses performing oneself as overperforming one aspect of self; see also Carlson, *Performance*, 6.

19. Citation from Menéndez Pidal, *Poesía juglaresca*, 93, 228. See also Ruth Harvey, "*Joglars* and the Professional Status of the Early Troubadours," *Medium Ævum* 62 (1993): 221–41; as she has noted, a *joglar* was expected to be a "courtier-companion. . .[with] the ability to oil the wheels of cultivated social intercourse in the *familia* of a great lord and to contribute to the reputation of the court as a place of gracious living" (225).

20. Citation from Butler, "Performative Acts and Gender Constitution: An Essay in Phenomenology and Feminist Theory," *Writing on the Body: Female Embodiment and Feminist Theory*, ed. Katie Conboy, Nadia Medina, and Sarah Stanbury (New York: Columbia University Press, 1997), 401–17, 410–11. Admittedly the medieval dinner table does not correspond to Butler's bus scenario, which she employs to indicate the casual and close albeit public contact between individuals of different ages, ranks, sexualities, etc., egalitarian contact that, to a greater or lesser extent, characterizes the modern urban condition. The medieval dinner table was certainly not a free and accessible space; rather, it was a restricted and hierarchically organized site in which social differences were palpably enacted and reinforced. Even as invited guests, *soldadeiras'* inferior social status would have been marked in their seating position and perhaps in the table service, food, and drink they were offered. For a discussion of fifteenth- and sixteenth-century mixed-rank banquets, see Teofilo R. Ruiz, *Spanish Society, 1400–1600* (Harlow, UK: Longman, 2001), 209–222.

21. Sigmund Freud, in *Jokes and Their Relation to the Unconscious*, trans. James Strachey (New York: Norton, 1963), suggests that sexual jokes function to express indirectly the socially unacceptable desire to see sexual organs; the verbal expression forces the target, the teller, and the audience to imagine the organs and acts referred to in the joke, satisfying the teller's desire and also giving him some relief from the internal pressures caused by repressing and displacing primal urges. The sexual joke is, in Freud's view, basically hostile and provides the teller and (male) audience pleasure as they imagine or, less frequently, see the embarrassment the joke causes the female target; their mutual pleasure cements homosocial bonds and further excludes women from the community of jokers/laughers. Freud also sees

the presence of low-class women, such as barmaids, as facilitating sexual joke-telling sessions. Not only may the barmaid, due to her profession and class status, herself participate in the joke exchange by replying ambiguously yet humorously to the veiled attempt at seduction, but after her departure (necessitated by the presence of other customers), the men feel greater license to continue telling sexual jokes. As my discussion of *soldadeiras'* role in Galician-Portuguese lyric shows, I see their presence at court as similarly facilitating sexual *cantigas*.

22. Ashurst, "Masculine Postures," has also discussed how poets depicted *soldadeiras* to enable them to assume poetically productive attitudes; he does not discuss how *soldadeiras* may have performed responses to their poetic depictions, nor explore in much detail the gap between poet, lyric 'I,' and performer/stage persona, essential questions to consider in order to understand the poetic treatment of *soldadeiras* in the *cantigas d'escarnho*. While Nodar Manso addresses the question of self-referential performances, arguing that for the most part composers of *Cantigas d'escarnho* performed their own work, he does not explore the gap between onstage and offstage identity (*Teatro menor galaicoportugués*, 29–99, esp. 32–34).

23. For stage names, see Menéndez Pidal, *Poesía juglaresca*, 27. Maria Pérez Balteira is the *soldadeira* most frequently interpellated in the *Cantigas d'escarnho*, although the exact number of songs that depict her is subject to critical debate. Lapa, *Cantigas d'escarnho e de mal dizer*, 282, lists fifteen songs that name her: RL 1, 11, 146, 147, 195, 245, 315, 321, 331, 337, 358, 376, 400, 425, and 428; the same character is called both Maria Pérez and Maria Balteira in RL 315. A. Martínez Salazar, "Una gallega célebre en el siglo XIII," *Revista crítica de historia y literatura españolas, portuguesas é hispano-americanas* 2.10 (October 1897): 298–304, includes four other songs that do not mention her by name, but which he interprets as referring to her. Menéndez Pidal agrees with Martínez Salazar's interpreting these songs as referring to la Balteira; he also considers Maria Leve another name for Maria Balteira, so he includes RL 244, 246, and 247 in the cycle (228–34). Alvar, "María Pérez, Balteira," excludes RL 1 since it does not refer to la Balteira but has been reconstructed by Michäelis and Lapa with her name (17); he also argues that there were at least two María Pérezes associated with Alfonso's court and denies that all fourteen Maria Pérez/Balteira poems refer to the same woman. Lacarra Lanz, "Sobre la sexualidad de las soldadeiras," agrees with Alvar.

24. Martín de Riquer, *Los trovadores: Historia literaria y textos*, vol. 1, 108, presents evidence that Guillaume IX performed his comic and obscene lyrics; Harvey, "*Joglars* and the Professional Status of the Early Troubadours," criticizes modern critics' overemphasis on the difference between the poetic and social functions of the amateur troubadour and the professional *joglar*, arguing that the magnitude of such differences is not supported by poetic or documentary evidence. Nodar Manso, *Teatro menor galaicoportugués*, 95–99, makes a similar assertion for Iberia, yet he explores the different

ranks of the stock characters of the *archimimus*, played by a *trovador*, and the *stupidus*, played by a *juglar*, in his discussion of the drama *Martín Joglar*, 63–64. The vast majority of Alfonso X's surviving profane lyrics are *Cantigas d'escarnho;* while many of these are personal invectives motivated by politics, the four *tenções* (poetic debates that were probably improvisational) in which Alfonso responds to a satiric query by a *trovador* and his ironic pieces directed against *segreis* like Pero da Ponte and *jograis* like Cítola show that the king was an active and good-natured participant in the more-or-less informal exchange of ritual insults across the courtly hierarchy. See also Joseph T. Snow's discussion of Alfonso's use of the *trovador* mask in the *Cantigas de Santa Maria* in his "Alfonso as Troubadour: The Fact and the Fiction," *Emperor of Culture*, 124–40, and Paredes's discussion of Alfonso's satires in his *El cancionero profano*, 59–71.

25. Reference to Osório, "«Cantiga de escarnho,»" 174–75. See my discussion of interpellation in chapter 1.

26. The referent for "torp'e desembrado" is deliberately ambiguous, since the unnamed "ome. . .ven da fronteira" is Ordonhez himself. I discuss the hostile effect of this song in "Jokes on *Soldadeiras*."

27. In my translation of this song, I have drawn on Arias Freixedo's modern Galician version in his *Antoloxía de poesía obscena*, 106. The word-play on *grave* makes this poem difficult to translate.

28. Arias Freixedo underlines the "Latinate" reading of *grave* that Coelho performs, explicating three connotations and showing himself as a *letrado* (*Antoloxía de poesía obscena*, 106).

29. It is worth noting that Soárez Coelho also initiated the famous *ama* cycle with his *cantiga d'amor on* an *ama*, playing on *ama/amada* (servant/beloved, LP 79, 9/CA 166). His song prompted Fernan Garcia Esgaravunha to respond with a *cantiga d'escarnho* mocking the treatment of an *ama* as an object of love (RL 130); Joan Garcia de Guilhade also mocked Soárez Coelho's love song to an *ama mamada* (wet nurse, RL 215). On this cycle, see Yara Frateschi Vieira, "O escândalo das amas e tecedeiras nos cancioneiros galego-portugueses," *Coloquio:Letras* 76 (1983): 18–27. The poetic evidence suggests that Soárez Coelho enjoyed playing with generic boundaries, especially those between the *Cantigas d'amor* and *d'escarnho*.

30. Once again, I prefer the LP reading to RL 384; I especially like the editor's punctuation because it increases the ironic humor of Negra's speeches. The word-play again makes this song difficult to render in English; vv. 16–18 in the third stanza are particularly difficult.

31. See Earnshaw, *The Female Voice in Medieval Romance Lyric*, 1–3, 11–15.

32. *Caldeira* can also be read as a knight's pendon, a nice phallic image; however, in this song, I believe the dominant image is the vagina as a cauldron/gaping mouth. Metaphors of blackening and burning signify loss of virginity and sexual activity; see my discussion of the *morena* burnt by sex in chapter 3. Donald McGrady, "Notas sobre el enigma erótico, con especial referencia a los *Cuarenta enigmas en lengua española*," *Criticón* 27 (1984): 71–108, includes

fuego, homicida, infierno, and *sepultura* (fire, murder, hell, and tomb) in his list of similes and symbols for female genitals in Golden Age riddles, 82.

33. See Pamela Robertson, *Guilty Pleasures: Feminist Camp from Mae West to Madonna* (Durham: Duke University Press, 1996), for an insightful discussion of feminist camp; while she focuses on twentieth-century performers, nonetheless many of the camp techniques she discusses are traditional performances of unruly female personas, such as the traditional female responses to phallic boasts that I discussed above.

34. In v. 4, Lapa changes *algun* (CV) and *algũ* (CB) to *algũa* in order to correct what he sees as an erroneous reading (*Cantigas d'escarnho e de mal dizer,* 46, n. 41.4); given this song's play on gender, body parts and sexuality, I believe the MSS readings are accurate. LP cites Lapa's edition [LP 2, 13]. Blackmore in his citation of this poem marks Lapa's emendation with square brackets, algũ[a], "The Poets of Sodom," 212. I draw on Blackmore's English translation in mine.

35. Reference to Blackmore, "The Poets of Sodom," 212–13; his reading of the narrator's stance toward Mari'Mateu's desires is similar to mine.

36. Arias Freixedo, *Antoloxía de poesía obscena,* 86; Ashurst, "Masculine Postures," 3; and Blackmore, "The Poets of Sodom," 211–13, all see the narrator's stance as tolerant; see Rosenstein, "The Voiced and the Voiceless," 67, for a different opinion. RL 62, 71, 73, 81, 83, 90, 91, 104, 116, 117, 127, 131, 132, 168, 188, 340, 342, 372, 377, 378, 381, 404, and 424 all treat same-sex desire.

37. The eroticized combat motif appears in JP 41 [RL 25], RL 71, 104, 188, 194, 331, and 342; I discuss JP 41 and RL 331 below.

38. Discussions of this song include Paredes, *El cancionero profano,* 75–76, 308–315, and his *Las cantigas de escario y maldecir de Alfonso X: Problemas de interpretación y crítica textual,* Papers of the Medieval Hispanic Research Seminar 22 (London: Queen Mary and Westfield College, 2000), 23; Lacarra Lanz, "Sobre la sexualidad de las soldadeiras," 84–86; and Liu, " 'Affined to love the Moor,' " 57. I take the phrase "sexual misalliance" from Liu. I cite Paredes's edition, and draw on his Castilian translation in my English one.

39. Lacarra Lanz, "Sobre la sexualidad de las soldadeiras," 85, reads the metaphorical language as acquiring a single, determinant meaning over the course of the song, although she also reads it as comic.

40. See Earnshaw, *The Female Voice in Medieval Romance Lyric,* my discussion of ventriloquism in chapter 1, and my discussion of female voicing in the *serranilla* in chapter 4. I survey female citations in the *Cantigas d'escarnho* in "Female Voices in the *Cantigas de escarnio.*"

41. I cite Paredes's edition and draw on his Castilian translation in my English one (*El cancionero profano,* 166–71). The first line, which probably named the angry *soldadeira,* is lost; Lapa assumes the female speaker is Maria Balteira and reconstructed the first line with her name in it.

42. While another possibility is that d'Ambroa refused to pay her after intercourse, I reject this because it is out of line with prostitute's business

practices as depicted in the *Cantigas d'escarnho*; they consistently demand payment in advance. The songs that complain of *soldadeiras*' fraud in never delivering the goods include RL 425, which depicts Balteira as defrauding the entire court, and RL 265, 266, and 267, a sequence of three songs by Don Lopo Lias in which the narrator tries to get a lady to 'meet' with him as promised and paid for; the mere existence of the sequence implies that she never complies with their agreement. Joseph T. Snow, "The Satirical Poetry of Alfonso X: A Look at Its Relationship to the 'Cantigas de Santa María,' " *Alfonso X of Castile, The Learned King (1221–1284)*; An International Symposium, Harvard University, November 17, 1984, ed. Francisco Márquez Villanueva and Carlos Alberto Vega, Harvard Studies in Romance Languages 43 (Cambridge: Harvard University Press, 1990), 110–31, reads the insult as "liberties taken in Pero's own house," 118, i.e., sexual assault.

43. Prostitutes as dishonorable women were not afforded legal protection against rape, insults, or assault. *Fuero Juzgo* 3.9.29 specifies that raping or insulting a prostitute is not a punishable offense, as shown by Miguel Jiménez Monteserín, *Sexo y bien común. Notas para la historia de la prostitución en la España Moderna* (Cuenca: Instituto Juan de Valdés, 1994), 25. Denis Menjot, "Prostitutas y rufianes en las ciudades castellanas a fines de la Edad Media," *Temas Medievales* 4 (1994): 189–204, mentions that it was not illegal to rape, insult, or kidnap prostitutes, 203. Madero, *Manos violentas, palabras vedadas*, 65–68, addresses the ideological construction of the *puta* as an essentially lascivious woman. Lacarra Lanz discusses *soldadeiras* as prostitutes and provides ample documentation to establish their identity as *personas viles* deprived of most legal rights and protection in "Sobre la sexualidad de las soldadeiras," 77–78, 80, 86; see also her "La evolución de la prostitución en la Castilla del siglo XV y la mancebía de Salamanca en tiempos de Fernando de Rojas," *Fernando de Rojas and Celestina: Approaching the Fifth Centenary*, ed. Ivy A. Corfis and Joseph T. Snow (Madison: Hispanic Seminary of Medieval Studies, 1993), 33–78, which addresses prostitution in fifteenth-century Castile.

44. Citation from Snow, "The Satirical Poetry of Alfonso X," 126.

45. Nodar Manso, *Teatro menor galaicoportugués*, reads lines such as "E diss' ela" as stage directions that signal the intervention of the nonnarrative voice (24, 50–53, 169).

46. To my knowledge no other critic has recognized that this dialogue is a ritual insult exchange charged with homoeroticism. Ashurst, "Masculine Postures," reads their insults as personal, while Osório, "≪Cantiga de escarnho,≫" 193–94, comments that the detailed attention to female body parts marks this *cantiga d'escarnho* as a countertext to the *Cantigas d' amor*, in which the *senhor's* body is absent.

47. Citations of Guillaume IX's "Farai un vers, pos mi somelh" from Frederick Goldin, *Lyrics of the Troubadours and Trouvères: An Anthology and a History* (Gloucester, MA: Peter Smith, 1983), 26–33. The repetition of 'b-b' sounds is a common Romance marker for foolishness or stupidity (as shown in words such as *bobo*, fool, in Spanish); the phonetic resemblance between the

nonsense uttered by Guillaume's poetic alter ego and Baveca's stage name underlines their self-mocking stances as tongue-tied poets. While we have no historical documentation for Joan Baveca, he is generally considered either a *jogral* or a *segrel*; the placement of his songs among those of other Galician *jograis* in the *Cancioneiro da Vaticana* combined with his comic sobriquet lead Oliveira to consider him a *jogral* (*Depois do espectáculo trovadoresco*, 358). Guillaume IX composed many comic-obscene songs similar to the *Cantigas d'escarnho*; see his repertoire and biography in Goldin, *Lyrics of the Tronbadours and Trouvéres*, 5–49.

48. This song also plays on *pastorela* conventions, hence my reference to the *locus amoenus* encounter between Diana and Orion. In Galician-Portuguese *pastorelas*, often the male narrator does not reveal himself but instead listens to the *pastora's* love-song, a *Cantiga d'amigo*, which he incorporates into his lyric (as in the *pastorelas* by Joan d'Avoin, CV 267/CB 665; Airas Nunes, CV 454/CB 868, 869, 870; Don Dinis, CV 102/CB 519 and CV 137/CB 534; and Lourenço, CV 867/CB 1262). Less often he reveals his presence and engages her in conversation; sometimes his love-suit is rejected (as in the works of Joan Airas de Santiago, CV 554/B 967 and Dinis, CV 150/B 547), sometimes accepted (as in Pedr'Amigo de Sevilha, CV 689/CB 1098). See Luciana Stegagno Picchio, "Entre pastorelas e serranas: Novas contribuições ao estudo da Pastorela galego-portuguesa," *Actas: II Congresso Internacional da Língua Galego-Portuguesa na Galiza, 1987* (La Coruña: Associaçom Galega da Língua, 1989), 409–424, who discusses the genre of the *pastorela* and provides the texts of the nine extant Galician-Portuguese *pastorelas*. I discuss this genre briefly in chapter 4. The Guillaume IX lyric I discuss here is also a parodic pastourelle; the encounter occurs on the road, but in an urban, not rural, context, and the ladies are noblewomen, not peasants. Baveca uses the angry *soldadeira* motif, already seen in JP 16 by Alfonso X, in RL 195, in which his narrator complains that Maria Balteira keeps harassing him because he insulted an old woman (i.e., Balteira herself).

49. Negotiating appears in RL 333 by Pero d'Ambroa, in which he advises the piecemeal sale of cunt, and RL 265, 266, and 267, discussed above in note 42. References to Liu, " 'Affined to love the Moor,' " 65, and Rosenstein, "The Voiced and the Voiceless," 70.

50. Citations from Nirenberg, *Communities of Violence*, 147, 154–55. I discuss prostitution further in chapter 3.

51. The other side of this metaphor, the significance of Christian men having intercourse with Muslim women, is seen above, in my discussion of agonistic phallic sexuality in Pero Viviaez's complaint to Marinha, LP 136.3.

52. Reference to Liu, " 'Affined to love the Moor,' " 65.

53. Reference to Osório, "≪Cantiga de escarnho,≫" 159 n. 18. Confession boxes did not appear until the sixteenth century; priests were urged to confess women in public and not to look directly at them, in order to avoid temptation. See Peter Biller, "Confession in the Middle Ages: Introduction," *Handling Sin: Confession in the Middle Ages*, ed. Biller and A.J. Minnis, York

Studies in Medieval Theology 2 (Woodbridge, UK: York Medieval Press, 1998), 3–33 esp. 5, 13. Maria Negra in LP 125.21, discussed above, also voices a deterministic construction of her sinful nature as caused by her bodily signs; Pero da Ponte in RL 358 identifies the loss of virginity (represented symbolically as breaking the lock on a box) as decisive in determining a prostitute's future trajectory, no matter what pious practices she engages in. See also Jacqueline Murray, "Gendered Souls in Sexed Bodies: The Male Construction of Female Sexuality in Some Medieval Confessors' Manuals," *Handling Sin*, 79–93, esp. 85.

54. In RL 47, Afons'Eanes do Coton similarly mocks a *soldadeira* who jokingly asks him for a cure to age; as in this song, that *soldadeira* is identified by name and her declaration, "Sõo velha" (v. 4), is directly cited, suggesting that this statement in the mouth of a *soldadeira* is always comic. The situation of a male witness to a female boast inverts the motif of a *soldadeira* who witnesses phallic boasts, found in RL 11 and 52. While the name Maria Leve does not appear in other *Cantigas d'escarnho*, Menéndez Pidal considers this to be another name for Maria Pérez Balteira (*Poesía juglaresca*, 233 n. 103). It is also possible that additional *Cantigas d'escarnho* on Maria Leve were not preserved.

55. I cite the edition of Paredes, *El cancionero profano*, 235–47. There are almost no marks of textual gender, with the exception of *coitado* in v. 23. Lapa read this as *coitada* in his 1965 edition of the *Cantigas d'escarnho*; while Paredes reads it as masculine, he acknowledges this ending cannot eliminate the possibility of female voicing. Voicing in this song has sparked intense critical debate; I, like many others, read this as a framed female monologue with the *soldadeira* speaking from v. 3 on. On the critical debate over voicing in this song, see Rodrigues Lapa, *Cantigas d'escarnho e de mal dizer*, 28 n. 14; Paredes, *Las cantigas de escarnio*, 30–31; and Manuel da Costa Fontes, "On Alfonso X's 'Interrupted' Encounter with a *soldadeira*" in his *Folklore and Literature: Studies in the Portuguese, Brazilian, Sephardic, and Hispanic Oral Traditions* (Albany: State University of New York Press, 2000), 27–34. Arias Freixedo, *Antoloxía de poesía obscena*, 111–14, places the discourse from v. 3 on in the *soldadeira's* voice and comments on the poet's surprise at her refusal to engage in intercourse, positing a previous relationship between the two. Nodar Manso also reads the song as voiced by the *soldadeira* (*Teatro menor galaicoportugués*, 179; see also his "La parodia de la literatura heroica y hagiográfica en las cantigas de escarnio y de mal decir," *Dicenda: Cuadernos de Filología Hispánica* 9 [1990]: 151–61). Lacarra Lanz argues that the male voice predominates, although she does not specify where the speech of the *soldadeira* ends. She reads this song as a parodic *Cantiga d'amor*, arguing that the narrator's expressions of frustration echo conventional love-laments and are absurd since the love-object is a prostitute who has merely asked him to wait a few days ("Sobre la sexualidad de las soldadeiras," 79–84). She does not cite Fontes so presumably is unfamiliar with his work on this text. If this song were voiced by the male narrator starting at any point after v. 5, then the suffering of which he complains would be the pressure in his groin. I persist in my reading of the voicing of this song; however, I

recognize the equivocal nature of its voicing. Different voicing options could have been developed in performance, to play with the expression of female sexual pleasure or male sexual frustration. Benjamin Liu, "Obscenidad y transgresión en una cantiga de escarnio," *Erotismo en las letras hispánicas: Aspectos, modos y fronteras*, ed. Luce López-Baralt and Francisco Márquez Villanueva (Mexico: Colegio de México, 1995), 203–217, esp. 203–207, discusses the very different critical reception of Lapa's two editions of this song due to the change in voicing. I have drawn upon Paredes's Castilian translation and on Fontes's English one in mine.

56. The question of whether this song is occasional is addressed by Fontes, "On Alfonso X's 'Interrupted' Encounter," 27–28 and by Liu, "Obscenidad y transgresión," 209–211, 216.

57. Reference to Vasvári, "Festive Phallic Discourse," 101–103.

Chapter 3   Negotiating Worth and Selling Sex: *Panaderas* as Marketplace Orators

1. Citation from Frenk, *Corpus*, no. 1165A. Mariana Masera, " 'Que non sé filar, ni aspar, ni devanar': Erotismo y trabajo femenino en el *Cancionero hispánico medieval*," *Discursos y representaciones en la Edad Media*, Actas de las VI Jornadas Medievales, ed. Concepción Company et al., Medievalia 22 (Mexico: Universidad Nacional Autónoma de México, 1999), 215–31, esp. 223–24, also discusses this lyric; she briefly mentions that it reflects the historical reality of the bread trade.

2. The one *panadera* lyric that contains taboo words is the *Coplas de la panadera*, a series of personal invectives voiced by a *panadera*-satirist; while she enunciates the taboo words, she applies them to the elite men she caricatures. Discussions of bread as sexual organs and especially the female organ in medieval and early modern Spanish literature and folklore include Louis Combet, "Doña Cruz, la panadera del ≪buen amor≫," *Ínsula* 294 (1971): 14–15; James F. Burke, "Again *Cruz*, the Baker-Girl: *Libro de buen amor*, ss. 115–120," *Revista Canadiense de Estudios Hispánicos* 4 (1980): 253–70; Vasvári, "La semiología de la connotación"; Márquez Villanueva, "Pan 'pudendum muliebris' "; Augustin Redondo, "De molinos, molineros y molineras. Tradiciones folklóricas y literatura en la España del Siglo de Oro," *Literatura y folklore: Problemas de intertextualidad*, Actas del segundo symposium internacional del Departamento de Español de la Universidad de Groningen, 28, 29, y 30 de octubre de 1981, ed. J.L. Alonso Hernández (Groningen: Universidad de Groningen; Salamanca: Universidad de Salamanca, 1983), 101–115; McGrady, "Notas sobre el enigma erótico"; Andre S. Michalski, "Juan Ruiz's *Troba Cazurra*: 'Cruz cruzada panadera,' " *Romance Notes* 11 (1969): 434–38; and Masera, " 'Que non sé filar.' "

3. Citations from *Ordenanzas de Sevilla* 73, *Ordenanzas de León* 39, and *Ordenanzas de Villatoro* 419, as cited by Pedro Chalmeta Gendrón, *El "señor del zoco" en España: Edades media y moderna, contribución al estudio de la historia del mercado* (Madrid: Instituto Hispano-Árabe de Cultura, 1973), 560, 566, 551.

It is worth noting that the growth of Castile, especially in the fifteenth century, was accompanied by the establishment of kingdom-wide standard measures, especially for bread; these standards held through the nineteenth century (Chalmeta Gendrón, *El "señor del zoco,"* 529).

4. On interpellation, see Butler, *Excitable Speech*, 5, 24–28; she draws principally on Althusser's theory of interpellation. See also my discussion of interpellation in chapters 1 and 2.

5. Reference to James Aho, *The Orifice as Sacrificial Site: Culture, Organization, and the Body* (New York: Aldine de Gruyter, 2002), 10–11. Claire M. Waters, "Dangerous Beauty, Beautiful Speech: Gendered Eloquence in Medieval Preaching," *Essays in Medieval Studies* 14, Online journal: http://www.luc.edu/publications/medieval/vol14/14ch5.html, cited August 23, 2001, discusses how female preachers' rhetoric was constructed as dangerous.

6. Reference to Vincent Barletta, "Context and Manuscript Discourse in Late Medieval Castile," *La corónica* 30.1 (Fall 2001): 3–35, 8. Entextualization and recontextualization are two movements in a complex process that involves the identification of phrases worthy of reuse. This process is an exercise of power; in the case of medieval popular lyric, the words of conventionally powerless characters are recontextualized in literate texts dating from the late fifteenth- to the seventeenth century, put to new use and infused with new meaning. Frenk's objective is to reclaim songs sung in the streets and fields during the Middle Ages that were mostly lost due to their oral and popular nature; the Renaissance interest in popular wisdom and poetry led to the incorporation of many popular songs in poems, dramas, and collections of refrains. While Frenk outlines a rigorous methodology to maximize the folkloric authenticity of the lyrics she cites, ultimately she relies on her judgment as to whether a particular verse is popular or not. Frenk describes her methodology and criteria for inclusion in the introduction to her *Corpus*, v–ix, in "La autenticidad folklórica de la antigua lírica ≪popular≫" and in "Problemas de la antigua lírica popular," both found in her *Estudios sobre lírica antigua* (Madrid: Castalia, 1978). My criticism is not meant to denigrate the monumental achievement represented by Frenk's compilation.

7. See Frenk, *Corpus*, 557–58.

8. References to Mikhail Bakhtin, *Rabelais and His World*, trans. Hélène Iswolsky (Bloomington: University of Indiana Press, 1984), 15–17, and to James Masschaele, "The Public Space of the Marketplace in Medieval England," *Speculum* 77 (2002): 383–421. Luis García de Valdeavellano, *El mercado. Apuntes para su estudio en León y Castilla durante la Edad Media*, 2nd rev. ed., Colección de bolsillo, 38 (Seville: Universidad de Sevilla, 1975), discusses the market cross adorned with the king's glove or other symbol of royal power, 111–12, 115, 131–33.

9. In my description of the medieval Iberian marketplace, I rely heavily on García de Valdeavellano, *El mercado*, esp. 57–102; see also Claudio Sánchez-Albornoz, *Una ciudad de la España cristiana hace mil años. Estampas de la vida en León*, 11th ed. (Madrid: Rialp, 1965), who reconstructs a day in a tenth-century Leonese marketplace, 30–56, and Dámaso Alonso, "Estilo y creación

en el *Poema de mío Cid*," *Obras completas*, 10 vols., vol. 2 (Madrid: Gredos, 1973), 107–143, in which he discusses marketplace performances, medieval and modern, 109. Within cities grain could be sold directly from warehouses as well as in the marketplace (García de Valdeavellano, *El mercado*, 73). For a map of a medieval marketplace in Navarre, see José Manuel Casas Torres and Ángel Abascal Garayoa, *Mercados geograficos y ferias de Navarra* (Zaragoza: Príncipe de Viana, 1948), 41. See a parallel discussion about the problem of animal and human waste in modern Moroccan marketplaces, in Kapchan, *Gender on the Market*, 30. While Chalmeta Gendrón's *El "señor del zoco"* focuses mainly on Al-Andalus, as he demonstrates in his careful comparison of Christian and Muslim documentary evidence (539–607), marketplaces in reconquered Christian areas probably adopted the organization established by Muslim rulers; certainly many of the titles for marketplace officials, such as the *zabazoque* and the *almotacén*, as well as *zoco*, marketplace, come from Arabic. Chalmeta Gendrón's *El "Señor del zoco"* 233–39, lays out the several factors that scholars should consider in a complete study of the market as a economic and social phenomenon. Much of what Masschaele says in his "The Public Space of the Marketplace" is also true for medieval Spain.

10. By 'private arrests,' I mean action taken by an individual against another, usually due to debt or other personal obligation; such arrests could include a lord recapturing an escaped serf or slave. On the *paz del mercado* and trade regulations, see García de Valdeavellano, *El mercado*, 33, 68, 76–83, 105–166, and Chalmeta Gendrón, *El "señor del zoco"*, 512–14, 549–52.

11. Masschaele, "The Public Space of the Marketplace," 391–98, discusses kings' and other magnates' use of the marketplace as a public forum for official announcements, news, and propaganda. José Manuel Nieto Soria, "Propaganda política y poder real en la Castilla trastámara: Una perspectiva de análisis," *Anuario de estudios medievales* 25 (1995): 489–515, mentions that political announcements were made publicly in marketplaces and *plazas*. See Madero, *Manos violentas, palabras vedadas*, on injurious speech in medieval Castile.

12. Citations from Alfonso Díaz de Montalvo, *Ordenanzas reales* 8.3, Huete, 1484, ADMYTE, Disk 1, 478, and from Masschaele, "The Public Space of the Marketplace," 408–409. Chalmeta Gendrón, *El "señor del zoco,"* 514, 529, 560, discusses the use of the market for official punishments.

13. Ruiz, *Spanish Society*, 217, 213, discusses bread in the medieval Spanish diet. Christina Segura Graíño, *Los espacios femeninos en el Madrid medieval*, Mujeres en Madrid (Madrid: Horas y horas, 1992), 62, argues that city officials maintained tight controls on *panaderas* in order to keep them in their inferior social position.

14. Citations from José Andrés-Gallego, "Economía, psicología y ética de un motín: Salamanca, 1764," *Hispania Sacra* 39.80 (1987): 675–711, esp. 707, and from Natalie Zemon Davis, *Society and Culture in Early Modern France* (Stanford: Stanford University Press, 1975), 146; see also 27–28, 72. Andrés-Gallego cites a contemporary account to demonstrate women's participation: "un grande alboroto de mujeres y niños que pedían pan, los cuales. . .se fueron

siguiéndole profiriendo entre otras cosas les diesen pan. . . . desde las nueve había empezado a acudir en tropel la gente, siendo de las primeras varias turbas de mujeres" (Archivo Histórico Municipal de Salamanca, *Gobierno*, Actas, 1764, fol. 79, sesión del 5 de marzo; A large mob of women and children who were demanding bread. . .they were following him and demanding among other things that they be given bread. . .from nine o'clock a group of people had begun to gather, various crowds of women being the first to gather). During this same demonstration, the chief protestors climbed a church tower and used for a flag a "manta roja, de un panadero" (a male bread baker's red cloak) to call the people to the market/ *plaza* to express their discontent (Villar and Macías, *Historia de Salamanca*, vol. 3, 109, as cited by Andrés-Gallego, 694–95). The use of a baker's cloak as an emblem of protest shows the alliance between professional bakers and their customers, who could have turned on the food sellers as complicit in the shortage; certainly there are examples of vendors who refused to sell grain during times of shortage in order to drive prices up, as Angus MacKay discusses in his "Popular Movements and Pogroms in Fifteenth-Century Castile," *Past and Present* 55 (1972): 33–67.

15. Discussions of the erotic connotations of *panadera* and of various bread-making activities include Márquez Villanueva, "Pan 'pudendum muliebris,' " 250–54 (yeast, heat, flour/wheat, action of kneading, and sexual connotations of bread); Burke, "Again *Cruz*, the Baker-Girl," 258–61, who particularly investigates semi-pagan and Christological associations; Vasvári, "La semiología de la connotación," 306–307 (*horno, pan, trigo*); Juan A. Frago Gracia, "Sobre el léxico de la prostitución en España durante el siglo XV," *Archivo de filología aragonesa* 24–25 (1979): 257–73, esp. 267–68 (*panadera* as prostitute); and Julio Caro Baroja, *Ritos y mitos equívocos*, 79–81. See also Camilo José Cela, *Diccionario secreto*, Hombres, hechos e ideas 15, 2 vols., vol. 1 (Madrid: Alfaguara, 1968), 282–83, for *bollo*, bun, as male or female genitals; José Luis Alonso Hernández, *Léxico del marginalismo del Siglo de Oro* (Salamanca: Universidad de Salamanca, 1977), 577, who lists *coño* (cunt) as the first meaning of *pan*; McGrady, "Notas sobre el enigma erótico"; and Redondo, "De molinos, molineros y molineras." Alicia María González, " 'Guess How Doughnuts Are Made': Verbal and Nonverbal Aspects of the *Panadero* and His Stereotype," *Perspectives in Mexican American Studies* 1 (1988): 89–107, discusses erotic bread names in modern Mexican folklore; I discuss her work below.

16. Jacques Rossiaud, *Medieval Prostitution*, trans. Lydia G. Cochrane (Oxford and New York: Basil Blackwell, 1988), 56-59, and Leah Lydia Otis, *Prostitution in Medieval Society: The History of an Urban Institution in Languedoc* (Chicago: University of Chicago Press, 1985), 18, discuss thirteenth- and fourteenth-century French decrees forbidding prostitutes to touch food in the marketplace; Rossiaud suggests that the view of prostitutes as ritually unclean waned in the fifteenth century, since at that time public prostitutes in Languedoc would make bread with their own hands to distribute to the poor (64). Rossiaud argues that prostitutes who solicited in the marketplace

were well-protected clandestine prostitutes who could operate in a scene of intense competition (7). The *panadera*-prostitutes I discuss all occupy an ambiguous space between public and clandestine prostitutes. Studies of prostitution in medieval Iberia include Heath Dillard, *Daughters of the Reconquest: Women in Castilian Town Society, 1100–1300* (Cambridge, UK: Cambridge University Press, 1984); Majorie Ratcliffe, "Adulteresses, Mistresses and Prostitutes: Extramarital Relationships in Medieval Castile," *Hispania* 67 (1984): 346–50; Ángel Galán Sánchez and María Teresa López Beltrán, "El «Status» teórico de las prostitutas del reino de Granada en la primera mitad del siglo XVI (Las ordenanzas de 1538)," *Las mujeres en las ciudades medievales*, Actas de las III Jornadas de Investigación Interdisciplinaria, ed. Cristina Segura Graíño (Madrid: Seminario de Estudios de la Mujer, 1984), 161–69; Tatiana Bubnova, "Estado, iglesia, universidad: Prostitución y proxenetismo como problema de conciencia en la vida cotidiana y en la expresión literaria," *Caballeros, monjas y maestros en la Edad Media*, Actas de las V Jornadas Medievales, ed. Lillian von der Walde et al. (Mexico: Universidad Nacional Autónoma de México, 1996), 415–31; Andrés Moreno Mengíbar and Francisco Vázquez García, "Poderes y prostitución en España (siglos XIV-XVII). El caso de Sevilla," *Criticón* 69 (1997): 33–49; Márquez Villanueva, *Orígenes y sociología del tema celestinesco*; and Lacarra, "La evolución de la prostitución en la Castilla del siglo XV." Other studies of medieval prostitution include Ruth Mazo Karras, *Common Women: Prostitution and Sexuality in Medieval England* (New York: Oxford University Press, 1996).

17. Menjot's discussion of the location of brothels in various Castilian towns indicates that in many cities brothels were found near commercial centers, marketplaces, and fair grounds ("Prostitutas y rufianes," 191). The location of the *mancebía* ('red-light district') varied from city to city, but they tended to be found in areas where men, especially single men and/or travelers, gathered: near cathedrals, especially those that attracted pilgrims, universities, ports, and commercial districts. While urban regulations throughout the Middle Ages restricted prostitutes to areas outside the city walls, many principal European cities located brothels (especially after the development of municipal brothels which enabled cities to control and profit from prostitution during the late fourteenth- and throughout the fifteenth- and sixteenth centuries) within the walls in central locations (Rossiaud, *Medieval Prostitution*, 60; Menjot, "Prostitutes y rufianes," 190–93). In the late fifteenth century several Castilian cities gathered brothels together into an isolated, walled zone at a distance from the city center, in order to assert more municipal control over public prostitution; the walls often had only one gate that was locked at night (Menjot, 192). In Seville, shortly after its 'Reconquest' in the thirteenth century, a *mancebía* administered by ecclesiastical authorities grew up near the cathedral on the location of a former mosque; the municipal *mancebía* was located near the port, the economic center of the city. In Valencia, by contrast, the *mancebía* was outside of the city walls (Moreno Mengíbar and Vázquez García, "Poderes y prostitución," 36–38).

18. Citation from Nirenberg, *Communities of Violence*, 154. Nirenberg also cites a commentator on Augustine's *De ordine* 2.4.12: " 'The public woman is in society what bilge is in [a ship at] sea and the sewer pit in a palace. Remove this sewer and the entire palace will be contaminated' " (154). As I comment in my discussion of the *Coplas de la panadera* below, the phrase *puta carcavera* identified prostitutes who solicited clients among the sewers outside of city walls. This type appears in the list of prostitutes who could be found in the city of Rome in Francisco Delicado's picaresque novel, *Retrato de la Lozana Andaluza*, ed. Claude Allaigre, 3rd ed. (Madrid: Cátedra, 2000), 270–72. On medieval medical theories of sexual hygiene, see Michael Solomon, "Catarsis sexual: *La Vida de Santa Maria Egipciaca* y el texto higiénico," *Erotismo en las letras hispánicas*, 425–37. See also my discussion of the prostitute as an identity marker in Christian Spain, in chapter 2.

19. Waferers appear on lists of entertainers generated by moralists who condemn minstrelsy in general, in Geoffrey Chaucer's "Pardoner's Tale," *The Canterbury Tales*, VI.479 (*The Riverside Chaucer*, 3rd ed., ed. Larry D. Benson, [Boston: Houghton Mifflin, 1987], 196) and in the cleric Peter of Blois's grumbling description of Henry II's household (cited in John Southworth, *The English Medieval Minstrel* [Woodbridge, UK and Wolfeboro, NH: Boydell, 1989], 46–47). Waferers seem to be particularly associated with noble households; payroll entries indicate their function as waferers, servants, and entertainers (Southworth, 80). Derek Pearsall mentions that waferers and their female counterparts, *wafresteres*, "were associated with taverns. . .and had a bad reputation" (William Langland, *Piers Plowman: An Edition of the C-Text*, ed. Pearsall, York Medieval Texts, second series [London: Edward Arnold, 1978], 144, n. 285).

20. Citation from Chalmeta Gendrón, *El "señor del zoco,"* 29.

21. In my discussion of haggling techniques I draw upon Kapchan's study of female marketplace orators in modern Morocco, *Gender on the Market*, esp. 2–3, 6–12, and 29–49, and on French, "The Symbolic Capital of Social Identities," who analyzes the verbal strategies of female Mayan vendors in interaction with customers of various class and ethnic identities.

22. Citation from " 'Guess How Doughnuts Are Made,' " 98. Vasvári, "Festive Phallic Discourse," 102, and "The Semiotics of Phallic Aggression," 139–40, also cites this joke; she reads the *panadero* as performing an upward punch with his closed fist (i.e., a reaming gesture), a reading with which I disagree.

23. This eroticized view of bread shapes proliferates in the examples María González, " 'Guess How Doughnuts Are Made,' " offers of *cuernos* (horns, either of the cuckold or phallic horns), *bollos* (white or blond people), *calzones* (pants/panties), *besos* (kisses), *chilindrina* (La Chilindrina was a beautiful prostitute who refused to sleep with the *panadero* who first made this bread in her honor), *conchas* (shells, a frequent image for female genitalia), *faldas* (skirts), *novias* (brides), *volcanes* (volcanoes, a phallic image), *monjas* and *viudas* (nuns and widows, both of whom are frequently associated with illicit

sexuality), and *abrazos* (hugs). In modern North American jokes, crullers and doughnuts connote male and female genitals.

24. Reference to *Sendebar*, ed. María Jesús Lacarra, 2nd ed. (Madrid: Cátedra, 1995), 89–90.

25. I use 'wily' here in a positive sense; I see the *moça's* behavior as a tactic used by the powerless to resist dominant cultural forces, as discussed by Michel de Certeau, *The Practice of Everyday Life*, trans. Steven F. Rendall (Berkeley: University of California Press, 1984), xix, 37–39.

26. For bread in medieval Iberia, see Richard Terry Mount, "Levels of Meaning: Grains, Bread, and Bread Making as Informative Images in Berceo," *Hispania* 76 (1993): 49–54, esp. 50; José Ángel García de Cortázar, *El dominio del monasterio de San Millán de la Cogolla (siglos X a XIII). Introducción a la historia rural de Castilla altomedieval* (Salamanca: Universidad de Salamanca, 1969), 286; Ruiz, *Spanish Society*, 2, 212; Gonzalo de Berceo, *Milagros de Nuestra Señora*, trans. Daniel Devoto, Odres nuevos, 7th ed. (Madrid: Castalia, 1996), 222; and Chalmeta Gendrón, *El "señor del zoco,"* 514.

27. Citations from *The Orifice as Sacrificial Site*, 18, 19, 135–37; reference to Mary Douglas, *Purity and Danger: An Analysis of the Concepts of Pollution and Taboo* (London: Routledge & Kegan Paul, 1966).

28. Citations from Berceo, *Milagros de Nuestra Señora*, trans. Devoto, 223.

29. I realize that the expression "quién comiera de su pan" carries great rhetorical weight; nonetheless, the fact that the strength of the speaker's desire is in direct proportion to the inaccessibility of the object and that the object itself is the highly ambiguous *pan* lead me to focus on the ludic connotations of these lyrics. While the 'innocent' meaning may seem the only tenable one, I read these lyrics as playing with innocent and taboo interpretations much like the erotic joke I discuss below.

30. On the other hand, in popular lyrics the *panadera* frequently is an itinerant figure, as I discuss below. María González, " 'Guess How Doughnuts Are Made,' " focuses on itinerant *panaderos* in modern Mexican folklore; as she comments in a footnote, *panaderas* also figure prominently in bread-making, yet they tend to be less mobile than their male counterparts. Millers like *panaderas* had reputations as thieves and as oversexed; *molineros* (nearly always male) were widely disliked and suspected of cheating their customers by retaining more than their share of the grain, of replacing high-quality wheat with lower-quality barley or rye, and of mixing sand or sawdust into the flour to conceal their thefts (Redondo, "De molinos, molineros y molineras," 102–105; H.E. Jacob, *Six Thousand Years of Bread: Its Holy and Unholy History*, trans. Richard and Clara Winston [New York: Doubleday, Doran & Co., 1944], 128–30). In the popular imagination, *molineros* were excessively potent sexually due to their association with grain and flour, both of which denote semen, due to the social function of the mill as a site for women's gatherings, especially prostitutes, and due to the constant grinding movement of the millstone, connoting sexual intercourse (Redondo, "De molinos," 106–110; Vasvári, "El hijo del molinero: Para la polisemia popular del *Libro del arcipreste*," *Erotismo en las letras hispánicas*, 461–77, esp. 468–71).

31. My comments in this section parallel those of Manuel da Costa Fontes, "Celestina as Antithesis of the Virgin Mary," *Journal of Hispanic Philology* 25 (1990): 7–41. While he mentions that fifteenth-century *conversos* (Jewish converts to Christianity) called the Virgin a *mujer común* or prostitute, I would argue that this idea is latent in medieval secular Christian culture and not specifically a reflection of Fernando de Rojas's *converso* identity.

32. Citation from José Luis Gárfer and Concha Fernández, *Adivinancero popular gallego* (Madrid: Taurus, 1984), no. 167.

33. McGrady, "Notas sobre el enigma erótico," 82–83, 85, discusses how both male and female genitals eat (*comer*) in Golden Age erotic jokes, although he sees *pan* as a symbol for male genitals consumed by the female.

34. For a more complete introduction to the popular lyric, see Vicenç Beltrán, "Poetry, Spanish, Lyric, Traditional," in *Medieval Iberia. An Encyclopedia*, ed. E. Michael Gerli, 662–664, and D. Gareth Walters, *The Cambridge Introduction to Spanish Poetry* (Cambridge, UK: Cambridge University Press, 2002), 108–117; both cite some popular lyrics in the original and in English translation. I know of no other English translations of medieval Spanish popular lyrics.

35. Cited from Frenk, *Corpus*, no. 120B. This lyric has also been discussed by Masera, " 'Que non sé filar,' " 226, and " 'Yo, mi madre, yo, que la flor de la villa me so': La voz femenina en la antigua lírica popular hispánica," *Voces de la Edad Media; Actas de las Terceras Jornadas Medievales*, ed. Concepción Company et al., Medievalia 6 (Mexico: Universidad Nacional Autónoma de México, 1993), 105–113, and by Vasvári, *The Heterotextual Body of the Mora Morilla*, Papers of the Medieval Hispanic Research Seminar 12 (London: Queen Mary and Westfield College, 1999), 16.

36. Her use of the imperfect determines this song's tone; if she had used preterites, then the tone would be exultant, as the female speaker told her mother about the eager welcome she received in the town and, through codes, about how she fell in love/had sex there.

37. Citations from Butler, *Excitable Speech*, 29, 27.

38. Cited from Frenk, *Corpus*, no. 1163. *Lleva* means both "to carry" and "to wear"; in this lyric, it plays on the relationship between the *panadera* and her *pan*, part of her body.

39. Cited from *Cancionero leonés*, ed. Miguel Manzano Alonso, 5 vols. (León: Diputación Provincial, 1990), no. 307; *Cancionero popular gallego*, ed. José Pérez Ballesteros [Madrid: 1886 (reprint Vigo: Galaxia, 1979)], no. 17; and Frenk, *Corpus*, no. 1589. Masera, " 'Que non sé filar,' " 227, also cites the first two lyrics.

40. On *morenas*, see Vasvári, *The Heterotextual Body*, 41–57.

41. Cited from Frenk, *Corpus*, nos. 131, 145A, and 1164.

42. For a more complete introduction to the *Libro de buen amor* in English, see Alan Deyermond's entry in *Medieval Iberia: An Encyclopedia*, 488–89. This book is widely available in English translation; I recommend the verse translation of Elisha K. Kane (New York: privately published, 1933), infamous for its amusing illustrations, and the far more accurate and comprehensible

paraphrase of Raymond S. Willis (Princeton: Princeton University Press, 1972). Discussions of Cruz include Combet, "Doña Cruz, la panadera del ≪buen amor≫"; James Burke, "Again *Cruz*, the Baker-Girl"; and Vasvári, "La semiología de la connotación," "Festive Phallic Discourse," and "The Semiotics of Phallic Aggression.' " I use 'Juan Ruiz' to identify the first-person narrator, a character not to be read as that of the historic author of the pseudo-autobiographical *Libro de buen amor*. See my discussion of his historical identity in chapter 1.

43. References to Menéndez Pidal, *Poesía juglaresca*, 268–83; Walsh, "The *Libro de buen amor* as a Performance-Text"; Stern, *The Medieval Theater in Castile*, 160–69. I discuss the performance of Ruiz's *cánticas de serrana* in chapter 4.

44. On mediated desire and erotic triangles, see René Girard, *Deceit, Desire, and the Novel: Self and Other in Literary Structure*, trans. Yvonne Freccero (Baltimore: Johns Hopkins University Press, 1961; reprint 1972), esp. 9.

45. *Libro de buen amor* citations from Alberto Blecua's edition (Madrid: Cátedra, 1992); line references included in the text. See Vasvári, "La semiología de la connotación," 310–11, where she provides a chart that illustrates the several levels of meaning and connotations in this episode.

46. Vasvári, "The Semiotics of Phallic Aggression,' " 139–42.

47. Nodar Manso, *Teatro menor galaicoportugués*, has discussed similarly riotous performances in Greek and Roman theatrical traditions, implying they continued into the Middle Ages, 173–74; he describes erotic miming in detail in his discussion of his reconstructed script of *Os Zevrões*, 149–70. In chapter 4, I argue that the *cuaderna vía* portions of the *serrana* episodes were not performed due to the references to the material book and to reading the text. However, in the Cruz episode, such references are not found in the *cuaderna vía* portions that surround the lyric, in st. 112–14 and 121–22.

48. Cited from Montoro, *Cancionero*, ed. Ciceri, no. 36. Throughout this book, I use D to refer to Brian Dutton's numbering system for fifteenth-century *cancionero* poetry, found in his *Cancionero del siglo XV*. Márquez Villanueva, "Pan 'pudendum muliebris,' " 252, also cites this *copla*. The rubrics for this lyric help contextualize it. In LB3 the rubric reads, "Otra del mismo porque le encerraron unas panaderas a quien devié dineros e non ge los pagava" (Another [song] by the same poet, because some *panaderas* to whom he owed money and hadn't paid surrounded him). The one in SV2 identifies the addressee: "Antón de Montoro al corregidor de cordoba porque le ençerraron a pedradas en san pedro unas panaderas a quien debia dineros porque non ge los pagava" (Antón de Montoro to the magistrate of Cordoba, because he had been confined to San Pedro by stones thrown by some *panaderas*, to whom he owed money, because he had not paid them). Dutton, 7:94 (D1793), cites these two rubrics. For a good introduction to Montoro's life and work, see E. Michael Gerli's entry in his *Medieval Iberia: An Encyclopedia*, 583–84.

49. References to Kaplan, *The Evolution of Converso Literature*, 44–45, to Márquez Villanueva, "Jewish 'Fools' of the Spanish Fifteenth Century," *Hispanic Review* 50 (1982): 385–409, esp. 387, 396–97, 402–4, and to Gerli,

"Antón de Montoro and the Wages of Eloquence," 272–73. Rodríguez Puértolas denies that Montoro frequented the royal court, although he knew and entered into poetic contests and exchanges with the Marqués de Santillana, Juan de Mena, Gómez Manrique, and Juan Poeta, among others, and addressed poems to Enrique IV and Isabel I (Montoro, *Cancionero*, ed. Ciceri, 14–24).

50. Montoro, a small city near Cordoba, was the birthplace of our poet whose family, like that of many *conversos*, replaced its Jewish patronymic with a place name. Rodríguez Puértolas discusses Montoro's *converso* heritage, the question of his own conversion, and his reaction to the 1473 uprisings, in Montoro, *Cancionero*, ed. Ciceri, 11–13, 15. Costa, *Bufón de palacio y comerciante de ciudad: La obra del poeta cordobés Antón de Montoro* (Córdoba: Diputación de Córdoba, 2001), 130, reads this composition as a comic piece on Montoro's indigence and dates it to the period of 1444–57. As MacKay's list of grain prices in Seville shows, throughout that period barley prices ranged from a low of 24 *maravedís* to a high of 47, not as bad as during 1472–73 (100–120 maravedís), but much higher than average ("Popular Movements and Pogroms," 35, 66–67). Montoro comments on the 1473 riots in *Cancionero*, nos. 97 and 98.

51. Sebastián de Horozco, father of the famous lexicographer Sebastián de Covarrubias y Horozco, was a prominent municiple authority in Toledo and a prolific writer of *cancionero* poetry and religious drama. His probable *converso* origin may have influenced his choice of fool persona, as discussed by Francisco Márquez Villanueva, "Sebastián de Horozco y la literatura bufonesca," *Homenaje al profesor Antonio Vilanova*, ed. Adolfo Sotelo Vázquez and Marta Cristina Carbonell, 2 vols., vol. 1 (Barcelona: Departamento de Filología Española, 1989), 393–431. Alonso Hernández defines *chipirrichape* as *coño*, cunt, and cross references *pan*, yet the only example he cites is this poem (*Léxico del marginalismo*, 262, 577). Frenk cites a popular lyric quite similar to the *viejo chiste* (old joke) that Horozco adapts: "Decí, damas arreboladas,/¿qué tenéis y a cómo vendéis / la onza del chípite, chápite, / la onza del chípite, chápite,/la onza del chípite, chápite, / chípite, chápite que os ponéis?" (*Corpus*, no. 1740A: Tell me, ruddy ladies, what do you have and for how much do you sell the ounce of chípite, chápete [etc.] that you put on?). In modern Spanish, *chipichape* onomatopoetically refers to the sound made by two bodies bumping together; the resemblance between *chipirrichape* and *chipichape* makes me believe the former is an onomatopoetic double-entendre for sex.

52. Cited from Horozco, *Cancionero*, ed. Weiner, no. 133, vv. 1–9, 93. All future line references in text.

53. Márquez Villanueva, "Sebastián de Horozco y la literatura bufonesca," discusses Horozco's fool persona.

54. I am indebted to Eileen Willingham for telling me about pennyroyal's use as an abortifacient. This use is expressed euphemistically as "limpiar la madre" (clean the womb) in medieval Spanish medical tracts. *Poleo* had other uses as well, principally to treat stomach and digestive disorders.

55. Florence Dumora, "Jeux de la parole féminine dans le *Cancionero* de Sebastián de Horozco," *Images de la femme en Espagne aux XVIe et XVIIe siècles*, ed. Augustin Redondo (Paris: Presses de la Sorbonne Nouvelle, 1994), 117–26, has discussed similarly aggressive rhetorical techniques employed by female characters in other dialogic poems by Horozco. The female speaker's strategies, such as her use of impersonal forms that downplay her agency, parallel those used by modern female vendors in Guatemalan markets as analyzed by French, "The Symbolic Capital of Social Identities," esp. 163–64.

56. Márquez Villanueva, "Pan 'pudendum muliebris,' " 251, reads this comment as an insult, indirectly labeling the female character a *panadera*.

57. On negotiating strategies, see French, "The Symbolic Capital of Social Identities," 161–63, 178–80; on prostitutes' income, see Lacarra, "La evolución de la prostitución," 39; on coinage values, see Earl J. Hamilton, *American Treasure and the Price Revolution in Spain, 1501–1650* (Cambridge, MA: Harvard University Press, 1934), 55 n. 3.

58. On Horozco's account of this street theater, see Márquez Villanueva, "Sebastián de Horozco y la literatura bufonesca," 420–25; Stern, *The Medieval Theater in Castile*, 215–16; and Ana María Álvarez Pellitero, ed., *Teatro medieval*, Colección Austral (Madrid: Espasa-Calpe, 1990), 402, 407–408. Sirera, "Diálogos de cancionero y teatralidad," argues that poetic dialogues are theatrical, although he does suggest that those in which each character voices a complete stanza, as in this poem, are less so than those in which the speeches do not conform to the poetic form.

59. The identity of the author has provoked much critical interest. Nilda Guglielmi, "Los elementos satíricos en las *Coplas de la panadera*," *Filología* 14 (1970): 49–104, 103–104, argues that it could have been Juan de Mena and certainly was a member of the courtly bureaucratic ranks. Antón de Montoro has also been mentioned as a possibility, although Rodríguez Puértolas rejects this (Montoro, *Cancionero*, ed. Ciceri, 29). For an introduction to *Coplas de la Panadera* in the context of late fifteenth-century satire, see Barbara F. Weissberger, "Protest Poetry in Castile (circa 1445-circa 1506)," *Castilian Writers, 1400–1500*, ed. Frank A. Domínguez and George D. Greenia, Dictionary of Literary Biography, 286 (Detroit: Gale, 2004), 340–47.

60. *Vender de barato* means to sell retail or piecemeal; it connotes a small-time, itinerant vendor. Citations of the *Coplas de la panadera* from Paola Elia, *Coplas hechas sobre la batalla de Olmedo que llaman las de la panadera* (Verona: Università degli studi di Verona, 1982). Line and stanza references included in the text. Other editions of this poem include Miguel Artigas, "Nueva redacción de las *Coplas de la Panadera* según un manuscrito de la Biblioteca Menéndez Pelayo," *Estudios eruditos in memoriam de Adolfo Bonilla San Martín (1875–1926)*, 2 vols., vol. 1 (Madrid: J. Ratés, 1927–30), 75–89; Vicente Romano García, *Coplas de la Panadera* (Pamplona: Aguilar, 1963); Eduardo Rincón, *Coplas satíricas y dramáticas de la Edad Media* (Madrid: Alianza, 1968); Julio Rodríguez Puértolas, "Poesía satírica medieval: 'Coplas de la

Panadera,' " *El comentario de textos*, 4: *La poesía medieval*, ed. Manuel Alvar et al. (Madrid: Castalia, 1983), 375–404; *Poesía crítica y satírica del siglo XV*, ed. Rodríguez Puértolas (Madrid: Castalia, 1989), 131–47; and F. Domínguez, "El manuscrito de las *Coplas de la panadera* de la Biblioteca Colombina y Capitular de Sevilla," *Hispanófila* 90 (1987): 81–98. I know of no complete English translation of this poem.

61. Reference to Filios, "Rewriting History in the *Coplas de la panadera*," *Hispanic Review* 71 (2003): 345–63. See my discussion of the definition of *soldadeira* in chapter 2. The official version is a first-person account of the battle narrated by Juan II and addressed to Luna found in MS 18697 / 73 of the Biblioteca Nacional; Elia appends this document to her edition, *Coplas*, 83–86. On the use of marketplaces for political propaganda, see Nieto Soria, "Propaganda política y poder real."

62. For more information about the partisan activity surrounding Álvaro de Luna, see Nicholas Round, *The Greatest Man Uncrowned: A Study of the Fall of Don Alvaro de Luna* (London: Tamesis, 1986). For contemporary views of Luna, see Fernán Pérez de Guzmán, *Generaciones y semblanzas*, ed. J. Domínguez Bordona (Madrid: Espasa-Calpe, 1965); Alonso de Palencia, *Crónica de Enrique IV*, trans. D.A. Paz y Melía, Biblioteca de autores españoles 257, 3 vols. (Madrid: Atlas, 1973–75); Pedro Carrillo de Huete, *Crónica del halconero de Juan II*, ed. Juan de Mata Carriazo, Colección de crónicas españolas 8 (Madrid: Espasa-Calpe, 1946); and the anonymous *Crónica de don Alvaro de Luna, Condestable de Castilla, Maestre de Santiago*, ed. Juan de Mata Carriazo, Colección de crónicas españolas 2 (Madrid: Espasa-Calpe, 1940). Pérez de Guzmán, Palencia, and Carrillo de Huete are anti-Luna; the *Crónica* that bears his name is pro-Luna.

63. Of the forty-one combatants presented in this poem, twenty fought on the side of Juan II, not including his son Enrique who appears in the first stanza: Diego López de Estúñiga, 3; Lope de Barrientos, Bishop of Cuenca, 4; Juan de Luna, Bishop of Toledo, 5; Alonso Carrillo de Albornoz, Bishop of Sigüenza, 6; Pero González de Ávila, Lord of Villatoro de Albalecha, 21; Alonso Pérez Vivero, 23; Diego Arias Dávila, 24; Pedro Fernández de Velasco, Count of Haro, 25; Pero Sarmiento, Count of Salinas, 26 & 44; Álvaro de Luna, 27; Íñigo López de Mendoza, Marqués de Santillana, 28; Juan Pacheco, 29; Fernando Álvarez de Toledo, Count of Alba, 30; Pedro García de Herrera, Lord of Asturias, 31; Rodrigo de Villandrando, Count of Ribadeo, 32; Pedro de Acuña, Count of Buendía and Lord of Dueñas, 33; Payo de Rivera, 34; Juan Ramírez de Guzmán, 35; Juan de Pimentel, Count of Mayorga, 36, and Juan de Silva, Lord of Cifuentes, 37. The rebels are represented by Alonso de Pimentel, Count of Benavente, 7; Rodrigo Manrique, Count of Paredes and father of the poet Jorge, 8; Fernando de Rojas, 9; Ruy Díaz de Mendoza, 10; Fernán López de Saldaña, 11; Mosén López de Ángulo, Marshall of Navarre, 12; Luis de la Cerda, Count of Medinaceli, 13; Pedro de Mendoza, Lord of Almazán, 14; Juan de Tovar, Lord of Berlanga and Astudillo, 15; Manuel de Benavides, Lord of Jabalquinto, 16; Enrique Enríquez, Lord of Bembibre and Bolaños, 17; Gutierre de Sotomayor,

Master of Alcántara, 18; Garci Sánchez de Alvarado, 19; Diego de Quiñones, Count of Cangas and Tineo, 20; Juan I of Navarre, 38 & 45; Infante Enrique of Aragon, 39; Diego Gómez de Sandoval, Count of Castro, 40; Fadrique Enríquez, Admiral of Castile, 41; Fernando de Quiñones, brother of Diego (20), 42; and Lope García de Rojas, 43. Only one of the individuals presented in the poem (in st. 22) has not been identified. See Elia, *Coplas*, 14, n. 4, and Rincón, *Coplas satíricas y dramáticas*, 63–65. The only characters caricatured twice are Pero Sarmiento (st. 26 and 44) and Juan I of Navarre (st. 38 and 45). Note that in MSS 3993 and 3788 of the Biblioteca Nacional of Madrid and in MS 9939 of the British Library, st. 43 and 44 are absent; complete versions of the *Coplas de la panadera* are found in MSS 10475 of the Biblioteca Nacional (lacking the first, unnumbered stanza), B-2347 of the Hispanic Society of New York, vol. 63-9-71 of *Varios* in the Biblioteca Colombina y Capitular de Sevilla (published by Domínguez, "El manuscrito de las *Coplas de la panadera*") and in MS 71 of the Biblioteca de Menéndez Pelayo. One complete MS, belonging to the Real Academia of Madrid and published by Sáez in 1805, has since been lost. For more information on the manuscript tradition, see Elia, *Coplas*, 13–31, and Domínguez.

64. Barbara F. Weissberger, "The Body as Contestant Site in *Cancionero* Poetry," MLA Convention, San Diego, CA, December 27, 1994, argues that the *panadera* is a victim of rape, construing the verses "quéntanos de aquel rebato/que te aconteció en la vera" (vv. 3–4) as indicating that she was the object of violent attack.

65. Reference to *Poesía crítica y satírica del siglo XV*, 130.

66. Citation from Kapchan, *Gender on the Market*, 2. In these comments I draw on Certeau, *The Practice of Everyday Life*, esp. xii–xix, 18, 34–39, who discusses consumption as resistance and tactics as the recourses of the powerless. On the Catalan *Cobles de la Panadera*, see Martín de Riquer, "Las «Coplas de la panadera» en Cataluña," *Philologica hispaniensia in honorem Manuel Alvar: III, Literatura*, 4 vols., vol. 3 (Madrid: Gredos, 1983–86), 435–50, and his *Història de la literatura catalana*, 3 vols, vol. 3 (Barcelona: Ariel, 1964), 93ff. I discuss these satires in "Women Out of Bounds: *Soldadeiras, Panaderas*, and *Serranas* in the Poetry of Medieval Spain," Diss. University of California at Berkeley, 1997, 128–45.

Chapter 4   Monstrosity in the Mountains, Courtesy at Court: Contesting Space in Poems on *Serranas*

1. I cite the version found in Frenk, *Corpus*, no. 86; Sebastián de Horozco (*Cancionero*, ed. Weiner, no. 281) includes this lyric in an *entremés* (comic skit) written for the feast day of St. John the Evangelist (December 27). Horozco puts this song in the mouth of a *villano* (rustic), who sings it as he walks the streets of Toledo looking for an open shop where he can buy his *zagala* a gift. The speech immediately following this song explains that the *villano* fell in love with his *zagala* while watching her dance; he depicts her

as aggressively flirting with him and himself as hopelessly in love with her. This lyric is in *sayagués*, the language spoken by rustic characters in Golden Age literature. *Sayagués* is purely a literary convention; authors would freely combine archaisms, dialectical traits, and made-up words to produce a sense of rusticity and uneducated language. As a result, it is impossible to translate this lyric completely accurately; I have approximated the sense as much as possible.

2. As Nancy F. Marino, *La serranilla española: Notas para su historia e interpretación* (Potomac, MD: Scripta Humanistica, 1987), 2–16, explains, *serranillas* narrate the bucolic encounter between a male traveler, usually a *cavallero*, and a *serrana*; while in some mid- to late fifteenth-century *serranillas* the female protagonist is noble, these poems use other *serranilla* conventions, such as the encounter in a rural setting and a dialogue between the two protagonists. I use the circumlocution "poetry about *serranas*" to refer broadly to all medieval Iberian lyrics that refer to or include *serranas* as characters, regardless of origin, narrative structure, and meter. I reserve the term *serranilla* for fifteenth-century courtly lyrics that narrate the encounter between a *serrana* and an elite male traveler; I call the *serrana* lyrics in the *Libro de buen amor cánticas*, as they are labeled in the subtitles. Other discussions of the *serranilla* as a genre include Ramón Menéndez Pidal, "La primitiva poesía lírica española," *Estudios literarios* (Madrid: Atenea, [1920]), 251–344, and Rafael Lapesa, *La obra literaria del Marqués de Santillana* (Madrid: Ínsula, 1957), 46–73. For a good introduction to the *serranilla* in English, see Marino's entry in *Medieval Iberia: An Encyclopedia*, 749–50. For the *serrana* lyrics I discuss in this chapter, I indicate the numbering found in standard, single-author editions in addition to Dutton's numeric identifications of *cancionero* lyrics, found in his *Cancionero del Siglo XV*. For Santillana's *serranillas*, I cite the edition of Miguel Ángel Pérez Priego [Marqués de Santillana (Íñigo López de Mendoza), *Poesía lírica* (Madrid: Cátedra, 1999)]; for those of Carvajal, I cite Emma Scoles's edition [Carvajal, *Poesie* (Rome: Ateneo, 1967)]. Additional *serrana* lyrics are found in the *Cancionero musical español de los siglos XV y XVI* [= *Cancionero musical de Palacio*, MP4], ed. Francisco Asenjo Barbieri (Buenos Aires: Schapire, 1945). I identify lyrics about *serranas* not included in Dutton by the collection and/or text within which they are found, most frequently Frenk, *Corpus*, and *Libro de buen amor*, ed. Alberto Blecua. Line references included in the text.

3. As Nieto Soria, "Aspectos de la vida cotidiana de las pastoras," 317–18, comments, it is odd that wolves do not appear in *serranillas*; not only is their absence unrealistic (and a sign that *serranillas* do not reflect historic reality) but, I would argue, their absence underlines the male protagonist's role as a sexual predator, a role assumed by aggressive *serranas* like La Chata, Gadea, Alda, and Menga de Mançanares. See my discussions of transgendered performances and parodic mimicry in chapter 1.

4. Reference to Blay Manzanera, "El varón que finge voz de mujer." See my discussion of interpellation in chapters 1 and 2. The three *cancioneros* Blay Manzanera studies in this article are the *Cancionero de Baena* [PN1], the

Cancionero de Palacio [SA7], and the *Cancionero de Estúñiga* [MN54]; out of the one thousand and eight poems contained in these three collections, only forty-eight cite female voices (20, 23). In "El discurso femenino," Blay Manzanera analyses an additional four *cancioneros* (the *Cancionero de Gómez Manrique* [MP3], *Cancionero general de Hernando del Castillo* [11CG], the *Cancionero musical de Palacio* [MP4], and the *Cancionero de Uppsala* [not included in Dutton]); unfortunately in this article she does not discuss the female characters' class status, a shame since MP4 includes many popular lyrics voiced by peasant women. Blay Manzanera does not include allegorical characters in her analysis of female voicing, nor has she incorporated the entire *corpus* of *cancionero* poetry in her statistics; nonetheless, I expect that her findings are representative of the *corpus* as a whole.

5. Menéndez Pidal argues that *serranas guiadoras* (mountain women who guide lost travelers) really inhabited medieval Spanish mountain ranges ("La primitiva poesía lírica española," 291–92, 295); Bruce D. Kirby, "Juan Ruiz's *Serranas*: The Archpriest-Pilgrim and Medieval Wild Women," *Hispanic Studies in Honor of Alan D. Deyermond*, ed. John S. Miletich (Madison: Hispanic Seminary of Medieval Studies, 1986), 151–69, more persuasively argues that the aggressive *serranas* in the *Libro de buen amor* are unrealistic and instead reflect medieval beliefs in wild women and carnival rituals. For additional discussions of mountains in medieval literature and culture, see *La montagne dans le texte médiéval: Entre mythe et réalité*, ed. Claude Thomasset and Danièle James-Raoul (Paris: Presses de l'Université de Paris-Sorbonne, 2000). Unfortunately *Inventing Medieval Landscapes: Senses of Place in Western Europe*, ed. John Howe and Michael Wolf (Gainesville, FL: University Press of Florida, 2002) does not include any discussions of mountains. René Jantzen, *Montagne et symboles* (Lyon: Presses Universitaires de Lyon, 1988) discusses the symbolic values of mountains in Enlightenment and nineteenth-century French literature and culture.

6. Citation from Bartholomaeus Glanville, *De proprietatibus rerum, Propiedades de las cosas*, Tolosa, 1494, ADMYTE, Disk 1, 343. While this encyclopedia was written in Latin by an Englishman, the Castilian translation is an adaptation that reflects the translator's knowledge and understanding of the source text. Joëlle Ducos, "Entre terre, aire et eau: La formation des montagnes," *La montagne dans le texte médiéval*, 19–51, discusses medieval French translations of Latin encyclopedias as a process of adaptation; she also addresses medieval accounts of the formation of mountains. John Rennie Short, *Imagined Country: Society, Culture and Environment* (London and New York: Routledge, 1991), 15, discusses medieval and early modern interpretations of mountains as products of man's sinfulness.

7. Citations from Bartholomaeus Glanville, *Propiedades de las cosas*, 344–45, and from Gauberto Fabricio de Vagad, *Crónica de Aragón*, Zaragoza, 1499, ADMYTE, disk 1, 59. Anthony D. Smith, "The Origins of Nations," *Becoming National: A Reader*, ed. Geoff Eley and Ronald Grigor Suny (New York and Oxford: Oxford University Press, 1996), 106–130, discusses how historicizing natural features and naturalizing historical features help create

the idea of nation, 120–21. The use of mountains as natural sites of refuge as well as the foundations for castles, especially in the territory known as Castile, helped nationalize the landscape.

8. References to *Cancionero musical español*, nos. 81 and 82.

9. Victoria A. Burrus discusses courtly love as a game appropriate only for the young; mature men who played the role of a lover at court often became targets of ridicule ("Poets at Play: Love Poetry in the Spanish 'Can-cioneros,' " Diss. University of Wisconsin at Madison, 1985, 89–93). See also her "Role Playing in the Amatory Poetry of the *Cancioneros*," *Poetry at Court in Trastamaran Spain*, 111–33. I discuss "Moçuela de Bores" at greater length below. Julian Weiss has demonstrated that, in Galician-Portuguese love lyric, the male speaker can only assume the role of desiring subject, never object, in contrast to female speakers of *Cantigas d'amigo*, who play both roles with respect to the *amigo* ["On the conventionality of the *Cantigas d'amor*," *La corónica* 26.1 (Fall 1997): 225–45]. In fifteenth-century Castilian love lyrics, male speakers most often play the frustrated desiring subject; when they assume the role of object of desire it is usually in comic pieces, as in *serranillas* or parodic verses that Hernando de Castillo located among the *Obras de burlas provocantes a risa* at the conclusion of his *Cancionero general*. I take the word "pornotopia" from Steven Marcus, *The Other Victorians: A Study of Sexuality and Pornography in Mid-Nineteenth-Century England* (New York: Basic Books, 1966), 271; see also Vasvári, "Peregrinaciones por topografías pornográficas," 1563–72.

10. I develop this theme in my discussion of the *Libro de buen amor* below. The text of the "Serrana de la Vera" is found in *El romancero viejo*, ed. Mercedes Díaz Roig (Madrid: Cátedra, 1985), 267–68; see also Julio Caro Baroja, "La serrana de la Vera, o un pueblo analizado en conceptos y símbolos inac-tuales," *Ritos y mitos equívocos*, 259–338. For fifteenth-century depictions of sexually aggressive *serranas*, see Marino, *La serranilla española*, 116–19.

11. Citations from Frenk, *Corpus*, nos. 979A, 1896, 38 vv. 1–2, 39B, 117, and from Shields, *Places on the Margin: Alternative Geographies of Modernity* (London and New York: Routledge, 1991), 3, 4. While the last four lyrics employ the future tense in the relative clause, the first three do so with a speculative sense in the present; only the fourth, which specifically questions what the young girl will be like when she's grown, uses the future tense in order to refer to future time.

12. Citations from Frenk, *Corpus*, nos. 985, 986, 987, 989; references to Laura R. Bass, "Crossing Borders: Gender, Geography and Class Relations in Three *Serranillas* of the Marqués de Santillana," *La corónica* 25.1 (Fall 1996): 69–84; and to Vasvári, "Peregrinaciones por topografías pornográficas." On the bewildering properties of the wilderness, see Short, *Imagined Country*, 6–9, 21. See also Marcus, *The Other Victorians*, whose work on Victorian pornotopias Vasvári draws on, and Darby Lewes, *Nudes from Nowhere: Utopian Sexual Landscapes* (Lanham, MD: Rowman & Littlefield, 2000), who discusses Victorian pornographic landscapes as "somatopias" (body-places, both places constructed as bodies and places where bodily desires are

indulged); she links a variety of feminized landscapes in seventeenth- to nineteenth-century British literature to changing attitudes toward the land, conditioned by the British experience of empire.

13. Citations from Frenk, *Corpus*, nos. 980, 981.

14. *Hable con ella*, dir. Pedro Almodóvar [El Deseo, 2002], Videocassette (Warner Bros. Pictures, 2003). In the screenplay, Alfredo sees Amparo's body as a landscape: "De perfil, el cuerpo de Amparo es un paisaje natural, con valles, montes, arbustos y claros, por cuya superficie Alfredo disfruta del mejor paseo que haya dado en su vida" [In profile, Amparo's body is a natural landscape, with valleys, mountains, bushes and clearings, on whose surface Alfredo enjoys the best walk of his life). (Almodóvar, *Hable con ella: el guión* [Madrid: El Deseo and Ocho y Medio, 2002], 141).

15. Citation from Nicolás Bratosevich, "Entornos y efectos de enunciación," *Homenaje a Ana María Barrenechea*, ed. Lía Schwartz Lerner and Isaías Lerner (Madrid: Castalia, 1984), 207–17, 210.

16. On the debate over the authorship of the four *cánticas de serrana* in the *Libro de buen amor*, see Marino, *La serranilla española*, 42–49.

17. Citation from Miguel Ángel Pérez Priego, "Sobre la transmisión y recepción de la poesía de Santillana: el caso de las *serranillas* y los *sonetos*," *Homenaje al profesor F. López Estrada*, spec. issue of *Dicenda* 6 (1987/90): 189–97, 192.

18. Citations from Lapesa, *La obra literaria del Marqués de Santillana*, 50, 52; reference to Battesti, "Tipología del encuentro en la serranilla medieval," *Mélanges à la mémoire d'André Joucla-Ruau*, ed. Jean Chalon et al., 2 vols, vol. 1 (Aix-en-Provence: Université de Provence, 1978), 405–42. Pérez Priego, ed., *Poesía lírica*, 44, follows Lapesa in suggesting that *serranillas* were usually performed orally in court upon a poet's return from a trip.

19. Citations from Bratosevich, "Entornos y efectos de enunciación," 210, and from Battesti, "Tipología del encuentro," 422–23.

20. References to Sirera, "Diálogos de cancionero y teatralidad," 356–57.

21. There are some extant *serrana* lyrics that seem to have been composed for performance by women. Three polyphonic compositions found in the *Cancionero musical de Palacio* [MP4] put popular lyrics into the mouths of *serranas*: D3926, "Sola me dejastes," attributed to the musician Gabriel, a female-voiced monologue; D4077, "Una montaña pasando," attributed to Garcimuñoz; and D3956, "Serrana del bel mirar," attributed to the musician Millán, which has a *serrana* sing two popular lyrics as the male narrator looks on sympathetically. These compositions were scored for polyphonic performance, probably by men as well as women; women could well have voiced the parts of the *serranas*. On the late fifteenth-century taste for reusing popular lyrics in courtly compositions, see Margit Frenk Alatorre, "¿Santillana o Suero de Ribera?," *Nueva Revista de Filología Hispánica* 16 (1962): 437. As I mention below in my discussion of Carvajal's *serranilla* XLVI/D0651, that composition could have been composed for dialogic performance, with a woman voicing the *serrana*'s song. Regula Rohland de Langbehn, "Íñigo López de Mendoza, Marqués de Santillana," *Castilian Writers, 1400–1500*,

ed. Frank A. Domínguez and George D. Greenia, Dictionary of Literary Biography, 286 (Detroit: Gale, 2004), 233–54, claims that two of Santillana's *serranillas* survive in oral tradition (236, 237).

22. Citation from Gerli, "Fernán Pérez de Guzmán, *Cancionero de Baena* 119, and the *Libro de buen amor*," *MLN* 105 (1990): 367–72, 368; see also his "Carvajal's *Serranas*." I provide a brief introduction to the *Libro de buen amor* in chapter 3. The Archpriest's *serrana* adventures include four episodes, each of which includes a *cuaderna vía* introduction and a lyric portion written in a different rhyme and meter. The first adventure, in which the male protagonist encounters La Chata, extends from st. 950 to 971 (*cuaderna vía* 950–58, *cántica* 959–71); the second adventure, which features Gadea de Riofrío, runs from 972 to 992 (*cuaderna vía* 972–86, *cántica* 987–92); the third, with Menga Lloriente, encompasses 993–1005 (*cuaderna vía* 993–96, *cántica* 997–1005); the final and perhaps most famous, featuring the grotesque Alda de Tablada, runs from 1006 to 1042 (*cuaderna vía* 1006–21, *cántica* 1022–42).

23. Citation from L. Jenaro MacLennan, "Sobre los orígenes folklóricos de la serrana Gadea de Riofrío (*Libro de buen amor*)," *Vox Romanica* 47 (1988): 180–83, 181; references to James F. Burke, "Juan Ruiz, the *Serranas*, and the Rites of Spring," *The Journal of Medieval and Renaissance Studies* 5 (1975): 13–35, and to Vasvári, "Peregrinaciones por topografías pornográficas."

24. Citation from Brownlee, "Permutations of the Narrator-Protagonist: The *Serrana* Episodes of the *Libro de buen amor* in Light of the Doña Endrina Sequence," *Romance Notes* 22.1 (1981):98–101, 100–101. See my discussion of interpellation in chapters 1 and 2. R.B. Tate, "Adventures in the *Sierra*," '*Libro de buen amor*' *Studies*, ed. G.B. Gybbon-Monypenny (London: Tamesis, 1970), 219–29, 223; Marino, *La serranilla española*, 42–49; and Vasvári, "Peregrinaciones por topografías pornográficas," 1564, also discuss the narrator-protagonist's changing identity in this sequence. Anthony N. Zahareas and Óscar Pereira, *Itinerario del Libro del Arcipreste: Glosas críticas al Libro de buen amor* (Madison: Hispanic Seminary of Medieval Studies, 1990), 278, do recognize that the *serranas* impose various identities upon the Archpriest.

25. In this quotation *juego* is a noun not a conjugated verb; in this context, it functions as a vague threat, so I translate it as a verb.

26. Vasvári, "Peregrinaciones por topografías pornográficas," 1567, explains the erotic connotations of Sotosalvos. Jacques Joset, in his edition of the *Libro de buen amor*, 2 vols. (Madrid: Espasa-Calpe, 1974), notes that 971g is ambiguous, meaning both 'I made a good bargain' and 'I got out of a tight spot for little money' (II: 40, 971g n.); as Zahareas and Pereira, *Itinerario del Libro del Arcipreste*, 270, note, the protagonist didn't have to pay money, but he did pay with sex. *Fiz* is also ambiguous, either first- or third-person singular preterite, adding to the comic possibilities of this verse.

27. Reference to Vasvári, "Peregrinaciones por topografías pornográficas," 1567–68.

28. References to Cano Ballesta, "¿Pretende casarse la serrana de Tablada?," *La corónica* 23.1 (Fall 1994): 3–11, and to Bass, "Crossing Borders," 79. Given that RL 193 parodies *pastorela* conventions, the fact that both male narrators

avoid sexual contact with the highly accessible yet degraded women is ironic, playing with the audience's horizon of expectations.

29. These interruptions occur in 959e, 961c, 991g, and 1031d; they do not occur in the third *cántica*, in which each characters' speeches are introduced with verbs of speaking.

30. Menéndez Pidal argues that the performance of the *Libro de buen amor* would have ressembled the French *chantefable* (*Poesía juglaresca*, 280); his performance scenario is based in part on his reading of a *Libro de buen amor* miscellany as a *juglar cazurro's* performance text (270, 277, 308–13, 487–93). As Alan Deyermond has shown, it is highly unlikely that miscellany was ever used by a *juglar* ["*Juglar's* Repertoire or Sermon Notebook?—The *Libro de Buen Amor* and a Manuscript Miscellany," *Bulletin of Hispanic Studies* 51 (1974): 217—27.] John Walsh, "The Genesis of the *Libro de buen amor* (from Performance-Text to *libro* or *cancionero*)," (unpublished manuscript), also argues the *juglar* spoke the *cuaderna vía* portions and sang the lyrics. For an opinion similar to mine, see Bruce Kirby, "Juan Ruiz's *Serranas*: The Archpriest-Pilgrim and Medieval Wild Women," who argues, "the recent discovery of a surviving melody for the metrical form in which the book is predominantly written [i.e., *cuaderna vía*], lends support to the idea that works composed in this meter were in fact *sung* (not merely recited) in public (162, emphasis in original). He cites an extant melody from the *Carmina Burana* to support this argument.

31. Reference to Bratosevich, "Entornos y efectos de enunciación." The autobiographical reading of Santillana's *serranillas* originated with José Amador de los Ríos, the editor of the first complete modern edition of the works of Santillana [*Obras de don Íñigo López de Mendoza, Marqués de Santillana*, ahora por vez primera compiladas de los códices originales e ilustradas con la vida del autor, (Madrid, 1852)]. Others who have examined the geography of Santillana's *serranillas* include José María de Cossío, "Geografía de una serranilla del Marqués de Santillana," *Correo erudito* 2 (1941): 52–53; José Terrero, "Paisajes y pastoras en las "serranillas" del Marqués de Santillana," *Cuadernos de literatura* 7 (1950): 169–202; Rafael Lapesa, *La obra literaria del Marqués de Santillana*; and Bass, "Crossing Borders." For a good English introduction to the life and work of the Marqués, see Rohland de Langbehn, "Íñigo López de Mendoza, Marqués de Santillana."

32. Cossío, "Geografía de una serranilla del Marqués de Santillana," discusses this conflict in detail. He also argues that the four place-names mentioned in this poem (Bores, Lama, Frama, and Espinama) are quite distant from each other, making the landscape of this poem unrealistic or imaginary; he argues these names were chosen for metrical reasons, not for geographic realism.

33. But see Marino, who reads this comment as a criticism of courtly ladies' use of cosmetics (*La serranilla española*, 88). Bratosevich, "Entornos y efectos de enunciación," 210–13, discusses the narrator's self-depiction as explicitly bringing the courtly code of love to bear on this encounter and as situating himself with respect to his courtly audience; he sees this elevating treatment

of the *serrana* as an attempt to make her worthy of attention by construing her as a *dama*.

34. Menéndez Pidal discusses the *serrana salteadora* along with other *serrana* types in his "La primitiva poesía lírica española," 283–95. Bratosevich, "Entornos y efectos de enunciación," 213–14, reads her speech as illustrating her wit and therefore her worth as an object of desire.

35. References to Bratosevich, "Entornos y efectos de enunciación," 216, and to Pérez Priego, ed., *Poesía lírica*, 15 n. 37, 15 n. 45.

36. Reference to Bratosevich, "Entornos y efectos de enunciación," 215. Burrus, "Poets at Play," 263–64, makes a similar argument in her discussion of the game of love.

37. Critics who have posited a direct allusion to Ruiz's *cánticas de serrana* in V/D3432 include Menéndez Pidal, "La primitiva poesía lírica española," 286; Rafael Lapesa, *La obra literaria del Marqués de Santillana*, 53; and Marino, *La serranilla española*, 91–92. Pérez Priego, ed., *Poesía lírica*, suggests Menga may have become a frequent name for *serranas* due to this composition by Santillana, which he sees echoed in two *serranas* in the Cancionero Musical de Palacio [MP4], nos. 350/D3981 and 380/D3826, named respectively Menga del Boscar and Menga del Bustar. Other similarities between these three compositions, such as the use of *par* as a rhyme word in no. 350/D3981 and the fact that in no. 380/D3826 Menga is singing a *cantar* (as she does in Santillana's poem), increase the likelihood of Pérez Priego's theory. Frenk includes these two anonymous compositions in her *Corpus*, nos. 997 and 998. Yet more Mengas appear in poems on *serranas*, including one found in the Cancionero de Baena, D1388 by Pedro González de Mendoza, "Menga, dame el tu acorro" (Dutton, *El cancionero del siglo XV*, 7:498).

38. Citations from Terrero, "Paisajes y pastoras," 181, and from Bass, "Crossing Borders," 79. References to Pérez Priego, ed., *Poesía lírica*, 115 n. 4, and to Lapesa, *La obra literaria del Marqués de Santillana*, 53.

39. The reference to *tomellares* is a veiled yet unambiguous indication that they had sex, similar to *flores* in the previous poem.

40. Citation from Pedro Rodríguez de Lena, *El passo honroso de Suero de Quiñones*, intro. and ed. Amancio Labandeira Fernández (Madrid: Fundación Universitaria Española, 1977), 9.

41. On the *Paso de la Fuerte Ventura*, see Rodríguez de Lena, *El passo honroso*, 14–15; this text also cites the *salvajes'* challenge at the 1459 *paso*, 19. Rico, "Unas coplas de Jorge Manrique," 519, cites the speech of *Ventura*. Manuel Criado de Val, *Historia de Hita y su Arcipreste: Vida y muerte de una villa mozárabe* (Madrid: Nacional, 1976), 136, discusses Santillana's role in the *Paso de la Fuerte Ventura*. Both Burrus, "Poets at Play," and Roger Boase, *The Troubadour Revival: A Study of Social Change and Traditionalism in Late Medieval Spain* (London and Boston: Routledge & K. Paul, 1978) discuss the increasing importance of chivalric games such as tournaments and *pasos de armas* in fifteenth-century aristocratic culture.

42. Lapesa does recognize that Menga issues a challenge that the *caballero* accepts; he also uses somewhat chivalric language in his discussion of this poem. However, he does not admit that she plays the role of a knight (*La obra literaria del Marqués de Santillana*, 53).

43. References to Menéndez Pidal, "La primitiva poesía lírica española," 282–86, and to Bass, "Crossing Borders," 78–82. The comment from Santillana's *Proemio e carta* to which I refer is: "En este reyno de Castilla dixo bien el rey don Alfonso el Sabio, é yo ví quien vió deçires suyos, é aun se diçe metrificava altamente en lengua latina," Santillana, *Poesías completas*, ed. Manuel Durán, 2 vols, vol. 2 (Madrid: Castalia, 1980), 219 (In this kingdom of Castile King Alfonso el Sabio wrote well, and I've seen someone who saw poems by him, and it is still said that he composed Latin poetry in a high style). See also Harold Livermore, "Santillana and the Galaico-Portuguese Poets," *Iberoromania* 31 (1990): 53–64, who opines that Santillana had read neither Alfonso el Sabio's Galician-Portuguese lyric, nor that of Don Dinis (54 n. 4, 55).

44. Citations from Bass, "Crossing Borders," 80–81, and from Kathryn Gravdal, "Camouflaging Rape: The Rhetoric of Sexual Violence in the Medieval Pastourelle," *Romanic Review* 76 (1985): 361–73, 364. Bass incorrectly calls her Karen Gravdal (81, 83).

45. Unfortunately very little is known about Carvajal (also called Carvajales); even his Christian name has not been preserved. According to Nicasio Salvador Miguel, who includes Carvajal's biography in the introduction to his edition of the *Cancionero de Estúñiga*, Carvajal was probably Castilian in origin, entered the service of Alfonso V at some time after the conquest of Naples in 1443, and remained in Naples until at least 1460, i.e., for a while after Alfonso's death in 1458 [Salvador Miguel, *La poesía cancioneril. El* Cancionero de Estúñiga (Madrid: Alhambra, 1977), 55–73, esp. 55–57]. Carvajal seems to have been the most productive and/or favored poet at Alfonso's court, since he is the poet with the greatest number of compositions included in the *Cancionero de Estúñiga*; what other duties he served is unknown, so Salvador Miguel considers him a professional poet of unclear class status (47). Scoles, in her edition of Carvajal's work, suggests he could be identified with a Captain Alfonso de Carvajal, a suggestion that Salvador Miguel considers promising albeit difficult to prove due to the lack of documentation (Carvajal, *Poesie*, ed. Scoles, 23 n. 15; Salvador Miguel, 55 n. 2). Carvajal's extensive repertoire includes love songs, encomiums to Alfonso, his queen María, and his lover Lucrecia d'Alagno, and political satires against courtly intrigues. Following Marino, *La serranilla española*, 110, I consider the following compositions *serranillas*: X/D0608, XVIII/D0618, XXII/D0622, XLI/D0646, XLV/D0650, XLVI/D0651, and XLIX/D0655. Salvador Miguel numbers these poems CIX (D0608), CXIX (D0618), CXXIII (D0622), CL (D0650), CLI (D0651), and CLV (D0655); he does not consider XLI/D0646 a *serranilla*, nor does Scoles.

46. Reference to Gerli and Weiss, eds., *Poetry at Court in Trastamaran Spain;* see esp. Weiss's introduction to this volume.

47. References to *Libro de buen amor*, ed. Blecua, 231 n. 952c, 238 n. 972b, and to Vasvári, "Peregrinaciones por topografías pornográficas," 1564; see also Vasvári, "Múltiple transparencia semántica de los nombres de la alcahueta en el *Libro del Arcipreste*," *Medioevo y Literatura*, Actas del V Congreso de la Asociación Hispánica de Literatura Medieval, ed. Juan Paredes, 4 vols, vol. 2 (Granada: Universidad de Granada, 1995), 453–63, esp. 459–60. Burke, "Juan Ruiz, the *Serranas*, and the Rites of Spring," 24, cites Daniel Devoto's argument that *troya* means 'sow,' referring to an oversexed person; Devoto also suggests this word could refer to the destruction and doom of Troy, implying that La Chata's victims are similarly doomed. Carvajal could be playing with all these meanings in his portrait of Cassandra. Gerli, "Carvajal's *Serranas*," sees similarly subtle references to the *Libro de buen amor* in Carvajal's two *serranillas* that feature grotesque *serranas*, XXII/D0672 and XLIX/D0655. Note that Troya is also a place-name close to Naples (Salvador Miguel, *La poesía cancioneril*, 32).

48. While Scoles, ed., *Poesie*, reads *camurra*, I agree with Marino, *La serranilla española*, 121, that the item in question is a *çamarra*, a lamb-skin coat. This detailed description is quite difficult to translate; I am indebted to Barbara Weissberger and Marino for their help in translating this stanza.

49. On *invenciones*, see Ian Macpherson, "The Game of Courtly Love: *Letra, Divisa*, and *Invención* at the Court of the Catholic Monarchs," *Poetry at Court in Trastamaran Spain*, 95–110.

50. Lapesa, *La obra literaria del Marqués de Santillana*, 287, considers it doubtful that Carvajal is referring to Santillana's "Cantar" in this composition. Another psuedo-*serranilla* often attributed to Santillana, "Por [En] una gentil floresta" (D2475), portrays three *damas* singing popular lyrics; however, I agree with Frenk Alatorre and Dutton that this composition is erroneously attributed to Santillana and is probably the work of Suero de Ribera, to whom it is attributed in two *cancioneros*. Suero de Ribera frequented Alfonso V's Neapolitan court alongside Carvajal. See Frenk Alatorre, "¿Santillana o Suero de Ribera?"; Dutton, *Cancionero del siglo XV*, 7: 441–42; and Pérez Priego, ed., *Poesía lírica*, 134–35 n.

51. Carvajal uses *serranilla* conventions to praise an actual woman in XVIII/D0618, dedicated to Eleanora of Aragon, the illegitimate daughter of Alfonso V. In that poem, he portrays her as Diana, goddess of the hunt: "topé dama que deesa / parescía en su fermosura" (vv. 3–4; I met a lady who seemed God-like in her beauty).

52. See Scoles, ed., *Poesie*, 208; Salvador Miguel, *La poesía cancioneril*, 66–68; Marino, *La serranilla española*, 116–17; Gerli, "Carvajal's *Serranas*"; and Pilar García Carcedo, "Las serranillas de Carvajal," *Medioevo y Literatura*, vol. 2, 345–58.

53. Citation from Black, "Poetic Taste at the Aragonese Court in Naples," *Florilegium Hispanicum: Medieval and Golden Age Studies Presented to Dorothy Clotelle Clarke*, ed. John S. Geary et al. (Madison: Hispanic Seminary of Medieval Studies, 1983), 165–178, 167.

54. As Marino notes in *La serranilla española*, 28–32, 112–13, Carvajal's citation of a *serrana*'s song is unusual for Castilian *serranillas*. The motif of a traveler who watches a singing shepherdess and incorporates her song into his appears in a Galician-Portuguese *pastorela* by Airas Nunes (CV 454) and in late fifteenth-century Castilian *cancionero* poetry, especially in the *Cancionero musical de Palacio* [MP4] (Garcimuñoz, "Una montaña pasando," no. 351/D4077; "Serrana del bel mirar," no. 346/D3956). These heterogeneous songs are *ensaladas*, combinations of popular lyrics and courtly verses, and are frequently preserved with musical notation. "Por una gentil floresta" (D2475), the poem erroneously attributed to Santillana as I mentioned above, is also an *ensalada*. Given the length of the female speech in XLVI/D0651, I expect this *serranilla* was performed dialogically, with a woman voicing the *serrana*'s song. On Galician-Portuguese *pastorelas*, see Arlene T. Lesser, *La pastorela medieval hispánica: Pastorelas y serranas galaico-portuguesas* (Vigo: Galaxia, 1970), and Stegagno Picchio, "Entre pastorelas e serranas"; on the late fifteenth-century vogue for popular lyric, see Frenk Alatorre, "¿Santillana o Suero de Ribera?"

Conclusion

1. Those who have explored gender construction in the *Cantigas d'escarnho* include Blackmore, "The Poets of Sodom"; Liu, " 'Affined to love the Moor' " and "Obscenidad y transgresión en una cantiga de escarnio"; Rosenstein, "The Voiced and the Voiceless"; and Ashurst, "Masculine Postures and Poetic Gambits." Studies of gender construction in *cancionero* lyric include Weiss, "Alvaro de Luna, Juan de Mena and the Power of Courtly Love" and the essays in *Poetry at Court in Trastamaran Spain*.

2. Studies of female voices in poetry include Blay Manzanera, "El discurso femenino," and "El varón que finge voz de mujer"; Earnshaw, *The Female Voice in Medieval Romance Lyric*; and Lorenzo Gradín, *La canción de mujer*.

3. The six Martin Codax *cantigas* are found in MS Vindel, MS 979, Pierpont Morgan Library, New York; they are transcribed into modern notation in Manuel Pedro Ferreira, *O Som de Martin Codax*. Harvey Leo Sharrer, "Fragmentos de Sete Cantigas d'Amor de D. Dinis, musicadas; uma descoberta," reproduces the manuscript fragments of the seven Don Dinis cantigas. Manuel Pedro Ferreira, "Relatório Preliminar sobre o Conteúdo Musical do Fragmento Sharrer," *Literatura medieval*, vol. 1, 35–42, provides a comparative analysis of the musical content and notation of these seven *Cantigas d'amor*. Charles E. Brewer, "The *Cantigas d'amigo* of Martin Codax in the Context of Medieval Secular Latin Song," *La corónica* 26.2 (Spring 1998): 17–28, demonstrates that these *Cantigas d'amigo* are anomalous, differing significantly from both Dinis's *Cantigas d'amor* and from the *Cantigas de Santa Maria*. He finds closer parallels for the Codax melodies in two male-voiced Latin love songs; he does not explore the issue of gendered voicing in his study. On contrafacta, see William D. Paden, "Contrafacture between Occitan and Galician-Portuguese," *La corónica* 26.2 (Spring 1998): 49–63; while he does not look for

metrical similarities within the extant Galician-Portuguese notation, his methodology is applicable to such a study. For a good overview of studies on the music of the sacred and profane cantigas, see Pedro Manuel Ferreira, "A música das cantigas galego-portuguesas: balanço de duas décadas de investigação (1977–1997)," *Centro de Estudos de Sociologia e Estética Musical*, Online journal, http://www.fcsh.unl.pt/cesem/18_02_00/revistas/mpf_mus_cantig98.htm, ca. 1999, cited May 10, 2004. *Cantigas from the Court of Dom Dinis: Devotional, Satirical & Courtly Medieval Love Songs*, Theatre of Voices, Paul Hillier, dir., CD (Los Angeles: Harmonia Mundi USA, 1995) includes some *Cantigas d'escarnho* set to extant notation from the *Cantigas de Santa María*. See Frederic L. Cheyette and Margaret Switten, "Women in Troubadour Song," for an approach to analyzing musical gender in secular, vernacular lyric.

4. I do not know of any studies of music and gender for fifteenth-century Spain. Studies of performance of *cancionero* song include Tess Knighton, "The *a capella* Heresy in Spain: An Inquisition into the Performance of the *Cancionero* Repertory," *Early Music* 20.4 (1992): 560–81; María Carmen Gómez Muntané, "La música laica en el reino de Castilla en tiempos del Condestable don Miguel Lucas de Iranzo (1458–1473)," *Revista de Musicología* 19 (1996): 25–45; David Fallows, "A Glimpse of the Lost Years: Spanish Polyphonic Song, 1450–70," *New Perspectives in Music: Essays in Honor of Eileen Southern*, ed. Josephine Wright, Detroit Monographs in Musicology (Warren, MI: Harmonie Park Press, 1992), 19–36; and Robert Stevenson, *Spanish Music in the Age of Columbus*. Basic sources for the study of fifteenth-century musical cancioneros include Higinio Anglès, ed., *La música en la corte de los Reyes Católicos. Polifonía profana: Cancionero Musical de Palacio (Siglos XV–XVI)*, 2 vols., Monumentos de la Música Española, 5, 10 (Barcelona: CSIC, Instituto Español de Musicología, 1947, 1951); José Romeu Figueras, *La música en la corte de los Reyes Católicos. Cancionero Musical de Palacio III*, Monumentos de la Música Española, 14 (Barcelona: CSIC, Instituto Español de Musicología, 1965), and Miguel Querol Gavaldá, ed., *Cancionero musical de la Colombina (Siglo XV)*, Monumentos de la Música Española, 33 (Barcelona: CSIC, Instituto Español de Musicología, 1971).

5. *Cantar de mio Cid: Manuscrito de Per Abbat*, Tesoros de la Biblioteca Nacional, Colección de Facsímiles en CD-ROM, 1, 1 disk (Madrid: Biblioteca Nacional, 1998), includes music and a reading of the text as well as digital images of the manuscript with a hypertext transcription. *Teaching Medieval Lyric with Modern Technology: New Windows on the Medieval World*, Margaret Switten, dir., CD-ROM, 9 disks (North Hadley, MA: Mount Holyoke College, 2001), is designed for classroom use and private study; the Instructor's Manual includes sample class plans for high school teachers.

6. ADMYTE [Archivo Digital de Manuscritos y Textos Españoles], disk 0, includes six *cancioneros*, most notably the *Cancionero de Baena*; none of these *cancioneros* include musical notation. Disk 1 includes several of Juan del Encina's works, for none of which notation survives, although there are many surviving examples of his musical compositions; this disk includes digital images of the texts it contains, all of which are incunabulae.

LIST OF WORKS CITED

ADMYTE. See *Archivo Digital de Manuscritos y Textos Españoles*.

Aho, James. *The Orifice as Sacrificial Site: Culture, Organization, and the Body*. New York: Aldine de Gruyter, 2002.

Allegri, Luigi. "Aproximación a una definición del actor medieval." *Cultura y representación en la Edad Media*. Actas del II Festival de Teatre i Música Medieval d'Elx, 1992. Ed. Evangelina Rodríguez Cuadros. Alicante: Instituto de Cultura "Juan Gil Albert," 1994. 125–36.

———. "El espectáculo en la Edad Media." *Teatro y espectáculo en la Edad Media*. Actas Festival d'Elx, 1990. Ed. L. Quirante. Alicante: Instituto de Cultura "Juan Gil Albert," 1992. 21–30.

Almodóvar, Pedro. *Hable con ella: el guión*. Madrid: El Deseo and Ocho y Medio, 2002.

Alonso Hernández, José Luis. *Léxico del marginalismo del Siglo de Oro*. Salamanca: Universidad de Salamanca, 1977.

Alonso, Dámaso. "Estilo y creación en el *Poema de mío Cid*." *Obras completas*. 10 vols. Vol. 2. Madrid: Gredos, 1973. 107–143.

Alvar, Carlos. "María Pérez, Balteira." *Archivo de filología aragonesa* 36–37 (1985): 11–40.

Álvarez Pellitero, Ana María, ed. *Teatro medieval*. Colección Austral. Madrid: Espasa-Calpe, 1990.

Amador de los Ríos, José, ed. *Obras de don Íñigo López de Mendoza, Marqués de Santillana*, ahora por vez primera compiladas de los códices originales e ilustradas con la vida del autor. Madrid: J. Rodríguez, 1852.

Andrés-Gallego, José. "Economía, psicología y ética de un motín: Salamanca, 1764." *Hispania Sacra* 39.80 (1987): 675–711.

Anglès, Higinio, ed. *La música en la corte de los Reyes Católicos. Polifonía profana: Cancionero Musical de Palacio (Siglos XV–XVI)*. 2 vols. Monumentos de la Música Española, 5, 10. Barcelona: CSIC, Instituto Español de Musicología, 1947, 1951.

Archivo Digital de Manuscritos y Textos Españoles (ADMYTE). CD-ROM. 2 vols, disks 0 and 1. Madrid: Micronet, 1992–93.

Arias Freixedo, Xosé Bieito, ed. *Antoloxía de poesía obscena dos trobadores galego-portugueses*. Santiago de Compostela: Positivas, 1993.

Artigas, Miguel. "Nueva redacción de las '*Coplas de la Panadera*,' según un manuscrito de la Biblioteca Menéndez Pelayo." *Estudios eruditos in memoriam de Adolfo Bonilla y San Martín (1875–1926)*. 2 vols. Vol. 1. Madrid: J. Ratés, 1927. 75–89.

Ashurst, David. "Masculine Postures and Poetic Gambits: The Treatment of the *Soldadeira* in the *Cantigas d'escarnho e de mal dizer*." *Bulletin of Hispanic Studies* (Liverpool) 74 (1997): 1–6.

Bakhtin, Mikhail. *Rabelais and His World*. Trans. Hélène Iswolsky. Cambridge, MA: MIT Press, 1968. Reprinted Bloomington: Indiana University Press, 1984.

Barletta, Vincent. "Context and Manuscript Discourse in Late Medieval Castile." *La corónica* 30.1 (Fall 2001): 3–35.

Bass, Laura R. "Crossing Borders: Gender, Geography and Class Relations in Three *Serranillas* of the Marqués de Santillana." *La corónica* 25.1 (Fall 1996): 69–84.

Battesti, Jeanne. "Tipología del encuentro en la serranilla medieval." *Mélanges à la mémoire d'André Joucla-Ruau*. Ed. Jean Chalon et al. 2 vols. Vol. 1. Aix-en-Provence: Université de Provence, 1978. 405–442.

Beltran Pepió, Vicenç. "The Typology and Genesis of the *Cancioneros:* Compiling the Materials." *Poetry at Court in Trastamaran Spain*. 19–46.

Berceo, Gonzalo de. *Milagros de Nuestra Señora*. Trans. Daniel Devoto. Odres nuevos. 7th ed. Madrid: Castalia, 1996.

Bhabha, Homi K. "Of Mimicry and Man: The Ambivalence of Colonial Discourse." In his *The Location of Culture*. London and New York: Routledge, 1994. 85–92.

Biller, Peter. "Confession in the Middle Ages: Introduction." *Handling Sin*. 3–33.

Black, Robert G. "Poetic Taste at the Aragonese Court in Naples." *Florilegium Hispanicum: Medieval and Golden Age Studies Presented to Dorothy Clotelle Clarke*. Ed. John S. Geary et al. Madison: Hispanic Seminary of Medieval Studies, 1983. 165–78.

Blackmore, Josiah. "Locating the Obscene: Approaching a Poetic Canon." *La corónica* 26.2 (Spring 1998): 9–16.

———. "The Poets of Sodom." *Queer Iberia*. 195–221.

Blay Manzanera, Vicenta. "El discurso femenino en los cancioneros de los siglos XV y XVI." *Actas del XIII Congreso de la Asociación Internacional de Hispanistas. Madrid. 6–11 de Julio de 1998*. Ed. Florencio Sevilla and Carlos Alvar. 4 vols. Vol. 1. Madrid: Castalia, 2000. 48–58.

———. "El varón que finge voz de mujer en las composiciones de cancionero." *Cultural Contexts/Female Voices*. Ed. Louise M. Haywood. Papers of the Medieval Hispanic Research Seminar, 27. London: Queen Mary and Westfield College, 2000. 9–26.

Boase, Roger. *The Troubadour Revival: A Study of Social Change and Traditionalism in Late Medieval Spain*. London and Boston: Routledge & K. Paul, 1978.

Boynton, Susan. "Women's Performance of the Lyric Before 1500." *Medieval Woman's Song: Cross-Cultural Approaches*. 47–65.

Bratosevich, Nicolás. "Entornos y efectos de enunciación en una serranilla de Santillana." *Homenaje a Ana María Barrenechea*. Ed. Lía Schwartz Lerner and Isaías Lerner. Madrid: Castalia, 1984. 207–17.

Brewer, Charles E. "The *Cantigas d'amigo* of Martin Codax in the Context of Medieval Secular Latin Song." *La corónica* 26.2 (Spring 1998): 17–28.

Brownlee, Marina Scordilis. "Permutations of the Narrator-Protagonist: The *Serrana* Episodes of the *Libro de buen amor* in Light of the Doña Endrina Sequence." *Romance Notes* 22.1 (1981): 98–101.

Bruckner, Matilda Tomaryn. "Fictions of the Female Voice: The Women Troubadours." *Speculum* 67 (1992): 865–91.

Bubnova, Tatiana. "Estado, iglesia, universidad: Prostitución y proxenetismo como problema de conciencia en la vida cotidiana y en la expresión literaria." *Caballeros, monjas y maestros en la Edad Media.* Actas de las V Jornadas Medievales. Ed. Lillian von der Walde, Concepción Company and Aurelio González. Mexico: Universidad Nacional Autónoma de México, 1996. 415–31.

Burke, James F. "Again *Cruz*, the Baker-Girl: *Libro de buen amor*, ss. 115–120." *Revista Canadiense de Estudios Hispánicos* 4 (1980): 253–70.

———. "Juan Ruiz, the *Serranas*, and the Rites of Spring." *The Journal of Medieval and Renaissance Studies* 5 (1975): 13–35.

Burns, E. Jane. *Bodytalk: When Women Speak in Old French Literature.* Philadelphia: University of Pennsylvania Press, 1993.

Burrus, Victoria A. "Poets at Play: Love Poetry in the Spanish 'Cancioneros.' " Diss. University of Wisconsin at Madison, 1985.

———. "Role Playing in the Amatory Poetry of the *Cancioneros*." *Poetry at Court in Trastamaran Spain.* 111–33.

Butler, Judith. *Bodies that Matter: On the Discursive Limits of "Sex."* New York and London: Routledge, 1993.

———. *Excitable Speech: A Politics of the Performative.* New York and London: Routledge, 1997.

———. *Gender Trouble: Feminism and the Subversion of Identity.* New York and London: Routledge, 1990.

———. "Performative Acts and Gender Constitution: An Essay in Phenomenology and Feminist Theory." *Writing on the Body: Female Embodiment and Feminist Theory.* Ed. Katie Conboy, Nadia Medina, and Sarah Stanbury. New York: Columbia University Press, 1997. 401–417.

Cancioneiro da Ajuda. Ed. Carolina Michäelis de Vasconcelos. 2 vols. Halle: Max Niemeyer, 1904.

[*Cancioneiro da Ajuda.* Facsimile.] *Fragmento do Nobiliario do Conde Dom Pedro. Cancioneiro da Ajuda. Edição Fac-similada do códice existente na Biblioteca da Ajuda.* Ed. Instituto Português do Patrimonio Arquitectónico e Arqueológico. Lisbon: Távola Redonda, 1994.

Cancioneiro da Biblioteca Nacional (antigo Colocci-Brancuti). Ed. E. Paxeco Machado and J.P. Machado. 8 vols. Lisbon: Revista de Portugal, 1949–64.

Cancionero musical español de los siglos XV y XVI [= *Cancionero musical de Palacio*]. Ed. Francisco Asenjo Barbieri. Dutton MP4. Madrid, 1890. Reprint Buenos Aires: Schapire, 1945.

Cancioneiro Português da Vaticana. Ed. Theófilo Braga. Lisbon: Impresa Nacional, 1878.

Cancionero leonés. Ed. Miguel Manzano Alonso. 5 vols. León: Diputación Provincial, 1990.

Cancionero popular gallego. Ed. José Pérez Ballesteros. Madrid, 1886. Reprint Vigo: Galaxia, 1979.

Cano Ballesta, Juan. "¿Pretende casarse la serrana de Tablada?" *La corónica* 23.1 (Fall 1994): 3–11.

Cantar de mio Cid: Manuscrito de Per Abbat. Tesoros de la Biblioteca Nacional. Colección de Facsímiles en CD-ROM, 1. 1 disk. Madrid: Biblioteca Nacional, 1998.

Cantigas d'escarnho e de mal dizer dos cancioneiros medievais galego-portugueses. Ed. M[anuel] Rodrigues Lapa. 4th ed. Lisbon: João Sá da Costa, 1998. 1st ed., 1965; 2nd ed., rev., 1970.

"Las Cantigas de Santa Maria." [no name]. Online website. http://www.3to4.com/Cantigas/e_index.html. Updated February 4, 2004. Cited May 10, 2004.

Cantigas from the Court of Dom Dinis: Devotional, Satirical & Courtly Medieval Love Songs. Theatre of Voices. Paul Hillier, dir. CD. Los Angeles: Harmonia Mundi USA, 1995.

Carlson, Marvin. *Performance: A Critical Introduction.* London and New York: Routledge, 1996.

Caro Baroja, Julio. *Ritos y mitos equívocos.* Madrid: Istmo, 1974.

Carrillo de Huete, Pedro. *Crónica del halconero de Juan II.* Ed. Juan de Mata Carriazo. Colección de crónicas españolas, 8. Madrid: Espasa-Calpe, 1946.

Carvajal. *Poesie.* Ed. Emma Scoles. Rome: Ateneo, 1967.

Casas Torres, José Manuel and Ángel Abascal Garayoa. *Mercados geográficos y ferias de Navarra.* Zaragoza: Príncipe de Viana, 1948.

Cela, Camilo José. *Diccionario secreto.* Hombres, hechos e ideas, 15. 2 vols. Madrid: Alfaguara, 1968.

Certeau, Michel de. *The Practice of Everyday Life.* Trans. Steven F. Rendall. Berkeley: University of California Press, 1984.

Chalmeta Gendrón, Pedro. *El "señor del zoco" en España: Edades media y moderna, contribución al estudio de la historia del mercado.* Madrid: Instituto Hispano-Árabe de Cultura, 1973.

Chaucer, Geoffrey. *The Riverside Chaucer.* 3rd ed. Ed. Larry D. Benson. Boston: Houghton Mifflin, 1987.

Cheyette, Fredric L. and Margaret Switten. "Women in Troubadour Song: Of the Comtessa and the Vilana." *Women & Music* 2 (1998): 26–45.

Cohen, Judith R. "*Ca no soe joglaresa*: Women and Music in Medieval Spain's Three Cultures." *Medieval Woman's Song: Cross-Cultural Approaches.* 66–80.

Coldwell, Maria V. "*Jougleresses* and *Trobairitz*: Secular Musicians in Medieval France." *Women Making Music.* 39–61.

Combet, Louis. "Doña Cruz, la panadera del «buen amor»." *Ínsula* 294 (1971): 14–15.

Corominas, Joan and José A. Pascual. *Diccionario crítico etimológico castellano e hispánico.* 5 vols. Madrid: Gredos, 1983.

Corral Díaz, Esther. *As mulleres nas cantigas medievais.* Seminario de Estudios Galegos, 2. La Coruña: Castro, 1996.

Corral, Esther. "Feminine Voices in the Galician-Portuguese *cantigas de amigo.*" Trans. Judith R. Cohen with Anne L. Klinck. *Medieval Woman's Song: Cross-Cultural Approaches.* 82–98.

Cossío, José María de. "Geografía de una serranilla del Marqués de Santillana." *Correo erudito* 2 (1941): 52–53.

Costa, Marithelma. *Bufón de palacio y comerciante de ciudad: La obra del poeta cordobés Antón de Montoro.* Córdoba: Diputación de Córdoba, 2001.

Craddock, Jerry R. "The Legislative Works of Alfonso el Sabio." *Emperor of Culture.* 182–97.

Crane, Susan. *The Performance of Self: Ritual, Clothing, and Identity during the Hundred Years War.* Philadelphia: University of Pennsylvania Press, 2002.

Criado de Val, Manuel. *Historia de Hita y su Arcipreste: Vida y muerte de una villa mozárabe.* Madrid: Nacional, 1976.

Crónica de don Álvaro de Luna, Condestable de Castilla, Maestre de Santiago. Ed. Juan de Mata Carriazo. Colección de crónicas españolas, 2. Madrid: Espasa-Calpe, 1940.

Cusick, Suzanne G. "Feminist Theory, Music Theory, and the Mind/Body Problem." *Perspectives of New Music* 32.1 (1994): 8–27.

Dangler, Jean. *Mediating Fictions: Literature, Women Healers, and the Go-Between in Medieval and Early Modern Iberia.* Lewisburg, PA: Bucknell University Press, 2001.

Davis, Natalie Zemon. *Society and Culture in Early Modern France.* Stanford: Stanford University Press, 1975.

Delicado, Francisco. *Retrato de la Lozana Andaluza.* Ed. Claude Allaigre. 3rd ed. Madrid: Cátedra, 2000.

Desmond, Jane C. *Staging Tourism: Bodies on Display from Waikiki to Sea World.* Chicago: University of Chicago Press, 1999.

Deyermond, A.D. "*Juglar's* Repertoire or Sermon Notebook?—The *Libro de Buen Amor* and a Manuscript Miscellany." *Bulletin of Hispanic Studies* 51 (1974): 217–27.

———. "Sexual Initiation in Woman's Court Lyric." *Courtly Literature: Culture and Context.* Selected papers from the 5th Triennial Congress of the International Courtly Literature Society, Dalften, The Netherlands, 9–16 August, 1986. Ed. Keith Busby and Eric Kooper. Amsterdam and Philadelphia: John Benjamins, 1990. 126–58.

Diamond, Elin. "Mimesis, Mimicry, and the 'True-Real.'" *Modern Drama* 32.1 (March 1989): 58–72.

Díaz de Montalvo, Alfonso. *Ordenanzas reales.* Huete, 1484. ADMYTE. Disk 1.

Dicionário da literatura medieval galega e portuguesa. Organized and coordinated by Giulia Lanciani and Giuseppe Tavani. Lisbon: Caminho, 1993.

Dillard, Heath. *Daughters of the Reconquest: Women in Castilian Town Society, 1100–1300.* Cambridge, UK: Cambridge University Press, 1984.

Domínguez, F. "El manuscrito de las *Coplas de la panadera* de la Biblioteca Colombina y Capitular de Sevilla." *Hispanófila* 90 (1987): 81–98.

Douglas, Mary. *Purity and Danger: An Analysis of the Concepts of Pollution and Taboo.* London: Routledge and Kegan Paul, 1966.

Dronke, Peter. *The Medieval Lyric.* 3rd ed. Woodbridge, UK: D.S. Brewer, 1996.

Ducos, Joëlle. "Entre terre, aire et eau: La formation des montagnes." *La montagne dans le texte médiéval: Entre mythe et réalité.* 19–51.

Dumora, Florence. "Jeux de la parole féminine dans le *Cancionero* de Sebastián de Horozco." *Images de la femme en Espagne aux XVIe et XVIIe siècles.* Ed. Augustin Redondo. Paris: Presses de la Sorbonne Nouvelle, 1994. 117–26.

Dutton, Brian. *Catálogo-Indice de la poesía cancioneril del siglo XV.* 2 vols. Madison: Hispanic Seminary of Medieval Studies, 1982.

———. *El Cancionero del siglo XV, c. 1360–1520.* Biblioteca Española del siglo XV, 7. 7 vols. Salamanca: Universidad de Salamanca, 1990–91.

Earnshaw, Doris. *The Female Voice in Medieval Romance Lyric.* New York: Peter Lang, 1988.

Edwards, J. Michele. "Women in Music to ca. 1450." *Women & Music: A History.* 26–53.

Elia, Paola, ed. *Coplas hechas sobre la batalla de Olmedo que llaman las de la panadera.* Verona: Università degli studi di Verona, 1982.

Emperor of Culture. Alfonso X the Learned of Castile and His Thirteenth-Century Renaissance. Ed. Robert I. Burns, S.J. Philadelphia: University of Pennsylvania Press, 1990.

Erotismo en las letras hispánicas: Aspectos, modos y fronteras. Ed. Luce López-Baralt and Francisco Márquez Villanueva. Mexico: Colegio de México, 1995.

Fabricio de Vagad, Gauberto. *Crónica de Aragón.* Zaragoza, 1499. ADMYTE. Disk 1.

Fallows, David. "A Glimpse of the Lost Years: Spanish Polyphonic Song, 1450–70." *New Perspectives in Music: Essays in Honor of Eileen Southern.* Ed. Josephine Wright. Detroit Monographs in Musicology. Warren, MI: Harmonie Park Press, 1992. 19–36.

Ferreira, Ana Paula. "A 'Outra Arte' das Soldadeiras." *Luso-Brazilian Review* 30.1 (1993): 155–66.

Ferreira, Pedro Manuel. "A música das cantigas galego-portuguesas: balanço de duas décadas de investigação (1977–1997)." *Centro de Estudos de Sociologia e Estética Musical.* Online journal: http://www.fcsh.unl.pt/cesem/18_02_00/revistas/mpf_mus_cantig98.htm. Ca. 1999. Cited May 10, 2004.

———. "Relatório Preliminar sobre o Conteúdo Musical do Fragmento Sharrer." *Literatura medieval.* Actas do IV Congresso da Associação Hispânica de Literatura Medieval. Lisboa, 1–5 Outubro 1991. Ed. Aires A. Nascimento and Cristina Almeida Ribeiro. 4 vols. Vol. 1. Lisbon: Cosmos, 1993. 35–42.

———. *O Som de Martin Codax: Sobre a dimensão musical da lírica galego-portuguesa (séculos XII-XIV).* Lisbon: Unisys, 1986.

Filios, Denise K. "Female voices in the *Cantigas de escarnio e de mal dizer.* Index and Commentary." *Bulletin of Spanish Studies* 81 (2004): 135–55.

———. "Jokes on *Soldadeiras* in the *Cantigas de escarnio e de mal dizer.*" *La corónica* 26.2 (Spring 1998): 29–39.

———. "Rewriting History in the *Coplas de la panadera.*" *Hispanic Review* 71 (2003): 345–63.

———. "Women Out of Bounds: *Soldadeiras, Panaderas,* and *Serranas* in the Poetry of Medieval Spain." Diss. University of California at Berkeley, 1997.

Fontes, Manuel da Costa. "Celestina as Antithesis of the Virgin Mary." *Journal of Hispanic Philology* 25 (1990): 7–41.

———. "On Alfonso X's 'Interrupted' Encounter with a *soldadeira.*" In his *Folklore and Literature: Studies in the Portuguese, Brazilian, Sephardic, and Hispanic Oral Traditions.* Albany: State University of New York Press, 2000. 27–34.

Frago Gracia, Juan A. "Sobre el léxico de la prostitución en España durante el siglo XV." *Archivo de filología aragonesa* 24–25 (1979): 257–73.

French, Brigittine M. "The Symbolic Capital of Social Identities: The Genre of Bargaining in an Urban Guatemalan Market." *Journal of Linguistic Anthropology* 10 (2001): 155–89.

Frenk Alatorre, Margit. "¿Santillana o Suero de Ribera?" *Nueva Revista de Filología Hispánica* 16 (1962): 437.

———. *Estudios sobre lírica antigua.* Madrid: Castalia, 1978.

Frenk, Margit. *Corpus de la antigua lírica popular hispánica (siglos XV a XVII).* Nueva biblioteca de erudición y crítica, 1. Madrid: Castalia, 1987.

Freud, Sigmund. *Jokes and Their Relation to the Unconscious.* Trans. James Strachey. New York: Norton, 1963.

Galán Sánchez, Ángel and María Teresa López Beltrán. "El ≪Status≫ teórico de las prostitutas del reino de Granada en la primera mitad del siglo XVI (Las ordenanzas de 1538)." *Las mujeres en las ciudades medievales.* Actas de las III Jornadas de Investigación Interdisciplinaria. Ed. Cristina Segura Graíño. Madrid: Seminario de Estudios de la Mujer, 1984. 161–69.

García Carcedo, Pilar. "Las serranillas de Carvajal." *Medioevo y Literatura.* Vol. 2. 345–58.

García de Cortázar, José Ángel. *El dominio del monasterio de San Millan de la Cogolla (siglos X a XIII). Introducción a la historia rural de Castilla altomedieval.* Salamanca: Universidad de Salamanca, 1969.

García de Valdeavellano, Luis. *El Mercado. Apuntes para su estudio en León y Castilla durante la Edad Media.* 2nd ed, rev. Colección de bolsillo, 38. Seville: Universidad de Sevilla, 1975.

Gárfer, José Luis and Concha Fernández. *Adivinancero popular gallego.* Temas de España, 152. Madrid: Taurus, 1984.

Gaunt, Simon. *Gender and Genre in Medieval French Literature.* Cambridge, UK: Cambridge University Press, 1995.

Gerli, E. Michael. "Antón de Montoro and the Wages of Eloquence: Poverty, Patronage, and Poetry in 15th-c. Castile." *Romance Philology* 48 (1995): 265–76.

———. "Carvajal's *Serranas*: Reading, Glossing, and Rewriting the *Libro de buen amor* in the *Cancionero de Estúñiga*." *Studies on Medieval Spanish Literature in Honor of Charles F. Fraker.* Ed. Mercedes Vaquero and Alan Deyermond. Madison: Hispanic Seminary of Medieval Studies, 1995. 159–71.

———. "Fernán Pérez de Guzmán, *Cancionero de Baena* 119, and the *Libro de buen amor*." *MLN* 105 (1990): 367–72.

Girard, René. *Deceit, Desire, and the Novel: Self and Other in Literary Structure.* Trans. Yvonne Freccero. Baltimore: The Johns Hopkins University Press, 1965. Reprint 1990.

Glanville, Bartholomaeus. *De proprietatibus rerum, Propiedades de las cosas.* Tolosa, 1494. ADMYTE. Disk 1.

Goldin, Frederick. *Lyrics of the Troubadours and Trouvères: An Anthology and a History.* Gloucester, MA: Peter Smith, 1983.

Gómez Moreno, Ángel. *El teatro medieval castellano en su marco románico.* Madrid: Taurus, 1991.

Gómez Muntané, María Carmen. "La música laica en el reino de Castilla en tiempos del Condestable don Miguel Lucas de Iranzo (1458–1473)." *Revista de Musicología* 19 (1996): 25–45.

González, Alicia María. " 'Guess How Doughnuts Are Made':Verbal and Nonverbal Aspects of the *Panadero* and His Stereotype." *Perspectives in Mexican American Studies* 1 (1988): 89–107.

Gravdal, Kathryn. "Camouflaging Rape: The Rhetoric of Sexual Violence in the Medieval Pastourelle." *Romanic Review* 76 (1985): 361–73.

Guglielmi, Nilda. "Los elementos satíricos en las *Coplas de la panadera*." *Filología* 14 (1970): 49–104.

Gutiérrez, Laura G. "Gender Parody, Political Satire, and Postmodern *Rancheras*: Astrid Hadad's *Heavy Nopal*." Upublished manuscript.

Hable con ella. Dir. Pedro Almodóvar. El Deseo, 2002. Videocassette. Warner Bros. Pictures, 2003.

Hamilton, Earl J. *American Treasure and the Price Revolution in Spain, 1501–1650*. Cambridge, MA: Harvard University Press, 1934.

Handling Sin: Confession in the Middle Ages. Ed. Peter Biller and A.J. Minnis. York Studies in Medieval Theology, 2. Woodbridge, UK: York Medieval Press, 1998.

Harvey, Ruth. "*Joglars* and the Professional Status of the Early Troubadours." *Medium Ævum* 62 (1993): 221–41.

Hernández, Francisco J. "The Venerable Juan Ruiz, Archpriest of Hita." *La corónica* 13.1 (Fall 1984): 10–22.

Holsinger, Bruce W. *Music, Body, and Desire in Medieval Culture: Hildegard of Bingen to Chaucer*. Stanford: Stanford University Press, 2001.

Horozco, Sebastián de. *Cancionero*. Ed. Jack Weiner. Bern: Herbert Lang; Frankfurt: Peter Lang, 1975.

Inventing Medieval Landscapes: Senses of Place in Western Europe. Ed. John Howe and Michael Wolf. Gainesville, FL: University Press of Florida, 2002.

Jacob, H.E. *Six Thousand Years of Bread: Its Holy and Unholy History*. Trans. Richard and Clara Winston. New York: Doubleday, Doran and Co., 1944.

Jantzen, René. *Montagne et symboles*. Lyon: Presses Universitaires de Lyon, 1988.

Jenaro MacLennan, L. "Sobre los orígenes folklóricos de la serrana Gadea de Riofrío (*Libro de buen amor*)." *Vox Romanica* 47 (1988): 180–83.

Jensen, Frede, ed. and trans. *Medieval Galician-Portuguese Poetry: An Anthology*. Garland Library of Medieval Literature, vol. 87, series A. New York and London: Garland, 1992.

Jiménez Monteserín, Miguel. *Sexo y bien común. Notas para la historia de la prostitución en la España moderna*. Cuenca: Instituto Juan de Valdés, 1994.

JP. See Paredes, Juan. *El cancionero profano de Alfonso X el Sabio*.

Kane, Elisha K., trans. "*The Book of Good Love*" *of the Archpriest of Hita*. New York: Private publication, 1933.

Kapchan, Deborah A. *Gender on the Market: Moroccan Women and the Revoicing of Tradition*. Philadelphia: University of Pennsylvania Press, 1996.

Kaplan, Gregory B. *The Evolution of* Converso *Literature: The Writings of the Converted Jews of Medieval Spain*. Gainesville, FL: University Press of Florida, 2002.

Karras, Ruth Mazo. *Common Women: Prostitution and Sexuality in Medieval England.* New York: Oxford University Press, 1996.

Kay, Sarah. *Subjectivity in Troubadour Poetry.* Cambridge, UK: Cambridge University Press, 1990.

Kelly, Henry Ansgar. "Juan Ruiz and Archpriests: Novel Reports." *La corónica* 16.2 (Spring 1988): 32–54.

Kendrick, Laura. *The Game of Love: Troubadour Word Play.* Berkeley: University of California Press, 1988.

Kirby, Steven D. "Juan Ruiz's *Serranas*: The Archpriest-Pilgrim and Medieval Wild Women." *Hispanic Studies in Honor of Alan D. Deyermond.* Ed. John S. Miletich. Madison: Hispanic Seminary of Medieval Studies, 1986. 151–69.

Knighton, Tess. "The *a capella* Heresy in Spain: An Inquisition into the Performance of the *Cancionero* Repertory." *Early Music* 20.4 (November 1992): 561–81.

Krogstad, Jineen Elyse. "Cancionero Poetry and Its Musical Sources." Diss. University of Illinois at Urbana-Champaign, 1988.

Kruger, Steven F. "Conversion and Medieval Sexual, Religious, and Racial Categories." *Constructing Medieval Sexuality.* Ed. Karma Lochrie, Peggy McCracken, and James A. Schultz. Medieval Cultures, 11. Minneapolis: University of Minnesota Press, 1997. 158–79.

Labov, William. "Rules for Ritual Insults." *Studies in Social Interaction.* Ed. David Sudnow. New York: The Free Press, 1972. 120–69.

Lacarra, María Eugenia. "La evolución de la prostitución en la Castilla del siglo XV y la mancebía de Salamanca en tiempos de Fernando de Rojas." *Fernando de Rojas and* Celestina: *Approaching the Fifth Centenary.* Ed. Ivy A. Corfis and Joseph T. Snow. Madison: Hispanic Seminary of Medieval Studies, 1993. 33–78.

Lacarra Lanz, Eukene [María Eugenia Lacarra]. "Sobre la sexualidad de las soldadeiras en las cantigas d'escarnho e de maldizer." *Amor, escarnio y linaje en la literatura gallego-portuguesa.* Ed. Eukene Lacarra Lanz. Bilbao: Universidad del País Vasco, 2002. 75–97.

Langland, William. *Piers Plowman: An Edition of the C-Text.* Ed. Derek Pearsall. York Medieval Texts, second series. London: Edward Arnold, 1978.

Lapa, M[anuel] Rodrigues. *Lições de literatura portuguesa, Época medieval.* 7th rev. ed. Coimbra: Coimbra, 1970.

Lapesa, Rafael. *La obra literaria del Marqués de Santillana.* Madrid: Ínsula, 1957.

Léglu, Catherine. "Did Women Perform Satirical Poetry? *Trobairitz* and *Soldadeiras* in Medieval Occitan Poetry." *Forum for Modern Language Studies* 37.1 (2001): 15–25.

Lemaire, Ria. "Explaining Away the Female Subject: The Case of Medieval Lyric." *Poetics Today* 7 (1986): 729–43.

Lesser, Arlene T. *La pastorela medieval hispánica: Pastorelas y serranas galaico-portuguesas.* Vigo: Galaxia, 1970.

Lewes, Darby. *Nudes from Nowhere: Utopian Sexual Landscapes.* Lanham, MD: Rowman and Littlefield, 2000.

Lírica profana galego-portuguesa. Corpus completo das cantigas medievais, con estudio biográfico, análise retórica e bibliografía específica. Ed. Fernando Magán Abelleira et al. 2 vols. Santiago de Compostela: Xunta de Galicia, 1996.

Liu, Benjamin. " 'Affined to love the Moor': Sexual Misalliance and Cultural Mixing in the *Cantigas d'escarnho e de mal dizer.*" *Queer Iberia*. 48–72.

———. "Obscenidad y transgresión en una cantiga de escarnio." *Erotismo en las letras hispánicas*. 203–217.

Livermore, Harold. "Santillana and the Galaico-Portuguese Poets." *Iberoromania* 31 (1990): 53–64.

Lopes, Graça Videira. *A sátira nos cancioneiros medievais galego-portugueses*. Lisbon: Estampa, 1994.

Lorenzo Gradín, Pilar. *La canción de mujer en la lírica medieval*. Santiago de Compostela: Universidade de Santiago de Compostela, 1990.

LP. See *Lírica profana galego-portuguesa.*

MacKay, Angus. "Popular Movements and Pogroms in Fifteenth-Century Castile." *Past and Present* 55 (1972): 33–67.

Macpherson, Ian. "The Game of Courtly Love: *Letra, Divisa*, and *Invención* at the Court of the Catholic Monarchs." *Poetry at Court in Trastamaran Spain*. 95–110.

Madero, Marta. *Manos violentas, palabras vedadas: La injuria en Castilla y León (siglos XIII–XV)*. Humanidades/Historia, 341. Madrid: Taurus, 1992.

Malm, Ulf. *Dolssor Conina: Lust, the Bawdy, and Obscenity in Medieval Occitan and Galician-Portuguese Troubadour Poetry and Latin Secular Love Song*. Historia Litterarum, 22. Uppsala: Uppsala University Library, 2001.

Marcus, Steven. *The Other Victorians: A Study of Sexuality and Pornography in Mid-Nineteenth-Century England*. New York: Basic Books, 1966.

Marino, Nancy F. *La serranilla española: Notas para su historia e interpretación*. Scripta humanistica, 40. Potomac, MD: Scripta Humanistica, 1987.

Márquez Villanueva, Francisco. "Jewish 'Fools' of the Spanish Fifteenth Century." *Hispanic Review* 50 (1982): 385–409.

———. *Orígenes y sociología del tema celestinesco*. Barcelona: Anthropos, 1993.

———. "Pan 'pudendum muliebris' y *Los españoles en Flandes.*" *Hispanic Studies in Honor of Joseph H. Silverman*. Ed. Joseph V. Ricapito. Newark, DE: Juan de la Cuesta, 1988. 247–69.

———. "Sebastián de Horozco y la literatura bufonesca." *Homenaje al profesor Antonio Vilanova*. Ed. Adolfo Sotelo Vázquez and Marta Cristina Carbonell. 2 vols. Vol. 1. Barcelona: Departamento de Filología Española, 1989. 393–431.

Marshall, Kimberly. "Symbols, Performers, and Sponsors: Female Musical Creators in the Late Middle Ages." *Rediscovering the Muses: Women's Musical Traditions*. Ed. Kimberly Marshall. Boston: Northeastern University Press, 1993. 140–68.

Martínez Salazar, A. "Una gallega célebre en el siglo XIII." *Revista crítica de historia y literatura españolas, portuguesas é hispano-americanas* 2.10 (October 1897): 298–304.

Masera, Mariana. " 'Que non sé filar, ni aspar, ni devanar': Erotismo y trabajo femenino en el *Cancionero hispánico medieval.*" *Discursos y representaciones en la Edad Media*. Actas de las VI Jornadas Medievales. Ed. Concepción Company, Aurelio González, and Lillian von der Walde Moheno. Medievalia, 22. Mexico: Universidad Nacional Autónoma de México, 1999. 215–31.

———. " 'Yo, mi madre, yo, que la flor de la villa me so': La voz femenina en la antigua lírica popular hispánica." *Voces de la Edad Media*. Actas de las Terceras

Jornadas Medievales. Ed. Concepción Company et al. Medievalia, 6. Mexico: Universidad Nacional Autónoma de México, 1993. 105–113.

Masschaele, James. "The Public Space of the Marketplace in Medieval England." *Speculum* 77 (2002): 383–421.

Massip, Francesc. "L'actor en l'espectacle medieval." *Teatralidad medieval y su supervivencia*. Actas del III Festival d'Elx de Teatre i Música Medieval. Ed. César Oliva. Alicante: Instituto de Cultura "Juan Gil Albert," 1998. 27–40.

McDowell, John H. "Verbal Dueling." *Handbook of Discourse Analysis, III: Discourse and Dialogue*. Ed. Heurs Aven Digle. London: Academic Press, 1985. 203–211.

McGrady, Donald. "Notas sobre el enigma erótico, con especial referencia a los *Cuarenta enigmas en lengua española*." *Criticón* 27 (1984): 71–108.

Medieval Iberia: An Encyclopedia. Ed. E. Michael Gerli. New York: Routledge, 2003.

Medieval Woman's Song: Cross-Cultural Approaches. Ed. Anne L. Klinck and Ann Marie Rasmussen. Philadelphia: University of Pennsylvania Press, 2002.

Medioevo y Literatura. Actas del V Congreso de la Asociación Hispánica de Literatura Medieval. Ed. Juan Paredes. 4 vols. Granada: Universidad de Granada, 1995.

Menéndez Pidal, Ramón. *Poesía juglaresca y juglares. Orígenes de las literaturas románicas*. 1942. 9th ed. Madrid: Espasa Calpe, 1991.

———. "La primitiva poesía lírica española." *Estudios literarios*. Madrid: Atenea, [1920]. 251–344.

Menjot, Denis. "Prostitutas y rufianes en las ciudades castellanas a fines de la Edad Media." *Temas Medievales* 4 (1994): 189–204.

Michalski, Andre S. "Juan Ruiz's *Troba Cazurra*: 'Cruz cruzada panadera.'" *Romance Notes* 11 (1969): 434–38.

Moisala, Pirkko. "Musical Gender in Performance." *Women & Music* 3 (1999): 1–16.

La montagne dans le texte médiéval: Entre mythe et réalité. Ed. Claude Thomasset and Danièle James-Raoul. Cultures et civilisations médiévales, 19. Paris: Presses de l'Université de Paris-Sorbonne, 2000.

Montoro, Antón de. *Cancionero*. Ed. Marcella Ciceri. Intro. Julio Rodríguez Puértolas. Salamanca: Universidad de Salamanca, 1990.

Montoya Martínez, Jesús. "El carácter lúdico de la literatura medieval. (A propósito del 'jugar de palabra.' Partida Segunda, tít. IX, ley XXIX)." *Homenaje al profesor Antonio Gallego Morell*. Ed. C. Argente del Castillo et al. Granada: Universidad de Granada, 1989. 431–42.

Moreno Mengíbar, Andrés and Francisco Vázquez García. "Poderes y prostitución en España (siglos XIV–XVII). El caso de Sevilla." *Criticón* 69 (1997): 33–49.

Mount, Richard Terry. "Levels of Meaning: Grains, Bread, and Bread Making as Informative Images in Berceo." *Hispania* 76 (1993): 49–54.

Mourinho, Antonio María. "A Dança na Antiguidade e na Idade Média." *Revista de dialectología y tradiciones populares* 32 (1976): 373–403.

Murray, Jacqueline. "Gendered Souls in Sexed Bodies: The Male Construction of Female Sexuality in Some Medieval Confessors' Manuals." *Handling Sin*. 79–93.

Muscatine, Charles. "Courtly Literature and Vulgar Language." *Court and Poet*. Selected Proceedings of the Third Congress of the International Courtly

Literature Society, Liverpool, 1980. Ed. Glyn S. Burgess et al. Liverpool: Francis Cairns, 1981. 1–19.

Nieto Soria, José Manuel. "Aspectos de la vida cotidiana de las pastoras a través de la poesía medieval castellana." *El trabajo de las mujeres en la Edad Media Hispana.* Ed. Ángela Muñoz Fernández and Cristina Segura Graíño. Madrid: Asociación Cultural Al-Mudayna, 1988. 303–19.

———. "Propaganda política y poder real en la Castilla trastámara: Una perspectiva de análisis." *Anuario de estudios medievales* 25 (1995): 489–515.

Nirenberg, David. *Communities of Violence: Persecution of Minorities in the Middle Ages.* Princeton: Princeton University Press, 1996.

Nodar Manso, Francisco. "El carácter dramático-narrativo del escarnio y maldecir de Alfonso X." *Revista Canadiense de Estudios Hispánicos* 9.3 (1985): 405–441.

———. "La parodia de la literatura heroica y hagiográfica en las cantigas de escarnio y de mal decir." *Dicenda: Cuadernos de Filología Hispánica* 9 (1990): 151–61.

———. *Teatro menor galaicoportugués (siglo XIII): Reconstrucción textual y Teoría del Discurso.* Kassel: Reichenberger, 1990.

Oliveira, António Resende de. *Depois do espectáculo trovadoresco: A estrutura dos cancioneiros peninsulares e as recolhas dos séculos XIII e XIV.* Lisbon: Colibri, 1994.

Osório, Jorge A. "«Cantiga de escarnho» galego-portuguesa: sociologia ou poética?" *Revista da Faculdade de Letras, Linguas e Literatura* 3 (1986): 153–97.

Otis, Leah Lydia. *Prostitution in Medieval Society: The History of an Urban Institution in Languedoc.* Chicago: University of Chicago Press, 1985.

Paden, William D. "Contrafacture between Occitan and Galician-Portuguese." *La corónica* 26.2 (Spring 1998): 49–63.

Palencia, Alonso de. *Crónica de Enrique IV.* Trans. D.A. Paz y Melía. 1904. Biblioteca de autores españoles, 257. 3 vols. Madrid: Atlas, 1973–75.

Paredes, Juan. *El cancionero profano de Alfonso X el Sabio. Edición crítica, con introducción, notas y glosario.* Rome: Japadre, 2001.

———. *Las cantigas de escarnio y maldecir de Alfonso X: Problemas de interpretación y crítica textual.* Papers of the Medieval Hispanic Research Seminar, 22. London: Queen Mary and Westfield College, 2000.

Parker, Ian. "The Performance of Troubadour and Trouvère Songs." *Early Music* 5 (1977): 184–207.

Pérez, Martín. *Libro de las confesiones: Una radiografía de la sociedad medieval española.* Ed., intro. and notes, Antonio García y García, Bernardo Alonso Rodríguez, and Francisco Cantelar Rodríguez. Madrid: Biblioteca de Autores Cristianos, 2002.

Pérez de Guzmán, Fernán. *Generaciones y semblanzas.* Ed. J. Domínguez Bordona. 1924. Madrid: Espasa-Calpe, 1965.

Pérez Priego, Miguel Ángel, ed. *Teatro medieval, volumen 2: Castilla.* Barcelona: Crítica, 1997.

———. "Sobre la transmisión y recepción de la poesía de Santillana: el caso de las *serranillas* y los *sonetos.*" *Homenaje al profesor F. López Estrada.* Spec. issue of *Dicenda* 6 (1987/90): 189–97.

Poesía crítica y satírica del siglo XV. Ed. Julio Rodríguez Puértolas. Madrid: Castalia, 1989.

Poetry at Court in Trastamaran Spain: From the Cancionero de Baena *to the* Cancionero General. Ed. E. Michael Gerli and Julian Weiss. Tempe, AZ: Medieval & Renaissance Texts & Studies, 1998.

Queer Iberia: Sexualities, Cultures, and Crossings from the Middle Ages to the Renaissance. Ed. Josiah Blackmore and Gregory S. Hutcheson. Durham: Duke University Press, 1999.

Querol Gavaldá, Miguel, ed. *Cancionero musical de la Colombina (Siglo XV).* Monumentos de la Música Española, 33. Barcelona: CSIC, Instituto Español de Musicología, 1971.

Ratcliffe, Marjorie. "Adulteresses, Mistresses and Prostitutes: Extramarital Relationships in Medieval Castile." *Hispania* 67 (1984): 346–50.

Redondo, Augustin. "De molinos, molineros y molineras. Tradiciones folklóricas y literatura en la España del Siglo de Oro." *Literatura y folklore: Problemas de intertextualidad.* Actas del segundo symposium internacional del Departmento de Español de la Universidad de Groningen, 28, 29, y 30 de octubre de 1981. Ed. J.L. Alonso Hernández. Groningen: Universidad de Groningen; Salamanca: Universidad de Salamanca, 1983. 101–115.

Relación de los hechos del Condestable don Miguel Lucas de Iranzo (Crónica del siglo XV). Ed. Juan de Mata Carriazo. Colección de crónicas españolas, 3. Madrid: Espasa-Calpe, 1940.

Rey, Alfonso. "Juan Ruiz, Don Melón de la Huerta y el yo poético medieval." *Bulletin of Hispanic Studies* 56 (1979): 103–116.

Rico, Francisco. "Unas coplas de Jorge Manrique y las fiestas de Valladolid en 1428." *Anuario de estudios medievales* 2 (1965): 515–24.

Rincón, Eduardo. *Coplas satíricas y dramáticas de la Edad Media.* Madrid: Alianza, 1968.

Riquer, Martín de. "Las ≪Coplas de la panadera≫ en Cataluña." *Philologica hispaniensia in honorem Manuel Alvar: III, Literatura.* 4 vols. Vol. 3. Madrid: Gredos, 1986. 435–50.

———. *Història de la literatura catalana.* 3 vols. Barcelona: Ariel, 1980.

———. *Los trovadores: Historia literaria y textos.* 3 vols. Barcelona: Planeta, 1975.

Rivas, Félix A. "El significado de las imágenes de bailarinas en el románico aragonés." *De los símbolos al orden simbólico femenino (Siglos IV-XVII).* Ed. Ana Isabel Cerrada Jiménez and Josemi Lorenzo Arribas. Madrid: Asociación Cultural Al-Mudayna, 1998. 217–35.

RL. See *Cantigas d'escarnho e de mal dizer dos cancioneiros medievais galego-portugueses.* Ed. M. Rodrigues Lapa.

Robertson, Pamela. *Guilty Pleasures: Feminist Camp from Mae West to Madonna.* Durham: Duke University Press, 1996.

Rodríguez de Lena, Pedro. *El passo honroso de Suero de Quiñones.* Intro. and ed. Amancio Labandeira Fernández. Madrid: Fundación Universitaria Española, 1977.

Rodríguez Puértolas, Julio. "Poesía satírica medieval: 'Coplas de la Panadera.' " *El comentario de textos, 4: La poesía medieval.* Ed. Manuel Alvar et al. Madrid: Castalia, 1983. 375–404.

Rodríguez Velasco, Jesús D. *Castigos para celosos, consejos para juglares*. Madrid: Gredos, 1999.

Rohland de Langbehn, Regula. "Íñigo López de Mendoza, Marqués de Santillana." *Castilian Writers, 1400–1500*. Ed. Frank A. Domínguez and George D. Greenia. Dictionary of Literary Biography, 286. Detroit: Gale, 2004. 233–54.

El romancero viejo. Ed. Mercedes Díaz Roig. Madrid: Cátedra, 1985.

Romano García, Vicente, ed. *Coplas de la Panadera*. Pamplona: Aguilar, 1963.

Romeu Figueras, José. *La música en la corte de los Reyes Católicos. Cancionero Musical de Palacio III*. Monumentos de la Música Española, 14. Barcelona: CSIC, Instituto Español de Musicología, 1965.

Rosenstein, Roy. "The Voiced and the Voiceless in the *Cancioneiros*: The Muslim, the Jew, and the Sexual Heretic as *Exclusus Amator*." *La corónica* 26.2 (Spring 1998): 65–75.

Rossiaud, Jacques. *Medieval Prostitution*. Trans. Lydia G. Cochrane. Oxford and New York: Basil Blackwell, 1988.

Round, Nicholas. *The Greatest Man Uncrowned: A Study of the Fall of Don Alvaro de Luna*. London: Tamesis, 1986.

Ruiz, Juan. *Libro de buen amor*. Ed. Alberto Blecua. Madrid: Cátedra, 1992.

———. *Libro de buen amor*. Ed. Jacques Joset. 2 vols. Madrid: Espasa-Calpe, 1974.

Ruiz, Teofilo R. *Spanish Society, 1400–1600*. Harlow, UK: Longman, 2001.

Russo, Mary. *The Female Grotesque: Risk, Excess and Modernity*. New York and London: Routledge, 1994.

Salvador Miguel, Nicasio. *La poesía cancioneril. El* Cancionero de Estúñiga. Madrid: Alhambra, 1977.

Sánchez-Albornoz, Claudio. *Una ciudad de la España cristiana hace mil años. Estampas de la vida en León*. 11th ed. Madrid: Rialp, 1965.

Santillana, Marqués de (Íñigo López de Mendoza). *Poesía lírica*. Ed. Miguel Ángel Pérez Priego. Madrid: Cátedra, 1999.

———. *Poesías completas*. Ed. Manuel Durán. 2 vols. Vol. 2. Madrid: Castalia, 1980.

Saraiva, António José. "A poesia dos cancioneiros não é lírica, mas dramática." In his *Poesia e drama: Bernadim Ribeiro. Gil Vicente. Cantigas de Amigo*. Lisbon: Gradiva, 1990. 181–89.

Schechner, Richard. *Performance Theory*. Rev. ed. New York: Routledge, 1988.

Scholberg, Kenneth R. *Sátira e invectiva en la España medieval*. Biblioteca Románica Hispánica, 163. Madrid: Gredos, 1971.

Segura Graíño, Cristina. *Los espacios femeninos en el Madrid medieval*. Mujeres en Madrid. Madrid: Horas y horas, 1992.

Las siete partidas del sabio rey don Alfonso el nono, nueuamente Glosadas por el Licenciado Gregorio Lopez del Consejo Real de Indias de su Magestad. Salamanca, 1555. Facsimile. Madrid: Boletín Oficial del Estado, 1974.

Sendebar. Ed. María Jesús Lacarra. 2nd ed. Madrid: Cátedra, 1995.

Sharrer, Harvey Leo. "Fragmentos de Sete *Cantigas d'Amor* de D. Dinis, Musicadas; uma Descoberta." *Literatura medieval*. Actas do IV Congresso da Associação Hispânica de Literatura Medieval. Lisboa, 1–5 Outubro 1991. Ed. Aires A. Nascimento and Cristina Almeida Ribeiro. 4 vols. Vol. 1. Lisbon: Cosmos, 1993. 13–29.

Shields, Rob. *Places on the Margin: Alternative Geographies of Modernity*. London and New York: Routledge, 1991.

Short, John Rennie. *Imagined Country: Environment, Culture and Society*. London and New York: Routledge, 1991.

Sirera, Josep Lluís. "Diálogos de cancionero y teatralidad." *Historias y ficciones: Coloquio sobre la literatura del siglo XV*. Ed. R. Beltrán, J.L. Canet y J.L. Sirera. Valencia: Universidad de Valencia, 1992. 351–63.

Smith, Anthony D. "The Origins of Nations." *Ethnic and Racial Studies* 12.3 (July 1989): 340–67. Reprinted in *Becoming National: A Reader*. Ed. Geoff Eley and Ronald Grigor Suny. New York and Oxford: Oxford University Press, 1996. 106–130.

Snow, Joseph T. "Alfonso as Troubadour: The Fact and the Fiction." *Emperor of Culture*. 124–40.

———. "The Satirical Poetry of Alfonso X: A Look at Its Relationship to the 'Cantigas de Santa María.' " *Alfonso X of Castile, The Learned King (1221–1284): An International Symposium, Harvard University, 17 November 1984* .Ed. Francisco Márquez Villanueva and Carlos Alberto Vega. Harvard Studies in Romance Languages, 43. Cambridge, MA: Harvard University Press, 1990. 110–31.

Solomon, Michael. "Catarsis sexual: La *Vida de Santa Maria Egipciaca* y el texto higiénico." *Erotismo en las letras hispánicas*. 425–37.

Southworth, John. *The English Medieval Minstrel*. Woodbridge, UK and Wolfeboro, NH: Boydell, 1989.

Städtler, Katharina. "The *Sirventes* by Gormonda de Monpeslier." *The Voice of the Trobairitz*. 129–55.

Stegagno Picchio, Luciana. "Entre pastorelas e serranas: Novas contribuições ao estudo da Pastorela galego-poratuguesa." *Actas: II Congresso Internacional da Língua Galego-Portuguesa na Galiza, 1987*. La Coruña: Associaçom Galega da Língua, 1989. 409–424.

Stern, Charlotte. *The Medieval Theater in Castile*. Binghamton, NY: Medieval & Renaissance Texts & Studies, 1996.

Stevenson, Robert Murrell. *Spanish Music in the Age of Columbus*. The Hague: M. Nijhoff, 1960.

Tate, R.B. "Adventures in the *Sierra*." *"Libro de buen amor" Studies*. Ed. G.B. Gybbon-Monypenny. London: Tamesis, 1970. 219–29.

Teaching Medieval Lyric with Modern Technology: New Windows on the Medieval World. Margaret Switten, dir. CD-ROM. 9 disks. North Hadley, MA: Mount Holyoke College, 2001.

Terrero, José. "Paisajes y pastoras en las ≪serranillas≫ del Marqués de Santillana." *Cuadernos de literatura* 7 (1950): 169–202.

Vasvári, Louise O. " '*Chica cosa es dos nuezes*': Lost Sexual Humor in the *Libro del Arcipreste*." *Revista de Estudios Hispánicos* 24.1 (1990): 1–22.

———. "Festive Phallic Discourse in the *Libro del Arcipreste*." *La corónica* 22.2 (Spring 1994): 89–117.

———. *The Heterotextual Body of the* Mora Morilla. Papers of the Medieval Hispanic Research Seminar, 12. London: Queen Mary and Westfield College, 1999.

Vasvári, Louise O. "El hijo del molinero: Para la polisemia popular del *Libro del arcipreste*." *Erotismo en las letras hispánicas*. 461–77.

———. "≪La madeira certeira . . . a midida d'España≫ de Alfonso X: un *gap* carnavalesco." *Actes del VII Congrés de l'Associació Hispànica de Literatura Medieval: Castelló de la Plana, 22–26 de setembre de 1997*. Ed. Santiago Fortuño Llorens and Tomàs Martínez Romero. 3 vols. Vol. 3. Castelló de la Plana: Universitat Jaume I, 1999. 459–69.

———. "Múltiple transparencia semántica de los nombres de la alcahueta en el *Libro del Arcipreste*." *Medioevo y Literatura*. Vol. 2. 453–63.

———. "Peregrinaciones por topografías pornográficas en el *Libro de buen amor*." *Actas del VI Congreso Internacional de la Asociación Hispánica de Literatura Medieval*. Ed. José Manuel Lucía Megías. Alcalá: Universidad de Alcalá, 1997. 1563–72.

———. "La semiología de la connotación: Lectura polisémica de 'Cruz cruzada panadera.' "*Nueva Revista de Filología Hispánica* 32 (1983): 299–324.

———. "The Semiotics of Phallic Aggression and Anal Penetration as Male Agonistic Ritual in the 'Libro de Buen Amor.' " *Queer Iberia*. 130–56.

Vieira, Yara Frateschi. "O escândalo das amas e tecedeiras nos cancioneiros *galego-portugueses*." *Colóquio: Letras* 76 (1983): 18–27.

———. "Retrato medieval de mulher: a bailarina com pés de porco." *Estudos Portugueses e Africanos* 1 (1983): 95–110.

——— and Brian F. Head. "Obscenidade em Poesia de Língua Portuguesa." *Luso-Brazilian Review* 16.1 (1979): 91–103.

The Voice of the Trobairitz: Perspectives on the Women Troubadours. Ed. William D. Paden. Philadelphia: University of Pennsylvania Press, 1989.

Walsh, John K. "The Genesis of the *Libro de buen amor* (from Performance-Text to *libro* or *cancionero*)." Unpublished manuscript.

———. "The *Libro de buen amor* as a Performance-Text." *La corónica* 8 (1979): 5–6.

———. "Performance in the 'Poema de mio Cid.' " *Romance Philology* 44.1 (1990): 1–25.

Walters, D. Gareth. *The Cambridge Introduction to Spanish Poetry*. Cambridge, UK: Cambridge University Press, 2002.

Waters, Claire M. "Dangerous Beauty, Beautiful Speech: Gendered Eloquence in Medieval Preaching." *Essays in Medieval Studies* 14. Online journal: http://www.luc.edu/publications/medieval/vol14/14ch5.html. Cited August 23, 2001.

Weiss, Julian. "Alvaro de Luna, Juan de Mena and the Power of Courtly Love." *MLN* 106 (1991): 241–56.

———. "On the Conventionality of the *Cantigas d'amor*." *La corónica* 26.1 (Fall 1997): 225–45. Reprinted in *Medieval Lyric: Genres in Historical Context*. Ed. William D. Paden. Chicago: University of Illinois Press, 2000. 126–45.

Weissberger, Barbara F. "The Body as Contestant Site in *Cancionero* Poetry." MLA Convention, San Diego, CA. December 27, 1994.

———. "Male Sexual Anxieties in *Carajicomedia*: A Response to Female Sovereignty." *Poetry at Court in Trastamaran Spain*. 221–34.

Weissberger, Barbara F. "Protest Poetry in Castile (circa 1445-circa 1506)." *Castilian Writers, 1400–1500* .Ed. Frank A. Domínguez and George D. Greenia. Dictionary of Literary Biography, 286. Detroit: Gale, 2004. 340–47.

Willis, Raymond S., ed. and trans. *Libro de Buen Amor.* Juan Ruiz. Princeton: Princeton University Press, 1972.

Women & Music: A History. Ed. Karin Pendle. 2nd ed. Bloomington and Indianapolis: Indiana University Press, 2001.

Women in Music: An Anthology of Source Readings from the Middle Ages to the Present. Ed. Carol Neuls-Bates. Boston: Northeastern University Press, 1996.

Women Making Music: The Western Art Tradition, 1150–1950. Ed. Jane Bowers and Judith Tick. Urbana and Chicago: University of Illinois Press, 1986.

Wright, Janice. "The Galician-Portuguese *Cancioneiro* Poets: *Cantigas de amor, de amigo, de escarnho e maldizer.*" *Castilian Writers, 1200–1300.* Ed. Frank A. Domínguez and George D. Greenia. Dictionary of Literary Biography. Detroit: Gale, 2004. Forthcoming.

Zahareas, Anthony N. and Óscar Pereira. *Itinerario del* Libro del Arcipreste: *Glosas críticas al* Libro de buen amor. Madison: Hispanic Seminary of Medieval Studies, 1990.

Zenith, Richard, trans. *113 Galician-Portuguese Troubadour Poems in Galician-Portuguese and English.* Aspects of Portugal. Manchester: Carcanet, 1995.

Zumthor, Paul. *La lettre et la voix: De la "littérature" médiévale.* Paris: Seuil, 1987.

INDEX

UK 2002 - 2003
UK 2003 - 2004
UK 2004 - 2005
ESPAÑA 2005 - 2006
UK 2006 - 2007